Also by JAMES KITFIELD

Prodigal Soldiers: How the Generation of Officers Born of Vietnam
Revolutionized the American Style of War

WAR & DESTINY

How the Bush Revolution in Foreign and Military Affairs Redefined American Power

JAMES KITFIELD

Potomac Books, Inc.
Washington, D.C.

Library of Congress Cataloging-in-Publication Data

Kitfield, James.
  War and destiny : how the Bush revolution in foreign and military affairs redefined American power / James Kitfield.—1st ed.
    p. cm.
  Includes bibliographical references and index.
  ISBN 1-57488-959-1 (hardcover : alk. paper)
  1. United States—Foreign relations—2001–   2. United States—Military policy.   3. Bush, George W. (George Walker), 1946–   4. War on Terrorism, 2001–   5. Iraq War, 2003.   6. Kitfield, James.   7. Embedded war correspondent—United States—Biography.   8. Embedded war correspondents—Iraq—Biography.   I. Title.
E902.K58   2005
327.73'009'0511—dc22   2005003860

Printed in the United States of America on acid-free paper that meets the American National Standards Institute Z39-48 Standard.

Potomac Books, Inc.
22841 Quicksilver Drive
Dulles, Virginia 20166

First Edition

10   9   8   7   6   5   4   3   2   1

To my father, David Brewster Kitfield, former Marine Corps fighter pilot, for teaching me respect for the warrior spirit; to Lydia, for showing me the rest.

And to Michael Kelly
A good friend we had, a good friend we lost, along the way

"No cause has he to say his doom is harsh,
Who's made the master of his destiny."

FRIEDRICH VON SCHILLER
Wilhelm Tell

CONTENTS

ACKNOWLEDGMENTS

There are a number of people without whom this book could not have been completed. I would like to thank Nadia Schadlow and the Smith Richardson Foundation for the financial support that made the book possible. The publisher and editors of *National Journal* magazine not only regularly provide me with one of the more interesting jobs in all of Washington, D.C., but they were also supportive of this effort from the start. I would especially like to thank Charlie Green and Pat Pexton, the editor and deputy editor of *National Journal*, respectively. At the *Atlantic Monthly*, Cullen Murphy and P. J. O'Rourke were instrumental in helping me to visualize this story as a long-form narrative, and eventually a book. Lydia Pearce was a constant support and essential sounding board.

Special thanks go to Lt. Gen. William "Scott" Wallace and the men and women of V Corps; to Maj. Gen. Buford Blount and the commanders and troops of the Third Infantry Division; and to Col. Ralph "Rob" Baker and the officers and soldiers of Second Battalion, First Armored Division, all of whom embraced the essential spirit of the experiment to embed journalists into their ranks and into their confidences, the better to illuminate a seminal endeavor in U.S. military history.

PROLOGUE

There are no more slow news days for America. Each day's newspaper or nightly newscast seems filled to bursting with stories of political confrontation and partisan rancor at home, and strife, conflict, and gathering threats abroad. If our leaders and news merchants can be believed, each of those disjointed events may now have a direct or indirect bearing on the lives of ordinary Americans. Because we are a nation unlike any other, in a war without precedent.

Only sometimes it's hard to know exactly what that means. I have friends and loved ones, well-educated citizens who I deeply respect, who can no longer bring themselves to even read a daily newspaper. Sure, there are full-time jobs to attend and children to chauffeur, but in early twenty-first-century America forty-five minutes with the newspaper can seem like a week with an angry mob. Who needs the inevitable surge of fear and anger, and the disquieting sense that events are somehow spinning out of control? Presumably for different reasons, President George W. Bush himself, the leader of the free world, claims not to read newspapers, preferring to get the facts unabridged from his close circle of aides.

In my own home and office, there are piles of newspaper clippings defaced by yellow marker and curled at their edges like dead leaves. My computers—office, home, and laptop—are likewise clogged with "clipping" files of news reports of particular interest. All of my life as a chronicler I have trawled the endless stream of news, constantly searching for evidence of strong currents hidden beneath the torrents of ink.

A postelection article clipped from the *Washington Post* on George W. Bush's reelection outlined the now-familiar map of red and blue America, our national conscience now bifurcated into opposing caricatures. The article quoted political scientists who saw in Bush's victory in the 2004 presidential contest, and in commensurate Republican gains in the House and Senate, a "realignment election" that signaled a lasting majority and strong mandate for the Bush doctrine for fighting the war on global terrorism. As the *Christian Science Monitor* pointed out in a December 3 article, that mandate broke down in a recent Gallup poll to 51 percent of Americans who believed America was right to invade Iraq, and 47 percent who believed it was a mistake. I also highlighted articles on the shake-up of the Bush team in anticipation of a second term: Colin Powell out, Condi Rice in, Donald Rumsfeld, Paul Wolfowitz, and Dick Cheney staying put.

On a recent expedition I also noted an October 22 article in the *San Bernardino Sun* quoting a prominent member of the 9/11 Commission that terrorist mastermind Osama Bin Laden was hiding out in the South Waziristan region in Pakistan, and the Pentagon knew this with certainty. A December 5 article in the *Washington Post* quoted Pakistani president Pervez Musharraf insisting that Bin Laden's trail had gone stone cold, and blaming the United States for the inability to capture the terrorist because the U.S.-led coalition in Afghanistan lacked sufficient troops, which had left "voids" near its border with Pakistan. There might be an eddy there worth fishing.

Buried in the news stream was a November 21 article from the *Houston Chronicle* detailing the imminent deployment of the Bush administration's new national missile defense system, and another article on funds requested by the Bush administration to develop a new generation of nuclear weapons. October articles in the *Boston Globe* and *New York Times*, respectively, detailed the accelerated efforts of Iran and North Korea to develop their own nuclear weapons, and Russia's plans to introduce a new nuclear missile capable of thwarting U.S. defenses.

According to a December 2004 clipping from the *Washington Post* the Republican-controlled U.S. Congress was introducing legislation to limit the power and reach of the United Nation's International Criminal Court. The *New York Times* reported on November 13 that President Bush wanted to expand the Pentagon's role in clandestine operations that often circumvent international law and are the traditional purview of the Central Intelligence Agency. Meanwhile, a United Nations panel released a report in December publicly challenging the Bush doctrine of preemption, while the International Committee of the Red Cross found that same month that the U.S. military was bending the rules governing the detention of prisoners at Guantánamo Bay, Cuba, in ways that were "tantamount to torture." Those countervailing currents begin to suggest a whirlpool.

As part of an outreach to allies, President Bush in November visited Canada, where 45 percent of our northern neighbors reportedly now hold unfavorable views of the United States, up from 8 percent in the early 1980s. An October 21 article detailed a Middle Eastern country's efforts to acquire weapons of mass destruction. Britain, France, and Germany were pushing for international inspections, while hard-liners in the Bush administration talked about possible military action and regime change. Only this time the country was Iran. According to a November 23 article in the *Washington Times*, the European Union was considering lifting an arms embargo on China against U.S. objections. For its part, China was siding with erstwhile U.S. ally South Korea against the Bush administration's approach to negotiations with North Korea over its nuclear weapons program, according to the October 27 *New York Times*. All of which suggests a fork in the river long plied together by the United States and its closest allies.

There was better news from Afghanistan, where the *Washington Post* reported on successful October elections that brought eight million Afghans to the polling booths. The news was less good in an October 22 piece in *USA Today* noting Afghanistan's bumper crop of opium, which accounted for more than one-third of the country's entire economy. A November *New York Times* report quoted Michael Scheuer, the former chief of the CIA's Osama Bin Laden unit, to the effect that Al Qaeda had morphed into a "global Islamic insurgency" after being largely driven out of Afghanistan. On November 12, the *Washington Post* reported that Abu Musab Al-Zarqawi, the most wanted terrorist in Iraq, had begun referring to his group as "Al Qaeda in Iraq."

In anticipation of January elections in Iraq, U.S. military officials announced late in 2004 that they were upping the U.S. troop levels to one hundred fifty thousand, the highest level since the end of major hostilities. A page-one story in the *Washington Post* on December 6 quoted U.S. generals in Iraq to the effect that great gains had been achieved against the Iraqi insurgency as a result of fighting to retake the stronghold of Fallujah. A December 1 article in *USA Today* revealed that U.S. casualties in Iraq in November of 2004 matched the highest monthly level since the invasion. There was also this little noted report in the December 3 *New York Times:* The U.S. embassy in Iraq had barred its employees from using the five-mile stretch of highway that connected the Green Zone in Baghdad to the Baghdad International Airport. After twenty months of efforts to secure the road—which had been dubbed "Ambush Alley" by U.S. soldiers—it was deemed too dangerous to travel. Danger, white water ahead.

As a wise man once told me, when you're a superpower at war every damn thing that happens in the world is connected to every other damn thing. This book is about those connections and the backstory they reveal. Distilled to its essence it is the culmination of a nearly four-year journey to try and understand the powerful global forces, political movements, and individual motivations that conspired to bring America to a critical juncture. The end of an endeavor that President Bush has assured us will shape a generation of Americans is not yet in sight, and this book is not intended to presuppose or predict any final outcome in the global war on terrorism. Rather it is an attempt to inform the reader to the best of my ability how we came to this pass, the better to navigate and choose carefully the way ahead.

That road is obviously perilous because wars and revolutions change the course of history, often in unpredictable and unintended ways. They forge new international orders, and chart the ascent and decline of major powers and even empires. There's no reason to doubt that the United States' global war on terrorism, with Afghanistan as the opening campaign and Iraq as the Bush administration's chosen centerpiece, is destined to do the same. After all, it is a war led and waged by the only superpower on earth, and one designed from its inception to challenge and topple many of the orthodoxies of the old world order.

From the very beginning the Bush doctrine, with its attendant revolutions in foreign and military affairs, represented a radical strategy wedded to a bold and ambitious premise: that American power, unconstrained by traditional bonds and honed to a domineering edge by military transformation, could not just check or contain, but decisively defeat the great threats confronting Western civilization at the turn of the twenty-first century—nihilistic Islamic terrorism, the spread of doomsday weapons and technology, growing global instability, and the proliferation of failed or rogue states that nourish all those modern scourges.

At least on the matter of the stakes involved, and on that one point only, there was virtually unanimous consensus among the scores of senior Bush administration officials, U.S. military leaders, congressional lawmakers, foreign leaders, intelligence analysts, historians, strategists, and foreign affairs and national security experts that I spoke with in researching this book. Historians will one day look back on this relatively brief and violent period as a seminal moment in the American Project that decisively shaped the latter half of the twentieth century, and stands at a fateful crossroads at the beginning of the twenty-first century.

PART I

Revolution

"We used to think that revolutions are the cause of change. Actually it is the other way around: change prepares the way for revolution."

ERIC HOFFER
The Temper of Our Time

CHAPTER 1

Atlas Shakes

N THE SPRING of 2000 I returned from an extended reporting trip in Europe to Washington, D.C., and the transition was jarring in ways that had nothing to do with jet lag. One of my stops in Europe was The Hague, a windswept city on Holland's North Sea coast that was home to the United Nation's war crimes tribunal for the former Yugoslavia. There I had reported on the trial of Radislav Krstic, a middle-aged man in an ill-fitting suit who day after day sat impassively in a sterile, brightly lit courtroom separated from onlookers by bulletproof glass. As the general in charge of the Bosnian-Serb forces that overran the United Nations' "safe haven" of Srebrenica in July 1995, Krstic was accused of organizing the execution of roughly seven thousand Muslim civilians in Europe's worst atrocity since the Holocaust.

Tribunal prosecutors had carefully built their case for genocide, which included video footage of Krstic in Srebrenica and intercepted phone conversations between his top officers discussing the need to "distribute" thirty-five hundred "parcels," euphemisms for the disposal of human bodies. Witnesses told the tribunal's three international judges of lying in a field beneath bleeding corpses for hours as Bosnian-Serb soldiers methodically machine-gunned truckload after truckload of Muslim prisoners. As it happened, I had seen the partial aftermath of Srebrenica on an earlier reporting trip to Bosnia, when I stood on a sunny hillside in the Glumina Mountains and watched as United Nations and NATO officials excavated a mass gravesite, one of six in that area thought to hold the victims of nearby Srebrenica. The freshly unearthed bodies looked like clumps of misshapen clay at first, until you made out the shape of a hand or a grotesquely contorted leg poking through the pile.

I had traveled to The Hague in hopes of a dramatic confrontation, an epiphany to help explain how such darkness still lurked in the heart of Europe at the close of the twentieth century. Instead, there was a gray-haired man in a bad suit staring incessantly at his hands, unwilling even to look his accusers in the eye. After witnessing the cumbersome bureaucracy of international justice and the banality of a familiar evil in The Hague, it occurred to me that the post–Cold War era of boundless expectations had not advanced civilization nearly as far as many experts had predicted.

In contrast to The Hague, Washington, D.C., upon my return in the spring of 2000 was already deep in the grip of the presidential campaign season, a quadrennial celebration that had the capital humming like a tuning fork in anticipation of the ear-splitting crescendo to come in November. Presidential election season is to Washington what October is to baseball, only with campaign rallies and debates in lieu of playoff games and the World Series. And for a sizable portion of the inside-the-Beltway crowd, the crib sheet of choice for the contest, where they go for the latest play-by-play, polling, and analyses of all things political, is *National Journal* magazine, where I work as a senior staff correspondent.

The actual circulation of *National Journal* is only around ten thousand weekly copies, very small for an operation with more than 125 editors and reporters. As our sales department never tires of reminding advertisers, however, it is a very influential and committed readership. Most members of Congress and the cabinet, many senior staff in the White House, and myriad press secretaries, chiefs of staff, legislative directors, legal counsels, policy advisers, executive directors, think tankers, lobbyists, and assorted players in the capital all kindly plunk down $1,600 for an annual subscription. What they get for this business deduction is a weekly magazine with in-depth, nonpartisan, and hopefully insightful coverage of the news of most interest to Washington insiders. In lieu of a larger audience, writers at *National Journal* get the time and space in the magazine to delve into the combustible issues that fuel the world's longest-running experiment in democracy, in all their complexity and rich context, free from the dictates of a daily deadline. For journalists who don't mind toiling in relative obscurity, it's good work if you can find it. As the senior staff correspondent for foreign and military affairs, my editors approached me with a deceptively simple question in the spring of 2000: Just how would a Bush administration's foreign and defense policy differ from those of President Bill Clinton and Vice President Al Gore?

At first glance the distance between Gore and Texas governor George W. Bush on foreign affairs and national security didn't seem all that wide. Both men were committed free traders and internationalists. Neither had shown an instinct for the protectionism or isolationism that arose at times from the fringes of their respective parties. Both generally supported maintaining the world's strongest military.

As someone who had covered the increasingly vitriolic battles over foreign and defense policy between the Clinton administration and a Republican Congress, however, it was easy to discern very different instincts and attitudes on those issues between the Gore and Bush camps. An obvious example was how many congressional Republicans had objected to the Kosovo war to reverse Slobodon Milosevic's latest campaign of ethnic cleansing in the Balkans in 1999, and the Bush camp's promise to pull U.S. troops out of the region. They also strongly opposed international efforts to make the war crimes tribunal in The Hague permanent in the form of an International Criminal Court.

As I wrote in April of 2000, a Gore administration would very likely further advance a Clinton foreign policy characterized by a comfort with international institutions such as the United Nations, frequent engagement and compromise with major powers such as Russia and China, a belief in the utility of multilateral arms control agreements, and assertiveness in using the U.S. military to ease regional crises and humanitarian disasters. After two terms in office, the Clinton-Gore team had settled into the assertive engagement in international affairs that essentially defined the post–Cold War era, and they had coined a phrase for America's role in the world: The United States was the "indispensable nation."

Some other publications had focused on George W. Bush's promise of humility in foreign affairs in suggesting that he would follow in the footsteps of his father, a Republican moderate firmly in the internationalist wing of his party. "If we're an arrogant nation, [the world] will view us that way, but if we're a humble nation, they'll respect us," Bush said during the election campaign. Beyond the campaign platitudes, however, the Bush camp was advocating a sharp departure from the notion of America as the indispensable nation. They talked instead of an era of American "exceptionalism," arguing that the nation's predominant power dictated a singular approach to world affairs. As I wrote at the time, if elected, a President Bush would likely adopt a foreign policy more nakedly assertive of American interests. He was likely to take a harder line toward major powers Russia and China, and give voice to the Republican establishment's deep distrust of binding America too tightly to international bodies or multilateral agreements.

With regard to the military, the Bush camp signaled that it would no longer deploy U.S. troops on "do-gooder" humanitarian missions or to crises not vital to America's interests, including the Balkans and Haiti. Bush promised to hasten construction of a national missile defense system, fulfilling a plank of the Republican platform that dated back nearly two decades to Ronald Reagan's "Star Wars" vision of an impenetrable shield against nuclear missiles. Notably, the Bush campaign had also taken up the banner of a band of military reformers who had argued throughout the 1990s that the U.S. military needed to fundamentally transform itself into a more high-tech, agile, and lethal force in order to address new threats and exploit information-age technologies. By so fervently embracing this "revolution in military affairs" as their own, the Bush camp revealed both their distaste for the mundane toils of peace negotiations and peacekeeping operations, and an early penchant for rejecting the status quo in favor of revolutionary, even radical, change.

In an interview with me at the time, Condoleeza Rice, Bush's chief foreign and national security policy adviser, predicted that a President George W. Bush would transform the Pentagon more radically "than any President since Harry Truman," who established the Defense Department in the first place. "You would also see a foreign policy that is more focused on America's national interest in promoting prosperity and keeping the peace, and less prone to flying from crisis to crisis," said Rice, who had served as a Soviet specialist in the first Bush administration and had recently left her job as provost of Stanford University. "That means resorting to military force only in those special cases when important American interests are at stake. [The Clinton] administration seems to think an adequate justification for the use of force is simply if we can do some good. That's an odd criterion for military force, because it leads to rather ad hoc decisions about where to intervene and where not to."

As someone familiar with the considerable space between campaign rhetoric and reality, none of the Bush camp's positions seemed especially headline grabbing. Presidential candidates invariably embraced ambitious platforms, promised dramatic change, and adopted black-and-white positions in order to clearly distinguish themselves from the other guy. Once in office they usually discovered that the built-in system of checks and balances in Washington dilutes radical reforms and ideologies. Divided government and vested interests dictate compromises and temper revolutionary zeal. As another southern governor with big plans, Bill Clinton came into office promising to establish a national health care system and allow gays to serve openly in the military, only to discover that everything in the way Washington and the federal government works is geared to favor slower, more evolutionary change. Especially in an era of globalization, the world at large also frequently intervened to help shape a president's foreign policy through its own system of international checks and balances, and through crises that no one could anticipate. There was also the issue of a mandate. What support for a dramatic reordering of world affairs or transformation of American military power could a Bush administration hope to draw from a presidential campaign focused, as almost all were, on domestic issues?

In response to our early coverage of the Bush campaign, the publisher of *National Journal* received a very complimentary note. I have no idea if the message referred to our coverage that suggested rather different foreign policy instincts on the part of Bush the younger. The author of the handwritten note, however, thanked us for our profile and analysis, and said he had personally learned a lot about candidate George W. Bush from our coverage. The note was signed George Herbert Walker Bush, forty-first president of the United States.

At 10:00 P.M. on Tuesday, December 12, 2000, the Supreme Court split 5–4 along ideological lines and issued its ruling effectively declaring George W. Bush the forty-third president of the United States, ending one of the most tumultuous and bizarre episodes in American political history. For five weeks the public was riveted to their television sets by the spectacle of angry protesters clashing in Florida, lawyers scuttling back and forth between Tallahassee and the U.S. Supreme Court in Washington, and election workers peering at ballots and "hanging chads" as if to divine the secrets of the oracle. Along the way the red state/blue state map of America showing a country evenly yet deeply divided was indelibly seared into the national consciousness. In the end, the difference between red and blue America, a country of well over 250 million citizens, were 527 voters in Florida and five Supreme Court justices in Washington, D.C., who tipped the election toward Bush.

While most of my colleagues were focused on the election drama and its rancorous aftermath, I was researching what a Bush foreign affairs and national security team might look like. If nearly two decades of reporting in Washington had taught me anything, it was the truth in the saying that history *is* biography. Far more than campaign rhetoric, I believed the Bush administration's choices of who would helm the vast foreign policy and national security apparatus of the United States would best reveal its true nature. As part of my research I talked with a number of experts close to the Bush camp, including members of a group of close Bush foreign policy and national security advisers who collectively referred to themselves as the "Vulcans."

By the time of the Bush inauguration in January of 2001, I had already begun to sense a shift in the tectonic plates of world affairs. It wasn't just that revolutions require a triggering event, something to shake up the old order, though a bitterly contested election and constitutional crisis in the most powerful nation on earth was certainly a seismic event. Rather, I came to see the 2000 presidential election as a possibly decisive battle in an ongoing clash between opposing political movements with very different visions of America. Other major clashes included Newt Gingrich's Republican revolution and takeover of Congress in 1994; the shutdown of the federal government in 1995; the controversial 1998 Kosovo war; the 1999 battle to impeach Bill Clinton; and the Republican Senate's 1999 vote to defeat the Comprehensive Test Ban Treaty, its first such rejection since the 1919 Treaty of Versailles that would have established the League of Nations.

Despite its razor-thin margin, I believed then as I do now that the 2000 election represented a culminating moment in that clash of competing and largely incompatible worldviews. The reelection of George W. Bush in 2004 suggests that it will be a lasting victory. Thus in a *National Journal* cover story published in the Bush administration's first months in office, I wrote that the world order was indeed about to undergo a dramatic shake-up. The superpower was determined to change the rules in new, and yes, revolutionary ways. To understand why an America arguably at the zenith of its power would so desire to shatter the status quo, after a period of unprecedented prosperity at home and predominance abroad, requires reviewing a little history. Hopefully it will explain the conclusion I reached in my article: The post–Cold War period of great expectations was dead, and America was entering a new era that was rife with premonitions of conflict.

For the vast majority of Americans who grew up in a nation that always cast an oversized shadow, it's easy to forget just how recently the country was fit for that superpower suit of armor. As recently as the late nineteenth century the United States was still engrossed with Civil War reconstruction and Manifest Destiny, or the westward expansion to the Pacific Coast and Alaska, and eventually abroad to the Caribbean. The Spanish-American War of 1898 and President Teddy Roosevelt's launching of the "Great White Fleet" on a world diplomatic tour in 1907 were only the first steps of a rising, but hardly dominant, power. Throughout the latter half of the nineteenth century and first half of the twentieth, the United States remained largely a strategic ward of the British Empire on which the sun famously never set. Only at the end of World War II in 1945, with Europe in ruins and Great Britain exhausted by two world wars, did the United States truly assume the mantle of Western leadership. For the first time U.S. leaders were forced to focus in earnest on a grand strategy that would order the world to America's advantage and hopefully avoid the kinds of cataclysms that had made the first half of the twentieth century the most blood-soaked period in history. With the recent advent of nuclear weapons and the U.S. bombings of Hiroshima and Nagasaki near the end of the war, there were no guarantees at the time that mankind would even see the twenty-first century.

At important points in their ascent all great powers are blessed with visionary leadership, and in the United States' case it was supplied in that critical period of the 1940s by Presidents Franklin Roosevelt and Harry Truman, and by the foreign policy team that served them and became known simply as the "Wise Men." Drawn primarily from the worlds of finance, banking, statecraft, and the military, the group included, among others, the likes of Dean Acheson, George F. Kennan, Paul Nitze, and George Marshall. Together, these men responded to a post–World War II period of epic crisis with the strategic equivalent of a grand slam.

The Wise Men oversaw establishment of the United Nations in hopes of avoiding future world wars, the World Bank to fund postwar reconstruction, and the International Monetary Fund to promote free trade. By reaching out with the Marshall Plan to help rebuild Western Europe, as well as to defeated foes Germany and Japan, the United States avoided the mistakes of the interwar years of the 1920s and 1930s, when ostracizing the defeated Weimar Republic after World War I led to the resurgence of a belligerent Germany. The article Kennan published anonymously (under the name "X") in 1947 in *Foreign Affairs* magazine—together with Nitze's National Security Council Directive 68 and the establishment of the NATO alliance under Secretary of State Acheson—laid the foundation for the strategy of containment that successfully won the Cold War and deterred World War III.

Of all the U.S. military war colleges, my favorite is the Naval War College in Newport News, Rhode Island. With its well-preserved main street the town itself could be snatched out of a travel brochure for the New England coast, and the War College sits impressively on a bluff above town overlooking the ocean. It's a perfect perch for the contemplation of grand strategy, and on my occasional visits to speak to classes of officers I've always made it a point to visit with someone who has benefited greatly from the surroundings, Mackubin Owens, professor of strategy at the Naval War College.

"What you learn from history is that the emphasis on strategic thinking in the United States is really a recent, post–World War II phenomenon," Owens told me in one such discussion in 1999. "Before that time, we were really strategic free-riders on the British." As the framework for containment of the USSR, the United States constructed a ring of U.S. military commands and bases on the periphery of the Soviet Union and Warsaw Pact, bracketing the Eurasian continent from Europe to the Pacific. In the 1970s that ring was extended south to the Middle East after President Jimmy Carter, in response to the energy crisis and the Soviet invasion of Afghanistan, pronounced the doctrine that any attack on the vital oil supplies of the West would be considered an attack on the United States. "Over time, our geographical commanders in chief around the world became almost like British proconsuls in the days of empire," Owens continued. "In the process, we discovered that the U.S. military presence created what amounted to a transoceanic system of alliances and economic zones. And much like the British in the nineteenth century, in the second half of the twentieth century we engaged in a sort of imperial policing of those zones, because the United States reaped the greatest rewards from their stability."

When victory in the Cold War came in 1989 with the toppling of the Berlin Wall and subsequent dissolution of the Soviet Union, the United States was thus left with a superpower military and security commitments stretching in an arc from Norway south through the Persian Gulf and east into the Sea of Japan—and with no superpower rival. The American ideals of democracy and free markets spread like wildfire through Eastern Europe, Asia, and Latin America. In 1993 the neoconservative intellectual Francis Fukuyama wrote the book *The End of History and the Last Man*, which argued that the bitter ideological struggles that had dominated the twentieth century were over, and that the model of free-market capitalism and liberal democracy championed by the United States represented the logical "end state" of political evolution. In his book *The Grand Chessboard: American Primacy and Its Geostrategic Imperatives*, Zbigniew Brzezinski described the country at that moment as the rarest of historical anomalies: "America is the first, the only, and the last superpower in the history of international affairs."

One of my favorite historians is Donald Kagan, at that time the Hillhouse professor of classics and history at Yale University. Besides being a leading historian in his own right, Kagan is the father of Robert Kagan, a neoconservative intellectual and author of the excellent book on transatlantic relations *Of Paradise and Power*; and Fredrick Kagan, a professor of military history at West Point with whom Don Kagan coauthored the book *While America Sleeps*. To find a historical analogy to America in the post–Cold War 1990s, Donald Kagan argued for looking back as far as two thousand years ago. "I think you have to go all the way back to the Roman Empire to find a single power so preeminent compared to all others," Kagan told me in 1999, comparing the United States of the 1990s to a Roman Empire that at one point stretched from Britain and Germany in the north to the Persian Gulf in the south. The dangers a preeminent America faced, he said, were not unlike those that eventually brought down the Roman Empire: overextension and imperial hubris. Largely as a result of the arrogance of power and overreach, the Roman Empire saw its strength sapped by an onslaught of barbarian invaders—vandals, Visigoths, Huns, and Goths—finally falling in AD 476.

Don Kagan also saw similarities between a globe-spanning U.S. military that was unchallenged in the air or at sea, and the Royal Navy of the nineteenth century. "Even at its peak, however, Great Britain had more competition from other great powers such as Russia, Austria, and France," Kagan explained. "And, of course, it was the wholly unexpected emergence of Germany as a great rival that led to two world wars and ultimately the end of the British Empire."

With the end of the Cold War and collapse of the Soviet Union, the United States' political leaders might reasonably have reordered the world according to just such a historical "balance of power" blueprint, contenting themselves to let the country become just one among a number of competing major powers in a benign era of democratic expansion. After all, bringing the troops home after war and disbanding wartime coalitions was an American tradition and in keeping with the avoidance of "entangling alliances" about which Founding Fathers George Washington and Thomas Jefferson warned.

At another seminal moment in its history, however, the United States benefited from the foresight of leaders who had come of age during World War II and its aftermath. After Ronald Reagan pressed the Soviet Union toward collapse, George H. W. Bush helped engineer a soft landing, promoting the peaceful reunification of Germany and beginning the process of NATO's expansion eastward in a protective embrace of the new democracies of the former Warsaw Pact.

According to one of these latter-day Wise Men and a chief architect behind that deft statecraft, the idea that the United States was going out of the superpower business was never given serious thought. "If after the Cold War the United States had just pulled out of Europe, or Asia or the Middle East, things would have just gone to hell in a hurry," Gen. Brent Scowcroft (U.S. Air Force, ret.), former national security adviser for George H. W. Bush, told me in his office in downtown Washington in 1999. "Japan would have doubled its defense budget and probably gone nuclear, upsetting the balance in Asia. Israel would probably have soon been fighting the Palestinians and might have faced a united Arab coalition once again. In Kosovo and Bosnia, Europe would prove that it was not ready to tackle tough problems without U.S. leadership. So the United States still had to shoulder those burdens, because we had a better chance to construct a world representative of our core values than at any other time in a rather bloody century."

With characteristic strategic ineptitude, Saddam Hussein of Iraq chose exactly that moment to swim against the tide of history, invading Kuwait in August of 1990. After the Bush administration won unanimous U.N. Security Council approval for ousting Iraqi forces from Kuwait, and built a broad coalition of Western powers and Arab allies to do just that, Scowcroft and Bush thought they could glimpse a "New World Order" for the post–Cold War era. Scowcroft remembers the moment precisely. He and President Bush were fishing off the coast of Kennebunkport, Maine, and both men realized that for the first time the Soviet Union would stand with the United States and approve United Nations–backed military action to repel Iraq's aggression. "We were out on the water for about four hours without even a nibble, and it gave us a rare chance to talk philosophically about the state of the world, and where we were heading as a nation," Scowcroft told me. "And it occurred to President Bush and to me that a new vista was opening in terms of countering nation-state aggression against other states, one of the great scourges of mankind throughout history. That was the first time we used the phrase 'New World Order,'" he said before adding ruefully: "It didn't last long."

In fact, even as America stood at the height of its power and international influence, rumblings of a backlash against U.S. predominance and the phenomenon of "globalization" that helped fuel it soon began sounding both abroad and at home. After the United States' war with Iraq in 1991, failed states replaced state-on-state aggression as the primary source of global instability. Crises followed in rapid succession in Somalia, Haiti, and the Balkans, as civil wars of nationalism, tribalism, and self-determination that were held in check during the Cold War erupted with increased frequency during the 1990s.

The tide of democratic liberalization and free market capitalism that swept across the world at the end of the Cold War would begin to sputter and in some cases recede as Russia and countries in Eastern Europe, Asia, and Latin America struggled with democratic transitions and attempted to weather major disruptions in the world financial markets. The same dynamic forces that sped the movement of capital and goods also spread the technological and material ingredients of doomsday weapons. Islamic extremism and its attendant terror grew throughout the decade, as parts of the Muslim world in particular pushed back fiercely against the encroachment of modernity and what they saw as the imposition of corrupt Western culture and values.

The rumblings of discord and dissonance could be heard at home as well. One year after George H. W. Bush was lauded as a hero of the Persian Gulf War, he was defeated by Democrat Bill Clinton, whose campaign mantra was "it's the economy, stupid," and whose administration promised a "peace dividend." Even if their leaders were not looking inward, the American people wanted respite from the burdens of a Cold War that left them saddled with a sluggish economy and massive debt that had quadrupled during the Reagan-Bush years.

Most important, Clinton's election represented a generational passing of the torch as the World War II generation began to recede from center stage in Washington, D.C. In its place, a new generation was set to take power. Rather than the binding experiences of the Great Depression and World War II that were the seminal events of their fathers' generation, however, the baby boom politicians still carried within them the bitter divisions left over from the Vietnam War and the 1960s cultural upheaval.

At a critical moment, the bipartisan consensus on the United States' rightful role in the world, somehow held together during the tumultuous decades of the Cold War by the political center in Washington, was about to splinter. The Atlas of the post–World War II global order was about to be shaken by the inconsistencies of a superpower at war with itself.

Predictably, baby boom politicians on both sides of the partisan divide struggled with their newfound power and ascendance. Certainly during his first term Bill Clinton endured serious foreign policy foibles, a number of them associated with strong currents in the Democratic Party. A humanitarian impulse led to mission creep and nation building in Somalia, and then to ignoble military retreat. Unfettered belief in multilateralism resulted in undue faith in the United Nations' ability to manage violent conflict, leading to nearly two years of dithering as the Balkans burned. Horrendous genocide in Rwanda was greeted by indecision and inaction. Yet as they searched for their own lodestar to guide them through the unfamiliar shoals of the post–Cold War era, Democrats were aided mightily by a president riding herd on their fractious caucus from the White House, where the foreign policy and military tools of the superpower are so overwhelmingly concentrated that historians talk of the modern "imperial presidency."

The seminal event in the ascendance of baby boom Republicans was the Republican takeover of Congress in 1994 as part of Newt Gingrich's "Republican Revolution." Like Clinton's election, the Republican Revolution symbolized the generational passing of the torch from aging Cold War warriors in the Republican Party such as former Senate Leaders Howard Baker (R-TN) and Robert Dole (R-KS) to a new generation of baby boom Republicans such as Gingrich (R-GA), Trent Lott (R-MS), and Dick Armey (R-TX). The Republican Revolution changed the political dynamic in Washington in important ways. Owing his ascent in large part to a successful campaign to bring down former House Speaker Jim Wright (D-TX) on ethics charges, Gingrich embodied a take-no-prisoners approach to politics that has become a fixture of the Washington scene. With little stomach for the divisiveness such tactics ensure, centrists from both parties were driven away from national politics. At times the Republican revolutionaries overstepped and devoured their own, a common phenomenon in revolutions, leading to the 1995 shutdown of the federal government that helped reelect Clinton the following year. During the impeachment drama, both Gingrich and his designated successor, Bob Livingston (R-LA), were forced to resign for their own sexual imbroglios. But the revolutionary forces unleashed by the political battles of the 1990s persisted.

Part of Gingrich's genius was that he visualized how to demarcate the boundaries of red and blue America in ways that favored a Republican majority in Congress. It wasn't an altogether original idea: Richard Nixon got there first, subtly manipulating the issue of race to tap into deep resentments in the South over federally imposed desegregation during the 1960s, and breaking what had been a stronghold of the Democratic Party. But Gingrich expanded the franchise, masterfully pushing hot button issues touching on "God, guns and gays" to appeal to the innate social conservatism of the South and West. That in turn helped reshape a Republican coalition that was more reflective of, and beholden to, those regions and values, especially as embodied in Christian evangelicals that are the bedrock of the new Republican base. While the domestic social policies associated with that shift are well known, the attendant views on international affairs that went along with it were less well understood.

By instinct, the Republican revolutionaries were probably closest to the tradition of populist nationalism associated with Andrew Jackson, the champion of American "exceptionalism" abroad and states' rights at home. Philosophically, the newly ascendant Republicans were thus suspicious of the federal government and of multilateral engagement that could impinge on U.S. sovereignty, whether expressed in international treaties or undue deference to the United Nations.

For a time during the post–Cold War debate on America's role in the world, a Republican Party in opposition even flirted with the isolationism of its past under Henry Cabot Lodge and William G. Harding, which had culminated in Republican support for the Neutrality Act of 1935, legislation designed to keep the United States out of World War II. That was the message behind the Republican presidential candidacy of Pat Buchanan in 1996, and his book *A Republic, Not an Empire*, which argued that arrogant U.S. foreign policy elites had overcommitted America to go to war in regions where it has no vital interests, and betrayed U.S. sovereignty by tying its fortunes to agencies of "an embryonic new world government," such as the United Nations, the World Trade Organization, and the International Monetary Fund. Among Republican revolutionaries, that argument had considerable resonance.

The Republican revolutionaries' belief in the benefits of unfettered capitalism borrowed from the economic nationalists associated with Alexander Hamilton, only it was capitalism on a global scale and on steroids. Their faith in a values-based approach to foreign policy borrowed from the idealist internationalism of Woodrow Wilson. Only the neoconservatives prominent among the Republican revolutionaries showed little of Wilson's commitment to international institutions or patience in letting League of Nations-like diplomacy and soft power prevail in spreading the faith. As Walter Russell Mead, a historian and fellow at the Council on Foreign Relations, details in his excellent book *Power, Terror, Peace and War*, the Republican revolutionaries, or "American Revivalists" as he calls them, borrowed from all those traditional strains of U.S. foreign policy to fashion a powerful hybrid that prizes American individualism and devalues the rule-based global institutions that might impinge upon it; promotes the bare-knuckle global economic competition of "millennial capitalism"; and espouses a deep faith in the power of U.S. values such as democracy and freedom to transform the world.

In the mid-1990s all of those various strains were still coalescing in a Republican majority in Congress that mainly stood in opposition to a Democrat in the White House. They thus objected to the Clinton administration's nation-building interventions in places such as Bosnia and Haiti as international social work. They rejected Clinton's outreach to Communists and former Communists in China and Russia. After aligning themselves with powerful southern committee chairmen such as Jesse Helms (R-NC), chairman of the Senate Foreign Relations Committee, the Republican revolutionaries also began withholding dues from the United Nations, making the United States the world body's largest debtor by 2000. State Department funding and foreign aid were cut to the point where American diplomacy faltered and the United States ranked last among all industrialized nations in the share of gross domestic product devoted to foreign aid.

Most of all, however, the Republican revolutionaries objected viscerally, manifestly, to Bill Clinton himself, and they wasted no opportunity to utterly reject his vision of America as the indispensable nation leading alliances and paying homage to multilateral institutions in order to tame a fractious world. Months after the effort to impeach Clinton failed, the Republicans thus exacted partial revenge by bringing the Comprehensive Test Ban Treaty up to a vote despite the Clinton administration's pleas to let it lie dormant. The Republicans knew they had the votes to inflict an embarrassing defeat on the administration and land a blow against its favored multilateralism.

More than any other single factor, those deep political fissures dividing Washington during the 1990s produced a troubling inconsistency in U.S. foreign policy. During a critical period of transition, the United States sent confused signals to the rest of the world. The divisions also sapped America's own energies to act abroad to confront global problems, be they failed states, the spread of terrorism and drug trafficking, disruptions in the global capital markets, or the proliferation of weapons of mass destruction. Thus in one moment the United States was fighting a humanitarian war in Kosovo, expanding NATO, ratifying the Chemical Weapons Convention, and helping create the World Trade Organization. In the next, it was stiffing the United Nations for dues, rejecting both the test ban and anti-landmine treaties, imposing unilateral economic sanctions here and there, and threatening to abolish the International Monetary Fund. The result was a decade of uncertain American leadership and a troubling deterioration of global stability as chronic threats festered.

Norman Ornstein, the veteran congressional analyst at the American Enterprise Institute and a valuable part of Washington's institutional memory, told me in an interview in 1999, "What concerns me is the fact that this debate about America's role in the world is occurring at a time when a generation of very powerful congressional leaders from both parties who shared a broad internationalist perspective is passing from the scene. It's being replaced by a new generation of political leaders that don't see American leadership in the world as particularly important."

The late Rep. Herbert H. Bateman (R-VA), a kindly southerner and former chairman of the House Armed Services Military Readiness Subcommittee, was exactly the kind of centrist that had been counted on by both parties as the glue that held the Cold War consensus together behind a strong military and international engagement. When I talked with him before the 2000 election, Bateman was already planning to retire and feeling like the last of a vanishing breed. "I'm very much aware of a body of opinion within the Republican Party which holds that America is trying to be the world's policeman, and too often we do undertake missions that are not really vital to U.S. national security," Bateman said. "At the same time, I've certainly never been an isolationist or 'Fortress America' type, and it's a major embarrassment that a meaningful number of Republicans can be identified as the 'Get out of the United Nations' crowd. It embarrasses me that those people even exist in the Republican Party."

In the spring of 1999, with Bill Clinton trying to manage a crisis in Kosovo even while Senate Republicans were voting to oppose NATO air strikes and the Republican House was trying to impeach the president, support for Clinton arrived from an unexpected corner. In a blistering editorial, the editors of the *Weekly Standard*, the increasingly influential broadsheet for the neoconservative movement, weighed in on Clinton's behalf. "As a result of that vote, and of the neo-isolationist arguments that leading Republicans made to support their position, Republican foreign policy is now mired in pathetic incoherence," the editors wrote. "Is this the party of Reagan, or the party of [Patrick] Buchanan? Right now, it's hard to tell."

There was no question which way the *Weekly Standard* wanted to tip the balance, along with other neoconservatives whose views were gaining currency in the Republican caucus. As a political movement, neoconservatism traced its lineage most directly to Woodrow Wilson and his idealistic view of America as a nation with a special calling to promote the spread of democracy and liberty in the world. As Joseph Nye, a former dean of the John F. Kennedy School of Government and author of *The Paradox of American Power*, put it to me in an interview, there was one major difference between modern neoconservatives and Woodrow Wilson: Modern neoconservatives, he said, were "neo-Wilsonians with a sword."

After becoming disillusioned with the Democratic Party's antiwar stance and "bring the boys home" flirtation with isolationism in the 1970s, a number of leading neoconservatives had migrated from the Henry "Scoop" Jackson wing of the Democratic Party—moderate on domestic issues but fervently anticommunist and pro-defense—to Ronald Reagan's administration. The seminal experience of their professional lives was Reagan's decision to discard the policy of détente and accommodation with the Soviet Union for a more confrontational approach.

Reagan's launching of the largest peacetime defense buildup in American history; his support for anticommunist fighters in Central America and Africa as a way to push back against the spread of communism; his description of the Soviet Union as an "evil empire" and spirited demand in Berlin that Mikhail Gorbachev "tear down this wall"—all were enshrined in the neoconservative ideology and worldview. The neoconservatives believed that U.S. military power must be unsurpassed in order that evil empires and nations could be confronted and defeated, not accommodated, to prepare the path for the march of democracy.

Jonathan Clarke is the coauthor of *America Alone: The Neo-Conservatives and the Global Order*. "There are a number of strong themes which define neoconservative thought, including the idea that military power is really at the center of international relations and how states interact with one another," he said to me in 2004. "Philosophically, they tend to divide the world into good and evil, and to reject the shades of gray so common in state-to-state interactions. Thirdly, there is a strong sense in neoconservative thought that, for the United States to lead, its power must be unconstrained by international law and treaties—and even allies, unless those allies happen to agree with it completely."

Back in mid-1997 leading neoconservatives had launched the Project for the New American Century, a sort of think tank whose goal was to unite the neoconservatives with the more traditional "realist" wing of the Republican Party in support of Reaganite principles. Chaired by Bill Kristol, the project called for major increases in U.S. defense spending, more challenges to "regimes hostile to our interests and values," active promotion of "political and economic freedoms abroad," and recognition of

"America's unique role in preserving and extending an international order friendly to our security, our prosperity and our principles."

As I was researching the Bush administration's staffing of its foreign affairs and national security bureaucracies in the months after the Supreme Court's December 2000 decision, I was struck by the names that appeared at the bottom of that founding document of the Project for the New American Century. Among the twenty-five or so signatories were the names of Vice President Dick Cheney and Defense Secretary Designate Donald Rumsfeld. Lewis Libby, Cheney's designated chief of staff, and Zalmay Khalilzad, a senior National Security Council official in the new Bush administration, were also listed. Both had been former protégés of Paul Wolfowitz, who had served in the Reagan and George H. W. Bush administrations and was considered by many as the intellectual high priest of the neoconservative movement.

Of course, Wolfowitz's own name was on the founding document for the New American Century, and on another Project document that in 1998 called on Clinton to militarily overthrow Saddam Hussein. That "Iraq letter" included the names of Richard Armitage, slated to become Colin Powell's number two at the State Department, and Richard Perle, a key figure in the Reagan Pentagon who had been dubbed "the Prince of Darkness" for his hard-line approach to arms control negotiations. In the new administration of George W. Bush, Perle was slated for the Defense Policy Board, a group that would advise Secretary Rumsfeld on key issues. Meanwhile, a former Perle protégé, Douglas Feith, was tagged for the important position of Undersecretary of Defense for Policy, essentially the number three position in the Pentagon and the job that Wolfowitz had held in the first Bush administration. Like other prominent neoconservatives, Feith was a veteran of the Reagan Pentagon, had close ties with Israel's conservative Likud Party, and in testimony and writings was on record criticizing virtually the entire gamut of arms control agreements.

And so it went after the election, as the Bush transition team heavily stocked the new administration with the most prominent "neo-Wilsonians with a sword" and hard-line Jacksonians in the country. Among these hard-line nationalists was Vice President Dick Cheney himself, a Wyoming native whose mild demeanor belied a deep conservatism. As a congressman Cheney had actually once complained when a reporter referred to him as a moderate, and in *National Journal*'s analysis of voting records Cheney was at one time rated the most conservative member in Congress.

Other than Colin Powell and a few of his top aides at Foggy Bottom, the Bush foreign policy and national security team was nearly devoid of the moderate internationalists that dominated his father's administration, men and women in the tradition of the Wise Men of the post–World War II period. Even at the State Department some of the new administration's key picks seemed to reveal an ideological agenda that was at odds with any talk of a "humble" foreign policy. As the Assistant Secretary of State for Latin America, for instance, the Bush team nominated Otto Reich, a fervent anti-Castro crusader and Cuban-American hard-liner who the Senate judged too divisive even to confirm.

Another telling choice was John Bolton, who was nominated to serve as the Undersecretary of State for Arms Control and International Security. As I wrote in *National Journal* at the time, Bolton was also a curious and controversial choice, in that he had vociferously opposed in writings and testimony virtually all of the multilateral arrangements and arms control agreements that he would soon be responsible for overseeing, negotiating, and enforcing. His positions, in other words, fit comfortably with those of his chief congressional patron, Sen. Jesse Helms, who during the Clinton years had forced the State Department to abolish the Arms Control and Disarmament Agency (ACDA).

For my article on the new Bush team, I ran the Bolton choice by Joseph Cirincione, the feisty and always quotable arms control expert at the Carnegie Endowment for International Peace in Washington. "After razing the Carthage of arms control by abolishing ACDA and defeating the Comprehensive Test Ban Treaty, Senator Helms has now pushed Bolton for this position as a way to salt the fields so that no arms control will grow at the State Department for forty years," Cirincione was quoted in my story.

Designees for top-level positions will rarely talk to journalists until after they have been confirmed by the Senate, so after Bolton was confirmed on a largely party-line vote of 57–43, I called his office at the State Department to give him a chance to respond to his critics. After I gave my name to the secretary, Bolton came on the line.

"You're the one who quoted Joe Cirincione in that article?"

Well, I explained, the reason I had called was to give Bolton a chance to reply. I needn't have bothered. Before the words were out of my mouth Bolton had muttered an expletive and my receiver went dead. The post–Cold War era was dead too, I reasoned, and the United States was poised to offer a radical new answer to the question of how America would wield its preponderant power. The Bush revolution had begun.

CHAPTER 2

Three-Dimensional Chess

THE CHEYENNE MOUNTAIN Operations Center is the hub of a vast underground complex buried deep beneath Colorado's Rocky Mountains. Each day more than twelve hundred men and women enter the base of Cheyenne Mountain through massive twenty-seven-ton concrete-and-steel blast doors to toil in a subterranean city that boasts its own emergency food supply, a cavernous water reservoir, and a labyrinth of raised walkways and chambers that float on a bed of industrial-sized springs, cushioning the cave dwellers from a thermonuclear blast. The command-and-control room, the nerve center for the North American Aerospace Defense Command, is essentially the conductor's podium for Armageddon. If the Cold War had ever superheated, raising the curtain on the carefully rehearsed symphony of doom known as "mutually assured destruction," the men and women in Cheyenne Mountain would have served as the sorcerer's apprentices: tracking the blossoming arcs of missiles on giant electronic wall maps of the world, validating the satellite findings, cross-checking the trajectories with ground radars, and matter-of-factly advising the National Command Authority that yes, sir, unfortunately this was the real thing.

On a chilly afternoon in February 2001, I found myself in the Operations Center, watching a simulated, more modest attack staged for my benefit. Rehearsing the sequence of events exactly as they would actually occur—the rote drill by which the U.S. military prepared its Cheyenne troops for the unthinkable—a single missile launch was "detected" in North Korea. Using the largest and most complex command-and-control network in the world, consisting of more than two hundred computer systems and six hundred communications circuits, technicians tracked the missile's trajectory with a constellation of early warning satellites. After double-checking the data and fixing the missile's likely impact point in the United States, the Cheyenne commander calmly communicated the warning over redundant communications hotlines that in an actual attack would have connected to the White House, the Pentagon, and

U.S. Strategic Command in Omaha, Nebraska, where America's terrible retribution would originate. In fact, practically the only thing the Operations Center could not do during the missile's twenty-eight-minute virtual flight—and this was really the point of the demonstration—was to take any action to stop it.

In an era when the likes of North Korea's Kim Jong Il was acquiring long-range missiles and perhaps nuclear warheads, few could dispute the usefulness of a system capable of intercepting them if the occasion arose. In fact, the quest to develop a reliable defense against the world's most fearsome weapon—the Intercontinental Ballistic Missile (ICBM)—began shortly after the missiles themselves were introduced in the late 1950s. In the 1960s, the Johnson administration proposed building the Sentinel system, a limited antimissile system that employed interceptors with nuclear warheads. The United States even briefly deployed a one-site missile defense system called Safeguard in the early 1970s to protect its missile forces, but quickly closed the site down because of cost and reliability problems (the system's rocket failed on nearly half of its forty-two flights over a five-year period). Largely because of the technological difficulties and great expense involved in fielding a viable defense against a speeding, nuclear-tipped bullet, the United States and the Soviet Union both signed the Antiballistic Missile (ABM) Treaty in 1972, which greatly restricted both nations from testing and fielding an antimissile system.

President Ronald Reagan resurrected the idea of an umbrella against missile attack in 1983, however, proposing a combination of laser-equipped satellites and space-based weapons to get the job done. In the process Reagan captured the imaginations of an entire generation of Republican politicians and national security experts enthralled by the possibilities. The Pentagon spent $60 billion on the program, dubbed "Star Wars" by its critics, but never produced a single interceptor. The research on the system, however, apparently helped make the Soviets despair of keeping pace in the arms race, hastening the end of the Cold War. Ever since, Reagan's vision of an effective national missile defense system had become a pillar of Republican defense policy, enshrined as a major plank in Newt Gingrich's 1994 *Contract with America*. Pressured by a Republican Congress, the Clinton administration had spent billions of additional dollars on research in the 1990s and proposed a limited system that could fit within the confines of a renegotiated ABM Treaty.

Lingering and serious questions remained, however, about the cost and viability of such a system. As the head of the Pentagon's missile defense program once noted to me, this really *was* "rocket science." The nonpartisan Congressional Budget Office estimated that even Clinton's stripped-down system would require an investment of between $30 and $60 billion. The much more robust system proposed by the Bush administration would likely cost $120 billion or more, putting it on a par with the two most technologically ambitious projects ever undertaken by the U.S. government, the 1940s-era Manhattan Project to create the world's first nuclear weapons, and the 1960s Apollo Program to land a man on the moon. As missile defense proponents rightly pointed out, both of those programs also began amidst serious doubts and daunting technological challenges, and both ultimately succeeded in spectacular fashion.

Despite the unshakable faith in missile defense among Republicans, however, many experts in rocket science and physics remained highly skeptical that a national missile defense system could ever adequately contend with easily adopted and relatively cheap countermeasures. Because warheads and simple decoys such as balloons travel at the same speed and behave similarly in the vacuum of deep space, where missiles would almost certainly have to be intercepted, physicists had long recognized that interceptors could be tricked. For that reason, the Security Studies Program at the Massachusetts Institute of Technology and the Union of Concerned Scientists released a detailed study in 2000 opposing the system proposed by the Bush administration.

"We've been around this circuit twice before, first with the Johnson and Nixon administrations, and then with Ronald Reagan's 'Star Wars' episode. Each time the scientific community has reached a consensus that the national missile defense as proposed is a basically flawed concept because it is not capable of handling countermeasures," said Kurt Gottfried, a professor emeritus of physics at Cornell and chairman of the Union of Concerned Scientists. "There seems to be a sort of mythical attraction to the idea of a national defense against missiles that unfortunately we physicists find hard to understand. Maybe you should convene a convention of psychologists to find out what continues to motivate these efforts."

Beyond the nuts and bolts and dollars of missile defense, there were also a host of strategic imponderables that made the entire enterprise akin to three-dimensional chess. As the Bush administration pointed out, fielding their proposed missile defense system would require a total abrogation of the ABM Treaty, the first time in the nuclear age that America had rescinded an arms control treaty. Would Russia respond, as it had threatened, by tearing up the SALT and START missile limitation agreements, and begin again fielding multiple-warhead missiles that could easily overwhelm a defense system? Might Moscow pass on its sophisticated decoy technology to "rogue" clients with a relative handful of missiles such as North Korea and Iran, thus increasing the only threat the national missile defense could plausibly counter? Could such a system actually drive rogue regimes to pass nuclear weapons to terrorists instead as a surer and more surreptitious means of delivery? Or might they focus on cruise missiles that would literally fly under the radar of such a missile defense system? Would China react by greatly increasing its very limited arsenal of nuclear ICBMs, possibly igniting an Asian arms race that could sweep in India, Pakistan, and perhaps Japan?

Conversely, if those scenarios were avoidable, could a viable national missile defense actually discourage rogue nations from even trying to develop expensive ICBM arsenals, much less use them? Under which combination of scenarios would national missile defense actually make the United States a more secure nation? With its determination to begin fielding a robust missile defense system in its first term in the face of all the imponderables, the new Bush administration was essentially anteing up $60 billion for its opening gambit, revealing an early penchant for bold moves in the three-dimensional chess game of grand strategy. No one believed it would be their last.

In fact, the Bush administration's determination to rapidly deploy a missile defense system was only one reason I decided to visit Colorado Springs in February of 2001. The road that runs straight as an arrow from the eastern scrub plains of Colorado west to Cheyenne Mountain and the front range of the Rockies also passes by nearby Petersen Air Force Base, home to U.S. Space Command, the Pentagon's joint center for space operations. The separate headquarters of the Air Force and Army space commands also lie along that route. In terms of the military, that makes Colorado Springs "Space Town, USA," and thus perhaps the best place in the entire country to try and understand Secretary of Defense Donald Rumsfeld's vision for transforming the U.S. military.

The resurrection of Donald Rumsfeld's government career after a Rip van Winkle-like absence of nearly two decades was one of the more intriguing backstories of the Bush transition of early 2001. As James Mann details in his book *Rise of the Vulcans,* the surprise choice of Rumsfeld was largely due to the desire of neoconservatives and hard-liners in the new administration, and their powerful allies in Congress, to counterbalance and limit the influence over foreign policy of Colin Powell. At the press conference announcing his selection as Secretary of State in December 2000, Powell was seen by many conservatives close to the new administration as having upstaged President Bush. A noted, moderate internationalist, furthermore, was not the most welcome company at a revolution.

Rumsfeld, on the other hand, had never been accused of moderation when it came to doggedly pursuing his goals and interests. A legendary bureaucratic infighter, Rumsfeld had served in various top positions, including White House chief of staff and Defense Secretary, in the Nixon and Ford administrations. Rumsfeld and his then-protégé Dick Cheney, both strongly opposed to Henry Kissinger's policy of détente and arms

control agreements with the Soviet Union, had once so badly outmaneu-
vered Kissinger in bureaucratic battles in the Ford administration that
Kissinger had drafted a letter of resignation. In Republican circles, outma-
neuvering Kissinger was pretty much the gold standard of bureaucratic
infighting. Rumsfeld also saw to it that Cheney succeeded him as Ford's
chief of staff, the kind of career-advancing boost rarely forgotten in the
surprisingly tight-knit circles at the center of American politics and governance.

The choice of Donald Rumsfeld also sent an unambiguous signal to
the uniformed military that George W. Bush was actually serious about
defense transformation. Rumsfeld had resurfaced in the national defense
debate in the late 1990s, for instance, after he was named chairman of two
influential congressional commissions. The first commission focused on
the ballistic missile threat. What came to be known as the Rumsfeld Missile Commission concluded that the threat to the United States from
rogue states armed with ballistic missiles was "broader, more mature,
and evolving more rapidly than has been reported" by the intelligence
community. Soon after the release of that report, North Korea unexpectedly launched a multistage rocket that sailed over Japan and well into the
Pacific toward Alaska. That made Rumsfeld something of a hero with Republicans who for years had been advocating the need for a national missile defense system, and it undoubtedly solidified Rumsfeld's noted
skepticism of the reliability of U.S. intelligence.

The Rumsfeld Space Commission, on the other hand, was arguably
even more influential in shaping the new Defense Secretary's thinking on
defense transformation. The Commission concluded that the military's increased exploitation of outer space heralded revolutionary change in military operations. Rumsfeld and the other commissioners argued that the
U.S. military's control and dominance of space could prove as vital in the
Information Age as U.S. shipyards and factories were in manufacturing
"the arsenal of democracy" during the Industrial Age.

Retired Navy Adm. David Jeremiah served on the Rumsfeld Space
Commission, whose report was released in January 2000, and he spoke
with me about its findings. "The United States' utilization of space today
is enormous, and it is increasing at a rate that makes this nation very dependent on space assets for a host of services whose importance we don't
even fully recognize yet," he said. As just one example of the growing
dependency on space, Jeremiah cited the rapid proliferation over the past
decade of Global Positioning Systems (GPS) in everything from advanced
munitions and military aircraft to cars and recreational boats. Commercial imaging satellites now offered to the highest bidder high-resolution
photos that in the past were the exclusive purview of spy satellites. "History also tells us that, as we have increasingly explored every medium—

land, sea, and air—that medium has eventually seen military conflict," said Jeremiah. "Experience suggests that space will be no different."

The Rumsfeld Space Commission's finding that warfare in space was a "virtual certainty" predictably outraged arms control advocates who had long argued against the militarization of space, but very early on Rumsfeld displayed something of a taste for provoking outrage. More to the point, the Rumsfeld Space Commission report, with its emphasis on the technologies on display at Space Town USA, offered tantalizing insights into Rumsfeld's thinking on military transformation. The picture that emerged was of a U.S. military capable of projecting power rapidly anywhere in the world, using eyes, ears, and commands from outer space to shrink distances and pierce the ever-present "fog of war" from above, even while lowering that cloud over its adversaries with advanced jamming and space-denial technologies.

At the Space Control Center in Cheyenne Mountain, for instance, I watched technicians track the movement of each of the man-made objects currently orbiting the Earth—all eighty-three hundred of them. The wall-mounted video display in the control center showed swarms of satellites and space debris careening around the Earth in crisscrossing orbits, as the center's powerful computers constantly plotted and updated their positions. From inside that control center, experts in the esoteric science of "orbitology" used that data to regularly inform U.S. military commanders around the world exactly when they would have an open window over a potential adversary's territory, and when unfriendly spy satellites were lurking overhead.

To hear the experts at Space Command tell it, the Persian Gulf War was the watershed event that first alerted U.S. military commanders, and eventually the rest of the world, to the largely untapped military potential of space. With the Cold War suddenly over, secret imaging, missile-warning, and electronic intercept satellites that had been focused almost exclusively on the Soviet Union's strategic nuclear forces were aimed instead at Iraq. The Pentagon quickly discovered that those same satellites could help track the movements of the Iraqi Republican Guard and the launches of Iraqi Scud missiles. U.S. ground forces also used thousands of GPS receivers to navigate over the featureless Saudi and Iraqi deserts. And satellites carried 90 percent of the U.S. military's long-distance communications in and out of the Persian Gulf region.

After Desert Storm, the U.S. military's exploitation of space assets grew exponentially, as evidenced by the 1999 war over Kosovo. For the first time in combat, U.S. forces used the GPS-guided Joint Direct Attack Munition (JDAM), an all-weather, precision-guided bomb that, at roughly $21,000 each, offered an accurate alternative to the $1 million-plus Tomahawk cruise missile, presaging a new era of affordable precision-guided weaponry. U.S. commanders were also able for the first time to transfer satellite information directly into the cockpits of long-range bombers during the Kosovo war, including information on moving targets, threats, and the positions of friendly aircraft. The Air Force planned to outfit its entire bomber fleet with the new satellite links.

In many ways the exploitation of space was what most distinguished the U.S. military superpower from its distant competitors, much as the dreadnought once distinguished the British Navy from pretenders to the blue-water throne. Although many potential adversaries had modern armies, navies, and air forces, none came close to the U.S. military in their use of space for secure communications, missile warning, surveillance, navigation, intelligence gathering, and overall command-and-control.

Col. Robert Ryals, the deputy commander of the Air Force's Space Warfare Center in Colorado Springs, likened the U.S. position in space at the turn of the millennium to the early days of flight during World War I, when primitive airplanes were initially used primarily for observation and reconnaissance. "In the interwar years, a lot of smart people such as Gen. Billy Mitchell developed new concepts for arming aircraft and projecting airpower, so that when World War II came along, we had a plan on how to prosecute an air war," he told me in the windowless building, surrounded by a moat of barbed wire, that housed the Space Warfare Center. "Today, the United States is likewise using space assets primarily for observation and communication purposes. If called upon by the National Command Authority in the future, however, our mission is to be ready to prosecute space warfare."

By the time Space Town USA was in my rearview mirror, Donald Rumsfeld's vision for a transformed U.S. military was coming into clearer focus. As billed, it was very much in keeping with a band of military reformers who had argued throughout the 1990s that information-age technologies were creating a "revolution in military affairs" (RMA) that the U.S. services ignored at their own peril. With U.S. conventional military superiority unchallenged, those reformers advocated new strategies and doctrines to address the "asymmetrical" threats to the U.S. homeland from ballistic missiles, terrorists armed with weapons of mass destruction, and cyber-hackers intent on crippling U.S. computer networks.

Much like the men and women of Space Town, those reformers argued that the Pentagon needed to do more to protect its increasingly important constellations of space-based satellites, as well as its overseas bases and staging areas, from adversaries armed with missiles and biological and chemical warheads. They too put a premium on the cutting-edge technologies on display in Colorado Springs, such as national missile defense, space-based radars, airborne and space-based lasers, unmanned aerial vehicles and radar-evading stealth aircraft, ships, and ground-combat systems.

While the U.S. armed services had all adopted parts of that agenda, and were constantly upgrading their weapons with advanced information-age technologies, in general they resisted revolutionary change in favor of a more evolutionary approach. The reformers talked about the post–Cold War period as a "strategic pause," a period of relative calm when the services could abandon "legacy" weapons systems designed in the 1970s and 1980s such as conventional tanks, ships, and aircraft, in order to afford new, "leap ahead" technologies for the new millennium. In the midst of the anticipated strategic breather, however, the armed services had gone through a painful downsizing, cutting their forces by roughly a third so that the Clinton administration could reap a "peace dividend." The resultant "procurement holiday" in the early and mid-1990s, and a string of nearly continuous contingencies in Iraq, Somalia, Haiti, Bosnia, and Kosovo, left the U.S. military with rapidly aging arsenals worn from nearly nonstop use. The tumultuous post–Cold War decade of the 1990s seemed to the uniformed leadership like precarious ground from which to make any risky leaps into the technological unknown.

As traditionally conservative institutions responsible for the very survival of the republic, the U.S. armed services were also reluctant to accept the risks inherent in such radical change. Many of the concepts affiliated with Rumsfeld's proposed transformation constituted a direct threat to powerful and venerable constituencies in the uniformed services, including proponents of Navy aircraft carriers, Army heavy divisions, and Air Force tactical fighters. The revolutionaries who were flocking to Rumsfeld's "transformational" banner in the Pentagon had frequently argued in the past that aircraft carriers were too expensive and vulnerable, heavy divisions too slow and difficult to deploy, and tactical fighters too short-range to adequately address the threats of the future. All of which suggested a *battle royale* looming over Donald Rumsfeld's proposed transformation of the U.S. military.

Any doubts that Space Town USA offered valuable insights into Don Rumsfeld's thinking on military transformation were dispelled in his first months in office. Rumsfeld brought his chief of staff on the Missile and Space Commissions, Stephen Cambone, over to the Pentagon and installed him as a key figure in the transition. A briefing paper circulated from the Office of the Secretary of Defense soon after listed Rumsfeld's top five priorities, which included deploying a missile defense system; modernizing U.S. command, control, communications, intelligence, and space capabilities; and "transforming" the military with new technologies, many based on space systems. Later in the year, when Rumsfeld had his first opportunity to truly put his stamp on the top leadership of the U.S. military by naming a new Chairman of the Joint Chiefs of Staff, the highest-ranking officer in the land, Rumsfeld chose Air Force Gen. Richard Myers. Myers's previous job was as the four-star commander of U.S. Space Command in Colorado Springs.

Deep in the bowels of the Pentagon there is a small, in-house think tank and a group of iconoclasts collectively called the Office of Net Assessment. While the rest of the building primarily focuses on the day-to-day running of the U.S. military's vast empire, or the recruiting, training, and equipping of an organization over two million strong with a budget in the hundreds of billions of dollars, the tiny band of guerrilla analysts are paid to think outside the box and many years down the road. In 2001, they were led by seventy-nine-year-old Andy Marshall, a legendary futurist and one of the foremost advocates in military circles of the revolution in military affairs.

In the Defense Department's vast realm, the tiny Office of Net Assessment is hardly considered a major power center. Because it has no direct say in major procurement or budgetary decisions, Net Assessment offers only reflected light, its influence directly proportional to the size and power of the officials who find its arguments illuminating. In the spring of 2001, Andy Marshall and his iconoclasts were told that those officials included the new Defense Secretary and the Vice President of the United States, himself a former Secretary of Defense.

As a sort of real-life Yoda, the elderly Marshall had mentored many of the advocates of transformation who passed through the Office of Net Assessment on their way to jobs with influential think tanks and major defense contractors, and they had helped keep his vision of a revolution in military affairs alive during the 1990s. In the spring of 2001, many of those Marshall protégés and self-styled revolutionaries received phone calls asking them to come back to the Pentagon to take part in a secretive strategic review of the U.S. military. Everything was on the table, Marshall's office told them, and the stars were finally in alignment to realize truly transformational change of the U.S. military.

Put in the unusual position of being able to ram through the recommendations of his own recent commissions, Donald Rumsfeld and his close-knit team of civilians in the Office of the Secretary of Defense (OSD) quickly telegraphed to the uniformed leadership their intent to steer a course toward fundamental transformation. Those who didn't get the message were treated with sharp elbows. Privately, many of Rumsfeld's team believed that Bill Clinton had allowed the uniformed leadership to walk all over him, and they were quick to show who was boss. Rumsfeld's revolutionaries were also convinced that the powerful service chiefs and their mammoth staffs of thousands had become expert at gaming the system, using the glacier-paced Quadrennial Defense Review (QDR), a top-to-bottom analysis of U.S. force posture required by Congress every four years, to essentially ratify the status quo. Indeed, at the end of each major post–Cold War review of the U.S. military, the answer posited by the generals and admirals was essentially a smaller version of the Cold War force they had grown up with and were comfortable in, built around Navy carrier battle groups, Air Force tactical fighter wings, Army heavy divisions, and Marine amphibious groups.

Determined to hear a different answer, the Rumsfeld team asked the questions in a novel way. Rather than wait for completion of the QDR, Rumsfeld immediately launched Marshall's secretive strategic review and demanded a report back in just forty-five days, hopefully before service resistance to the ideas could coalesce. Much to their chagrin, U.S. service leaders were largely excluded from those early deliberations.

Andrew Krepinevich, the director of the Center for Strategic and Budgetary Assessments, a think tank in Washington, is one of the foremost authorities on the concepts behind RMA and military transformation. Another former protégé of Andy Marshall, Krepinevich was also pulled back into the Pentagon to do work on the guerrilla review. "The best way to ensure the survival of the status quo in military strategy is to ask all the factions in the Pentagon for their input, which is exactly what happens with the Quadrennial Defense Review," Krepinevich told me in an interview in 2001. "Because Rumsfeld was a Secretary of Defense when the current members of the Joint Chiefs of Staff were all majors and lieutenant commanders, however, they cannot intimidate him. So just as only Nixon could go to China, perhaps only Republicans have enough latitude on defense issues to realize change this dramatic. The key will be whether the new strategy reduces the risks we face from future threats, and whether or not there are sufficient resources identified to execute that strategy."

The issue of how Rumsfeld and company planned to pay for all their expensive transformation initiatives was the source of great unease among service leaders. According to inside sources, when Rumsfeld had crossed the Potomac for his first full cabinet meeting, he was carrying budget estimates that showed that even an essentially zero-growth defense budget would require an extra $113 billion to cover inflation, rising fuel costs, and increased maintenance for the Pentagon's aging arsenal. Just to adequately sustain the U.S. military force that existed in 2001, Rumsfeld told his fellow cabinet officers, the Pentagon would need an extra $245 billion above the Clinton administration's proposed six-year budget plan.

Like the other cabinet members present, however, Rumsfeld was told
by the Office of Management and Budget that the Pentagon would have
to live under tight spending ceilings so that President Bush could afford
his immediate priorities of a $1.35 trillion tax cut and proposed domestic
reforms in education, Social Security, and prescription drug insurance. In
the budget released on February 28, 2001, Bush asked for $310 billion for
the Pentagon in fiscal 2002, essentially hewing to the defense budget proposed by the Clinton administration and disappointing high expectations
in the military raised by Dick Cheney's campaign pledge that "help is on
the way."

As the stewards of their services, the chiefs of the Army, Air Force,
Navy, and Marines all understood those numbers better than just about
anyone in Washington, D.C., and their staffs of "iron majors" were expert
at reading the tea leaves. Most senior uniformed officers were lukewarm
about national missile defense precisely because they saw it draining
badly needed funds from more pressing needs and priorities. If the Bush
administration wasn't going to significantly increase defense spending,
and with Rumsfeld apparently serious both about missile defense and
transformation, then the OSD was obviously going to need a "bill payer."
In essence, that meant Andy Marshall's strategic review would have to be
funded either by cuts in the overall size of a U.S. military force structure
that was already strained by ongoing operations, or by the cancellation
of major weapons systems badly needed to replenish an aging arsenal.
Realistically, Rumsfeld and his team would probably need to fashion an
unpopular combination of both approaches, plus some future increase in
defense spending. Little wonder that the honeymoon for the new Rumsfeld team inside the Pentagon was short.

Because it was the least high-tech and most troop heavy of the services, the U.S. Army felt by far the most vulnerable among the services.
Cuts in Army troop strength and force structure, for instance, yield relatively immediate and substantial cost savings because the Pentagon's payroll costs are so huge and funding for major weapons programs is spaced
out over many years. The Army force structure of ten divisions also didn't
translate into home-state programs such as big shipbuilding or airplane
manufacturing contracts, and thus didn't enjoy the same level of support
on Capitol Hill.

In 1999, because of its massive logistics requirements, the Army had
struggled mightily to deploy a single Apache gunship unit to the Kosovo
war. After this "Task Force Hawk" debacle, the impression had grown
that of all the services, the Army had been slowest to adjust to a post–
Cold War era that favored more rapidly deployable and expeditionary
forces. More recently, Army Chief of Staff Eric Shinseki had launched his
own transformation effort aimed at making Army forces lighter and more

rapidly deployable with a plan to create new "Stryker Brigades" built around lighter, wheeled, Stryker armored vehicles as opposed to the tracked M-1 Abrams tanks and Bradley Fighting Vehicles in heavy and mechanized divisions. With the emphasis of the Rumsfeld team on radical transformation, however, there was a growing alarm among greensuiters that whatever questions were asked by the Marshall strategic review, the answers would spell trouble for the Army.

Those fears crystallized on Saturday, May 12, when the Joint Chiefs of Staff met with Rumsfeld for a briefing on one of the most eagerly awaited of the many secretive ongoing reviews of U.S. defense posture, the blueprints for Rumsfeld's transformation of the U.S. military. The particular briefing was on the future of conventional war-fighting, the mission the services spent the vast majority of their energies preparing for and contemplating. Leading the briefing was David Gompert, a vice president at the RAND Corporation think tank who had answered Andy Marshall's call for all revolutionaries on deck.

According to sources familiar with the briefing, Gompert emphasized the future value of long-range, precision-strike capabilities, meaning missiles and bombs that airplanes and ships could launch from safe altitudes or distances. The review defined weapons as either suitable to a future battlefield dominated by rapidly deployable forces with such over-the-horizon firing capability, or as marginal or even irrelevant to that scenario. In the latter categories, reportedly, were the Army's seventy-ton M1-A2 Abrams battle tank and the still-in-development Crusader mobile artillery system. The Gompert review also raised the possibility of eliminating two heavy Army tank divisions in order to fund military transformation.

All of the service chiefs were smarting over being excluded from the early stages of what were being called the "Rumsfeld Reviews," and they gave the briefing a frosty reception. To senior Army leaders, however, the review seemed like nothing less than a warning shot across the bow, calling into question their fundamental relevance. As I reported at the time, a week after the May 12 briefing former Army Chief of Staff Gen. Gordon Sullivan (ret.), president of the Association of the U.S. Army, an alumni group that retains very close ties to senior Army leaders, took a rare public swipe at the new Defense Secretary. Rumsfeld seemed headed, Sullivan said, toward "the easy but erroneous conclusion that by spending hundreds of billions of dollars weaponizing space, developing a national missile defense, and buying long-range precision weapons, we can avoid the ugly realities of conflict."

With the Bush revolution only months old, institutional resistance to its restructuring of the accepted order was already growing inside the Pentagon. The episode also revealed that in terms of Donald Rumsfeld's vision for a transformed military, the battle lines would most clearly delineate a confrontation between Rumsfeld and his OSD staff and the U.S. Army.

Events in the spring and summer of 2001 also proved conclusively that Rumsfeld's reforging of the sword of the republic was only part of a much broader effort to redefine the nature of American power and how it was wielded on the international stage. At the same time the Pentagon was moving rapidly to build a missile shield and announcing it wanted to restart research on a new generation of nuclear weapons, for instance, the Bush administration began systematically unshackling the United States from a host of international treaties and peacekeeping commitments. To those on the other side of the three-dimensional chessboard, it looked very much like history's most dominant power was about to unilaterally press its advantage.

CHAPTER 3

A Darker Prism

O N A MAY EVENING in 2001 at the Russian Embassy in
Washington, I found myself standing beneath a massive tap-
estry bearing the Russian double-headed eagle and talking
with the last Communist czar of the Soviet Union. With the Soviet hammer and sickle retired as a symbol of one of history's great failures, the
eagle had been resurrected from the time of the royal czars to serve as the
mascot of the new Russian state. As in centuries past, one of the eagle's
heads looked left and the other right, a proclamation of Russia's central
position on the Eurasian continent straddling the Eastern and Western
worlds. Lately, the visage looking to the West had been scowling.

For the man who fed the Russian eagle its first taste of glasnost, and
was as responsible as any individual for the peaceful dissolution of the
Soviet empire, the turn of events by the spring of 2001 were perplexing
indeed. Almost nothing that had transpired since Russia's hopeful birth
of freedom and democracy in the early 1990s had unfolded in the way
once envisioned by Mikhail Gorbachev.

Many of the aspirations of Russia in those days of optimism had
faded after a decade of disappointments and humiliations. The Western-
prescribed privatization of Russia's state-owned industries in the mid-
1990s had gone disastrously awry, giving corrupt oligarchs and criminal
mafias a near stranglehold on the economy. A visibly enfeebled President
Boris Yeltsin, hero of the democracy movement, retired in June 2000 with
single-digit approval ratings and a reputation for drunkenness and odd
behavior. His replacement was the increasingly authoritarian populist
Vladimir Putin, an ex-KGB official who since assuming the Russian presidency had cracked down on the independent media, waged a scorched-
earth war in Chechnya, and openly intimidated Russia's neighbors by
cutting off their energy supplies.

In Washington, meanwhile, the son of the man with whom Gorbachev negotiated the final terms of the Soviet Union's "surrender" had
taken to wagging a disapproving finger at Russia's prostrate figure. In a

few short months, high-ranking Bush administration officials had termed Russia a "threat" and unscrupulous arms merchant, significantly cut U.S. funding for dismantling and securing Russia's nuclear stockpile, and kicked out fifty Russian "diplomats" in the largest expulsion of suspected spies since the height of the Cold War. Next on the U.S. agenda was a further expansion of NATO to Russia's very borders and the construction of a missile defense system, moves that Russian officials bitterly opposed but were helpless to stop.

"The direction of the U.S.-Russian relationship recently has clearly not been good, and I think it would be a mistake for either the Americans or Russians to treat irresponsibly the legacy of ending the Cold War," Gorbachev told me through an interpreter after a dinner in his honor in May 2001. "I believe it all started after the Soviet Union broke up and the United States rejected the strategy we had developed together for ending the Cold War. Up to that point, we were signing peace treaties in Paris, reuniting Germany, reducing arms in Europe, and turning the Warsaw Pact and NATO into more political rather than military alliances."

The turning point in the eyes of Gorbachev and many Russian elite had been the 1990s decision made by the United States to retain a histori-cally large military and expand the NATO alliance to secure the gains of liberty, essentially remaining a superpower without superpower rivals. Ironically, that was one of the last truly consequential foreign policy deci-sions made before the Cold War consensus in Washington fractured along America's widening domestic political divide. The growing resentment of that new unipolar international order peaked during the Kosovo war, when a U.S.-led NATO alliance acted without putting the matter to the U.N. Security Council, where both Russia and China had permanent seats and would surely have vetoed action to stop Slobodan Milosevic's ethnic cleansing.

During the 1990s the Clinton administration had sought to soften the blow of American hegemony by reaching out to Beijing and Moscow. Clinton called Beijing a "strategic partner" and advocated China's entry into the World Trade Organization, an approach that infuriated neocon-servative commentators and hard-line anticommunists in Congress. The Clinton administration also made Russia's democratic transition and entry into the Western fold the primary reclamation project of the post–Cold War 1990s.

The Bush revolutionaries had wasted no time in rejecting that soft-power outreach and recasting the world through the darker prism of "new realism." In just its first one hundred days in office, the Bush ad-ministration challenged the major powers, confronted regional rogues, rocked venerable alliances in Europe and Asia, stepped away from peace negotiations in Northern Ireland and the Middle East, and rejected out of hand a series of international treaties that collectively represented decades of painstaking diplomacy. For one hundred days and more the world watched and waited, and then slowly began reordering itself accordingly. As the Bush administration would discover, that was one of the disquieting powers of an unrivaled America: simply perceiving the world in a certain way was almost an act of self-fulfilling prophecy.

Not surprisingly, given the history and pedigree of the "neo-Wilsonians with a sword" and hard-line nationalists stacked deep in Bush administration ranks, Russia was first to feel the chill of the colder wind blowing out of Washington. After the Russian "diplomats" were sent packing in the largest expulsion of suspected spies since the Reagan administration, Deputy Defense Secretary Paul Wolfowitz publicly characterized Russia as a world-class arms merchant willing to "sell anything to anyone for money." The State Department added insult to the injury of the expulsions by meeting with representatives of Chechnyan rebels who were locked in a bloody war of succession with Russia.

As soon as the State Department successfully retrieved the crew of an accidentally downed U.S. Navy EP-3 reconnaissance plane from China with some conciliatory language, the Bush administration likewise began dropping all Clinton-era references to the Middle Kingdom as a "strategic partner." In the future, China would be considered a "strategic competitor." The administration quickly approved a major arms sale to Taiwan, and President Bush publicly announced that the United States would use its full military might to defend the island from Chinese attack. That seemed to abandon the diplomatic ambiguity of the three-decade-old "one-China" policy, a favorite target of neoconservatives throughout the 1990s. China was a communist country to be confronted, after all, and not appeased with a version of Henry Kissinger's hated détente.

The rogue states also quickly came in for a dose of the Bush administration's new "realism" (White House spokesman Ari Fleischer used a variation of the word a dozen times in his explanation for the expulsion of Russian diplomats and spies). In a snub to visiting South Korean president Kim Dae Jung, who won a Nobel Peace Prize for his "sunshine" policy of engagement with North Korea, Bush announced at a joint press conference that he was shelving an almost-completed deal between the United States and North Korea designed to curtail Pyongyang's long-range-missile program. North Korean president Kim Jong Il simply could not be trusted to honor agreements, Bush said in a bit of blunt speak that was seen in South Korea as a major affront and loss of face for Kim Dae Jung.

Saddam Hussein received the message not through diplomatic cables, but rather through the largest bombing raid on Iraqi air defense forces in the past two years of U.S. flights enforcing the "no-fly" zones over southern and northern Iraq. In his first trip to the Middle East as Secretary of State, Colin Powell proposed a new sanctions regime designed to tighten leaky Iraqi borders against the import of goods that could be used for military weapons, thus strengthening the cage of Saddam's containment.

European allies already shaken by U.S. rejection of the Comprehensive Test Ban Treaty and the Bush administration's pledge to withdraw unilaterally from the ABM Treaty, were further rattled by administration plans to withdraw U.S. military forces from the NATO peacekeeping operation in the Balkans. The Bush team was unable to follow through, given Clinton's ironclad pledge to NATO of "in together, out together" in the Balkans, but they did symbolically withdraw 750 U.S. peacekeepers from Bosnia even as the secretary-general of NATO was pleading for more troops from allied nations to handle a crisis in Macedonia. The secretary-general's call went unanswered in Washington.

In a visit to Washington in the spring of 2001, British Parliament member Francis Maude, the Conservative Party's shadow foreign secretary, carried an unusual warning to the Bush White House from a natural political ally and America's closest friend in Europe: Anti-Americanism was rising at such an alarming rate in Europe, Maude warned, that it threatened to "strike at the very heart of the trans-Atlantic relationship" and "drive the United States into the chill embrace of isolationism."

Major allies in the Arab world such as Egypt, Jordan, and Saudi Arabia were likewise confounded by the Bush administration decision to step away from the Middle East peace process. The new Bush team clearly hoped to distance itself from Bill Clinton's most identifiable foreign policy initiative, as well as disassociate themselves from the mess left in the wake of the failed Camp David summit of 2000. Like nearly all of the Bush administration's early moves rejecting the status quo in international relations, however, the new policy carried significant risks and potential downsides. By rejecting the traditional U.S. role as good-faith mediator between the two parties, the Bush administration was de facto aligning itself more closely with the Israelis, led by the hard-line Likud Party and Prime Minister Ariel Sharon. Sharon was the father of the settlement movement in the occupied territories and architect of the early 1980s Israeli invasion of Lebanon, which resulted in the massacres of Palestinians in two refugee camps in Beirut. Such an alignment between the United States and Israeli hard-liners, in fact, was a theme running through much of the writing of the neoconservatives in the Bush administration during the 1990s, many of whom had close ties to Israel in general and the conservative Likud Party in particular. Israel, after all, was a feisty Western-style democracy unafraid to press its military advantage against autocratic and tyrannical Arab regimes, and thus a natural champion for neoconservatives.

Such a realignment certainly had no downside on the domestic political scene, where strong support for Israel is taken for granted in both political parties and viewed by a powerful Israeli lobby and many Jewish voters as a make-or-break issue. For that reason Israel for more than two decades had ranked as the number one recipient of U.S. foreign aid, receiving roughly $3 billion annually, two-thirds of it in the form of state-of-the-art U.S. tanks, aircraft, and weaponry that make the small Israeli army one of the best in the world. Other forms of aid, such as loan guarantees, drive the actual total of American support for Israel much higher. Certainly that strong support and the close cultural, political, and military ties between the United States and Israel are not lost on the rest of the world or the Middle East region.

The traditional U.S. diplomatic position, standing between the two sides and pressuring each to reach a lasting peace, provided just enough equilibrium to allow Washington to both continue its strong support of Israel and retain relatively good relations with Arab allies in the Middle East region, and with European allies inclined to see the Palestinian populace as the more aggrieved party in the conflict. By contrast, the Bush administration position, stepping away from the fray and de facto aligning the United States more closely with Sharon, especially at a time when Palestinians and Israelis were engaged in a bloody cycle of terror and retribution and Israeli settlers continued to grab more of the occupied territories, risked alienating Arab allies and incurring the undying animosity of the Arab masses.

Lee Hamilton is the director of the Woodrow Wilson International Center for Scholars, formerly the chairman of the House International Relations Committee, and one of the most thoughtful foreign policy experts in Washington. When I spoke with him in the spring of 2001, Hamilton too was struck by the Bush administration's willingness to turn up the heat dramatically in international relations in order to forge a new international order that they had yet to even define, risking any number of miscalculations and crises in the process.

"Every Administration I can remember has tried to disentangle themselves from the Mid-East peace negotiations, and they've all eventually been pulled into the process," Hamilton said. "As is so often the case in foreign policy, you quickly learn in the Middle East that every issue is connected to some other issue. And while it's very early to judge, there's no question the harder line the Bush administration has adopted has raised tensions in a number of regions to a level that falls short of an international crisis, but that is bringing issues to a head very quickly. What remains to be seen is whether this new hard line will produce the intended results."

Reporting on the Bush administration initiatives in the months that followed, I was determined to let that be the final arbiter: Did the Bush revolution and the new order it proposed actually make the United States stronger and safer as a nation? An obvious place to start in searching for an answer was in the realm of multilateral treaties and arms control agreements, which the Bush revolutionaries began immediately rejecting outright.

In only its first months in office the Bush team dismissed or rejected the Comprehensive Test Ban Treaty, the Kyoto global warming treaty, the International Criminal Court, a verification protocol for the Biological Weapons Convention, a U.N. accord on the proliferation of small arms, and the Antiballistic Missile Treaty. In fact, if the Bush team were actually determined to unshackle American military power from the entire architecture of international arms control and nonproliferation agreements constructed with the support of both Republican and Democratic administrations over the course of forty years, then the early moves of the Bush administration were exactly how you would start.

Just south of Nevada's Great Basin desert is a dry lake bed called Frenchman Flat that served as ground zero for the first atmospheric nuclear weapons tests of the 1950s. Skeletons of cement-block buildings still stand like twisted sculpture on the flats, the remnants of the so-called survival village, where scientists tested the fragile resilience of man and his habitat against nuclear attack. On the day I visited the Nevada Test Site, light desert breezes rustled the sagebrush where nuclear winds once stripped those buildings bare. No trace remained of the monkeys dressed in human clothing that were placed downrange on the flats to gauge the effect of radiation flash on living tissue and organs.

The United States stopped aboveground nuclear tests in the early 1960s, hence testing only below the surface. Over a nearby ridge from the flats was Yucca Valley, a moonscape of massive craters that attested to some three decades of underground nuclear tests. In 1992, however, George H. W. Bush declared, and Congress wrote into law, a moratorium on nuclear tests. The era of "thinking the unthinkable," and preparing for it at Frenchman Flat, was seemingly coming to a close.

As a result of those decisions, the United States' nuclear research infrastructure had shrunk dramatically since 1992. Base Camp Mercury, once a bustling town near Frenchman Flat that boasted more than eight thousand scientists, engineers, and other workers in the heyday of nuclear testing, had the feel of a ghost town. The bowling alley and other recreational facilities had long since been closed and shuttered. The United States had not designed, produced, or tested a new nuclear weapon in the decade hence, and it had mothballed or retired much of the nuclear weapons complex.

Immediately upon taking office, however, the Bush revolutionaries signaled a new course that could put the Nevada Test Site and Base Camp Mercury back in business. As part of a major strategic review that included constructing a national missile defense, the Bush team suggested that the United States may need to design and test a new generation of low-yield nuclear weapons that could place the underground arsenals of potential adversaries at risk without the threat of massive collateral damage. The Pentagon also asked the nuclear weapons labs to examine ways to more quickly resume testing beneath the Nevada desert if it was deemed necessary to develop this new class of nuclear "bunker busters," designed to make the unthinkable thinkable again, at least in the minds and calculations of America's adversaries.

Once again there was a blueprint for the Bush strategic review, and once again it was signed by a number of leading neoconservatives and hard-liners with top jobs in the new administration. As would quickly become apparent, the Bush administration's new strategic review drew heavily on the ideas contained in a January 2000 report by the National Institute for Public Policy, a conservative think tank that billed itself as a nonprofit "public education organization." That report argued that the United States should no longer be limited by Cold War–style treaties, but instead should move unilaterally to reconfigure its strategic nuclear forces for a new era and new threats. The report also suggested that the nation would likely need to develop new, lower-yield nukes to deter rogue states armed with weapons of mass destruction.

Senior Bush administration officials who took part in the National Institute report included Deputy National Security Adviser Stephen Hadley, Condoleeza Rice's number two on the National Security Council; National Security Council missile defense expert Robert Joseph; and Stephen Cambone, Defense Secretary Donald Rumsfeld's right-hand man at the Pentagon. Thanks to hard-liners in the Bush administration and Congress, at the State Department John Bolton was settling in as Undersecretary for Arms Control and International Security, where he could apply his own interpretation of international treaties as not legally binding on the United States.

David Smith was a chief arms control negotiator in the first Bush administration, and a participant along with key Bush officials in the National Institute report. "The dirty little secret that no one likes to talk about in polite society is that deterrence doesn't work if your threat to use these weapons is not credible, and to make them credible in the future, we're going to have to design new nuclear weapons," Smith told me at an arms control conference in the summer of 2001. Like many of the Bush revolutionaries, Smith argued the case for a new generation of nuclear weapons by citing American "exceptionalism," suggesting that the nation's unique power and its commensurate responsibilities should exempt the country from traditional constraints such as arms control treaties. "European allies who object to that idea are going to have to face some harsh realities, namely that the United States plays a unique stabilizing role around the world that brings with it special requirements," said Smith. "It's not the French navy that keeps the Straits of Malacca open, it's the U.S. Navy. And if we argue that, along with the kinds of sweeping unilateral reductions in nuclear weapons that President Bush has talked about, the United States will also need to develop some new nuclear weapons, that is something the Europeans are going to have to come around to accepting."

As I knew well from my discussions with them, however, the European allies were little inclined to accept the radical premise that history's most preponderant conventional power needed to tilt the strategic calculus more in its favor with new nuclear weapons and a missile defense shield, while the rest of the world should reasonably forgo such weapons. That the Bush administration was forging ahead regardless suggested at the very least that they were willing to pay a steep price in alliance cohesion in order to realize their new vision of a more powerful and unconstrained United States. At the same conference where I spoke with authors of the influential National Institute report, for instance, I listened to Uta Zapf, a visiting member of the German parliament.

"A lot of nonnuclear states believe that without the commitment to eliminate nuclear weapons and abide by the Comprehensive Test Ban, the Nonproliferation Treaty is really just a convenient way for the nuclear states to keep the club exclusive," said Zapf. "Nor do we Europeans find persuasive this argument that the United States is somehow exceptional and deserves a special status. After listening to all of the Bush administration's comments on the ABM and CTBT treaties, missile defense, and the need to put weapons in space, the fear is growing in Europe that the United States is heading in a direction of rejecting all treaties that hinder its ability to pursue its own narrow interests."

As part of my coverage of the arms control debate, I visited the White House and spoke with a senior Bush administration official about the strategic review and plans to fundamentally recalculate the strategic nuclear weapons equation. At that point the Bush administration was already moving ahead with a missile defense system that would surely require abrogation of the ABM Treaty, raising the possibility of a new generation of nuclear weapons, and floating the idea of unilateral cuts in the size of the U.S. strategic nuclear arsenal. As they were boldly dismantling the architecture of agreements and treaties that had been assembled by nine previous U.S. administrations over a half century to rein in the nuclear arms race and the proliferation of weapons of mass destruction, however, the Bush revolutionaries were at pains to describe exactly what they planned to construct in its place.

"We haven't worked out all the modalities yet, but I think it's a legitimate question to ask whether arms control is still relevant in an era when the Soviet Union has disappeared and the Cold War is over," the senior White House official said in July 2001, arguing that such treaties had locked both the United States and Russia into the adversarial mind-set of mutually assured destruction. "Despite all of the arms control advocates in the Clinton administration, for instance, they did not succeed in reducing one single nuclear weapon. Cold War–style arms control has been an abysmal failure for the past eight years because it no longer works."

The Clinton administration's decidedly mixed record on arms control agreements was due in large part to fierce resistance by a Republican-dominated Congress, but there was no denying that strategic arms reductions between the United States and Russia had stalled badly during the 1990s. The Russian legislature had refused to ratify START II, for instance, due to its pique over NATO expansion and the Kosovo war. The Bush administration was gambling that its own willingness to make significant unilateral reductions in the U.S. nuclear arsenal would act as a sweetener, masking the more bitter medicine of new U.S. nuclear weapons and a new missile defense system, and hopefully provoking Russia to make its own unilateral cuts in its nuclear arsenal. To grasp what a radical departure that approach represented, it's important to understand a bit about the arms control house the Bush administration was determined to dismantle.

Multilateral efforts to limit the spread of weapons of mass destruction began in earnest almost immediately after World War II, while the horrors of Nagasaki and Hiroshima remained fresh in memory. President Dwight D. Eisenhower proposed creation of the International Atomic Energy Agency, which promotes the peaceful use of atomic energy and now polices compliance with the Nuclear Nonproliferation Treaty (NPT).

In terms of the existential threat those agreements were designed to protect against, John F. Kennedy was perhaps most eloquent on the subject when he famously worried in the early 1960s that by the end of the decade somewhere between fifteen to twenty-five nations would join the nuclear club (then consisting of the United States, the Soviet Union, the United Kingdom, and France). The specter raised by his words is one that has haunted the thoughts of all who have occupied the Oval Office in the nuclear age and era of doomsday weapons. "I ask you to stop and think for a moment what it would mean to have nuclear weapons in so many hands, in the hands of countries large and small, stable and unstable, responsible and irresponsible, scattered throughout the world," Kennedy said. "There would be no rest for anyone then, no stability, no real security, and no chance of effective disarmament."

In his short White House tenure, Kennedy thus secured the Limited Test Ban Treaty, ending nuclear tests in the atmosphere, under water, or in space. Lyndon Johnson successfully negotiated the multilateral NPT, the foundation of the nonproliferation regime that essentially locks all of the signatory nations into the 1960s status quo of a very few nuclear "haves" and a great many "have-nots." Under the terms of the NPT, however, the United States and other nuclear "haves" agreed to reduce their nuclear arsenals with an aim of eventually eliminating them at some undefined date, a pledge undercut by Bush proposals for a new generation of nuclear weapons.

Richard Nixon signed and secured Senate approval of the NPT in 1970 as well as the multilateral Biological Weapons Convention in 1972. Separately, on a bilateral track the United States and the Soviet Union negotiated a series of treaties to put limits on the Cold War nuclear arms race. Nixon signed both the Strategic Arms Limitation Treaty, or SALT I, limiting long-range weapons in the arsenals of both superpowers, and the companion ABM Treaty limiting missile defenses. After campaigning at first as an arms control skeptic, Ronald Reagan went on to negotiate and sign the landmark Intermediate-Range Nuclear Forces Treaty in 1987, which eliminated a whole class of missiles with ranges between 500 and 5,500 kilometers. Reagan also negotiated START I, the first strategic treaty that actually reduced (rather than capped) the number of deployed nuclear warheads.

George H. W. Bush signed START I in 1991, which was followed in 1993 with START II, the most sweeping arms reduction pact in history (which then bogged down in the Russian legislature). The elder Bush also set a precedent in 1991 by announcing that the United States would unilaterally withdraw most of its tactical nuclear weapons deployed around the world, and take much of the U.S. bomber force off high alert, moves that were then matched by Soviet president Mikhail Gorbachev. The first President Bush completed the nonproliferation trifecta by signing the Chemical Weapons Convention (prohibiting development or stockpiling of chemical weapons) in January 1993, just before Clinton took office, with Senate ratification coming under Clinton in 1997. For its part, the Clinton administration negotiated the Agreed Framework with North Korea to halt its nascent nuclear weapons program, helped persuade three states of the former Soviet Union to relinquish their nuclear weapons and sign on to the Nuclear Nonproliferation Treaty, and managed the indefinite extension and strengthening of the NPT in 1995.

By the end of 1999, when that steady construction of a nonproliferation regime came to an abrupt halt with the Republican Senate's rejection of the Comprehensive Test Ban Treaty (CTBT), there were only eight nations armed with nuclear weapons rather than the fifteen to twenty-five John F. Kennedy had feared by the end of the 1960s, including the recent additions in the 1990s of India and Pakistan. After the Senate vote, I spoke with retired Army Gen. John Shalikashvili, the former Chairman of the Joint Chiefs of Staff who had been tapped by the Clinton administration to recommend ways to improve the CTBT's future chances for ratification. The opposition to the CTBT, General "Shali" told me, certainly didn't originate in military ranks. "The Joint Chiefs were supportive of the test ban treaty when I was chairman, and from my talks with the current Chiefs, I believe they still are," Shalikashvili told me in an interview in July 2001. "Looking back, I think some Senators voted against CTBT simply because it was the Clinton administration pushing it, so they had to be against it. For others, however, it is like a religious issue: They never saw an arms control treaty they liked, because they simply don't believe in arms control."

Once again, the breakdown in the bipartisan consensus in the United States for arms control could largely be traced back to the Reagan administration, and the ascendance within the Republican Party at that time of neoconservatives and hard-liners who became ideologically opposed to arms control agreements in virtually any form. In their view, arms control treaties needlessly constrained U.S. freedom of action and were inherently unverifiable. Worse, they lulled signatories into a false sense of security, punished law-abiding nations, and lacked adequate enforcement measures to deter rogue nations even when they were caught cheating. Leading neoconservatives who advanced those arguments and served in the Reagan administration were once again listed in the who's who of Bush administration appointees and officials close to the administration, chief among them Paul Wolfowitz and Richard Perle and their numerous protégés.

Fred Iklé was a former Undersecretary of Defense for Policy in the Reagan administration, and a participant in the National Institute for Public Policy report on strategic forces that served as an early blueprint for the Bush administration strategic review. "Diplomats have an attachment to arms control treaties because they judge the success of their careers on how many they can put on their resumes," Iklé told me in an interview in July 2001. "Unfortunately, enforcement always gets left out of the equation." Whether it was the former Soviet Union's building of a radar facility clearly in violation of the ABM Treaty, or Iraq's dogged pursuit of nuclear weapons despite its membership in the NPT, Iklé said, the history of arms control was rife with examples of cheaters insufficiently deterred or punished.

While no treaty is 100 percent verifiable and Ronald Reagan's admonition to "trust, but verify" made sense even to ardent arms control advocates, the most pertinent issue for many experts is whether treaties are sufficiently verifiable to make it difficult for a nation to cheat over the long run, and to keep cheating once they are caught. After Desert Storm, for instance, when it became clear that Iraq had been much further along in its nuclear program than was widely believed at the time, the International Atomic Energy Agency, which polices the NPT, significantly strengthened its inspection and verification regime. North Korea sparked a crisis in 1994, meanwhile, precisely because it gave notice of withdrawing from the NPT, signaling an intent to step up its nuclear weapons program. Iran has long been thought to harbor a clandestine nuclear weapons program in violation of the NPT, but international inspections conducted in accordance with the treaty make it more difficult for Iran to bring the program to fruition and easier for the international community to threaten sanctions. After all, without the architecture of nonproliferation treaties there would be no cheaters to pressure with sanctions.

Amy Sands was deputy director of the respected Monterey Institute's Center for Nonproliferation Studies, and a participant at the 2001 arms control conference sponsored by the Carnegie Endowment for International Peace. "There is an apparent assumption at the senior levels of the Bush administration that proliferation is inevitable, and we should thus turn our focus to missile defense and military solutions, and away from traditional diplomacy and establishing international norms of behavior," she said. "If this approach continues, I fear the future world order could turn very ominous. The entire nonproliferation regime could collapse, leaving nations without an international nonproliferation bulwark to stem regional arms races and proliferation. That would be disastrous."

There was another aspect of the debate over the Bush administration's seemingly wholesale rejection of international treaties that was revealing. In those formative early months in office, Republican moderates who spoke up in defense of treaties or soft-power mechanisms were repeatedly overruled. When Secretary of State Colin Powell announced that the administration would continue the Clinton-era negotiations with North Korea over limiting its long-range-missile program, for instance, he was forced days later to recant in public, explaining somewhat sheepishly that he had gotten too far out over his "ski tips." After Environmental Protection Agency head Christine Todd Whitman assured European environmental ministers that Bush was committed to the Kyoto accord for reducing greenhouse gases and global warming, she was likewise forced to publicly reverse herself, declaring to reporters less than a month later that the Kyoto treaty "was dead."

It was in those early, formative days of the Bush administration that close observers first began noticing a furious tug-of-war behind the scenes between moderate internationalists and the neoconservatives and hardline nationalists. And just as clearly, President Bush, who was still learning his own instincts in international affairs, was more often swayed by the arguments of the latter. The revolutionaries were winning.

In the summer of 2001 while reporting on the Bush foreign policy revolution, I found myself in a smoky *gasthaus* near Potsdammer Platz in what was formerly East Berlin. Sitting in a large booth over tall steins of beer and plates of schnitzel, a group of German and American diplomats, journalists, and academicians gathered to talk about the extraordinary transformation that was reshaping both Germany and transatlantic relations. Formerly cut off from the West by the Berlin Wall, the once-grimy section of the city we were in was fast reclaiming its place as the epicenter of Berlin nightlife and café society. Nearby the massive German Reichstag, or federal parliament building, had reopened for business as the centerpiece of the new German Republic. The structure's imposing facade and dark Wagnerian dimensions were newly counterbalanced by a modern glass-domed atrium and visitor center. Everywhere, cranes punctuated the skyline and attested to the construction boom that had accompanied the relocation of the German government and capital from Bonn to Berlin. To visit the German capital was to understand just how fundamentally the physical and psychological landscape of Germany and Eastern Europe had changed in the post–Cold War era.

That transformation was underscored by the discussion around our table that night. The conversation inevitably turned to the U.S.-German relationship, which had also changed dramatically from the Cold War era, when Bonn could largely be counted on to defer to Washington on matters of transatlantic security. Just as in America, a new generation of baby boom politicians had taken the helm of the German government and other European capitals, and they had little direct memory of World War II or the Marshall Plan, and thus less instinctual deference toward Washington.

On matters of security, foreign policy, and economics, in fact, Berlin was looking increasingly toward Brussels, where Germany and France served as the twin cylinders of the engine driving European integration. European integration through an increasingly powerful European Union (EU) was seen in Paris as the only way to retain even a vestige of its former influence as a major power, and in Germany as the sole solution to making its size and power palatable to its neighbors. Especially since the successful launch in 1999 of the common "euro" currency, the continued integration of Europe, often referred to as the "European project," had become the dominant organizing principle on the European continent, and the prism through which Europeans increasingly viewed the world. By 2001, the view across the Atlantic as seen through that glass was of a darker and more menacing America.

"Where in the past, Germany felt pulled between Washington and Brussels, today Germans increasingly equate their own national interests with this European project, which is enormously popular," said a foreign affairs editor with the *Suddeutsche Zeitung*, one of Germany's largest newspapers. Unfortunately, he continued, talk of European integration had increasingly been accompanied by anti-American rhetoric. "The whole debate in Europe is now dominated by charges of U.S. 'hegemony' and 'unilateralism,' by transatlantic trade disputes, and by European disdain for the death penalty," the editor said. "Germans are rallying to the common cause of 'Euronationalism,' fueled in part by anti-American sentiment."

"It's a fact," the deputy director of a Berlin think tank agreed, "that we are beginning to catch the 'French disease,' which holds that you can only build greater European unity around anti-American rhetoric. Primarily, the French use it for domestic political consumption, and they can still be counted on in times of crisis. But I think we Germans must resist this creeping French disease, because it leads nowhere."

At that point a German diplomat broke in with a comment that gave me pause. "You know, Germany will never side with the French against the United States. We see how the French are. We know they would act impossibly if they had all the power," he said. "On the other hand, we will never side with the United States against France. We see our national interests as being in the middle, between you two."

Personally, I wasn't so sure. Certainly the U.S. government had always managed transatlantic relations and the NATO alliance by counting on Germany as a counterweight between the pro-American British and the always obstreperous French. Yet the Bush revolution had purposely rattled that old order by looking on NATO and Europe as less central to their strategic deliberations, and the repercussions were already unmistakable across the Atlantic. As I wrote in an article entitled "A Tale of Two Allies," one impact of that dramatic shift was to push a Germany already in flux as a result of reunification more rapidly toward the waiting French, which could spell serious trouble in transatlantic relations. That was just one way the world was reconfiguring itself to the Bush revolution.

For its part, the European Union in Brussels had accelerated an ongoing effort to create its own independent foreign and defense policy, and an EU rapid-reaction military force that some in the Pentagon saw as a potential challenge to NATO, the cornerstone of the Western alliance. Meanwhile, piqued at the rejection of numerous U.N. treaties and the U.S. arrears in dues, members at United Nations headquarters in New York had recently voted the United States off the U.N. Commission on Human Rights for the first time since it was established in 1947. Angered over the U.S. withdrawal from the Middle East peace process, Arab allies rebuffed Colin Powell's attempts to revitalize sanctions against Saddam Hussein. The conquering hero of Desert Storm was sent home from his first trip to the Middle East as Secretary of State empty-handed to fight a rearguard action against neoconservatives and hard-liners who continued to view the retired four-star general as insufficiently committed to the revolution.

Russia and China, long estranged during the Cold War, were also drifting closer to one another and attempting to form a counterbalance to a United States viewed as throwing its weight around. Early in the Bush tenure, Russian and Chinese forces thus held joint exercises during a mock nuclear showdown between Beijing and Washington over Taiwan, with Moscow practicing coming to the aid of China. In July, Russian and Chinese leaders also signed a treaty of friendship and cooperation aimed at countering U.S. power.

By the summer of 2001, South Korean president Kim Dae Jung was still smarting over the loss of face from Bush's criticism of his "sunshine" policy, and a Japan made grumpy by a decade-long flirtation with recession was made grumpier still by the Bush administration's outright rejection of the Kyoto treaty on global warming, which was negotiated under Japan's auspices. Even at the Pentagon, senior uniformed leaders were in near open revolt and had teamed with congressional allies in opposing Defense Secretary Rumsfeld's transformation as just another exercise in budget cutting, weapons cancellations, and force structure reductions.

Given the amount of external and internal blowback as the old world order resisted such radical change, the Bush revolution might well have sputtered or at the very least moderated in the summer of 2001. That seemed to be the fighting hope of Colin Powell, who in a later interview with me pointed to examples where the Bush administration reached a sort of yin and yang balance between soft-power moderates and hard-power revolutionaries, including his negotiations for the return of the U.S. aircrew from China, and the deal cut to win Russian acquiescence of the U.S. withdrawal from the ABM Treaty and sharp unilateral cuts in both nations' nuclear arsenals.

However, history doesn't offer alternate realities or views around the bend down the road not taken. The Bush revolutionaries looked through a prism darkly and saw a world full of gathering threats and existential dangers. The rest of the world perceived an increasingly menacing America intent on unilaterally pressing its military advantages. As President George W. Bush retired to his ranch in August 2001 for a monthlong working vacation, unseen forces were already poised to confirm everyone's worst fears.

PART II

Cataclysm

"All civilization has from time to time become a thin crust over a volcano. . . ."

HAVELOCK ELLIS
Little Essays of Love and Virtue

Conclusion

CHAPTER 4

Assassins at the Gate

EVERYONE REMEMBERS how blue the sky was that morning. Later we would recall the indelible silhouette of the New York City skyline with its gleaming towers reflecting sky, water, and the unsurpassed wealth of lower Manhattan; the broad-shouldered brawn of the Pentagon and the feelings of strength it evoked; the confident swagger of Washington, D.C., the capital city on a hill whose beacon of freedom was supposed to shine into virtually every corner of the globe. On the morning of September 11, 2001, Americans tasted firsthand the venom of those who rejected the light and all that it represented. And just like that the sky turned threatening, the once-proud skyline was gap-toothed and broken, and smoke hovered over the deserted and eerily quiet streets of Washington, D.C. Even the sense of what it meant to be an American seemed somehow altered. Everything had changed.

Because my car was due in for repair, I likely missed seeing American Airlines Flight 77 fly low over my normal route to work from Arlington into downtown Washington, and rip into the Pentagon with an explosive force that demolished three of the building's five concentric rings. By the time I dropped my car off the radio was already reporting that an airplane had flown into one of the World Trade Center towers on a sunny morning. I was at work and watching on television as the second airliner, United Airlines Flight 175, disappeared into the second tower in a cauldron of flame, and everyone knew with certainty what was happening. My colleagues watched with me as our fellow citizens jumped to their deaths and the towers crumbled, all of us numbed by an estimated death toll in the thousands, and stricken by the knowledge that the number was swollen by hundreds of New York City firemen and police who entered the doomed skyscrapers willingly in hopes of saving others. I wondered whether friends and colleagues of mine had perished at the Pentagon. Only later would we hear of the courageous passengers on United Airlines Flight 93 who rushed the hijackers and prevented them from landing another shattering blow to the city we loved.

At one point word came to evacuate *National Journal*'s offices, which were located five blocks from the White House. Outside on the streets of downtown Washington, D.C., deserted but for some scattered National Guard troops, I saw the sunlight catch and glint off an aircraft flying high above the normally restricted airspace above the capital. I wondered that such an impossibly blue sky could turn so menacing. Like countless millions of other Americans I wanted to know how this possibly could have happened, and what it meant for my country.

Of course it meant war, but fought in what fashion and against whom, exactly? Just by witnessing the attacks on the World Trade Center and Washington, most experts in and out of the government concluded immediately that they were the work of arch-terrorist Osama Bin Laden and his Al Qaeda terrorist organization. All summer the CIA's threat warning system for terrorist attack had been blinking red. National Counterterrorism Coordinator Richard Clarke had repeatedly cited intercepted "chatter" and intelligence indicating the high probability of a near-term, "spectacular" terrorist attack. As detailed in the *9/11 Commission Report*, on June 12 a CIA dispatch indicated that a top Al Qaeda operative was recruiting terrorists to travel to the United States to meet with colleagues already there so that they might conduct terrorist attacks on Bin Laden's behalf. On June 28, Clarke wrote to National Security Adviser Condoleeza Rice that the pattern of Al Qaeda activity pointing to an attack "had reached a crescendo." On August 6, 2001, a report in the classified Presidential Daily Brief given to President George W. Bush was headlined, "Bin Laden Determined to Strike in U.S."

The Bush team simply assumed they had more time to address an Al Qaeda threat that was way down their list of first-order priorities. Although the Bush Principals Committee met frequently in the administration's first nine months on topics ranging from Russia, the Persian Gulf, and the Middle East peace process, no Principals Committee meeting was held on Al Qaeda until September 4, 2001, less than a week before the attacks. For the Bush revolutionaries who were intent on reordering the global strategic chessboard, Bin Laden had seemed like a pawn at best. A pawn, that is, until September 11, 2001, changed everything.

Even experts not privy to the latest classified intelligence recognized in the 9/11 attacks the unmistakable signature of Al Qaeda: meticulously planned and well-financed suicide operations designed to inflict mass casualties. One of the first I spoke with after the attacks was Peter Bergen, a terrorism expert who authored *Holy War Incorporated* and who once interviewed Bin Laden in Afghanistan. "When the second jet hit the World Trade Center, I knew immediately that Bin Laden was behind it, because no other terrorist organization in the world combines that level of planning, sophistication, and organization with people willing to martyr themselves," Bergen told me. "What makes Al Qaeda so dangerous is that these people have a level of belief that we in the West have lost."

Within days of the attacks a sizable armada of U.S. ships and aircraft was already heading toward southwest Asia, where Al Qaeda ran its operations and training bases in Afghanistan under the protection of the fundamentalist Islamic Taliban regime. At the very least, it seemed, the United States was poised to do what it had hesitated doing in response to Al Qaeda attacks throughout the 1990s—track the terrorists and their operational commanders back to their lairs in Afghanistan.

While the rest of the world had its eye on the movements of U.S. military forces toward Afghanistan, the first clandestine skirmishes against Al Qaeda had already begun with FBI arrests of a number of suspected conspirators and accomplices in the September 11 attacks, and CIA moves to coordinate operations with intelligence services worldwide that had tracked Al Qaeda cells in as many as sixty different countries. The CIA also asked the Bush administration and Congress to relax restrictions on the recruitment of unsavory informants, and perhaps to drop the ban against assassinations. The Justice Department pressed Congress to vote on a hastily assembled package of counterterrorism measures that would dramatically expand the FBI's ability to wiretap telephones and computers, target money-laundering operations, and prosecute terrorists and those who harbored them. No request was denied. Meanwhile, Congress gave President Bush a $40 billion emergency supplemental spending bill and sweeping authority to pursue the antiterrorism campaign. Legal experts characterized the measure as comparable to granting the President new war powers.

As I wrote at the time, that war was likely to include multiple counterterrorism operations by an international coalition of law enforcement and intelligence agencies, plus commando raids, aerial bombing strikes, and intense diplomatic arm-twisting that employed all the tools of U.S. power and persuasion. The possibility of a full-blown war against a nation or nations that supported the terrorists also loomed as a distinct probability.

President Bush made clear in the early days after the attack that the global "war on terror" that his administration already anticipated would be unlike any ever fought by the United States. "The message to every country is that there will be a campaign against terrorist activity, a worldwide campaign, and there is an outpouring of support for such a campaign," Bush said on September 19, the day before addressing a joint session of Congress. "The mind-set of war must change. [This] is a different type of battle, a different type of battlefield, and a different type of war. . . . The challenge is to redefine the terms of the conflict and campaign in a way that leaders understand and in a way that the people of the world understand. This is a new type of struggle. It's really the first war of the twenty-first century."

Devising a strategy for that new kind of war, however, meant first understanding the nature of an enemy that had not even arisen on the threat radar screens of U.S. intelligence services until the mid-1990s. Without such a thorough understanding, the United States couldn't hope to identify the strengths and potential weaknesses of Al Qaeda, nor predict with any certainty whether the organization and its model of pan-Islamic terrorism would survive the destruction of its base of operations and the death or capture of its leader. The United States would have to do what Osama Bin Laden and Al Qaeda had already so clearly done: We would have to go to school on our adversary.

As I knew from earlier reporting, Bin Laden's ability to construct an agile terrorist network that rapidly learned both from its own mistakes and from its enemies' successes long ago won the grudging respect of Western counterterrorism experts. When I called one such senior intelligence source in the days after the September 11, 2001, attacks, he illustrated the challenge presented by Al Qaeda with a backstory behind Operation Infinite Reach. In response to the bombing of two U.S. embassies in Africa by Osama Bin Laden's terror network in August 1998, the United States had fired seventy-nine cruise missiles at a terrorist training camp in Afghanistan and a pharmaceutical plant in Sudan suspected of making chemical weapons. The Clinton administration was roundly criticized at the time for ineffectively firing million-dollar missiles at mud huts and relying on faulty intelligence to target what Sudan claimed was an aspirin factory.

In responding to the intense criticism, a U.S. counterterrorism official let out that they had used communications intercepts to place Bin Laden directly at the camp and had narrowly missed killing him and many of his top lieutenants. Although the leak somewhat muted the immediate criticism, it caused intelligence operatives at CIA headquarters in Langley, Virginia, to gnash their teeth. They feared the disclosure could compromise one of their prized "sources and methods" of intelligence collection. In actual fact, they had reaped a bonanza of information by intercepting and decoding calls that Bin Laden routinely made on a satellite telephone that he used to communicate with his far-flung network from remote hideaways in Afghanistan. Intelligence analysts hoped the leak about the phone intercepts would be buried unnoticed in the daily avalanche of information emanating from Western media outlets. Within days of the leak, however, Bin Laden's satellite telephone went dead. According to my intelligence source, it was never heard from again.

"That's just one of many examples of how we're constantly peering into the opaque world these terrorists inhabit, while they are using our own high-tech tools and openness, and a keen interest in our methods, to see us in full transparency. They've gone to school on us," the senior intelligence source told me. Because the CIA was originally founded to ensure that the United States would never again suffer a Pearl Harbor–like surprise attack, my source was somewhat contrite. "We failed the nation this week. The real failure, however, was one of policy and political will," he said. "For two years, we've pointed to Bin Laden as a terrorist targeting the United States. For two months, we've warned that something big was brewing. We've known where he was, and the American people have paid for the forces that can reach out and get him. So the policy makers have to explain to the people at the bottom of the World Trade Center towers why they declined to take him out."

When the Soviet Union withdrew from Afghanistan in 1989 and disintegrated soon after, and the CIA-supported mujaheddin groups took to fighting among themselves, the United States largely washed its hands of Afghanistan. Policy makers were preoccupied by an invasion of Panama in 1989, the 1991 Persian Gulf War, and the dissolution of the Soviet Union in December of 1991. At the time, U.S. intelligence officials failed to recognize just how effectively the worldwide system they helped establish to recruit and train radicalized Muslims and funnel them to wage jihad against the Soviets could be reversed to export terrorism from Afghanistan in a holy war against the West. It is part of Bin Laden's genius that he came to see it very clearly.

Seasoned by war and infused with fundamentalist fervor, most of the Arab mujaheddin returned to their homes in the Middle East determined to overthrow secular regimes and monarchs alike. Their vision was to install theocracies devoted to the Arabs' fundamentalist view of Islam. While Iran circa 1979 represented the revolutionary model, their extreme interpretation of Islam owed more to the ultraconservative Wahabi brand of Islam practiced in Bin Laden's home of Saudi Arabia, and exported with Saudi oil wealth to madrassas, or religious schools, throughout the Muslim world. By the mid-1990s, that worldview and the ideals of the Afghan Arabs, as they came to be called, would find expression in the almost medieval Taliban of Afghanistan.

Like the other Afghan Arabs, Bin Laden returned to his home and began to agitate against the Saudi royal family. He was soon even more distraught, however, over the deployment of U.S. troops to Saudi Arabia to help defend the kingdom against Iraqi forces that invaded Kuwait in 1990. Bin Laden was outraged when U.S. troops stayed in the Muslim holy land even after the 1991 Persian Gulf War was over, in order to protect the Saudi oil fields and keep Saddam contained. Thus, while other

Afghan Arabs were consumed by their opposition to local governments in places such as Egypt, Jordan, Algeria, and Tunisia, Bin Laden began very early to focus on the United States as the primary target and impediment to their dreams of a united Islamic caliphate, or theocracy. The Afghan mujaheddin had defeated and helped destroy one superpower, and Osama Bin Laden was convinced as a matter of religious certitude that they could defeat another.

As early as 1992 Al Qaeda issued its first threats against the United States, declaring that U.S. military forces in Saudi Arabia, Yemen, and Somalia should be attacked. U.S. officials hardly took notice. In the spring of 1993, Bin Laden dispatched his senior aide, Ali Mohamed, a naturalized American citizen and former member of the U.S. Army Special Forces, to Somalia to establish training camps to teach Somali tribes how to fight U.S. forces deployed there on a famine-relief mission. Somali tribesmen, many of whom had been trained in Al Qaeda camps, killed eighteen U.S. servicemen in Mogadishu in October 1993, in a battle that led to the ignoble retreat of U.S. forces from Somalia soon after. Bin Laden clearly believed he had identified a weakness in U.S. resolve and national will that he could exploit in the future.

Pressured by the government of Saudi Arabia in 1991, Bin Laden moved his base to Sudan, where he allied himself with Hasan al-Turabi, the radical leader of the fundamentalist National Islamic Front. During Bin Laden's time in Sudan his mentor Turabi, who was the power behind the Islamic regime in Khartoum, declared jihad on the Christian south in a civil war that eventually killed hundreds of thousands if not millions of Sudanese. Turabi taught Bin Laden something important in the process— the synergy possible when Islamic revolutionaries of different stripes were united under a common banner. Thus it was during this period that Al Qaeda began to serve as an important link in the cross-pollination between various radical Islamic groups, offering its finances and giving them global reach.

In turn, Bin Laden in this period also came to view seemingly isolated pockets of Islamic jihad—in Sudan, Kashmir, Chechnya, Uzbekistan, Algeria, and in the occupied Palestinian territories—as related battles in a single struggle. That apocalyptic vision of a war between Western and Islamic civilizations, with the United States as the great Satan and Al Qaeda as a conduit to pan-Islamic jihad, made Osama Bin Laden a very dangerous man.

Michael Swetman is the chief executive officer of the Potomac Institute for Policy Studies, and coauthor of *Osama Bin Laden's Al-Qaeda: Profile of a Terrorist Network.* "This radical ideology of Bin Laden's that dictates the overthrow of all governments that do not adhere to his strict interpretation of Islam is what makes him so lethal, because there is nothing quite so dangerous in this world as a religious zealot with means and a method to his madness," Swetman told me not long after 9/11. "That grand vision is what allowed Bin Laden to essentially merge with fourteen different terrorist organizations. The reason Al Qaeda developed so quickly is that rather than starting from scratch, it established itself as a super-coalition of existing terrorist organizations."

Bin Laden in the mid-1990s was also the beneficiary of significant luck and timing. Faced with a crippling embargo and under intense pressure from the United States, the Sudanese government put Turabi under house arrest and forced Bin Laden to leave the country. Though the expulsion reportedly cost Bin Laden much of his fortune, the Sudan experience clearly made a lasting impression on him. By 1996, Bin Laden was once again established in the familiar and, for him, fertile sanctuary of Afghanistan. There, he put down deep roots and built close ties to the ruling Taliban while erecting a network of Al Qaeda training camps. During this period in the mid- and late 1990s, most experts agree, Al Qaeda blossomed into a truly strategic threat to U.S. national security.

After being kicked out of Saudi Arabia and Sudan, for instance, Bin Laden largely eschewed the direct state sponsorship that had nourished traditional terrorist organizations in the past. As an intelligence source told the 9/11 Commission, Afghanistan under the Taliban was less a state sponsor of terrorism than a state sponsored by terrorists. Bin Laden contributed heavily to a Taliban regime that was a pariah among the community of nations, augmenting contributions from his personal fortune with creative financing schemes that ranged from diamond smuggling, drug running, and extortion to siphoning off money from legitimate Islamic charities. Significantly, that financial independence freed Al Qaeda from the constraints state sponsors had traditionally imposed on the terrorist organizations they harbor and support. In the past, for instance, state sponsors assiduously avoided crossing an invisible line of lethality that could provoke a direct backlash on their governments from the United States or the West. Bin Laden was under no such constraints, and provoking the United States into lashing out was very much a part of his plans.

With sanctuary and a free hand to operate in Afghanistan, and after already running six training camps during the Afghan war with the Soviet Union, Bin Laden established his revitalized network of terrorist training camps. From experience he understood the usefulness of such camps not only as a means of indoctrination and training, but also as a way to evaluate and promote the most promising talent. According to intelligence estimates, as many as fifteen thousand to twenty thousand Islamic extremists passed through Afghan terrorist training camps, many of them run by Bin Laden and Al Qaeda, or "The Base."

Revealing a penchant for innovation, Bin Laden organized his training camps almost as a "Terrorism University." Far-flung scouts, many of them working out of radicalized Islamic mosques scattered around the world, recruited students to travel to Pakistan. The role that radical Islamic clerics played in Al Qaeda's evolution was conclusively revealed in the mid-1990s after blind Egyptian cleric Sheik Omar Abdel Rahman, who was considered the religious leader of the Afghan Arabs, was sentenced to life in prison in the United States for using his New Jersey mosque to help plan a foiled bombing plot targeting the U.N. headquarters building and several tunnels in New York. Two of Abdel Rahman's sons later moved to Afghanistan to work at Bin Laden's side.

Students recruited to Al Qaeda bases often had to wait for weeks while undergoing thorough background checks to weed out possible Western intelligence agents. Recruits then passed through a series of specialized camps for religious indoctrination and small-weapons training. Largely uneducated youths from Pakistani madrassas might be deemed best-suited as frontline fighters. These undergraduates were often funneled to ongoing conflicts in Chechnya, Kashmir, Bosnia, or northern Afghanistan. The most educated and promising of recruits were groomed from the beginning to operate terrorist cells in potential target countries.

The emphasis of Al Qaeda leaders on the cell structure was another refinement on the old model of terrorist operations. Because most terrorist organizations of the 1960s and 1970s were focused on local struggles against domestic governments, they paid relatively little attention to learning how to embed operatives in foreign countries. And because many of those groups were leftist, they also tended to follow the Leninist model of hierarchical organizations with strict central control. With a far more global agenda, Bin Laden apparently drew his inspiration from those few terrorist organizations that strove to acquire a reach beyond their immediate region, including the Palestinian Black September group, which carried out terrorist operations in Europe in the 1970s; the Irish Republican Army, which mounted effective terrorist bombings in Britain in the 1980s; and especially the Lebanese Hezbollah, a terrorist organization supported by Iran that was responsible for bombing Israeli targets in Argentina in 1992 and 1994.

Among the centers within the U.S. government that had focused on the rising threat of terrorism was the Marine Corps' Center for Emerging Threats and Opportunities, at Quantico, Virginia. The director of the center was retired Col. Gary Anderson. "The best and most-ambitious terrorist groups tend to adopt a cell structure as a way to harden themselves to penetration by their enemies—otherwise they wouldn't survive," Anderson told me in the fall of 2001. "The process takes a lot of patience, because you have to build up a network of operatives that you trust, and have a good feel if any outsider is trying to break into the organization. The cell structure also has significant drawbacks in terms of command-and-control and reacting to dynamic events. They require a lot of careful and patient advance planning. That's why Bin Laden can't just wake up one day and decide he wants to bomb the Statue of Liberty in two weeks."

The timing of Bin Laden's relocation to Afghanistan in the mid-1990s was important for another reason. Around 1996, a major strategic shift occurred when established regimes in Egypt, Algeria, and elsewhere brutally defeated the Islamic radicals and Afghan Arabs who sought to dethrone them. At the very time when the remnants of those Islamic extremist groups were looking for a way out of their deadly predicament at home, Bin Laden rallied them to his banner in Afghanistan and to Al Qaeda, blaming their defeat on the United States and its support for the established political order in the Middle East.

That message and timing led to a watershed merger with Egyptian Islamic Jihad, for instance, bringing to Al Qaeda the prodigious organizational skills of Ayman al-Zawahiri, a medical doctor and one of the brains behind the Egyptian group's often spectacular terrorist attacks, which included the 1997 terror attack at Luxor that killed fifty-eight tourists, and the 1981 assassination of Egyptian president Anwar el-Sadat. From Algeria, Al Qaeda attracted members of the Armed Islamic Group, known for their fanaticism and ruthlessness in that nation's bloody civil war and for their skill in setting up logistical cells in foreign nations funded through credit card fraud and petty crime. Contacts with the Lebanese Hezbollah, meanwhile, exposed Al Qaeda to the skills of the undisputed masters of bomb making and their tactics for suicide bombing. Significantly, it was also around this time in 1998 that Bin Laden and al-Zawahiri, backed by senior leaders of other jihad movements, issued their famous "fatwa." In the "International Islamic Front for Jihad on the Jews and Crusaders," Bin Laden called on all Muslims to kill Americans, including civilians.

Bruce Hoffman is a longtime terrorism expert and analyst at the RAND Corporation, a think tank with close ties to the U.S. military. "Throughout history, there have been terrorist leaders who aspired to create a *'Terrorist Internationale,'* but before Bin Laden, no one has ever succeeded," said Hoffman, who is author of the book *Inside Terrorism*. By constantly refining and broadening his list of grievances against the United States and the West, Bin Laden was able to attract the best talent in the terrorist pantheon, tapping the know-how of various groups to hone the expertise of the Al Qaeda organization as a whole. "In terms of terror, Bin Laden is the fabled right person, at the right place, at the right time. He had a vision for uniting the disparate threads of Islamic extremism into a coherent force, and he found the money and people with the right organizational skills to realize it."

That rapid evolution of Al Qaeda as a base for a terrorist pantheon led by veterans of the Afghan war, and peopled by fanatical foot soldiers recruited from radicalized mosques, helps explain how a fledgling group developed in the short space of only a decade into the most lethal terrorist organization in history. Al Qaeda's somewhat amateurish first attack on a hotel in Yemen in 1992, for instance, was bungled when the bombers failed to note that U.S. troops on their way to Somalia had already vacated the hotel. By 1998, Al Qaeda operatives were able to successfully attack the U.S. embassies in Kenya and Tanzania in carefully synchronized bombings that killed 224 people and wounded more than 5,000 others. The 2000 attack on the USS *Cole* that crippled a state-of-the-art U.S. warship, and the catastrophic strikes on the World Trade Center and the Pentagon, followed like ominous drumbeats. Only a few lucky breaks, and some deft counterterrorism and police work by the FBI, CIA, and the Customs Agency, kept Al Qaeda attacks planned to coincide with millennium celebrations from adding to that grim dirge.

During that evolution Al Qaeda developed a unique signature and style of terrorism. There was the articulation of a grand anti-Western vision that resonated in Pakistani madrassas and the palaces of the Islamic elite alike; a time-tested recruiting, training, and indoctrination system; and decentralized and innovative operations that combined careful and patient strategic planning with largely autonomous operations designed to inflict maximum death and destruction.

When I asked him what most stood out in that hybrid model of terrorism, Lt. Gen. James Terry Scott, the retired commander of U.S. Army Special Operations Command, was unequivocal. In the Darwinian process by which terrorist organizations learn and constantly improve or else are crushed and fall by the wayside, Al Qaeda had proven that it could constantly adapt and learn. "What separates this guy from all his one-trick predecessors is, he really has developed a learning organization," said Scott in September 2001. "They learn from their successes and failures, as well as ours. Each time, we've prepared to defend ourselves against his last operation, and each time, he's discovered a new, asymmetric way to get at us. And if he's not stopped, he'll strike again."

When a seemingly innocuous letter arrived in the office of Senate Majority Leader Thomas Daschle (D-SD) on October 15, 2001, with a cryptic note and a small amount of white powder, it seemed as if Al Qaeda might indeed have struck again, and the prospect dealt a severe psychological blow to a capital already badly on edge. Immediately the letter tested positive for anthrax, leading to the closure of the Senate and House offices and throwing Capitol Hill into near panic. In the initial sweep, thirty-three Senate staffers tested positive to exposure to anthrax. Not surprisingly, suspicions immediately focused on Al Qaeda and intelligence reports that Osama Bin Laden had proclaimed that acquiring chemical and biological weapons was a "religious duty." There had also been reports that Mohammed Atta, the tactical ringleader of the September 11 hijackers, had made inquiries about crop dusters, possibly as a delivery mechanism to dispense chemical or biological agents.

Something about those initial reports on the Capitol Hill attack seemed odd to me. From earlier reporting, I knew that the anthrax must have been of an extremely high quality to spread through the air without detection and infect so many people. As opposed to the work of amateurs working in makeshift labs, the quality of the anthrax used in the attack on Capitol Hill suggested a very sophisticated germ weapon and an advanced biological weapons program such as a state might operate, which brought to mind Iraq. Yet if Al Qaeda had gotten its hands on such a lethal germ agent from a state sponsor like Iraq, why had it chosen a crude delivery mechanism such as a letter? Why would a terrorist organization that specialized in inflicting mass casualties alert its victims that they had been infected with a crude note, allowing them to seek early and effective treatment?

For answers to those questions, I called a longtime acquaintance who had once worked for the Arms Control and Disarmament Agency, Michael Moodie. "One quandary that I find difficult to explain is this use of an apparently sophisticated biological agent, coupled with a rather primitive means of delivery," said Moodie, president of the Chemical and Biological Arms Control Institute in Washington. "I'm not sure what that implies about the motivations and capabilities of the perpetrators. However, the attack on Capitol Hill suggests a level of sophistication and expertise in developing the anthrax agent—whether it was done by a state actor or by terrorists themselves—that is well beyond where most experts assumed terrorists or most state actors had advanced. That's something we have to worry about."

According to Moodie, the only previous incident of bioterrorism in the United States occurred in 1984, when a religious cult in Oregon spread salmonella at restaurant salad bars in an attempt to sway a local election. Although roughly 750 people fell ill, no one was seriously injured and the incident seemed more bizarre than apocalyptic. The October 15, 2001, anthrax attack that closed Capitol Hill, on the other hand, ushered in a new, far more ominous chapter in the annals of bioterrorism. For the first time, a sophisticated germ weapon was used successfully as a weapon of terror in America. An enemy with large quantities of such a form of anthrax, coupled with an efficient means of delivering it, could potentially inflict casualties on a truly horrendous scale.

"The reason this latest attack is so worrisome is that once you have the technology to mill a pure form of anthrax with the correct spore sizes, you're a major step closer to being able to put that into an aerosol form," Moodie told me. "At that point, all you need is some sort of industrial sprayer in order to have a potentially catastrophic impact. Osama Bin Laden and his Al Qaeda network have clearly been seeking chemical and biological weapons of mass destruction, and he has articulated an elaborate rationale for using them against America and the West. The possibility that Al Qaeda is behind these anthrax attacks is thus a scenario that has to be looked at very, very carefully."

While leads in the anthrax case would eventually point to the likelihood that the agent was stolen from a U.S. Army laboratory, the specter of terrorists armed with weapons of mass destruction that had been raised in so many past studies and reports was inescapable for policy makers in the fall of 2001. Certainly it was a danger long foreshadowed. Myriad national commissions, congressional task forces, and blue-ribbon reports had warned in recent years of a catastrophic terrorist attack on the United States using weapons of mass destruction. Those warnings all made note of transnational networks of terrorists, fueled by religious or ideological fervor and united in their hatred of the United States, that would seek to inflict casualties so massive as to undermine "our constitutional system of government," in the words of a report by the National Commission on Terrorism.

In their 1999 book *Preventive Defense*, former Defense Secretary William J. Perry and former Assistant Defense Secretary Ashton B. Carter made a similar prediction: "Even though an instance of catastrophic terrorism has not yet occurred, such an event seems inevitable. . . . Like the attack on Pearl Harbor, it would divide our past and future into 'before' and 'after.' The effort and resources we have so far devoted to averting or containing this threat now, in the period 'before,' would seem woefully inadequate when viewed with hindsight after an incident of catastrophic terrorism."

The Gary Hart-Warren Rudman Commission on National Security/ Twenty-first Century, which reported in early 2001, echoed those concerns: "A direct, catastrophic attack against American citizens on American soil is likely. . . . The risk is not only death and destruction, but also a demoralization that could undermine U.S. global leadership." Retired Air Force Gen. Chuck Boyd, the staff director of the Hart-Rudman Commission, recalled in an interview in September 2001 that members of the bipartisan commission reached their dire conclusion after traveling extensively around the world talking to security experts in twenty-eight different countries. "The theme we repeatedly heard from potential adversaries and friends alike was that the United States was resented for what we stood for, and that managing that resentment would be a major challenge of the twenty-first century," said Boyd. "Add to that resentment the proliferation of deadly technology and weapons of mass destruction into the hands of people who never in history had the ability to inflict serious damage on a great nation such as ours, and you have a lethal combination."

As the Bush administration scrambled to formulate a strategy for fighting the "first war of the twenty-first century" in the days and weeks following the 9/11 attacks, those threat analyses and the profile of Al Qaeda that began to emerge suggested the monumental challenges ahead. In response to America's overwhelming conventional and strategic power, Bin Laden had fashioned an "asymmetric" arrow and sent it straight into the nation's solar plexus, exposing vulnerabilities for all the world to see, and for other terrorist organizations and adversaries to exploit. The attacks pointed to obvious weaknesses in America's last line of defense—the Customs Agency, Immigration and Naturalization Service, Border Patrol, the Coast Guard, etc. All of those agencies and bureaus worked independently and often at cross-purposes with one another. That suggested the need for the establishment of a Department of Homeland Security, an idea that had been knocking around in security circles for some time, and which the Bush administration initially resisted. Eventually in 2002, however, Bush endorsed the new mega-department, paving the way for the consolidation of twenty-two separate agencies in the largest reorganization of the U.S. government since just after World War II.

Bin Laden likewise turned on its head the U.S. strategy of treating terrorism as a criminal matter, and bringing terrorists to justice before U.S. courts. What use was the threat of tough sentences or even the death penalty against a seemingly endless stream of martyrs who sought death in exchange for mass murder? Those Al Qaeda sleeper cells had also become adept at operating in the shadowy gaps between the United States' vast intelligence, defense, and domestic law enforcement bureaucracies, exploiting legal boundaries and distinct cultures that kept those agencies from effectively cooperating with one another. The CIA was barred from spying on individuals inside the United States, for instance, while the FBI lacked the overseas presence and expertise to pick up the trail of terrorists heading for U.S. borders. The tweedy academic types at Langley and the blue-collar beat cops at FBI headquarters in Washington were also notoriously bad at playing well together. That suggested the need for a fundamental reform of disparate U.S. foreign and domestic intelligence agencies that is still pending.

As the Al Qaeda résumé made clear, Osama Bin Laden had also

tapped into a deep sense of anger and humiliation in the arid Middle East, where autocratic rulers and tyrants had kept the cleansing tides of liberty and prosperity at bay through brutal repression and corruption. The only permissible outlet for the rage of a people who could view the post–Cold War flood of globalization but never quench their thirst for its freedoms was an Islamic fundamentalism that rejected them outright, and Bin Laden had twisted and perverted Islam until hatred of the United States seemed a religious duty. The message behind the countless thousands of Bin Laden posters that began papering the walls of kiosks and cafés throughout the Islamic world in the aftermath of the 9/11 attacks was that the United States confronted an ideological struggle the likes of which it hadn't seen since the Cold War. Somehow America was going to have to neutralize the terrorists without unnecessarily adding to Bin Laden's mythology or fueling the apocalyptic vision of a "clash of civilizations."

Most importantly, the portrait of Al Qaeda that emerged in the weeks and months after 9/11 revealed an enemy that could not be bargained with or contained, but which must be utterly destroyed. In going on the offensive the United States had some advantages. The horror of the 9/11 attacks had rallied much of the world to America's cause, for instance, and the Al Qaeda profile suggested serious weaknesses. The cell structure and careful planning that made Al Qaeda so difficult to penetrate and deadly would also make it hard for Bin Laden to rapidly adjust and retarget his forces once the fight was taken directly to him. Bin Laden's dependence on a sanctuary to operate effectively throughout his career, either in Pakistan during the Afghan war or in Sudan and Afghanistan in the 1990s, also suggested a potential vulnerability. Once Al Qaeda was deprived of such sanctuary, there was reason to hope that it would have trouble effectively planning new waves of attacks or indoctrinating new recruits.

At the time of the 9/11 attacks, David Kay was the longtime counterterrorism expert at Science Applications International Corporation, a contractor with close ties to the U.S. intelligence community. "Unlike the Irish Republican Army, which essentially learned to operate in hostile territory at a very early stage, Al Qaeda's real weakness is that it has become addicted to operating in a permissive environment," Kay told me. "If we're effective at denying Bin Laden that sanctuary in Afghanistan, it's not at all clear that he will be able to rapidly learn to operate effectively underground or rebuild that infrastructure elsewhere."

While seemingly a major strength, the cult of personality that surrounded Bin Laden was also a potential weakness. Only a few terrorist organizations in the past had been as dependent on a single figurehead as Al Qaeda, and most of those had foundered when that leader was killed or arrested. The rapid demise of Peru's Shining Path terrorist organization after the 1992 arrest of leader Abimael Guzman, and the equally quick end to the reign of terror in Turkey by the PKK (Kurdistan Workers' Party) after its leader Abdullah Ocalan was captured in 1999, stood as prime examples. Clearly the United States would have to give top priority to killing or capturing Osama Bin Laden himself.

As the Bush administration formulated its strategy and doctrine for fighting the global war on terrorism, however it decided to define such a struggle, all of those challenges had to factor into its thinking and high-level counsels. The success or failure of their efforts was likely to determine the shape and tenor of American life, and the quality of U.S. leadership in the world, for many years into the future. The stakes could not have been higher.

Anthony Cordesman, the sometimes acerbic but insightful Middle East analyst for the Center for Strategic and International Studies in Washington, talked with me shortly after the 9/11 attacks about those challenges confronting U.S. policy makers. "What occurred on September 11 will play out over decades, because you can no more win a war on terrorism than you can win a war on history. The American people need to understand that the United States must now use every asset at its command in a campaign that is both very lethal, and above all else, persistent," said Cordesman.

The fight was no longer just about terrorism, he cautioned, nor was the September 11, 2001, attack a worst-case scenario. "States who possess biological and chemical weapons of mass destruction, and who never thought of confronting our conventional military or nuclear strength head-on, have now been shown where our vulnerability lies," Cordesman continued. "The problems of asymmetrical warfare and terrorism have now been joined, and the battle has begun. I think that struggle will present a challenge and increased risk to every American who was alive to witness September 11, for every single day of the rest of their lives."

CHAPTER 5

A Fork in the Road

WHEN PRESIDENT BUSH'S top advisers gathered at Camp David on September 15, 2001, it was as if the violent terrorist attacks on the World Trade Center and Pentagon had rent the cloak of time. Many of those present had gathered in that exact spot a decade earlier during another national crisis. Colin Powell, Dick Cheney, Paul Wolfowitz, and many of their right-hand deputies must have felt the sense of déjà vu acutely. Even the President was a reflection, passed through time, of his father and namesake, their former commander in chief. It was fitting, then, that the September 15 discussion at Camp David quickly veered to the threat that had united them once, yet divided them still: What to do about Saddam Hussein?

Just as he had done a decade earlier as Chairman of the Joint Chiefs of Staff, Colin Powell argued for restraint. Broadening the strategy for the coming "war on international terrorism" to include toppling Saddam could cripple the coalition-building effort. Better to focus on Osama Bin Laden, his Al Qaeda organization, and similar terrorist networks that could threaten U.S. interests.

Much as he had done in 1991 as a senior Pentagon official, Deputy Defense Secretary Paul Wolfowitz argued just as strenuously that Saddam Hussein was simply too dangerous to leave in power. The 9/11 attacks were an opportunity to depose Saddam once and for all, a position Wolfowitz had advocated throughout the 1990s. Secretary of Defense Donald Rumsfeld suspected that Iraq was probably involved in the September 11 attacks in Washington and New York City, and his instinct was also to hit Saddam in their initial counterstrikes. A Defense Department paper included in the Camp David briefing book on potential strategies for the war on terrorism specified three priority targets for initial action: Al Qaeda, the Taliban, and Iraq.

After being tasked by President Bush on the day after the 9/11 attacks to explore a possible Iraq connection, National Counterterrorism Coordinator Richard Clarke concluded that there was anecdotal evidence at best of such a connection, and no compelling case that Iraq had either planned or perpetrated the attacks. Zalmay Khalilzad, the chief National Security Council official on Afghanistan who was also at the Camp David meeting, shared those doubts about Iraq's complicity.

That internal split on just how broad a strategy and target list to adopt in prosecuting the war on terrorism broke into rare public display in the days after Camp David. The war's goal would not be limited to killing terrorists, Wolfowitz told Pentagon reporters; it must include "ending states that sponsor terrorism." Powell, the former four-star general and Vietnam combat veteran, had long felt that the neoconservative intellectual was too quick to resort to the use of military force. Powell thus quickly amended the public record on the Bush administration's strategic goals: "I think 'ending terrorism' is where I would leave it, and let Mr. Wolfowitz speak for himself."

The fact that Iraq emerged literally in the hours and days after the attacks as the critical fault line between the Bush revolutionaries at the Pentagon and more moderate internationalists at the State Department was revealing. At the very least it suggested that the 9/11 attacks had failed to bridge fundamentally different worldviews that had become so evident in the Bush administration's first nine months in office. At some point the two camps were obviously going to confront a fork in the road over just how ambitious and aggressive a strategy to adopt, and how broad a war to wage on international terrorism.

"The disagreement over what to do about Iraq is real, but that shouldn't be surprising," a senior State Department source told me in the weeks after the attacks. Many of the foreign leaders who were passing through Washington since September 11, he said, had warned that a campaign to overthrow Saddam would doom the antiterrorism coalition and destabilize an already volatile Middle East. "We're focused on long-term coalition-building, and the Pentagon is focused on fighting a war. At the end of the day, both sides will give President Bush our best advice, and that's healthy. Ultimately, he'll make the decision."

Certainly in that critical period following the 9/11 attacks, no one seemed more decisive or changed than the man at the center of the maelstrom. A President Bush who was initially ill at ease and easily caricatured on the world stage, who had trouble remembering and pronouncing the names of fellow world leaders, seemed to find his métier. In his moving speech before a joint session of Congress shortly after the attacks, Bush struck the perfect pitch of steadfast faith and quiet determination in pulling the country out of its grief and rallying the world to the U.S. cause.

The new tone coming out of the White House and the horror of the September 11 attacks led to an outpouring of support from around the world, and a palpable hunger for U.S. leadership by a Western alliance shaken by the spectacle of its military and economic standard bearer brought momentarily to its knees. In Germany, more than 200,000 Berliners marched under the Brandenburg Gate in a show of solidarity with the United States. In London, the Coldstream Guards played the "Star-Spangled Banner" during the changing of the guard outside Buckingham Palace. The Paris-based *Le Monde* newspaper, often critical of the United States, famously proclaimed "We are all American."

That outpouring of international support extended to the United Nations, where the Security Council quickly passed a resolution unequivocally condemning the attacks and those behind them. For its part, the NATO alliance went into emergency session immediately upon learning of the attacks, and within twenty-four hours had for the first time in its long history invoked its bedrock Article 5 clause of collective defense, pledging that the attacks on the United States would be treated as an attack on all NATO allies.

As a result of the tremendous show of sympathy and support that flowed in the wake of the September 11 attacks, a Bush administration that had riled much of the international community with its revolutionary ideas and unilateralist tendencies was offered a rare second chance to make a good first impression. For a while at least, it seemed determined to make good on the opportunity.

Despite the faint rumblings of disagreement over Iraq, Bush's experienced foreign policy and national security teams for a time played to their collective strengths in the period after the attacks, generally displaying a unity of purpose that had eluded them in the first nine months in office. A day after *Time* magazine proclaimed Colin Powell as the "Odd Man Out" in the Bush administration on its cover, he was engaged in the largest coalition-building campaign since World War II. By taking the lead in assembling that unprecedented international counterterrorism coalition of more than one hundred nations, Powell suddenly seemed poised to put his stamp on the Bush legacy. In planning to take out the Taliban and Al Qaeda in remote Afghanistan with an innovative melding of U.S. space and airpower with Special Forces and Northern Alliance troops on the ground, Defense Secretary Donald Rumsfeld was seizing a real-world opportunity to put his ideas of "transformational warfare" to the test.

Almost immediately the extent of the crisis also revealed opportunities for a favorable reordering of international affairs. Leaders and foreign ministers from around the world shuttled through the White House and State Department for tense consultations in the weeks after the attacks. After taking a decidedly harder line toward the major powers in his first months in office, Bush reached out to Russian president Vladimir Putin and Chinese president Jiang Zemin immediately after the attacks, as well as to other permanent members of the U.N. Security Council. There were early signs that the crisis could potentially push Russia, China, India, Indonesia, and other regional powers that were threatened by their own radical Islamic movements closer to the United States.

Meanwhile, nations such as Pakistan, an Islamic country with a large fundamentalist population and an intelligence service that had close ties to the Taliban, were forced to make a difficult choice: Are you with the United States, or against it? Staring into the eyes of a United States bent on retribution against Al Qaeda and its Taliban protectors, and backed by a growing coalition of major powers that included archrival India, Pakistani president Gen. Pervez Musharraf sided with the United States. Other state sponsors of terrorism figured to confront similar difficult choices.

A week after the 9/11 attacks I found myself on a Lufthansa flight to Moscow in what amounted to one of the more tense international flights of my life. Along with a number of U.S. officials and academics, I had committed months earlier to attend a conference with senior Russian national security and military officials on the future of U.S.-Russian relations. Because of the attacks, I was one of only a couple of American representatives who actually made the flight, which consisted of scattered male passengers eyeing each other suspiciously for nearly fifteen hours. In Moscow, however, I came to realize for the first time just how powerful a catalyst 9/11 and its aftershocks might prove in molding a new international order, though not necessarily in the way originally anticipated by the Bush revolutionaries.

With its towering orthodox churches, traffic-snarled streets, and fashionably dressed pedestrians, Moscow appeared at first glance like any other European capital. Yet the upscale mall that abutted Red Square prominently displayed goods whose price tags exceeded the annual income of many Russians. Moscow's outward prosperity also cloaked a powerful Russian underworld and creaky infrastructure in the hinterlands that could barely support its aging arsenal of nuclear weapons. Beyond the glitter of central Moscow, colorless Soviet-era apartment blocks dominated the skyline, and behind them stretched a nation that spanned eight time zones and a vast, sparsely populated, and profoundly destitute interior. In both geography and mind-set, Moscow still straddled the uneasy divide between East and West, and after 9/11 that figured to be shifting and uncertain ground. Certainly, few nations were confronted with a more perplexing choice after President Bush divided the world between those nations willing to join a U.S.-led coalition against international terrorism, and those who were not.

Feeling marginalized in its relations with the United States and Europe in recent years, the Kremlin had continued strengthening its ties eastward toward China as a counterweight to perceived U.S. "hegemony." Moscow was similarly focusing again on the Middle East, where it was increasing its economic ties with former clients and trading partners Iraq and Iran, both listed by the State Department as terrorist sponsors. Despite cordial relations with Bush, Russian president Vladimir Putin also nursed a list of grievances with the United States, including U.S. criticism of his brutal war against Islamic separatists in Chechnya; the U.S.-led effort to expand NATO to Russia's borders; and the Bush administration's plans to build a national missile defense system.

When I sat down in the conference room of the Moscow Kempinski Hotel as practically the sole American in a room full of senior Russian generals and security officials, I was thus treated to an almost endless harangue about the arrogance of American power. Did I understand now, after the 9/11 attacks, how enraged the rest of the world was by U.S. arrogance? Was it finally clear the terrible price the United States would pay for its unequivocal support of a land-grabbing Israel in the heart of the Arab Middle East? How did it feel to finally be on the other side of the bombs? At some point I half-expected the Russians to take off their shoes and start pounding on the conference table à la Nikita Khrushchev.

"In my view, the extreme chilliness of U.S.-Russian relations in recent years has not been the fault of Russia," retired Gen. Fyodor Ladygin, former head of Russian military intelligence, told me during a break in the conference. "Rather, it has resulted from a misunderstanding in the United States about the meaning of the word 'partnership,' which is bandied about frequently on the banks of the Potomac and Moscow rivers. I only hope the tragic events of September 11 will force the U.S. leadership to change its perceptions of Russia, because if we're going to be partners against international terrorism, we also have to act like partners on all issues between us."

Even as the conference met, Russian president Vladimir Putin was pondering a fateful decision on whether to acquiesce in the deployment of U.S. troops to Central Asian bases on Russia's borders. To many of the Russian officials at the conference, the idea of green-lighting the deployment of U.S. military forces in Russia's "near abroad" in order to wage war in Afghanistan was unthinkable. Russia's Duma, or parliament, had already expressed grave concerns about Russia joining any U.S.-led counterterrorism coalition. The Russian public was also skeptical. According to a poll by the All-Russia Public Opinion Center in September of 2001, a majority of Russians favored neutrality in the conflict between the United States and Islamic terrorists. Nearly 70 percent felt that Russia should try and deny U.S. forces the use of bases in Central Asia.

A U.S.-Russian counterterrorism alliance undoubtedly presented potential risks as well as rewards for both countries. For the United States the risk was very real that such an alliance with Russia would eventually splinter over a lack of shared values, just as it had in the 1990s over the war in Kosovo. Only next time the fracture could come over what to do about Iraq, a longtime Russian client, or the issue of whether to seek approval for military action from the U.N. Security Council, where Russia held a permanent seat. If such a break occurred, the United States risked strengthening the already strong hand of hard-liners in the Russian government, endangering Russia's nascent experiment with democracy.

On the other hand, Russian officials had reason to fear that a botched campaign in Afghanistan to capture Osama Bin Laden or topple the ruling Taliban could prompt the United States to withdraw and leave Russia with even more radicalized Islamists on its unstable southern borders. Conversely, if the United States were successful, it could gain a foothold and lasting presence near the oil-rich Caucasus. "If the United States wants to use military infrastructure in Central Asia, Russia has every reason to be afraid the Americans will want to maintain a continued presence in that strategic region," said Michal Kreimer, president of the Colloqium of Military Experts, a Moscow think tank. "We can't just be neutral observers to such a threat."

Not everyone at the Moscow conference, however, believed that the risks of a U.S.-Russian antiterrorism partnership overshadowed the potential rewards. Wjatscheslaw Nikonow, a member of the Council for Foreign and Defense Policy in Moscow, was convinced that the September 11 attacks were momentous enough to shatter hardening positions on both sides of the U.S.-Russian divide. If he was right, the 9/11 attacks might have the effect of finally tipping Russia decisively into the Western camp, realizing one of the United States' primary strategic goals of the post–Cold War era. "This crisis is of a kind that happens very rarely in history, and their impact is usually to greatly accelerate change in the international system," Nikonow told me. "Already we've seen President Putin come to a decision point in a matter of weeks that normally would have taken years to arrive at. This crisis presents an opportunity to break out of the traditional agendas and old frameworks, and make a significant step forward not only in fighting terrorism, but in building a new world order for the twenty-first century."

In a dramatic September 24 televised address, Putin announced his decision to an expectant nation: Russia was joining the antiterrorism coalition. He offered to support the U.S. campaign in Afghanistan with search-and-rescue operations, the use of Russian airspace for humanitarian flights, and additional weapons transfers to the Northern Alliance forces allied against the ruling Taliban. Putin also offered the cooperation of Russian intelligence forces in tracking terrorists. Perhaps most surprising, he took the unprecedented step of supporting the use by U.S. forces of staging bases in Central Asia.

For a nation with a knack for consistently choosing the side of history's losers—from the embrace of communism, to Josef Stalin's pact with Adolf Hitler, to Russia's more recent backing of former Yugoslavian strongman and indicted war criminal Slobodan Milosevic—Putin's address seemed to mark a historic departure. Within days U.S. aircraft and Special Forces would begin pouring into the Central Asian region around Afghanistan by sea and air, including the small nation of Tajikistan, roughly a thirty-minute flight from the Afghan capital of Kabul. Once there, U.S. forces in Tajikistan would be protected by a vanguard of some twenty-five thousand Russian troops situated along the border between Tajikistan and Afghanistan.

I wondered if that was what the Russian meant, an acceleration of history so dramatic that at times it seemed to be looping back on itself like an old newsreel, its flickering images recalling long-ago battles and a war yet to begin. Only two decades earlier it was an ascendant Soviet empire that was invading Afghanistan, and Russian troops that were fighting and dying in a war with Islamic "holy warriors." Some of them were led by a warrior prince of Saudi Arabia named Osama Bin Laden.

After U.S. aircraft, Special Forces, and CIA operatives launched Operation Enduring Freedom in Afghanistan on October 7, marrying U.S. space and airpower with Northern Alliance troops mounted on horseback, the Bush administration continued to stress that the campaign was just the opening salvo in a much larger war. In fact, in the months after the 9/11 attacks Americans heard some of the strongest rhetoric from a U.S. president since John F. Kennedy pledged, during one of the darkest periods of the Cold War, to "pay any price, bear any burden, meet any hardship" in defense of liberty.

Daring skeptics to look into his eyes for any sign of doubt, President Bush declared his intention to impose a new set of rules on the relations between nations. "I promise you this: I will enforce the doctrine that says, 'If you house a terrorist, you're just as guilty as the terrorists themselves,'" Bush said in an October 4 address to the Department of Labor. "This is our calling. This is our nation's time to lead the world, and we must do so in a bold, strong, and determined fashion. We will not waver." Behind Bush's unflinching rhetoric about denying global terrorists safe havens or the succor of state sponsorship, however, a heated debate was raging within his administration and the international coalition about what it even meant to fight a "war on terror." Because terrorism had long been a tactic of the weak against the strong, trying to end it outright did in some sense seem like fighting a war against history.

As senior administration sources admitted to me at the time, the goal of ending state sponsorship of international terrorism and shattering a status quo where terrorism was too often viewed as a legitimate tactic, was widely agreed upon. The strategy for achieving such a long-sought aim was anything but. "President Bush has clearly signaled we're going after terrorists with global reach and those states that support them, and everyone understands that problem is much broader than Al Qaeda and Afghanistan," a senior National Security Council source told me. "So we know where we want to end up. We're still figuring out, however, how to get from here to there."

The difficulty of even describing the enemy, much less what victory would look like, underscored the challenges facing the Bush administration as it sought to formulate a strategy and build an international coalition for this self-described "new kind of war." The definition of what constituted a terrorist organization or act, for instance, had long been a prickly issue in diplomatic circles as a result of the dispute at the center of the Israeli-Palestinian conflict. Many Arabs insisted that Palestinian suicide bombers living under occupation were actually "freedom fighters," and thus would not support a blanket definition condemning all terrorism.

Officially, the State Department cited Title 22 of the U.S. Code, concluding that "international terrorism" was premeditated, politically motivated attacks on civilians of another country, whether through hijackings, hostage taking, assassinations, bombings, or the use of weapons of mass destruction. To avoid getting bogged down in scores of civil wars and separatist conflicts around the world where terror against civilians was all too common, however, the Bush administration officials narrowed the definition of the enemy as terrorists such as Al Qaeda with "global reach," plus those who support such organizations. Officials hoped that definition would help the United States avoid getting sidetracked by domestic terrorism centered around various separatist movements and civil wars, whether in Kashmir, Chechnya, Northern Ireland, Spain's Basque region, or especially the Palestinian territories. "We have to speak out against terrorism in broad terms because all terrorism is bad, but there's a danger of people trying to use that broad language to lure the U.S. into policing all the world's domestic conflicts," the senior NSC source said. "That war would never end for America. Especially when we're contemplating using U.S. military force, we need a definition of the enemy that reflects our direct national interests."

Unofficially, U.S. officials were well aware that since the 1979 Islamic revolution and seizure of the U.S. Embassy in Iran, the driving ideology of the most active international terrorist groups and their state sponsors had been radical Islam, and much of that terrorism was targeted at Israel and the United States. As noted by a 2000 Congressional Research Service report, for instance, most of the high-profile acts of terrorism against American citizens and targets in the past twenty years had been conducted by radical Islamic groups in the Middle East, aided and abetted by their state sponsors. Meanwhile, five of the seven nations on the State Department's list of terrorist sponsors, and many of the other acknowledged "states of concern," were in the Middle East. For that reason, many U.S. allies and senior State Department officials argued that addressing the Israeli-Palestinian conflict was the best way to change the dynamic of state-supported terror.

From the beginning, Bush administration officials also understood that the most difficult and crucial balancing act in the war on terrorism would likely be keeping a broad antiterrorism coalition together that cooperated on critical law enforcement and intelligence issues at the same time that Washington was threatening state sponsors of terrorism with military force. Moderate Arab regimes in the Middle East, for instance, warned early and often that military strikes on another Islamic or Arab regime such as Iraq would separate them from the coalition.

Richard Fairbanks was chief U.S. negotiator for the Middle East peace process in the Reagan administration and more recently a counselor at the Center for Strategic and International Studies in Washington. "This war on terrorism is going to take very adept and subtle diplomacy, careful coordination to keep the shifting coalitions together for whatever task is at hand, and very detailed and believable intelligence that we can share with the various nations involved to keep them on board," he told me in an interview in October 2001. "That's one hell of a challenge. While I applaud President Bush's forceful rhetoric, it has also set the bar very high, and there's tremendous risk for him politically and for the United States geopolitically. If we're seen as leaping for that bar and not making it, then the world's only superpower will be perceived as an impotent giant against the terrorist threat."

As New Year 2002 approached, disagreements over the proper strategy for the war on global terrorism were growing between the more cautious moderates at the State Department and the Bush revolutionaries in the Pentagon and Vice President's office. State Department officials continued to press for building the largest possible global coalition in order to isolate and track Al Qaeda, and to make terrorist sponsors pariah states in a new world order that rejected terrorism outright. Such a strategy, they argued, would magnify the coercive effect of all facets of American power, from the carrots of increased aid and trade, to the sticks of diplomatic isolation, economic sanction and, as a last resort, military action. According to that strategy, state sponsors of terrorism would be forgiven for past misdeeds and judged primarily on their actions post-9/11.

There was certainly precedent for such a view. Confronted with severe diplomatic isolation and sanctions as a result of the role its intelligence services played in the bombing of Pan Am Flight 103 over Lockerbie, Scotland, in 1988, Libya had worked in recent years to mend its international image and was generally viewed as trying to get out of the terrorism business. In 2000, Libya thus surrendered to international authorities two intelligence officers complicit in the downing of Flight 103. Similar economic and diplomatic pressures exerted on Sudan had also led to what U.S. officials characterized as a "constructive dialogue" on ending that nation's sponsorship of terrorist organizations.

The State Department's first major salvo in its campaign to marshal support for the United States' war on terror and institutionalize a worldwide rejection of terrorism had come with the passage of U.N. Resolution 1373 in September 2001. U.S. Ambassador to the United Nations John Negroponte successfully established a special Security Council committee on terrorism to monitor compliance with Resolution 1373, which under Chapter Seven of the U.N. Charter bound all members to its provisions. Significantly, the United States insisted that the British ambassador to the United Nations chair the new committee, thus putting the United States' closest ally in charge of the U.N.'s war on terrorism.

"Resolution 1373 was really unique in the history of the United Nations, in that it seeks to make proactive steps against terrorism mandatory for all member states," Jeremy Greenstock, committee chairman and British ambassador to the United Nations, told me at the time. "In the past, many of the sins of nations in terms of terrorism were of omission as well as commission," he added. "The aim is to eradicate this laxity among governments that allowed terrorist finances to filter through their systems; that led to inadequate sharing of information on terrorists; and that provided safe haven to terrorists. Those states that refuse to respond favorably will be reported back to the U.N. Security Council for whatever action it deems appropriate. But I think they will represent a tiny minority."

Along with many top State Department officials, Greenstock believed that given time, the application of diplomatic and economic pressure by a determined America, coupled with blanket international condemnation and the implied coercion of forcible regime change in Afghanistan, could dissuade many state sponsors of terrorism. "I have deliberately taken the temperature of the United Nations because this campaign is so important to London, and I sense more support for the United States as a nation on this issue than on any other I've witnessed," Greenstock told me in the late fall of 2001. "That comes both from the sympathy everyone feels for the loss of three thousand Americans, and also from the realization that this horror could be visited upon any of us."

Even before the Taliban fell and Osama Bin Laden and his top lieutenants were scattered into the mountains of Tora Bora, however, the Bush revolutionaries began agitating for a more ambitious and confrontational strategy for fighting the war on terrorism. The antiterrorism coalition being assembled by Secretary of State Powell at the United Nations, they argued, was so broad that it could be construed as including some nations that were on the State Department's own list of terrorist sponsors, thus diluting America's moral authority.

After entering office bent on unshackling American power and leading a revolution in world affairs, the Bush revolutionaries were determined to make the most of events that had conspired to thrust war upon the United States, and revolutionary change on the international system. In their view, the 9/11 attacks were an opportunity to permanently transform the international order into a more values-based system where the United States and its handpicked posses would be free to confront rogue states and "evil" non-state actors. "The post–Cold War period after the collapse of the Soviet Union was really a period of transition, when it wasn't really clear what the new challenges were going to be," a senior White House official later told me, recalling those seminal post-9/11 discussions within the Bush administration. "September 11 was the kind of shock that put into sharper relief what our key interests were. All of a sudden, it became clear that the focus needed to be on the nexus between terrorism, weapons of mass destruction, and the link between values and national security."

The Bush revolutionaries' focus on that shadowy nexus of rogue states, weapons of mass destruction, and terrorists became their post-9/11 compass for charting a bold and strategically ambitious course. Almost by definition the links between the rogues and terrorists would prove sketchy and circumstantial—that was how terrorist organizations operated. In their view, the United States could not afford to wait for proof of such linkages that would stand up in a court of law, or for that matter, in the court of international opinion. America had unsurpassed military power, and 9/11 had given it purpose and momentum. The way to shatter the nexus decisively was not to subject the likes of Saddam Hussein or Kim Jong Il to the tender mercies of diplomacy, the Bush revolutionaries argued, but to confront the evil head-on with the hard sword of U.S. military power.

"This war will not end in Afghanistan," Robert Kagan and William Kristol wrote in the October 29 issue of the *Weekly Standard*, reflecting the views of many influential neoconservatives within the Bush administration. "It is going to spread and engulf a number of countries in conflicts of varying intensity. It could well require the use of American military power in multiple places simultaneously. . . . It is going to resemble the clash of civilizations that everyone had hoped to avoid. And it is going to put enormous and perhaps unbearable strain on parts of the international coalition that today basks in contented consensus."

In early January of 2002, with President Bush preparing to publicly unveil for the first time the U.S. strategy for fighting the greater war on terrorism in his State of the Union address, I found myself in a trendy pizzeria in Georgetown with a senior official from the French embassy. The European allies, who had proven critical in assembling the broad counterterrorism coalition, had become increasingly uneasy over the Bush administration's heated rhetoric about Iraq. The fact that the coalition's partners had been largely left in the dark on U.S. plans suggested to some European leaders that the Bush administration was returning to unilateralist form after a post-9/11 period of outreach. Privately, the French official said, they had conveyed to the administration their fears that broadening the military campaign beyond Afghanistan would play into Osama Bin Laden's hands, casting the fight as a war against Islam.

"Europeans understand that this is a vital matter of life and death, and we're standing shoulder to shoulder with Americans in this global war," the French official said, noting his country's contribution of French commandos to the fighting in Afghanistan, and French support for a possible NATO force to police that war's aftermath. After being driven out of Algeria in the late 1950s in a bloody war of independence, however, the French had firsthand experience and bitter memories of the seething anticolonial, anti-Western sentiments of the region. "The question surrounding phase two of the campaign is about means. Given the irrational emotions of the Arab street, we believe an attack on an Arab nation will be exploited by the extremists as a war on all of Islam. That's why we support a combination of diplomatic, economic, and financial pressures rather than military force."

With the Taliban regime toppled and Al Qaeda scattered from its bases in Afghanistan, the world watched and waited expectantly for the Bush administration to outline the next phase in the global war on terrorism. Many observers sensed that President Bush had come to the long-anticipated fork in the road. He would have to choose between moderates in his administration who argued for keeping the diplomatic pressure on state sponsors of terror with the broadest international coalition, and finishing the job of capturing or killing Bin Laden and his top Al Qaeda lieutenants, and hard-liners and neoconservatives pressing for a confrontation with Iraq as the logical next step.

In the midst of that debate, I called Richard Perle, a member of Rumsfeld's Defense Advisory Board and a leading neoconservative intellectual close to many senior officials in the Pentagon. "I think you'll see a broad consensus begin to emerge in the Bush administration that it's futile to go after individual terrorists or terrorist organizations one at a time, because new ones will emerge faster than the old ones can blow themselves up," Perle told me. "So we're going to have to go after the state sponsors, who find it more difficult to hide. Iraq tops the list."

At 9:15 P.M. on January 29, 2002, President Bush took to the podium in the U.S. Capitol to deliver the State of the Union address to a nation waiting to hear which fork in the road he had chosen. In both tone and substance, the speech he delivered that night might have been lifted from a neoconservative manifesto, and to much of the rest of the world it sounded remarkably like the standard bearer of the West was looking beyond even Iraq and issuing a call to global war.

"What we have found in Afghanistan confirms that, far from ending there, our war against terror is only beginning," Bush said. While reiterating that the United States would continue to target Al Qaeda and other terrorists, he broadened the enemy to include "regimes who seek chemical, biological or nuclear weapons" and who might threaten the United States. Of these, he singled out Iraq, Iran, and North Korea as "an axis of evil, arming to threaten the peace of the world. By seeking weapons of mass destruction, these regimes pose a grave and growing danger. They could provide these arms to terrorists, giving them the means to match their hatred. They could attack our allies or attempt to blackmail the United States. In any of these cases, the price of indifference would be catastrophic."

In the next breath, Bush offered a glimpse of the preemptive tactics that would become an integral part of the Bush doctrine and the administration's strategy for continuing the war on terrorism, later outlined in the seminal 2002 National Security Strategy document. "We'll be deliberate, but time is not on our side. I will not wait on events as dangers gather. I will not stand by, as perils draw closer and closer. The United States will not permit the world's most dangerous regimes to threaten us with the world's most destructive weapons."

In closing, Bush espoused his faith in an America entrusted with an almost divine mission. After all, Bush was a man almost preternaturally disposed to see the world in terms of good and evil, and in confronting a monstrous act on September 11, Bush seemed convinced at last of his own purpose and a nation's calling. The United States had no intention of imposing its culture, Bush said, but "those of us who have lived through these challenging times have been changed by them. We've come to know truths that we will never question: evil is real and it must be opposed. . . . And many have discovered again that even in tragedy—especially in tragedy—God is near. In a single instant, we realized that this will be a decisive decade in the history of liberty, that we've been called to a unique role in human events. Rarely has the world faced a choice more clear or consequential."

President Bush's evocation of an America anointed to confront a spreading evil around the world, preemptively and unilaterally if need be, played well in the heartland of red state America, and with the Christian evangelicals with whom the President always seemed to viscerally connect. For much of the rest of the world the speech struck a somewhat messianic and decidedly menacing tone. An unsurpassed American superpower, fresh from victory in the bloody battlefields of Afghanistan was, with little consultation with allies or coalition partners, suddenly brandishing its sword at all the rogue states in the world. In retrospect, the January 2002 State of the Union address represented the decisive fork in the road for the U.S.-led war on international terrorism. Afterward, as the Bush revolutionaries beat the drums ever louder over war with Iraq, few seemed to notice or care that many of America's closest friends and allies had left the formation.

CHAPTER 6

A Familiar Nemesis

SABER, VAMPIRE is in the box."

"Roger that, Vampire. Knife and Blade are at your 9 o'clock."

After sucking on the extended nipple of a British midair refueling aircraft, and confirming altitude and heading with a nearby U.S. Air Force AWACS command-and-control aircraft called Saber, Vampire banked sharply and descended as the sun glinted off its silvery skin. From the window of the refueling aircraft, I watched the aircraft disappear along the bright ribbon of the Great Zab River as it flowed from the snow-blanketed mountains of southeastern Turkey onto the plains of northern Iraq. It was late February in 2002.

Because of the dangers that awaited in Iraq, the aircraft of Operation Northern Watch followed a well-orchestrated order of battle. Leading the way were dolphin-nosed U.S. Navy EA-6B Prowlers to jam Iraqi electronic signals, followed by sleek Air Force F-16CJ Falcon strike aircraft armed with distinctive HARM (high-speed anti-radiation) missiles to home in on enemy radars. High overhead, twin-engine F-15C Eagle air superiority fighters—"Knife" and "Blade"—flew "cap" or air cover. Wasp-like A-10 Warthogs with antitank missiles and armor-piercing 30 mm cannons followed, ready to strike any air-defense batteries that engaged the coalition aircraft. British Jaguars outfitted with special camera pods for reconnaissance duty completed the full-up strike package.

The battle formation was not for show. On average, Iraqi air-defense forces fired at Northern Watch aircraft thirty-four times each month as the allied planes patrolled the skies over northern Iraq to make sure Iraqi combat aircraft stayed on the ground. Both the U.S.-patrolled Northern and Southern Watch no-fly zones had been established in the early 1990s after Saddam's forces exploited a loophole in the 1991 surrender agreement and used helicopter gunships to slaughter northern Kurds and southern Shiites who had risen up against his rule. Thus while the debate continued back in Washington over whether war was justified to finally topple Saddam Hussein, for U.S. and British pilots flying out of Incirlik Air Base in southeastern Turkey the issue was largely moot. In Operation Northern Watch the pilots went to war with Saddam a little bit each day.

Once the strike package was safely back on the ground at Incirlik, I spoke with Brig. Gen. Edward "Buster" Ellis, commander of the Northern Watch Combined Task Force at the time. Ellis was still in his flight suit after the morning's mission, revealing the Air Force's ethos that encouraged even its senior officers to lead from the cockpit. "If the Iraqis didn't shoot at us, this would be a boring mission, because the Iraqi air force won't dare enter the no-fly zone," Ellis told me in his spare office. "The fact is, however, that not only do they shoot at us on nearly every mission, but Saddam has put a bounty on our heads payable to anyone who brings down one of our airplanes. After ten years, the Iraqis have also gotten smarter about parking their air-defense weapons near mosques and even in amusement parks for children, knowing that we won't strike back at them."

Besides facing a foe seasoned by that decadelong game of cat and mouse, Northern Watch patrols also confronted a mission that had become increasingly complicated as the international sanctions regime designed to contain Saddam had steadily eroded over time. "The one common denominator is that the same bad guy is still occupying the seat of power in Baghdad as ten years ago," Ellis said. "And rather than accept the status quo or rules of containment, he continues to test our limits and throw everything but the kitchen sink at us."

Because of domestic and regional sensitivities about the Northern Watch mission, Turkish officials had granted few requests from journalists to visit Incirlik, and the frequent Iraqi antiaircraft attacks and reprisal bombings had long ago been relegated to the inside pages of most U.S. newspapers. I had traveled halfway around the world and been given access to Incirlik, however, in search of answers to a deceptively simple question: Why were the United States and Iraq once again embarked on a seemingly irrevocable collision course toward war?

All of my reporting instincts told me that was the case, and indeed I had written that Iraq was the likely next phase in the war on terrorism back in October of 2001 in a cover story for *National Journal*. With much of the world warning against such a confrontation, however, I wanted to test the arguments and assumptions the Bush administration was relying on to make its case for regime change in Baghdad. To build a viable coalition for disarming Iraq and possibly even dethroning Saddam, and keep nations together for the wider war against international terrorism, the Bush administration was going to have to explain precisely what made Iraq such a unique threat.

Certainly the weapons of mass destruction that the United States now saw as a glaring threat had long been central to Saddam Hussein's thinking. Saddam was one of the few world leaders who had actually used nerve gas and chemical weapons, both against the Iranians during the Iraq-Iran war and against his own restive Kurdish population. Iraq was also in violation of numerous United Nations resolutions passed in the 1990s demanding that its weapons programs be unambiguously opened to international inspectors as agreed upon in the 1991 surrender document, leaving a legal and investigative paper trail to follow. There were also tantalizing but mostly unsubstantiated stories of ties between Iraqi intelligence officials and terror groups, including Al Qaeda. Other than Saddam's publicly acknowledged payments to the families of Palestinian suicide bombers, however, there was little hard proof of such ties.

Some observers suspected that the real reason behind the war drums was a decade of enmity between the United States and Iraq in general, and between Saddam Hussein and the Bush team in particular. After Saddam suffered one of the most lopsided defeats in modern history in his self-proclaimed "Mother of All Battles," Iraqi intelligence services had plotted in 1993 to assassinate George H. W. Bush on one of the former President's trips to Kuwait. When the plot was exposed the Clinton administration responded with cruise missile strikes on the headquarters of the Iraqi intelligence services in Baghdad. Now the son was President and the architects of an unfinished victory in the Persian Gulf War were back in power—including Vice President Dick Cheney, Secretary of State Colin Powell, and Deputy Defense Secretary Paul Wolfowitz.

Perhaps most intriguingly, the neoconservatives inside the Pentagon and close to the Bush administration were positing Iraq as the lynchpin for breaking the authoritarian mold of the Middle East, and thus key to the Bush grand strategy of transforming the region with freedom and democracy. Backed by Iraqi exile Ahmed Chalabi and his Iraqi National Congress, they argued that Iraq was ripe for a democratic revolution. With their close ties to Israel's hard-line Likud Party, the neoconservatives had long rejected the conventional wisdom that the road to peace and greater stability in the Middle East ran through Jerusalem, meaning a negotiated peace that would require painful concessions of territory by Israel, and lead to the establishment of a Palestinian state.

Ever the "Vulcans," the Bush revolutionaries believed instead that the road to a transformed Middle East ran through Baghdad. With just a little encouragement and support by the U.S. military, Chalabi assured his friends in the Pentagon, Iraqis would rise up against Saddam's tyranny just as they had following the Persian Gulf War of 1991. Then democracy would flourish in Iraq and sweep through the region in domino-like fashion. The Bush revolutionaries were eager to believe.

I intended to investigate all of those assumptions and had traveled to

Turkey specifically to test two premises: that Iraq and the region were ready for a democratic reformation of sorts, and the Bush administration's argument that the status quo was unsustainable because the sanctions regime designed to keep Saddam contained in his "box" was breaking down. On that final point, at least, the evidence was pretty clear.

Once upon a time anything that flew in the northern no-fly zone was fair game for Northern Watch patrols. U.S. officers at Incirlik told me, however, that commercial air traffic and trade routes between Baghdad and its neighbors hummed with activity by early 2002. Northern Watch pilots had to distinguish between potential Iraqi "bogies," for instance, and regular international commercial flights between Syria and Iraq, and domestic civilian flights between Baghdad and the northern Iraqi city of Mosul. The Iraqi government had also begun unauthorized crop dusting by helicopter in the northern no-fly zone, raising the possibility of sarin nerve gas attacks such as those launched from the air by Saddam against Iraqi Kurds in the city of Halabja in March 1988.

Any counterstrikes by Northern Watch pilots also had to steer clear of a recently reopened rail line between southern Turkey and Iraq that had been closed for many years. Likewise, U.S. pilots were told to avoid bombing near an oil pipeline running between Iraq and their host nation of Turkey. That pipeline was clear indication of a flourishing trade in oil, much of it bartered on the black market, between Iraq and its neighbors. That black market trading circumvented the United Nations' oil-for-food program and put as much as $2 billion in illegal revenue into Saddam's coffers each year, where it could be spent solely at his discretion.

An independent panel investigating the oil-for-food program would later reveal that it, too, was riddled with corruption, and that Saddam was steering oil deals to Russia and France especially, two permanent members of the U.N. Security Council that had continually urged that sanctions on Iraq be eased during the 1990s. The panel's report on companies purchasing Iraqi oil showed that Russian companies were the primary business partners of the Hussein regime, followed in order by French, Swiss, British and, Turkish companies. Four U.S. companies also purchased Iraqi oil in this time frame, including Chevron and Texaco.

Because the black market trade in cheap Iraqi oil helped regional allies Turkey and Jordan compensate for billions of dollars in trade lost due to the sanctions on Iraq, U.S. officials willingly turned a blind eye to the obvious leakage in the sanctions regime. There was no hiding the lavish palaces Saddam was constructing all over Iraq with the money, however, or assuaging concerns about what else the dictator might be purchasing with the ill-gotten gains.

Northern Watch pilots I talked with also chaffed at strict rules of engagement and operational conditions imposed by host-country Turkey, revealing the deep ambivalence Ankara felt as a Muslim country serving as a staging base for confrontations between the United States and an Arab neighbor. In an effort to avoid provoking Saddam, for instance, Turkey insisted on restrictive "rules of engagement" that severely limited the response of Northern Watch pilots to Iraqi fire, putting U.S. pilots in greater danger. The net effect of those restrictions was that Northern Watch pilots responded only rarely to Iraqi gunners who routinely tried to shoot them down. In the ten months before I visited Incirlik, Northern Watch pilots had fired back only eight times at Iraqi air-defense sties despite being targeted nearly thirty-five times each month. "I'm proud of the discipline my guys have shown in deciding not to take a shot because the risks of collateral damage were too high or the rules of engagement hadn't been met," Lt. Col. Tim Strawther, commander of an F-16 fighter squadron taking part in Northern Watch, told me on the Incirlik flight line. "But I do worry that the Iraqis are going to get lucky and down one of our people with a 'Golden BB.' The Las Vegas odds makers will tell you that sooner or later, your luck will change."

In fact, fear that Iraqi air-defense gunners would get lucky, or that mechanical failure might force a U.S. aircrew down inside Iraq, permeated Operation Northern Watch, which had launched more sorties over Iraq than were flown over Korea during the Korean War. One F-16 pilot involved in a Northern Watch mission had indeed suffered an engine failure that forced him to eject, but luckily he was picked up by a U.S. search-and-rescue helicopter. No one wanted to contemplate the public relations spectacle Saddam would undoubtedly put on if Iraqis ever actually captured a coalition pilot.

General Ellis conceded that the rules of engagement were frustrating for his pilots, whose natural reaction when they get shot at was to level something. "But anyone who thinks that military action shouldn't be governed by political constraints is naïve," Ellis told me. "The political reality is, we're not at war with Iraq at this point, and if we reacted rashly, we could force the hand or limit the options of U.S. policy makers who are trying to figure out what to do about Saddam Hussein. Having said that, I do think there is merit to the argument that the policy makers might want to address this issue sooner rather than later, because of the inherent jeopardy of this mission. The bottom line is, we continue to fly and the Iraqis continue to shoot at us. Nobody should be especially surprised if eventually they happen to hit something."

Five times a day, the eerie incantation of the Islamic *ezan* wafted over the staggered rooftops of Ankara and through the window of my hotel room in the Turkish capital, the loudspeakers calling the devout to prayer under the massive domes and towering spires of the nearby Kocatepe Mosque. Occasionally I would follow the faithful crowds and admire the mix of traditional dress and modern suits as they flocked to the mosque. In Muslim Turkey, those with a practiced eye claimed the ability to discern the level of a woman's devotion by how tightly she tied her head scarf.

Yet in a jarring bit of juxtaposition, directly below the Kocatepe Mosque thousands of shoppers respond to an altogether different call—the full-throated cry of modern capitalism. In an opulent shopping mall beneath the mosque, shoppers glided between the multiple levels on escalators, crowding around garish cosmetics counters and home electronics displays. On Arjantin Caddesi Street near the Sheraton Hotel in the capital, the chic fashions on display at trendy restaurants and bars rivaled those seen in London or Paris. After sunset one evening, I was invited to join a group of revelers at Ankara's Kashmir disco as they drank and danced until dawn to the incessant beat of European techno-rock.

Those contrasts between Eastern traditionalism and Western modernity were apparent everywhere I went in Ankara, and indeed they are integral to Turkey's unique character. As a geographical and metaphorical crossroads of Christian West and Muslim East, of rich north and poor south, and of liberalism and traditionalism, Turkey felt acutely its precarious position on the fault line of any post-9/11 "clash of civilizations." Certainly the internal dilemmas and contradictions between democratic secularism and Islam that Turkey had long struggled to reconcile were now central to the Bush administration's long-term strategy for winning the war on global terrorism. Meanwhile, two of the nations the Bush administration labeled an "axis of evil," Turkey called neighbors. All of which explained why the Bush administration's somewhat matter-of-fact rhetoric about "regime change" and potential war in Iraq was greeted with great fear and trepidation in Ankara.

At the U.S. embassy in Ankara I spoke with a senior diplomat about those concerns. "The Turks and many others in this region are very worried that this enormously powerful, but sometimes bumbling superpower that is the United States now believes it can apply the Afghanistan model to Iraq—which is a recipe for disaster," he told me in February 2002. If the United States used air strikes and local opposition groups in an effort to topple the leadership of a major Arab country possessing a large army, he warned, it would not have enough troops on the ground to manage the inevitably messy aftermath. After enduring a terrorist campaign by Kurdish separatists in the 1990s that claimed more than thirty thousand lives, Turkey was especially sensitive to the possibility that Iraq could fracture along its ethnic and religious divides following a war to oust Saddam. "That raises what for Turks is a truly horrifying possibility of an independent Kurdistan emerging in northern Iraq to unite the Kurds of the Middle East. The Saudis have similar concerns about Shiites in southern Iraq breaking away and aligning themselves with Iran," the diplomat said. "So while I still think the Turks could be with the United States at the end of the day if it came to war with Iraq, the quid pro quo is likely to be, 'No more half-measures or trying to accomplish this on the cheap.'"

With Vice President Dick Cheney scheduled to travel to Turkey and the Middle East in early 2002 for what many analysts predicted would prove a war council, the Turks were already prepared to drive a hard bargain. The entire region was deeply fearful, Turkish officials told me, that the United States was about to shatter an uneasy status quo and plunge the region back into chaos. Since the 1991 Gulf War, Turkish officials estimated that they had lost more than $30 billion in trade that once crossed their southern border bound for Baghdad or transiting to other Persian Gulf states. Nor had anyone forgotten that part of the blowback from Desert Storm was a massive influx of more than five hundred thousand Iraqi refugees across Turkey's already volatile southeastern border, near where many of the nation's twelve million Kurds lived. "At the time, the 1991 Iraqi exodus was the biggest refugee crisis the United Nations had ever witnessed," Metin Corabatir, Turkish coordinator for the U.N. High Commissioner for Refugees, told me. "And we're now reviewing our contingency plans in case it happens again."

In their talks with Cheney, Turkish officials told me they would stress three overriding concerns. "First, Turkey continues to shoulder a very heavy economic burden as a result of international sanctions on Iraq," a senior government official said, noting that any conflict in the region would also likely further hurt Turkey's economy in unforeseen ways, such as deterring the millions of visitors who fed the nation's increasingly important tourism industry. "Secondly, these sanctions and tensions are severely damaging the social fabric in Iraq," he said. An Iraqi child that was ten years of age in 1991 was now twenty-one, the Turkish official pointed out, and thus half of his or her life had been spent under severe economic hardships that the Iraqi propaganda machine had blamed primarily on the United States. "So we're going to face a very difficult and unpredictable generation of young Iraqis. Finally and most importantly, we have continually stressed that if Iraq is ever again to be a force for stability in this region, its territorial integrity must be maintained. If a conflict were to splinter or fragment Iraq, it would produce an earthquake that will shake this entire region."

The message I took away from my talks with numerous Turkish officials was sobering. America's longtime NATO ally and closest friend in the region suggested that far from being greeted with open arms, U.S. forces would likely confront a generation of Iraqis raised on hatred of the United States. That painted a very different picture, I knew, from the liberation scenario being advanced by Pentagon neocons and their friends in the Iraqi diaspora. At the very least, it also seemed that winning critical Turkish support would require a massive commitment of U.S. and coalition forces in order to hold Iraq and its fractious populace of Shiites, Sunnis, and Kurds together in the war's aftermath. The message also came through loud and clear that Turkey would need generous compensation for serving as a launching base for another risky war on its borders.

While in Ankara I visited the massive mausoleum that holds the remains of Kemal Ataturk, the founding father of modern Turkey and the inspiration for the "Turkish model" of Islamic democracy. Perched on a hillside in an extensive park with the skyline of Ankara spread out all around it, the many-columned Ataturk Memorial and museum complex suggests the omnipotent place Ataturk occupies in the national consciousness. The power of his vision of a secular Islamic nation and hold on the Turkish psyche would be hard to overstate. For Americans, it would be as if all the Founding Fathers were rolled into a single figure whose greatest deeds had occurred within living memory. Or as one U.S. official in Turkey put it: "You still can't sling a chicken in this country today without hitting a portrait or photograph of Ataturk."

After Turkey's crushing defeat in World War I on the side of the Germans, and the humiliating disintegration of the Ottoman Empire and partition of Turkey, Mustafa Kemal Ataturk led the revolutionary forces that eventually ousted occupying allied forces and carved out an independent Turkey. Breaking with hundreds of years of Ottoman tradition, Ataturk then abolished the ruling religious caliphate; replaced *sharia*, or Islamic law, with Western civil and penal codes borrowed, respectively, from Switzerland and Italy; and substituted the Latin alphabet for Arabic script. By the force of his considerable will and his stature as the nation's liberator, Ataturk thus almost single-handedly set Turkey on the path to secular democracy.

Sedat Ergin, the longtime Ankara bureau chief for Turkey's *Hurriyet* newspaper, met me for lunch while I was in the capital. Kemal Ataturk's insistence that Turkey weld its Islamic religious practices and centuries-old traditions to the framework of secular democracy and modernism, he told me, was the greatest single factor in Turkey's unique evolution. "I think the September 11 terrorist attacks were an eye-opener for many American intellectuals and policy makers in terms of seeing the significance of this transformation that Turkey has been undergoing virtually since its founding in 1923," said Ergin. "That separation of religion and governance that happened quite abruptly for Turkey nearly eighty years ago took centuries and many wars for the Western European countries to achieve, and in truth, except for the Turkish revolution, the Islamic world has never been subjected to a similar reformation project. Unfortunately, that explains to a large degree why Islam is suffering so much today. No other Islamic country has achieved major progress in fields such as technology and science, nor come to terms with contemporary civilization and modernity. Only Turkey has proved an exception."

Yet for all the pride and reverence bestowed on Kemal Ataturk, and all the hopeful talk that Iraq or other Muslim nations might adopt the "Turkish model" of Islamic democracy, there was a palpable sense inside Turkey that the country had advanced only partway down the path toward modernity. As a result of Turkey's determination to join the European Union, for instance, Turks had recently been forced to contemplate anew the still unfinished legacy of the Ataturk revolution, with its difficult and imperfect melding of an overwhelming Islamic society and democratic ideals. The Turkish government's policies regulating religion; the army's prominent role as the final guarantor of secularism, which had resulted in two military coups in Turkey in the past thirty years; the fear of fundamentalist and separatist dissent that had bred limits on free expression and a culture of police brutality—all the tensions that defined the essential duality of Turkish life would confront in spades any nascent Islamic democracy in Iraq or elsewhere in the Middle East.

So even while the Bush administration was looking to Turkey as a hopeful model for a democratic transformation of the Middle East, the Turks themselves feared that if the country could not successfully negotiate the next difficult stretch in their evolution and gain acceptance into the "Christian Club" of the European Union, then the country might still backslide into increased repression, separatist-inspired instability, or even religious fundamentalism. "American secularism is based on a consensus in your society that church and state should be separate, but in the Islamic world, quite the opposite view is held by most religious scholars," Ergin told me. "Especially among Islamic fundamentalists, the ultimate goal is to establish a state governed by the religious elite according to a strict interpretation of the Koran. So as an Islamic democracy with strong fundamentalist forces in our society, Turkey is caught in a dilemma. The more democratic freedoms we extend, the greater latitude we give to fundamentalist groups bent on destroying our democracy."

That dilemma figured to play prominently in a post-Saddam Iraq, given the secular dictator's long and brutal suppression of the country's Shiite religious majority in particular. In advocating the liberation of Iraq as a catalyst to democratic reform in the Middle East, President Bush would talk about a "generational commitment" on the part of Americans. After visiting Turkey and witnessing firsthand its struggles to reconcile secularism and Islam nearly eighty years after Ataturk's own fateful fork in the road, it occurred to me that President Bush might have underestimated the challenge by at least a couple of generations.

Where in Iraq's blood-soaked political culture of ruthless oppressors and the ruthlessly oppressed, I wondered, was there a surviving patriot with the stature and vision of a Kemal Ataturk? If the Bush revolutionaries were to be believed, Iraq did have a founding father in waiting, though he was not to be found in Baghdad or Karbala or even among the northern Kurds. Somewhat improbably, the man they thought qualified to lead Iraq out of Saddam's dark shadow could be found among the expensive town houses, boutiques, and woodsy pubs of fashionable Kensington, in the city of London.

There was no plaque or sign outside the London offices of the Iraqi National Congress (INC), a loose confederation of Iraqi exile groups, Kurdish factions, and an underground resistance inside Iraq of indeterminate size. Visitors had to make a prior appointment in order to get the address, where I was buzzed in by a security guard. Given the INC's prominent role in agitating for a war to unseat Saddam Hussein, the precautions were probably prudent. Though there primarily to speak with a top INC aide, once inside I ran into Ahmed Chalabi, the INC leader in whom the Bush revolutionaries had placed such high hopes.

Like many U.S. journalists, I had interviewed Chalabi before at the INC's Capitol Hill office in Washington, D.C. Wise to the ways of Washington, Chalabi had made outreach to the American press an integral part of his sophisticated campaign to build U.S. support for unseating Saddam Hussein. In 1998, Chalabi and the INC had been instrumental in convincing Congress to pass the Iraqi Liberation Act, for instance, which authorized hundreds of millions of dollars for the INC to train and equip Iraqi rebels and democratic forces. More recently, Chalabi had personally put a number of prominent U.S. reporters in touch with Iraqi defectors who claimed to have visited biological and nuclear weapons labs inside Iraq, and witnessed terrorist training camps specializing in the hijacking of airplanes.

An intelligent man with the air of an aloof professor, Chalabi could cite American as well as Iraqi history in persuasively making the case that Iraq was uniquely suited among nations in the Middle East for a democratic reformation. Iraqis were educated and secular, Chalabi explained, and had some history of democratic governance before Saddam and his military predecessors had violently seized power in the 1950s.

Early in 2002, Chalabi was stressing his oft-repeated case that the United States could overthrow Saddam on the cheap, using the Afghan model of transformational warfare by marrying U.S. airpower with Iraqi insurgent forces on the ground. The INC leader claimed that his organization could put under arms more than forty thousand Kurdish troops from the northern region of Iraq already protected by the Northern Watch no-fly zone. Chalabi likewise predicted that huge numbers of Iraqis in regions now under Saddam's control would rise up against his dictatorship if they believed the United States was serious about driving him from power this time, just as they had following the 1991 Persian Gulf War, when Shiites in southern Iraq and Kurds in the north captured fourteen of Iraq's eighteen provinces.

Though our discussions were off the record, Chalabi's comments mirrored those he made publicly at a conference we both attended in early 2002 hosted by the Council on Foreign Relations. "We believe we were the authors of the Afghan model, because what the United States did in Afghanistan was something that we proposed several years earlier for Iraq," Chalabi said. "A number of U.S. military leaders went through our plan and told Congress that they would stake their military reputation on its success. The plan calls for the United States to train a limited number of Iraqis, integrate that operation with U.S. airpower, and confront Saddam on the ground with opposition forces that would draw the Iraqi army out and thus defeat Saddam. We could do that."

Chalabi rightly noted that the United States was finding it increasingly difficult to marshal international support for continued sanctions on an impoverished Iraqi people, and that routine "maintenance" bombing of Iraq antagonized the Arab street against the United States. "I would remind you that the United States has been at war with our country for the past decade under the guise of maintaining the no-fly zones and protecting American aircraft, with weekly bombings of Iraq," said Chalabi. "That is not a stable situation that can perpetuate itself indefinitely. The United States cannot pull out of this strategic conundrum with Saddam in power, so therefore it should make up its mind to get rid of Saddam. The best way to do that is by helping us to get the job done."

Though Chalabi talked a good game, every time I had dug into his veracity and background, or talked with former acquaintances in the U.S. government, the unmistakable scent of scandal and blatant opportunism clung to him stubbornly. There was the indictment for bank fraud in Jordan, obviously. Ever since the INC launched an offensive against Iraqi forces in northern Iraq in 1995, relations between the opposition group and U.S. intelligence officials had also been severely strained. When hoped-for U.S. air support failed to materialize, the INC offensive led by Chalabi had stalled after a few initial victories. Exploiting a split between the two frequently quarreling Kurdish factions in northern Iraq (the Kurdistan Democratic Party, or KDP, led by Massoud Barzani; and the Patriotic Union of Kurdistan, or PUK, led by Jalal Talabani), Saddam had sent his armored forces to assault INC headquarters in August 1996. They captured nearly one hundred INC officials, executed them, and sent Chalabi fleeing into exile in London. Around the same time, Iraqi intelligence forces infiltrated a CIA-supported group that was poised to attempt a military coup against Saddam, exposing the operation and executing many of the dissident military officers.

Ever since those traumatic setbacks, U.S. diplomatic, intelligence, and military officials had been deeply skeptical of the INC as a viable opposition force. Retired Marine Gen. Anthony Zinni, a Middle East envoy for George W. Bush and his administration and a former commander of U.S. Central Command with responsibility for the Middle East, famously predicted that even with U.S. support, any INC-led operation would likely turn into a "bay of goats." Relations between the Bush State Department and the INC had also been strained over Colin Powell's fears that opposition activities undertaken by Chalabi's organization inside Iraq were designed to provoke a confrontation before U.S. policy makers were ready to deal with Saddam.

When I asked Chalabi why Turkey also continued to reject any direct dealings with the INC and viewed very dimly any U.S. battle plan that relied heavily on INC-led forces, Chalabi scoffed. Turkish leaders were happy to receive the leaders of the Kurdish factions with great ceremony, he said, "but when it comes to dealing with the democratic Iraqi opposition in the INC, which includes the Kurdish parties, they refuse on the basis of this fear of Kurdish independence," said Chalabi. "Unfortunately, Turkey's view of Iraq is both one-dimensional and somewhat schizophrenic."

After having just returned from Ankara, I found the views of the Turks just the opposite—both nuanced and deeply informed by dangerous currents swirling in the Middle East region. Those forces were far removed from the friendly bustle of traffic in Kensington high street, however, or the finer restaurants of Georgetown where "regime change" was a favored topic of discussion of Richard Perle, the influential Pentagon adviser and noted epicurean who was a close confidant and occasional dinner companion of Ahmed Chalabi.

One of the premises of the Bush revolutionaries that I had the most difficulty reconciling with the facts was their wholehearted faith in Chalabi and the INC, despite his checkered history and clear self-interest in a U.S.-led war to unseat Saddam. Certainly no one seemed to doubt Chalabi's ambitions to lead a liberated Iraq. He was also known to have close relations with senior officials in the Iranian government, which had its own reasons to wish Saddam gone. There was no question whose arguments better fit the ideological mind-set of the Bush revolutionaries, however, Chalabi's optimistic prediction of a welcome liberation on the cheap or the Turks' dire warnings of a potentially destabilizing earthquake.

At the Pentagon Paul Wolfowitz continued to make the case for Iraq's likely complicity in the attacks of September 11, 2001. He began pressing that point in a memo to Rumsfeld just days after the attacks, insisting that even if there was only a one in ten chance that Saddam was involved, he should be taken out. As evidence of likely complicity, Wolfowitz cited Saddam's praise of the 9/11 attacks, his venerable ties to terrorism, and theories that Ramzi Yousef, the mastermind of the 1993 attack on the World Trade Center, was an Iraqi agent. On the latter point, Wolfowitz was repeating the contention of Laurie Mylroie, the author of *Study of Revenge: Saddam Hussein's Unfinished War against America*. Mylroie was a fellow at the American Enterprise Institute, the intellectual home of many neoconservatives close to or inside the Bush administration, including Richard Perle, Undersecretary of Defense for Policy Douglas Feith, and the Vice President's wife, Lynn Cheney.

In a conversation I had with her in October 2001, Mylroie described Ramzi Yousef as the proverbial smoking gun pointing to Iraq as the culprit in the 1993 World Trade Center attacks. Though no one seemed to know exactly where Yousef came from, Mylroie noted that he arrived in New York in 1993 on a first-class ticket from Pakistan, using an Iraqi passport. His coconspirators in the first World Trade Center bombing reportedly referred to him as "Rashid, the Iraqi." Only Yousef and one other conspirator initially escaped capture. The other terrorist, Abdul Rahman Yasin, flew to Jordan after the attacks and then reportedly traveled overland to Baghdad. The stolen passports, the assuming of false identities, the carefully rehearsed escape routes—all of it, Mylroie argued, pointed to the tradecraft of a state intelligence service, and Iraq was the usual suspect.

There were other tantalizing anecdotes that seemed to tie Iraq to Al Qaeda. At first, Czech officials suggested that Mohammed Atta—the ringleader of the 9/11 hijackers—met in Prague with an Iraqi intelligence official named Ahmed Khalil Ibrahim Samir Al-Ani, though they later recanted the report. The *Washington Post* reported that Al-Ani was expelled from the Czech Republic in April of 2001 for activities "incompatible with his diplomatic status." The October 15, 2001, issue of *Newsweek* reported that Atta also met with Iraq's ambassador to Turkey, who was called back to Baghdad before September 11.

Did all of the circumstantial evidence compiled by Mylroie and other investigative journalists, many of them receiving tips from Chalabi's sources and defectors, paint a convincing picture of Iraqi complicity in the September 11 attacks? One person who seemed to think so was Vice President Dick Cheney, who persistently cited such anecdotal evidence in speaking engagements in 2002 calling for action against Saddam. A number of those engagements were hosted by the American Enterprise Institute, where Cheney's wife, Lynne, was a trustee and Laurie Mylroie worked.

Senior intelligence and counterterrorism experts, on the other hand, were far more skeptical. They pointed out that most of the evidence of Iraqi involvement was highly circumstantial and potentially misleading. There was a reason why the intelligence community relied on a carefully constructed pyramid of collection and analysis, so that unsubstantiated bits of "chatter" and anecdotal evidence were either filtered out or qualified before they reached the desk of senior policy makers. Many intelligence analysts believed that Pentagon civilians had essentially circumvented that filtering process and were relaying sensational intelligence gathered from Ahmed Chalabi directly into Vice President Dick Cheney's office, where it soon found its way into Cheney's speeches.

Noted Pentagon neocons Paul Wolfowitz and Douglas Feith, Undersecretary of Defense for Policy, had in fact established their own intelligence shop on Iraq called the Office of Special Plans. It was known to have close ties both to Ahmed Chalabi and his network of defectors, and to Vice President Dick Cheney's office, which was run by Cheney's chief of staff and de facto national security adviser, L. "Scooter" Libby. Libby was a protégé of Paul Wolfowitz, with whom Libby had worked at the Pentagon in the early 1990s as a specialist on the chemical and biological weapons programs of Saddam Hussein.

Although Cheney continued to stress Iraq's potential ties to the 9/11 attacks, that part of the Bush administration's brief on Iraq seemed highly questionable. The Bush revolutionaries seemed to be on much firmer ground, however, in pointing to Saddam as a growing threat by virtue of his thirst for weapons of mass destruction. As the man who had once tried to wrestle those weapons from Saddam's grip put it to me at the time, "The fundamental problem with Iraq remains the nature of the regime itself: Saddam Hussein is a homicidal dictator who is addicted to weapons of mass destruction."

I caught up to Ambassador Richard Butler, head of the last U.N. inspections teams in Iraq, in the plush offices of the Council on Foreign Relations in New York's Upper East Side. An affable and slightly rumpled Australian, Butler described how, almost from the beginning, U.N. weapons inspectors tasked with cataloging and destroying Iraq's residual

stockpile of chemical and biological weapons and long-range missiles in
the 1990s sensed that Saddam had another agenda entirely.

Time and again Iraqis would block inspections at gunpoint and pro-
test loudly about the indignities of inadequate notice. They would stall
inspections at the front gate of facilities and complain about the "wicked
inspectors" to the United Nations, even while U.S. spy satellites showed
massive amounts of materials being hurriedly loaded into a caravan of
waiting trucks at the back exit. The Iraqis would concoct elaborate lies
and when confronted with proof to the contrary, would shift into even
more-elaborate falsehoods. "In dealing with the Iraqis, you quickly
learned that their resistance to having the truth about a program revealed
had a direct, proportional relationship to the importance of that program," Butler told me in an interview in October 2001. "Given that fact, I
concluded that Iraq's biological weapons program was Saddam Hussein's
biggest self-indulgence and top priority. The ludicrous lies, false documentation, and pure effort the Iraqis employed in order to prevent us
from getting a handle on their biological-weapons program was an absolute wonder to behold."

The defection in August 1995 of Saddam's son-in-law Hussein Kamil,
who had been in charge of Iraq's unconventional weapons program, revealed for the first time the extent of Iraq's biological weapons program.
Iraq was forced by the incontrovertible evidence Kamil supplied to admit
that at one time it had produced significant quantities of both botulinum
and anthrax and had experimented with the Ebola virus. Given evidence
of massive amounts of biological-growth culture purchased by Iraq, UNS-
COM (United Nations Special Committee) experts suspected that Baghdad stockpiled far greater amounts of the agents than it had admitted. Yet
between Kamil's defection in 1995 and UNSCOM's expulsion from Iraq
on December 16, 1998, Iraq never turned over any of its suspected stockpile of biological agents, claiming instead that the material had been destroyed. When Kamil was lured back to Iraq from exile with promises
that all had been forgiven, Saddam's agents shot his son-in-law to death.

Jonathan Tucker was the director of the respected Chemical and Biological Weapons Nonproliferation Program at the Monterey Institute in
California. "We know for sure that Saddam had an extensive stockpile of
chemical weapons, that he had been busily acquiring biological weapons,
and that since 1998 he has probably been reconstituting those capabilities," Tucker told me in an interview in 2001. "What we don't know is
whether Saddam would take the enormous risk of providing those weapons to terrorists, because if we found that out, it would put his survival at
stake."

Why would Saddam Hussein risk so much and endure a decade of
crushing sanctions in his pursuit of weapons of mass destruction? As one

of the few people to personally try to take those weapons away, Richard Butler had a theory: "Saddam Hussein's behavior has made it manifestly clear that he is compulsively addicted to weapons of mass destruction. There has never been a moment when these weapons were not important in his life, and he's never had a weapon of mass destruction that he hasn't used, including on his own people," Butler told me. As a man whose rise to power was born of violence and bloodshed, who in the past year alone had reportedly killed an estimated three thousand Iraqis in order to retain his grip on power, Butler suggested that Saddam viewed doomsday weapons as the ultimate tool of intimidation. "These hideous adult toys play to Saddam's self-image and muscularity as the strongman with big weapons," said Butler. "They add to his credentials as the self-proclaimed leader of a pan-Arab movement against the Zionists, the United States, and what he calls the 'dwarves on Arab thrones' in Saudi Arabia and Egypt."

Throughout the spring and summer of 2002, the Bush revolutionaries made their case for regime change in Iraq even while skeptics inside and outside the administration raised yellow flags. Saddam had a well-known predilection toward doomsday weapons, but that didn't necessarily mean that Iraqi officials were lying about destroying residual stockpiles. Former U.N. inspectors feared that Iraq had taken the opportunity of their absence to develop ever-deadlier weapons, but their concerns were based on dated intelligence. There was anecdotal evidence pointing to past links between Iraq and Al Qaeda, but it was highly circumstantial. The sanctions regime designed to isolate and contain Saddam was fraying, but it might be rebuilt with determined U.S. leadership and post-9/11 international support. Regime change in Iraq might lead to a flowering of freedom and democracy in the region, but history suggested that bloodshed in the Middle East was more often followed by instability, chaos, and cycles of retribution.

With the momentum of the 9/11 attacks at their backs, however, the Bush revolutionaries were determined to press ahead in their global campaign of transformation, and they had the support of a fearful nation. Victory in Afghanistan had reinforced the Bush doctrine that governments protecting terrorists were as guilty as the terrorists themselves. Another catalyst was needed to sunder the nexus of doomsday weapons and rogue-state evil, and implement the Bush grand strategy of reforming the Middle East with democracy. Given the biography of the Bush revolutionaries and a history of unfinished business, perhaps it was inevitable that they chose as a catalyst a familiar nemesis in Baghdad.

CHAPTER 7

Pox Americana

O N A DREARY AFTERNOON in the fall of 2002, a small group of U.S. journalists and foreign policy specialists emerged from a smoky *Ratskeller* in the eastern German town of Rostock into a cold September drizzle. We were there to catch a glimpse of history, and as we took our places in the cobblestoned town square amidst a sea of raincoats and umbrellas, our mood was as gray as the dismal German weather. For the first time in living memory, the leader of an allied nation was about to sweep to electoral victory based on a campaign of thinly veiled anti-American rhetoric and staunch opposition to the United States.

Just weeks earlier German chancellor Gerhard Schroeder had been trailing badly in the polls and written off by political commentators. With the craven opportunism of a politician in trouble, Schroeder had refocused his campaign on opposing the Bush administration's growing confrontation with Iraq, tapping into a deep vein of pacifism and anti-Bush sentiment among Germans. Schroeder denounced Bush's push for "regime change" in Iraq and ruled out joining any U.S.-led effort, even if it had the blessings of the United Nations. "We say openly: The Middle East, Iraq included, needs a lot of peace but not a new war," Schroeder told an enthusiastic crowd in Rostock at what was his final campaign rally before the next day's election.

The choice of Rostock as the campaign's final stop was not happenstance. A former shipbuilding center in what had been East Germany, the city suffered from 17 percent unemployment despite nearly a decade of massive government subsidies lavished on major eastern cities since German reunification. Schroeder's Social Democratic Party (SDP) viewed outreach to those disaffected former East Germans as critical to party growth and the success of the chancellor's center-left coalition. More than a decade after the fall of the Berlin Wall, the unfamiliar currents that reunification had introduced into the German body politic were thus rocking the stodgy, tradition-bound and oh-so-predictable Germany that the United States had counted on throughout the Cold War.

Standing in the rain and listening to Schroeder's voice over a loud-speaker, I struck up a conversation with Reinhard Dankert, an SDP representative in the German parliament, or Bundestag, from the city of Rostock. "You have to remember that we eastern Germans had forty years of Communist rule, during which it was drummed into us by the state that we brought the world a lot of terror during World War II, and we should hate war above all else," Dankert told me in explaining the pacifist tendencies so prevalent in the region, and in Germany as a whole. "We were also taught that America was an imperialist nation, and thus you still find a more deep-seated anti-Americanism here that has been made stronger by our impression of Bush as someone who is very confrontational."

Schroeder's antiwar rhetoric and campaign were bolstered both by timing and the Bush administration's unstinting drive to force a confrontation with Iraq onto the international agenda despite rising resistance in Europe. Many Europeans had been alarmed by an August 26 speech by Vice President Dick Cheney that made the case for preemptive war to halt Iraq's suspected nuclear weapons program. Though most experts considered intelligence pointing to an Iraqi nuclear program as especially weak, Cheney dismissed a return to U.N. inspections as a useless and dangerous delay. The speech made headlines in Europe, where national leaders and the media criticized it as bellicose and unilateral, and it gave Schroeder a ready excuse to assume the mantle of antiwar populist.

What made that posture so politically tempting were polls showing that a scant 12 percent of Germans believed military action was justified in Iraq. By the fall of 2002 the Bush administration's assertive pursuit of a foreign policy largely unfettered by the traditional constraints of multilateralism, coupled with the propensity of center-left European politicians to caricature the American president as a gun-toting cowboy, had cost the United States dearly in world public opinion. A survey by the Pew Global Attitudes Project that polled fifty-four thousand people in sixty-five countries during the fall of 2002 and spring of 2003, for instance, would find that fewer than half of the people in traditionally allied countries such as Germany (45 percent), France (43 percent), Spain (38 percent), and Turkey (15 percent), even viewed the United States favorably.

A week before the Rostock rally, President Bush had put the issue of Iraq squarely before the U.N. Security Council, a move met by ambivalence in Europe. While it signaled that the United States was going to at least consult the world body before launching a war with Iraq, Bush strongly implied that if the United Nations failed to deal decisively with Saddam's defiance, it risked joining the League of Nations on history's dust heap. Nor had Bush left any doubt that the United States was prepared to act on its own lacking a U.N. resolution. Just days earlier the

U.S. Congress had granted Bush the authority to use military force in Iraq, essentially signing away in advance its once-precious war powers.

Meanwhile, just the day before the September 21 rally in Rostock, the White House had unveiled its new National Security Strategy, its seminal blueprint for the post-9/11 reordering of world affairs. The Bush strategy, which received wide play in the international press, essentially downgraded the defensive doctrines of containment and deterrence that had triumphed in the Cold War, arguing that they were inadequate to new threats posed by terrorists and rogue states armed with weapons of mass destruction. The new Bush strategy thus anticipated preemptive U.S. military action against terrorists and rogue states and asserted unchallenged U.S. military superiority in the name of democracy. Though the strategy gave a nod to the importance of U.S. alliances, the fact that it was fundamentally faithful to the tenets of neoconservatives and "revival Wilsonians" who advocated the spread of democracy at the hard point of American power was certainly not lost on the neocons themselves.

After the release of the new Bush strategy document, I spoke with Robert Kagan, a leading intellectual light of the neoconservative movement and a senior fellow at the Carnegie Endowment for International Peace. "I think the Bush administration's new National Security Strategy will stand alongside the Truman doctrine and National Security Council Directive 68—which were the clearest and boldest statements of America's Cold War goals—as one of the defining documents in U.S. foreign policy history," Kagan told me. The criticisms being leveled at the Bush doctrine were nearly identical to those once aimed at the Truman doctrine, he said, namely that it would require that the United States use military force to prop up nascent democracies around the world. "But the way America always assumed these global commitments is by never admitting what's truly involved going in," said Kagan. "In 1949 Secretary of State Dean Acheson promised, for instance, that we would only stay in Europe for two years." Similar assumptions were made before the United States intervened in the Philippines, Korea, and Bosnia, Kagan noted, all representing deployments of U.S. forces that would stretch into many years and even decades. "I suspect that we're going to see a similar expansion of U.S. forces into the Middle East and Central Asia, because especially in Iraq, the strategic importance of the region and the risk of pulling out [after regime change] and letting Iraq fall apart will force us to stay."

The idea that Americans should be led into a generational commitment in Iraq that dare not speak its name or true nature troubled me. Witnessing events unfold in Europe in the tumultuous fall of 2002, it was also clear just how unsettling the Bush administration's doctrine of preemption and call to global war was to close allies who had little input in formulating the doctrine or arriving at the life-and-death decisions. Many of the principles behind Bush's revolutionary doctrine were obviously anathema to Europeans who were major stakeholders in the old international system, and thus still attached to its assumptions and norms of behavior.

"Our position is that if a crisis comes to the point that you have to act preemptively, you just do it and don't try and write it into doctrine. We think that approach is flawed," a senior German diplomat told me. "Making it a doctrine that you can strike another country preemptively immediately raises the question of how it fits with the United Nations, which most Europeans still see as the critical legal framework for international affairs. The United States can't simply argue that other signatory nations need to comply with the U.N. charter, but they don't have to."

German officials pointed out that they and other NATO allies were contributing troops to stabilize Afghanistan in the wake of Operation Enduring Freedom, even though the United States had dismissed NATO's offer of a collective response to the 9/11 attacks, instead choosing to fight in Afghanistan leading a handpicked, six-nation "coalition of the willing." Chancellor Schroeder had even put his political coalition on the line in a very close vote on whether German troops should participate in operations in Afghanistan. The Europeans were also cooperating in the global campaign to track down Al Qaeda cells. Few European officials I spoke with, however, accepted the direct linkage between Iraq and the global war on terrorism that U.S. officials kept pressing, and many were simply unconvinced that Iraq represented the clear and present danger the Bush administration described.

Hans-Ulrich Klose, chairman of the German Bundestag's foreign policy committee, spoke with me in his office adjacent to the renovated German Bundestag building. "If the United States leads a handpicked coalition into Iraq, they should be prepared to stay for a very long time and not expect other nations to come in behind them and conduct the nation building," he said. "To do otherwise would be to repeat the example of Afghanistan, when I think the United States made a big mistake of refusing NATO's offer to make it an alliance campaign."

Along with many of their European counterparts, whose sympathies tended toward the Palestinians in the Israeli-Palestinian conflict, German officials were also dismayed by President Bush's decision to shun Palestinian leader Yasser Arafat after his Palestinian Authority was caught smuggling weapons from Iran. Bush's frustration with the calculating and duplicitous Arafat was certainly understandable and shared by many in the diplomatic community. I had recently attended a conference with Arafat hosted by the Council on Foreign Relations, during which the Palestinian firebrand had flown into a sputtering rage at the most innocuous perceived slight. The new U.S. position proclaiming him persona non grata effectively stopped negotiations for a peace settlement in their tracks, however, and further tied the Bush administration to the policy of hard-line Israeli leader Ariel Sharon, whose forces had surrounded and isolated Arafat in his charred West Bank compound. Nor did the Bush administration or Sharon show the least inclination toward supporting moderate Palestinians who might replace Arafat in talks. European officials feared that the new U.S. position and Israeli tactics, combined with a U.S.-led showdown with Saddam Hussein, would inflame an already volatile Middle East.

On the rainy night of September 22, the group of American and German observers I was with shuttled between the Berlin headquarters of the two main political parties as the election results poured in, indicating a razor-thin victory for Schroeder in one of the most closely contested elections in German history. The election night swings and Schroeder's miniscule victory all had a "hanging-chad" familiarity, with the fate of a major democracy once again swinging dramatically on the thinnest of electoral threads.

In publicly opposing Washington and staking out a foreign policy position in direct opposition to the United States for the first time in Germany's post–World War II history, Schroeder had broken an unspoken rule of German politics, with unpredictable repercussions. Throughout the Cold War, it was understood that neither major political faction in Germany would play politics with a nuanced foreign policy that was anchored in a special relationship with the United States and close ties to European institutions, positioning a prosperous and unthreatening Germany safely between the twin strategic pillars of a U.S.-led NATO alliance and an increasingly integrated European Union.

As the final days of the election proved, Schroeder had untethered Germany from its strategic moorings and was charting a new and unfamiliar course in foreign affairs that would be decided in Berlin based on a narrow reading of German interests. How that independent "third way" squared with a country whose ghosts of fascism and nationalism lurked in the shadows, able to frighten friends, neighbors, and not least of all the Germans themselves, was unclear. Certainly in the waning days of the election those restless demons of Germany's past had run amok, with one coalition candidate making comments about German-Jewish leaders and Israel that were widely interpreted as anti-Semitic, even while the German Justice Minister accused President Bush of adopting the tactics of Adolf Hitler, leading to her resignation. After watching his own advantage in the polls evaporate from the heat of Schroeder's anti-American rhetoric, the candidate of the center-right Christian Democrats, Edmund Stoiber, had launched a ferocious attack on Germany's immigrants and their alleged links to Islamic terrorism, resurrecting the xenophobia of the German right.

Revolutions upset the established order in unpredictable ways, and in Europe in the fall of 2002 the ripple effect of the Bush revolution and the war on global terrorism were shattering long-accepted notions and riling political demons that had long lay dormant. For someone who had watched the tremendous outpouring of European sympathy and support for the United States in the weeks and months after the September 11 attacks, that reversal of favor was dizzying. Whereas a scant year ago American flags had sprouted in the windows of shops and houses in Germany, and hundreds of thousands of Germans had marched together to the Brandenburg Gate in a show of solidarity with America, by the fall of 2002 U.S. business executives in Germany and elsewhere in Europe were complaining that companies identifiable as American were shunned by European consumers. Foreign correspondents talked of their disquiet at hearing European movie audiences cheer whenever an American on the screen met a violent end. Gerhard Schroeder was just the first European leader to ride that rising tide of anti-Americanism to political victory. There was little reason to believe he would be the last.

"You know, this is the Berlin-Moscow road," the taxicab driver said over his shoulder as we inched through one of the ubiquitous traffic jams in Warsaw, Poland, where the newfound enthusiasm for driving far outstripped roadways fallen into disrepair during Communist rule. The day after the German elections I had boarded a train from Berlin to Warsaw to cover a critical NATO summit on transformation and war taking place September 24–25, 2002. As the taxi driver pointed out, the road to the Summit grounds was also the major east-west causeway between Germany and Russia. "Our bad luck," said the Polish taxi driver wryly. "Throughout our history, we've sat between those two, with one or the other always trying to eat us alive."

The curse of voracious neighbors and a flat, defenseless geography largely explained why Warsaw exuded little of the old world charm of other European capitals. During World War II, Poland had been conquered first by the Germans and then by the Soviets, and between the two its past had literally been crushed into rubble. Although Germany was now an ally and the threat from Russia had receded dramatically with the end of the Cold War, the scars and continued costs of being caught between those goliaths of East and West were everywhere apparent in this nation of thirty-eight million Poles. That national trauma helped explain Poland's fervent outreach to the NATO alliance and other Western security and economic structures. Poland had been part of NATO's first wave of post–Cold War expansion in 1999, along with the Czech Republic and Hungary. Now the United States was pushing a further "big bang" expansion of the alliance to be voted on in Prague in November of 2002, which would extend NATO's borders southward to Romania and Bulgaria and all the way north to the three Baltic nations of Latvia, Lithuania, and Estonia, directly on Russia's border. Not altogether coincidentally, the Bush administration was also finding those newly liberated nations of the former Eastern bloc receptive to its message that the forces of tyranny must be confronted in this time of crisis.

When a high-level U.S. delegation led by Defense Secretary Donald Rumsfeld arrived in Warsaw for the NATO defense ministerial summit, its convoys and Secret Service detachment parting the traffic-snarled streets with wailing sirens, the Poles thus witnessed a diplomatic juggernaut the likes of which the city had not seen since the Soviet Union gathered its satellites together in 1955 to sign the Warsaw Pact. At every stop Rumsfeld and company emphasized the point that after the terrorist attacks of September 11, America was a changed nation. The Pentagon was transforming U.S. military forces and reconfiguring its security structures to confront the new threat posed by terrorists and rogue states armed with weapons of mass destruction. Now it was NATO's turn.

U.S. officials in Warsaw were thus not content to simply lay the groundwork for a historic expansion of NATO. Rumsfeld and company were determined to forcefully reshape NATO into a continent-spanning alliance with global military reach and the capability to respond rapidly and preemptively if necessary to new threats. As part of that transformation, Rumsfeld was pushing for creation of a NATO rapid-response force of some twenty-one thousand troops that could quickly deploy anywhere in the world. With the United States pressuring NATO to take command of stability operations in Afghanistan to free up U.S. forces for Iraq, a defensive alliance was also going to have to leave behind its venerable reluctance to deploy military forces "out of area."

If the NATO allies embraced such fundamental changes, it would result in the most profound reconfiguring of the alliance's charter and security architecture since 1949, when the United States first proposed creating NATO as a defensive bulwark against Soviet expansion. If the allies were not willing to transform NATO into a more offensive oriented alliance, Rumsfeld was quick to imply that the United States was prepared to go its own way.

"Those September 11 attacks were more than tragedy—they were a wake-up call warning us all of greater dangers lying ahead," Rumsfeld told the assembled NATO defense ministers on the Warsaw Summit's opening day. "We owe it to those killed to recognize that the world has changed." Although Rumsfeld stressed that the United States wanted

NATO to transform itself to better confront the challenges of that new security environment, he left little doubt about the consequences if it did not change. "If we fail to do so, it will send a harmful signal to the world about our alliance," Rumsfeld said. "If NATO doesn't have a force that is quick and agile, that can deploy in days and weeks rather than months and years, then it will not have much to offer the world in the twenty-first century."

Despite generally supporting U.S. calls for a rapid-response force and a big bang expansion of the alliance, the Europeans predictably had deep misgivings about where the Bush administration's new security strategy and post-9/11 global war on terrorism were leading the alliance. Those misgivings were exacerbated by Rumsfeld's characteristic brusque style, as the Secretary of Defense gave a cold shoulder to the German contingent in Warsaw, refusing to meet with his German counterpart as payback for Schroeder's antiwar platform.

With the Bush administration having secured the largest defense spending increase in over two decades in response to the 9/11 attacks, greatly bolstering an already unrivaled U.S. military, the allies gathered in Warsaw also despaired of closing an already wide gap between U.S. and European military capabilities. A 1990s decade that had seen the U.S. economy expand dramatically, for instance, had largely been a period of recession and stagnation for more socialized European economies struggling in an era of global competition. Thus only seven of nineteen NATO allies had met the modest goal of spending 2 percent of gross domestic product on defense in the previous year. Nor, under the circumstances, were governments in Europe likely to be reelected on a platform of significantly increasing defense spending in order that their militaries could better fight side by side with the United States.

That growing military capabilities gap, in turn, exacerbated very different perceptions within the alliance about the nature of the terrorism threat and what reasonably could be done about it. The United States was in full wartime mode after 9/11 and was contemplating its second invasion of a Muslim country in as many years as part of that effort. European nations, somewhat inured by their own plague of terrorism in the 1970s and 1980s, continued to treat terrorism as largely an intelligence and law enforcement matter. Those divergent views added to the significant forces tugging at transatlantic cohesion.

Ambassador Nicholas Burns was the U.S. permanent representative to NATO at the time of the Warsaw Summit. "The capabilities and technology gap is one of the most serious problems facing NATO today, because if you trace the continuum of conflict through the Persian Gulf War, Bosnia, Kosovo, and Afghanistan, what you see is that, with the notable exception of Britain, the European allies don't have sufficient capability

in areas such as strategic lift, precision-guided weapons, secure communications, and special forces," Burns told me in an interview. "So whether
the Europeans want to fulfill their commitments to NATO, or employ the
European Union's rapid-reaction force for crisis management or peacekeeping, they must address significant weaknesses in these areas."

In a well-coordinated campaign that included formal meetings, pri-
vate dinners, and bilateral discussions, for instance, the U.S. delegation in
Poland also laid out its case for war with Iraq in dramatic fashion. Deputy
CIA Director John E. McLaughlin briefed alliance defense ministers in un-
usual detail about U.S. intelligence on Saddam Hussein's suspected weap-
ons programs and possible links with Al Qaeda. At the same time that
NATO defense ministers were being briefed in Warsaw on September 24,
British Prime Minister Tony Blair was publicly releasing in London the
United Kingdom's extensive dossier on Iraq's illegal weapons programs.

As part of the well-practiced protocol peculiar to a nineteen-member
alliance of sovereign and often hypersensitive nations, both Rumsfeld and
NATO Secretary General Lord George Robertson told reporters in Warsaw with straight faces that they had not given any thought to what part
NATO might play in a U.S.-led war with Iraq. The truth was that both
men and their staffs had thought long and hard about the issue, and their
conclusions were not altogether comforting to an alliance poised at a critical crossroads: NATO would not likely have any substantive role in a war
with Iraq beyond possibly deploying forces to Turkey to protect it from
any Iraqi reprisals.

In terms of the Europeans, even in opposition to the war Germany
was highly unlikely to veto NATO participation. Enough other allies
shared its deep misgivings, however, to make formal NATO participation
unlikely even if the Americans were interested in it. If the United States
was successful in winning a U.N. resolution authorizing war, the majority
of NATO allies figured to join an anti-Saddam coalition. As for the U.S.
delegation, their message at Warsaw was the same as the bruising verdict
it delivered before the Afghanistan war, when NATO invoked its "all-for-
one" clause of collective defense for the first time in its history, only to
have their extended hand rejected by U.S. officials who insisted that "the
mission will define the coalition."

"I said last year that the mission defines the coalition, and I think that
was not only a correct statement, but it has been an enormously helpful
concept in this war on terror," Rumsfeld said at a press conference in
Warsaw. This was in response to a question I posed about whether the
United States could sustain this approach of launching wars largely on a
unilateral basis with a few handpicked and acquiescent allies, and then
asking NATO as a whole to help police the violent aftermath. "Every nation is different, with different cultures and geographies, and the thought

that they should all agree at the same moment how to contribute to this war is nonsense," Rumsfeld said. "That will never happen, and it never has. Countries ought to decide individually what they can do."

On background, U.S. officials in Warsaw sketched in this new Pentagon concept of NATO as a sort of farm team from which it would cherry-pick coalition partners and elevate them to the big leagues for specific operations. "In terms of NATO's role in any future scenario, I would stress the importance of the alliance in providing training, doctrine, and the interoperability that allow our militaries to work together in environments far distant from Europe," said a senior U.S. defense official in Warsaw. "We couldn't accomplish what we're doing in Afghanistan today, for instance, without NATO. If NATO didn't exist for that purpose today, we'd have to invent it."

European allies who were still under the mistaken impression that NATO was, in the words of former Secretary of State Henry Kissinger, "the keystone of the foreign policy of its members for a generation," the new U.S. approach essentially downgrading the alliance to a debating society, intramural practice squad, and cleanup crew was unnerving. After hostilities ended in Iraq, the Europeans were well aware that they could expect intense U.S. pressure to contribute troops and funds to Iraq's reconstruction, just as they had in Afghanistan. If they were going to constantly be in on the crash landings in the U.S.-led global war on terrorism, however, many Europeans preferred to be consulted more closely on the takeoffs.

"This new American approach suggests that the United States is increasingly coming to view NATO as a stabilizing influence in Eastern Europe rather than as a real military alliance. We find that direction very frustrating and worrisome," a senior official from a major NATO ally told me. "That's why I think European leaders must go to Prague willing to discuss with the Americans exactly what the purpose of the NATO alliance is? What exactly do we want NATO to become? The choices between the paths now before NATO are that fundamental."

While in Warsaw, I sought out Javier Solana, NATO's former secretary general who was there in his capacity as the European Union's chief for foreign and security policy. An affable Spaniard and longtime friend of the United States, Solana was as agitated as I had ever seen him and clearly worried about the underlying message the United States was sending to its closest allies at a critical moment for the Western alliance. "After September 11, the United States had the right to conduct its military operations in any manner it felt was right," Solana said. "After all, the twin towers were yours, and most of the people killed were Americans. But I don't like this principle that 'the mission defines the coalition.' The transatlantic community already has a coalition that has proven its worth over many, many years. The United States could have used it as the basis for forming a bigger coalition, or at some point to discuss perhaps breaking off a smaller coalition. But at no point has [Central Command Commander] Gen. Tommy Franks even talked to anyone at NATO! Instead, NATO invoked its most sacred covenant—*that no one had dared touch in the past*—and it was useless! Absolutely *useless!*"

CHAPTER 8

A Perfect Storm

S THE CHRISTMAS holiday season approached near the end of 2002, I attended a reception for visiting French dignitaries at the French ambassador's residence, a gated, villalike mansion that might have been plucked from the Riviera and placed on the corner it occupies on a tree-lined street in northwest Washington, D.C. Despite talk of Iraq dominating the cocktail chatter, the mood at the reception was buoyed by the sense that after an extremely rocky period in transatlantic relations the West was once again united behind U.S. leadership.

After steering the issue of Iraq to the United Nations that fall, Secretary of State Colin Powell had successfully secured unanimous Security Council backing on November 8, 2002, for U.N. Resolution 1441, which demanded that Iraq declare its weapons of mass destruction and open its programs to U.N. inspectors or suffer "serious consequences"— diplomatic speak for war. As one of the five permanent, veto-wielding members of the Security Council, France was intent on preserving the prestige of the body as the final arbiter of international conflict. Before the 15–0 vote French president Jacques Chirac had even lobbied Syria not to abstain in order to present a united front to Saddam Hussein.

France's intervention on the vote convinced many Bush administration officials that if it came to war, France would support a second U.N. resolution authorizing the use of force in Iraq and take part in any coalition. In fact, a senior French government official told me, a French general had been dispatched to the Pentagon to deliver a message of solidarity: If the U.N. Security Council decided to authorize military action against Iraq, France was prepared to contribute fifteen thousand troops, one hundred aircraft, and an aircraft carrier to the coalition.

A few years earlier I had written a critical article on the growing tensions in the always fractious U.S.-French relationship, after which the French ambassador had graciously subjected me to a charm offensive, which explained my invitation to the reception. I was more interested, however, in two of the other attendees. Both Defense Secretary Donald Rumsfeld and Deputy Secretary of Defense Paul Wolfowitz took time away from harried preparations for a possible war to stop by the French residence and pay their respects. That same afternoon I had attended a speech on Iraq that Wolfowitz gave at the Ronald Reagan Center for International Trade, and I complimented him on the presentation. Wolfowitz had movingly recounted the horrors of a children's prison Saddam ran for the offspring of enemies of his regime. The story of young children imprisoned in hopeless squalor had come from a book by former U.N. weapons inspector Scott Ritter, and it was indeed heartrending. I was also struck by the fact, however, that even in late 2002 with the United States on another collision course with Iraq, Wolfowitz was relying on accounts of life inside the country that were at least five years old, when the last of the U.N. inspectors had been kicked out of the country.

Noting the presence of Rumsfeld and Wolfowitz at the French ambassador's residence, a noted neocon writer told me that it proved the wisdom of the Bush revolutionaries' muscular approach to diplomacy—the best way to coax consensus out of reluctant allies was not endless debate, he said, but simply to demonstrate to them that the United States was prepared to act alone if necessary.

A senior State Department source I spoke with depicted the unanimous U.N. resolution on Iraq as a sign that Powell had triumphed in the internal debate against the Bush hawks and neocons, who opposed even taking the issue of Saddam's doomsday weapons to the Security Council. That indicated a growing realization within the White House, he said, that the magnitude of the likely challenge in post-Saddam Iraq made winning support of the wider international community critical. "The entire administration is now reading from the same page on the need to disarm Iraq," the senior State Department official told me. "But we felt all along that the benefits of making a good-faith effort to win U.N. authorization—in terms of gaining domestic support, bringing on allies to help manage the aftermath, and avoiding an overload of anti-American sentiment in the region—outweighed the risks involved that it might throw off any time lines for military action. Others," he conceded, "concluded differently."

In truth the issue of how much blood and national treasure a war with Iraq might require was still hotly debated among the Bush revolutionaries and Foggy Bottom moderates. Pentagon neocons like Wolfowitz were convinced that a transformational war-fighting model based on the lessons of Afghanistan could ensure a quick victory using a relatively small U.S. military force, and they were persuaded by Iraqi exiles who predicted a benign liberation. In congressional testimony, Wolfowitz had thus calculated that Iraq's own oil exports could fund the lion's share of its postwar reconstruction.

In outlining their vision for Iraq, however, Bush administration officials had frequently cited the post–World War II Marshall Plan for the reconstruction of Europe as a model. As I reported at the time, in 2002 dollars the Marshall Plan would cost roughly $100 billion over four years, a figure no administration official was willing to propose. A *Wall Street Journal* calculation in November 2002 added in reconstruction and humanitarian assistance to the costs of a war, concluding that even under the most favorable circumstances an intervention in Iraq would cost in the neighborhood of $141 billion. Putting the annual cost of supporting each peacekeeper at $250,000, and estimating that seventy-five thousand to two hundred thousand troops might be needed to police a post-Saddam Iraq, the nonpartisan Congressional Budget Office estimated peacekeeping costs alone at $1 billion to $4 billion a month. If anything like that level of commitment and funding was necessary, the United States would need the support of a broad international coalition to share the burden and make operations in Iraq sustainable over the long run.

As the former head of the U.S. Central Command with responsibility for the Middle East, retired Marine Corps Gen. Anthony Zinni had thought long and hard about the looming conflict with Iraq and about the lessons offered by Gen. George C. Marshall and the Marshall Plan. "Marshall is one of my heroes, not just because he led America to victory in the Great War, but also because he didn't look to fight other wars, nor was he willing to leave the situation in Europe as a breeding ground for future wars," Zinni said, speaking at a November 2002 conference I attended that was sponsored by the Middle East Institute, a think tank in Washington. "The same is true of Gen. Douglas MacArthur in Japan, who reached out to the Japanese people for help in re-creating stability and prosperity in that country."

A former special envoy to the Middle East for President Bush, Zinni had recently broken with the administration over the apparent decision to confront Iraq militarily; he argued that Saddam was not the top priority in the war on global terror, and that the risks of invading Iraq outweighed the probable benefits. If it came to war, however, Zinni shared the view that the United States should be prepared for the kind of commitment that characterized the post–World War II reconstruction of Germany and Japan. "Certainly, military success in Iraq will just be the beginning of the beginning," Zinni said. "I think we'll need the equivalent of a Marshall Plan for Iraq that is multinational with our European friends, and cooperative with our Arab allies in the region, and which addresses the economic, social, and political needs of that country and that troubled region. Because the mark of what America stands for,"

Zinni asserted, "will be measured in political rather than military terms. We will be judged by what we leave behind in Iraq."

The debate over Iraq among Middle East experts was spirited, with opinions varying widely. There was general agreement that any successful, long-term strategy in America's war against Islamic terrorism had to eventually address the root causes of Islamic extremism and anti-American fervor in the region. Prominent among them was America's close association with Israel and the festering Israeli-Palestinian conflict. Bush himself had apparently accepted the arguments of neoconservatives, however, that the road to peace in the Middle East ran through Baghdad. In a meeting with visiting Iraqi dissidents, Bush reportedly told them that "I truly believe out of this [war with Iraq] will come peace between Israel and the Palestinians."

The root causes of Islamic terrorism also included decades of U.S. support for Arab despots who stymied democratic reforms, free markets, and human rights—and thus their societies' ability to cope with the challenges of modernity. Bush supporters argued that ousting Saddam and building a viable democracy in Iraq might finally break that cycle. Of course, one of the challenges the Bush administration would confront in that regard was the great irony that in most Arab countries, the strongest opponents to autocratic regimes were Islamic fundamentalist parties that are at least as resistant to change and as repressive in outlook.

Barry Rubin, editor of the *Middle East Review of International Affairs*, nevertheless believed that if the Bush administration was truly determined to advance democratic ideals and assist in the reconstruction of a democratic Iraq, it could ignite a "third revolution" in the Middle East, a successor to the failed Arab nationalism of the 1950s and 1960s, and the largely discredited Islamist revolution ushered in with the overthrow of the Shah of Iran in 1979. "If the United States were to achieve an outstanding success in Iraq by overthrowing Saddam Hussein and helping to create a better system of governance, however imperfect, it could bring about a turning point in Middle Eastern history. Now that [the nationalist and Islamist movements] have failed to take power elsewhere or fulfill their promises, a new era in Iraq could spark a third revolution, persuading people that democratic and moderate approaches are best."

The more common view of Middle East experts I spoke with was skepticism of the idea that positive reforms and democracy would likely flow from a U.S.-instigated war in the region. One such expert was Ambassador David Mack, the vice president of the Middle East Institute and a former Foreign Service officer with long ties to the region. In his view, Middle Eastern history suggested that the kinetic energy of war would ripple through the region and through the decades with unforeseeable and possibly dire consequences, for the region and for the United States itself.

In that way, the Arab-Israeli wars of 1967 and 1973 and staunch U.S. support for Israel, had led directly to the Israeli-Palestinian impasse, Mack noted, and to America's increasing stake in that seemingly endless conflict. Americans were taken hostage at the start of the 1979 revolution in Iran largely because of anger over U.S. support for the former Shah of Iran. The Iran hostage crisis began decades of enmity that led to the murder of hundreds of U.S. Marines in Lebanon, the taking of numerous civilian U.S. hostages there, and the Iran-Contra scandal that rocked the Reagan administration. Iraq grew militarily strong enough to threaten its neighbors in the 1980s largely because of U.S. support for Saddam Hussein during his war with Iran. The presence of U.S. troops in the Muslim holy land of Saudi Arabia—so central to Osama Bin Laden's fevered visions of jihad—was a direct outgrowth of the 1991 Persian Gulf War with Iraq. The battle-hardened mujaheddin whom Bin Laden drew to his cause, meanwhile, had been trained and equipped by the CIA during their fight against the Soviets in Afghanistan. And on and on and on, each war begetting new enemies and sowing the seeds for future conflict.

"In the early 1980s, I was personally responsible as the State Department official in charge of the region for selling Congress on the presence of U.S. forces in Lebanon," Mack told me in late 2002. "And we used the same arguments then that I hear in selling 'regime change' in Iraq. We said it would be easy, that the people in the region would embrace us, and that wonderful developments would flow from our spreading democracy in the region. That doesn't mean we don't need to get rid of Saddam Hussein and his weapons of mass destruction," Mack said, "but I would caution against viewing that as a panacea for our troubles in the region. Given our sometimes disastrous past history in the Middle East, we should be a little gun-shy over what is about to come down in Iraq."

As an early down payment on what may prove the most ambitious postwar nation-building campaign in a generation, the State Department had launched a "Future of Iraq" project that highlighted the challenge and complexity of trying to export the institutions and structures of democratic governance and civil society in a country that had known neither. Gathering Iraqi opposition leaders along with prominent members of the Iraqi diaspora for the first time, State Department officials conducted workshops in the fall of 2002 to discuss the possible outlines of an Iraqi democracy.

The conference of more than one hundred Iraqis was broken down into various working groups whose titles alone indicated the many fundamental challenges that would face a post-Saddam government: democratic principles and procedures; transitional justice and legal reforms; public finance and accounting; public health and humanitarian needs; foreign and national security policy; oil and energy; state and private media; education; economic and physical infrastructure; water, agriculture, and environment; and refugees.

"This project led us into totally uncharted territory, because when you start talking seriously about the future of Iraq, you quickly realize that the whole debate is based on a foundation of unknown variables," a knowledgeable State Department official told me at the time. "The exercise was very helpful in opening our eyes, however, to the immense challenges we face, and in helping us grasp the kinds of difficult decisions the United States might have to make in a post-Saddam Iraq."

State Department officials steadfastly refused to take the project a step further by using it to establish a provisional Iraqi government—despite pressure from Ahmed Chalabi, as well as from his Pentagon backers. Such a "government-in-exile" would be viewed as a U.S. puppet, State Department officials feared, and would lack legitimacy within a post-Saddam Iraq and within the region. In general, State Department officials remained wary of the Pentagon neocons and their close embrace of Chalabi. Rather, Foggy Bottom saw participants in the "Future of Iraq" project as a cadre of knowledgeable experts who could act as interlocutors with whatever government might emerge in Iraq, and who might perhaps vie for power themselves during a transition to democracy. "We made it very clear that this was a totally exploratory and nonbinding project that did not represent official U.S. policy, and we made no promises that participants would even have a role in a future Iraqi government," said the State Department official. "Primarily, that's because we continue to believe that during the course of regime change, some individual or group inside Iraq is likely to emerge with significant political or military power and legitimacy. Who that will be is a matter of intense speculation, but we expect some leader to emerge."

As part of the "Future of Iraq" project, the State Department also planned and proposed funding a "unity conference" to bring the far-flung Iraqi diaspora together under one roof as a symbol of the collective hopes of Iraqis for a democratic future. Originally scheduled for late October in Brussels, the conference was continually postponed. When I asked the State Department why, a knowledgeable source told me that internal squabbling between the various Kurdish, Shiite, and Sunni factions threatened to make a farce of any show of supposed unity.

The critical diplomacy surrounding Iraq began to unravel with a mid-January phone call from Berlin to the German Embassy in Washington,

D.C. German officials were preparing for their first ministerial meeting as new members of the U.N. Security Council, poring over the Pentagon's schedule of troop deployments to the Middle East to answer a simple but all-important question: Had the Bush administration already decided that war with Iraq was inevitable?

The fact that German officials had to divine the answer using troop-deployment schedules like so many tea leaves—rather than accept Secretary of State Colin Powell's public assurances that no such decision had been made—spoke volumes about the precipitous decline in trust that underpinned the once solid German-American relationship. By January 2003, Germany was feeling increasingly isolated and jittery, frozen out by the Bush administration and convinced that in the end France would join with the Americans, British, Spanish, and Italians in a coalition against Iraq, leaving the Germans dangerously marginalized within the Western alliance. U.S. officials were already pushing a critical January 27 ministerial meeting on Iraq as the critical decision-making point, and as the date approached German Ambassador to the United States Wolfgang Ischinger and his staff were trying to discern whether the Bush administration had already decided to go to war. Based on U.S. troop deployments, they concluded that the point of no return had not yet been reached.

The uncertainty of the Germans was also testament to the great difficulty other nations were having trying to read the signals of a Bush administration that was split between hard-liners and revolutionaries in the Pentagon and the Vice President's office, and the traditional internationalists in the State Department. Until Bush stepped in at the final moment to decide on a true course, that split created a U.S. foreign policy working at cross-purposes with itself, lurching first one way and then another and confounding friend and foe alike.

The phone call from Berlin was to relay French intelligence to the effect that Bush had made a decision. According to a senior French official just back from Washington, President Bush had apparently decided on war. Within days, French Foreign Minister Dominique Villepin requested a meeting of foreign ministers at the United Nations on January 20, one week before the fateful January 27 briefing of the Security Council by chief U.N. weapons inspector Hans Blix. From the back-channel signals the French were sending, German officials believed that they were about to become far less isolated in their opposition to an Iraq war.

What intelligence had the French picked up on? It might have been a January 6 meeting of Bush and Republican congressional leaders. As Bob Woodward details at great length in his book *Plan of Attack*, Bush told Republicans "There's a good chance I'll have to address the nation and commit troops to war. It's clear Saddam Hussein is not disarming." Or the tip-off might have been a January 10 meeting between Bush, Cheney, and three leading Iraqi dissidents, in which Bush said unequivocally that the United States was going to remove Saddam from power. Or the French might have caught wind of a January 11 meeting between Rumsfeld, Chairman of the Joint Chiefs Gen. Richard Myers, and Saudi Ambassador Prince Bandar bin Sultan. Rumsfeld reportedly assured Bandar that a war to topple Saddam was going to happen—"You can take that to the bank."

In later interviews conducted in 2004, both Secretary Powell and National Security Adviser Condi Rice described the mixed signals as the inevitable duality involved in coercive diplomacy, where the growing threat of military action was used to ratchet up the pressure on Saddam to come clean about his weapons. They insisted that there were still actions that Saddam Hussein might have taken in January and February of 2003 that could have avoided war, and thus their public proclamations that no final decision had been made were not false per se. It was just that almost no one in the Bush administration believed by mid-January that Saddam would choose those actions.

In fact, by early January the fundamental differences on Iraq that had been purposely papered over with ambiguity in U.N. Resolution 1441—differences not only within the international community but inside the Bush administration itself—were coming into stark relief. At the insistence of Vice President Dick Cheney, for instance, the original U.N. resolution required that Saddam make a detailed declaration of his chemical, biological, and nuclear weapon programs, a sort of catch-22 clause that Cheney believed would lead to a "material breach" and war no matter how Saddam responded. After Iraq delivered a declaration on December 8 that clearly fell short of complying with the U.N. resolution—Blix called the declaration evasive and said it failed to answer important questions about Iraq's weapons of mass destruction (WMD) programs—U.S. Ambassador to the United Nations John Negroponte quickly labeled Iraq's declaration a "material breach."

While agreeing that Iraq's declaration was insufficient, France insisted that the Security Council should decide whether it constituted a "material breach," a phrase that could trigger the resolution's "serious consequences." Far from a spat over semantics, the differing interpretations of Iraq's December 8 declaration began to unravel the consensus that had been reached a month earlier. France and other nations on the Security Council thought inspections could still work. The Bush administration hard-liners clearly took the declaration as a signal that Saddam Hussein's regime was intent on reverting to its old policy of endless "cheat and retreat," and Bush himself apparently agreed.

Soon after the declaration, Negroponte began to argue that an already scheduled January 27 briefing to the Security Council by Blix should constitute a final report from the inspectors and a logical launching point for the debate on a second U.N. resolution authorizing war. "Frankly, that shocked us, because Resolution 1441 subsumed earlier resolutions that outlined a return to inspections over a period of months stretching into the summer of 2003," a senior French official told me. "That was a complete change of the rules of the game."

With the January 27 deadline approaching, another important factor emerged. Assurances by U.S. officials that American intelligence would soon lead U.N. inspectors in Iraq to unearth a "smoking gun" in regard to weapons of mass destruction proved wildly optimistic. Even in surprise searches of Saddam's palaces nothing was found. With each new dry hole the U.N. inspectors dug based on U.S. intelligence, opposition to war grew in Europe.

As timing and luck would have it, France was also serving in the rotating presidency of the U.N. Security Council for January. In the past, Chirac had made no secret of his neo-Gaullist ambitions, nor of his desire to see France lead a European counterweight to the American "hyperpower." In practical terms, however, France had never found many takers for such an opposing bloc, and Britain and Germany could normally be counted upon to counterbalance France's Gaullist tendencies in NATO and the European Union.

In mid-January, however, Germany was feeling lonely in its staunch opposition to an Iraq war, even though opposition to the war was prevalent among European publics. The French were facing a U.S.-imposed January 27 deadline that Paris found unacceptable, and it held the gavel in the Security Council. Opportunity was clearly knocking. At that point, French Foreign Minister Dominique Villepin called the unscheduled January 20 ministerial meeting at the United Nations, ostensibly on terrorism. The French knew that they were about to marginalize their closest ally among U.S. officials, but in their minds Colin Powell had already lost the internal battle in the Bush administration on inspections versus war with Iraq.

"By mid-January, it was clear to us that Powell had only won a battle when he convinced Bush to take the issue of Iraq to the U.N. Security Council," a senior French official told me. Cheney and Rumsfeld had essentially won the wider debate over war with Iraq, this source believed, by persuading Bush that Iraq's December 8 declaration was cause enough for war, and by deploying so many troops so rapidly to the region. The brusque manner and dismissive attitude Cheney and Rumsfeld had adopted in dealing with NATO allies had also clearly taken a toll, depleting the goodwill and trust essential for greasing alliance interactions in times of crisis. "The troop deployments were quickly closing the window on inspections, and we were not going to be railroaded into war on Rumsfeld's timetable," the French official said. "As for Powell, it's true that he was reluctant to attend the January 20 meeting, but by that time I think Powell knew that war was inevitable and he had to start aligning himself with Rumsfeld. We just gave him the justification to do so."

January 20 was Martin Luther King's birthday, and as the nation's most prominent African American, Powell took both pride and pleasure in speaking at celebrations about his "American journey" growing up as the child of Jamaican immigrants and rising to the pinnacles of power as a four-star general and Secretary of State. Powell was thus loath to cancel his speaking engagements to attend a ministerial meeting on terrorism at U.N. headquarters in New York. In the end, he relented because of Villepin's assurances that the subject would be terrorism and not Iraq, and because he had worked especially hard to form a bond of trust with the French foreign minister. When Villepin had come to Washington as the new foreign minister the previous fall, for instance, Powell had made a point of attending a special dinner in his honor, exactly the kind of diplomatic schmoozing he disliked and usually avoided.

At the January 20 U.N. meeting, Villepin initially kept his word, steering the agenda back toward terrorism whenever it inevitably veered toward Iraq. After the meeting was finished and Powell had left U.N. headquarters for the airport, however, Villepin held a press conference that was the reason behind the meeting all along. There, he accused the United States of "impatience" in the confrontation with Baghdad, and for the first time strongly implied that France would use its veto power if the United States tried to bring the issue of Iraq to a head after the January 27 ministerial meeting.

"Powell was very upset, because he felt that Villepin had pulled a 'bait and switch' and acted in bad faith," a senior State Department source close to the secretary told me. Said another department source: "January 20 was an important moment, because for the first time we became convinced not only that France would not support military action in Iraq, but that it was determined to actively oppose us in a way that we felt undermined our diplomacy and made war and the possibility of American casualties more likely. That put a lot of strain on our relationship."

Any doubts that France intended to lead a bloc of nations directly opposing the United States on Iraq were dispelled two days later, when Chirac and Schroeder met just outside Paris to celebrate the fortieth anniversary of the French-German Élysée Treaty. "Chirac gave Schroeder a great gift that day," a senior German official told me. "Schroeder went from being isolated to being part of a French-German-Russian bloc whose position was supported by a majority on the Security Council. He was no longer alone." Shaking hands with the German chancellor, Chirac stated at the Élysée celebration that on the Iraq crisis, veto-wielding France had adopted a view that virtually mirrored that of Germany, which had ruled out military action under almost any circumstances. Anyone who ever wondered what the future would look like if France's neo-Gaullists put their vision of a European counterweight into practice against the United States was about to find out.

During the final countdown to war, the French insisted that even one more month of inspections might win their support for another resolution. U.S. officials no longer trusted or believed them. "Even before the inspectors had finished their work, France was saying that they were going to veto any resolution that led to war, so it was pretty obvious that some members of the Security Council weren't going to be supportive even if we waited," Powell told me in a later interview. "Our concern was that if we didn't get to closure in this U.N. session, we'd be right back in the Security Council the following September for another round of desultory consultations, and yet another resolution warning the Iraqis."

When U.S. officials attempted to win over a majority on the Security Council for a second resolution authorizing force, primarily to bolster the politically tenuous position of British Prime Minister Tony Blair, the French actively opposed them. With U.S. and British troops perched on the knife-edge of war, Bush and Chirac were both calling individual members of the Security Council and trying to cajole them to vote against the other. Having positioned France as the head of a bloc in opposition to the United States, Chirac was desperate that France not lose a vote on the Security Council and be forced to exercise its veto from a minority position while American troops prepared for battle. "That would have been disastrous for U.S.-French relations for twenty years!" a senior French official told me.

In the end, Chirac gathered enough votes for a majority, and the effort to win a second U.N. resolution authorizing war was dropped. It was a Pyrrhic victory, however, ensuring that during the diplomatic run-up to war in Iraq the Western alliance was essentially at war with itself. Of course, Chirac and Schroeder bristled at Donald Rumsfeld's remarks relegating France and Germany to "old Europe," for instance, but once they formed a bloc in opposition to the United States, it was inevitable that the Bush administration would seek to split Europe into separate camps, thus making a mockery of French-German aspirations that Europe "speak with one voice" on security matters. When Eastern European nations known as "the Vilnius 10," as well as eight other European countries, published letters strongly supporting the United States on Iraq, Chirac even provided a preview of how a French-led E.U. counterweight to the United States might function: He threatened the pending membership of the Vilnius 10 in the European Union and suggested that the candidate countries had missed a good opportunity to "shut up."

When the United States and Ankara both insisted that NATO live up to its collective-defense clause by providing Patriot missile batteries to Turkey before the war, it also revealed just how contradictory was Germany's stance of having one foot firmly planted in the transatlantic alliance and one in a French-led opposition bloc. After paralyzing NATO and helping create one of the greatest crises in its history by refusing for eleven days to authorize the deployment, Germany finally relented under intense pressure. Nevertheless, German officials were incensed. "We promised to supply the Patriots to Turkey bilaterally and asked the United States please not to force us to be an obstruction within NATO," said a senior German official in July 2003. "But the Bush administration was determined to make life difficult for Schroeder by having Germany vote yes to the deployment, thus undermining the chancellor's own position against the Iraq war. That was a really nasty bit of political game-playing, and we viewed [it] as bullying, pure and simple."

Despite the contentious split with France and Germany, U.S. officials were confident after securing NATO's Patriot deployment that they could at least count on the support of the one ally that was viewed as critical for the war effort itself. Almost no one doubted that as Turkey's closest strategic ally, the United States would be granted permission to launch the important northern front of the Iraq invasion out of Turkey. Once again bad timing and dismal diplomacy interceded, however, this time in the form of an Islamic party sweeping into power in Ankara in November of 2002, along with an Islamic majority in the Turkish parliament.

Negotiations over the U.S. troop deployments bogged down over Turkish requests for as much as $6 billion in compensation, and polls that once again showed the vast majority of the Turkish public opposed to a war with their Muslim neighbors. Throughout the negotiations the Turkish military, which in the past wielded great influence on strategic matters and was viewed as closely aligned with U.S. policy, remained strangely quiet. In a close and confused vote on March 1, 2003, the Turkish parliament handed the United States a stunning diplomatic defeat, voting against the U.S. troop deployments.

"It was clear to us that the November election of an Islamic executive and parliament represented a huge change in Turkey, and that Iraq would be a very tough issue for them to contend with so soon," a senior State Department source involved in the negotiations told me. "When the Turkish military seemed to sit on its hands during this critical period, it was also unclear to us whether that was the result of democratic reforms, or whether the military simply wanted the Islamic party to fail. Ultimately, however, I think everyone involved was surprised the motion failed to pass."

Conceding those points, Turkish officials told me that the failure of the United States to win a second U.N. resolution and the staunch opposition to the war by two powerhouses of the European Union—which Turkey desperately hoped to join—helped doom the vote. "America's failure to convince the Security Council added to the impression we got that the United States was simply determined to oust Saddam at all costs, because we certainly didn't perceive an imminent threat from Iraq, and we live next door," a senior Turkish official told me. "The depiction by the U.S. press of Turkey as greedily bargaining for money at the bazaar also played disastrously back home, where it was picked up by the Turkish media. In our part of the world, the greatest insult you can deliver is to suggest that our blood is for sale. The idea of another war on our doorstep was simply abhorrent to the Turkish people."

In my interviews and close contacts with key players involved in what amounted to a diplomatic debacle of historic proportions, many of the officials involved described the diplomatic equivalent of "the perfect storm": a rare confluence of opposing currents in international affairs, bad political timing, and questionable political leadership. As it swirled, the tempest gathered strength from the volatile global climate that had existed since the 9/11 terrorist attacks, with a wounded U.S. superpower determined to confront perceived threats head-on, and a growing backwash of world opinion reflecting increasing anxiety about the Bush revolution and its combative focus on American military power.

Almost everyone agreed that the diplomatic failure was not preordained. None of the key players actually wanted it to happen. Given the circumstances, timing, and personalities involved, however, no one seemed capable of avoiding it in the end. In that sense it resembled the failed diplomacy that preceded the outbreak of World War I, and many of those involved believed it would likewise have a lasting, though unpredictable, impact on the international order.

Even before a single shot was fired, for instance, the showdown over Iraq had seriously damaged international institutions and the strategic relationships that underpinned them, shaking the pillars of the old world order. A U.N. Security Council that united to oppose Iraq's invasion of Kuwait in 1990, and showed initial signs of repeating that performance in the early stages of the Iraq diplomacy, fractured over what a majority of members came to see as a U.S.-led preemptive war. A NATO alliance that unanimously invoked its founding principle of collective defense on behalf of the United States following the September 11 terrorist attacks, had convulsed into near-paralysis. A European Union determined to develop a common security policy and to speak with one voice on foreign affairs, split into acrimony over whether to side with or against the United States on Iraq.

Perhaps the most striking aspect of the debate over Iraq was the extent to which it caused many senior officials on both sides of the Atlantic to fundamentally question the strategic relationships that anchored the Western alliance, and the assumptions behind them. Before Iraq, conventional wisdom held that France was a troublesome but ultimately reliable "foul weather friend" that could be counted upon in times of crisis. Yet in the Iraq debate U.S. officials came to view China as a more reliable partner than France among the U.N. Security Council's exclusive club of veto-wielding members. Germany and Turkey, two strategic bulwarks of the Western alliance, had sided against the United States at a critical moment in history, with unpredictable long-term implications. In opportunistically siding with France and Germany, Russia had shown that ad hoc coalitions lack the glue of common values that holds together traditional alliances.

Charles Kupchan was the professor of international relations at Georgetown University and the author of *The End of the American Era*. "I think we're witnessing a historic watershed for the international order, because the Western alliance that was predicated on the notion that U.S. and European security were indivisible is unraveling day by day," he told me in an interview in early 2003. "The damage already done to our relations with France and Germany is likely irreversible, for instance, because both have revealed their desire to end this era of Pax Americana. The likely midterm result is withdrawal of American troops from Germany and a gradual end to our willingness to be Europe's protector." In such a scenario, Kupchan believed transatlantic relations would become increasingly competitive and possibly even adversarial. "More broadly, what we're witnessing may also prove an incremental change in the global perception of the United States. People who once saw American power as a benign force may be starting to see us as predatory," he said. "Such a loss of international legitimacy for the global superpower would change the world."

As the national security adviser to President George H. W. Bush and a prime architect of the 1991 Persian Gulf War, retired Gen. Brent Scowcroft was also wary of the current Bush administration's post-9/11 approach, which seemed to devalue traditional alliances and relationships as overly restrictive on American power. "At this point I'm puzzled as to where President Bush stands on the issue of our traditional alliances such as NATO, because during the campaign he made some strong statements about putting more stock in them. Clearly, that hasn't happened," Scowcroft told me in early 2003. "Part of the Bush administration clearly believes that as a superpower, we must take advantage of this opportunity to change the world for the better, and we don't need to go out of our way to accommodate alliances, partnerships, or friends in the process, because that would be too constraining." That doctrine of the United States acting on its own at the head of hastily assembled coalitions of the agreeable, Scowcroft told me, is "fundamentally, fatally flawed. As we've seen in the debate about Iraq, it's already given us an image of arrogance and unilateralism, and we're paying a very high price for that image. If we get to the point where everyone secretly hopes the United States gets a black eye because we're so obnoxious, then we'll be totally hamstrung in the war on terror. We'll be like Gulliver with the Lilliputians."

By March of 2003, it was clear that the United States and Britain alone were going to assert a neocolonial position in Iraq, which was carved out of the remnants of the Ottoman Empire by British colonial rulers in the early 1920s, and ever since had lacked any ethnic, religious, or even constitutional coherence. There would be no U.N. resolution to bestow legitimacy, no grand coalition of Western powers, no major Arab nations to supply regional cover, not even a northern front from Turkey.

Fawaz Gerges is the chair of Middle Eastern Studies at Sarah Lawrence College and one of the most thoughtful commentators on the Middle East in the country. Before booking a flight to Kuwait in March of 2003, I asked for his assessment of the looming war with Iraq. "James, what alarms me about this debate we've just had on Iraq at a very historic juncture is that it seems to be driven more by neoconservative ideology than by a sober analysis of the complex realities on the ground and in the region," Gerges told me. Iraq was one of the most complicated and fragmented societies, not just in the Middle East, he said, but in the entire world. "Iraq has a blood-soaked political history," Gerges cautioned. "The deepening anti-American sentiment in the region will also foster a perception that this is a cynical American adventure to dominate the region's oil resources and assist Israel in its struggle against the Palestinians. So while I say that this is a great day if the United States is truly willing to expend massive amounts of national treasure and many years to create a civil society in Iraq and a new order in the Middle East, I would also humbly warn: Even the most powerful nation in the world should be very anxious about trying to construct a peaceful post-Saddam democracy, and thus becoming militarily engaged in the daily lives of millions of Arabs and Muslims."

At the very least a second Iraq war seemed destined to put the underlying tenets of the Bush revolution decisively to the test. Unconstrained by traditional alliances, the United States was going to preemptively confront a known evil armed with a transformational military and the power of American ideals. On a personal level such a historic endeavor seemed worth the considerable price of admission, and shortly after talking with Gerges I boarded a flight for the Middle East, where the U.S. military was gathering from points all around the world. After seeing the failure of diplomacy, I would now have an opportunity to witness the consequences firsthand.

PART III

War

"There are two things which will always be very difficult for a democratic nation: to start a war and to end it."

ALEXIS DE TOCQUEVILLE
Democracy in America

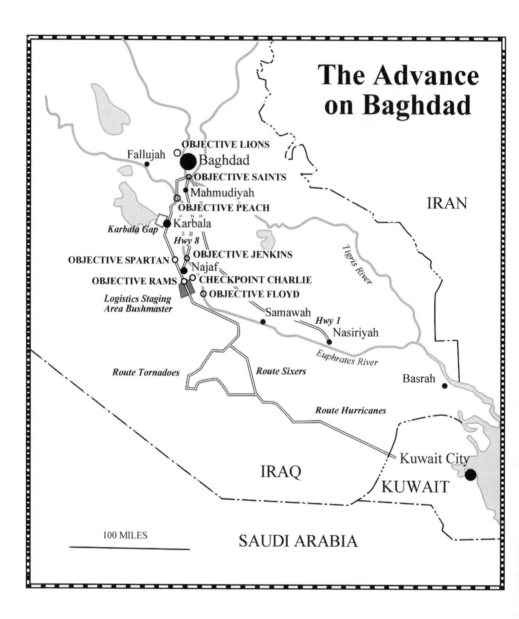

The Advance on Baghdad

OBJECTIVE LIONS

Fallujah

Baghdad

OBJECTIVE SAINTS

Mahmudiyah

OBJECTIVE PEACH

IRAN

Karbala Gap

Karbala

Hwy 8

OBJECTIVE SPARTAN

OBJECTIVE JENKINS

Najaf

OBJECTIVE RAMS

CHECKPOINT CHARLIE

Tigris River

OBJECTIVE FLOYD

Logistics Staging Area Bushmaster

Samawah

Hwy 1

Nasiriyah

Route Tornadoes

Route Sixers

Euphrates River

Basrah

Route Hurricanes

Kuwait City

IRAQ

KUWAIT

100 MILES

SAUDI ARABIA

CHAPTER 9

Fear City

A S THE KUWAITI AIRLINER banked in low on its approach to Kuwait International Airport, the city below seemed to rise from the nothingness of the desert in a gentle swell of two- and three-story buildings and modest dwellings, squat and baked mud-brown in the rays of an early morning sun. In the distance, the dusty sprawl gave way to the brilliant blue crescent of the Persian Gulf. Once on the ground the aircraft discharged a group of bleary-eyed American journalists of every conceivable stripe, interspersed with Kuwaiti businessmen in traditional Arab garb and the odd family. In early March of 2003, Kuwait City was not a popular destination for leisure travelers.

The Kuwait International Airport is a gleaming, ultramodern affair that bespeaks oil wealth and modernity, and the security personnel in their starched green uniforms were friendly enough as they ran our passports and visas through the computer. After my *National Journal* colleague George Wilson filed a missing bag report, we approached the customs station where agents were running all bags entering the country through giant X-ray machines. As a dodge, I slipped my bags into the mix of a CBS television crew that was transporting a small mountain of electronic equipment. A sharp-eyed agent singled the offending bag out immediately, however, and confiscated the bottle of Glenlivet scotch I had purchased at a duty-free shop in New York. If I had been a Kuwaiti, one of the CBS crew commented, they probably would have arrested me. Still, I was duly impressed with the lengths to which the Kuwaitis—reputedly among the most modern of Middle Easterners—were willing to go in order to keep the corrupting influences of the West out of their country.

The Kuwaiti government had set up a press bureau at the Sheraton Kuwait, and the hotel became an unofficial press center for many of the hundreds of international reporters pouring into the country in early March of 2003. You knew a media circus had come to town when Ollie North was spotted strolling through the lobby in full safari regalia and a camera crew in tow, and Geraldo Rivera was rumored to be close behind.

Our Atlantic Media colleague and friend Michael Kelly met us in the Sheraton lobby, looking characteristically disheveled. Though clearly disappointed, Mike took the news about Glenlivet's capture like a man. Since the 9/11 attacks, Kelly's regular opinion column in the *Washington Post* put him squarely in the camp of the neoconservative intellectuals who argued that ending Saddam's tyranny was a necessary first step toward reforming the Middle East, and I was interested to hear his impressions. Kelly had also written an excellent book on the 1991 Persian Gulf War and he was an expert on the region. As one of the first journalists to enter a liberated Kuwait after its occupation by the Iraqi Republican Guard, Kelly was also familiar with the brutal nature of Saddam's regime.

In a scene from his book *Martyrs' Day*, Kelly described himself after an entire Iraqi platoon tried desperately to surrender to him and another journalist. "I am five feet six inches tall and bespectacled, and running slightly to poundage," Michael wrote. "I don't think of myself as the sort of man who takes other men prisoner." Of course that description omitted an intellectual keenness and wit that all who knew him recognized in Mike Kelly, and he was obviously thrilled to be out from behind the editor's desk at the *Atlantic Monthly* and back in the field reporting. Briefing George Wilson and I, Kelly's compact frame was in a state of something akin to perpetual motion, as he patted down his pockets for his notepad and car keys, cleaned his eyeglasses, and simultaneously gave us a situation report on Kuwait and the media embed process.

In the weeks since his arrival in Kuwait, Kelly had conducted valuable reconnaissance for the company's operations in Kuwait, and employing a venerable war correspondent's tactic he had enlisted the services of a loyal man-Friday named Hamouda. A local taxicab driver and former official in the Kuwaiti government, Hamouda served as our guide to the labyrinth of electronic chop shops, camera stores, and clothing tailors in Kuwait City, as we outfitted ourselves for the war to come. Any friend of Mike's was a friend of Hamouda's, you bet.

One day while Hamouda and I were driving around Kuwait City trying to find a converter to power my laptop from a car battery, I tried out the Bush administration's idea of a war with Iraq as a catalyst to democratic reform in the Middle East. After all, Hamouda was about as representative of the "Arab street" as I could imagine. Did he think it was possible that the United States could topple Saddam and install a democracy in neighboring Iraq as a first step toward trying to reform the region? Hamouda's bitter memories of the 1991 Persian Gulf War and his conflicted view of America's motives were indicative of the widespread cynicism I gleaned from other man-on-the-street interviews.

"As a Muslim I have no problem with Americans, but everyone is now afraid of war and wondering why Bush insists on ousting Saddam," he said. "If it's not for oil, then what? Does Bush want to change all the leaders in the Middle East?" Yet when I asked if there were any Middle Eastern leaders he would particularly miss, Hamouda responded with a derisive snort. "You know, the reasons we Arabs hate each other is because our governments are all so bad. Even as an Arab and a Muslim it's very difficult for me to obtain a visa to travel or conduct business in the region. Why should this be so? Why do I have to kiss so many hands to get a fundamental courtesy even from my own government? Why do the police treat me with such abuse, like an animal? And the situation is much better in Kuwait than in many places. Believe me, it's much worse in Saudi Arabia, or Syria or Egypt."

To make his point, Hamouda recounted his experiences in the first Gulf War. At the time, he held a relatively prestigious job in the Ministry of Finance with paid vacations and generous health insurance. Despite growing up in Kuwait as the son of a Lebanese merchant, however, he was still considered one of the foreign workers who make up 60 percent of Kuwait's population of 2.2 million, and who conduct virtually all of the work in the country. The pampered native-born Kuwaitis acted mainly as managers and deal makers. Hamouda, on the other hand, would never be allowed to vote in Kuwait, and after reaching retirement age he and his wife would be told to leave the country.

With the Iraqi army bearing down on Kuwait City in August of 1990, Hamouda had stopped at a gas station in near panic in order to fill his family's getaway car. A Kuwaiti policeman turned him away with an insulting gesture, shouting that the gas was reserved only for true Kuwaitis. Unable to flee, Hamouda was eventually captured by Iraqi soldiers who were pillaging the city and torturing many of their captives. Once they learned he was Lebanese by birth, however, Hamouda was allowed to go on his way. Their fight, the Iraqis said, was only with the Kuwaitis.

When the Kuwaiti government returned to a city liberated by U.S. forces, many of the foreign workers—especially Palestinians whose leader Yasser Arafat had publicly supported Saddam's invasion—were roughly expelled as suspected Iraqi collaborators. Hamouda was allowed to stay, but he was fired from his prestigious government job, which in the future was reserved for native-born Kuwaitis. Looking back on the Persian Gulf War of 1991, Hamouda was thus nearly bankrupted by a conflict in which the marauding invaders treated him with more dignity and respect than the government of his adopted homeland. Little wonder that Arabs were cynical about the progress that the United States was likely to bring to the region at the point of a gun.

While in Kuwait I also contacted Saad Al-Ajmi, the former Kuwaiti Minister of Information, to get the perspective of the local elite on the looming war. In his view almost anything would be preferable than the stagnant status quo in the region. "Deep in the subconscious of the Middle East is a distrust of outsiders and tendency towards conspiracy theories which are the direct result of living under these brutal dictatorial regimes," Al-Ajmi told me. The Iraqis themselves, he said, were a perfect example. "No people have fought off dictatorship like the Iraqis, but they have faced a regime so brutal that opposition risks forfeiting not only your life, but also the life of your family, your cousins and even your neighborhood. The unprecedented tyranny of regimes willing to wipe out whole cities to stay in power has crushed Arab self-determination. The only way to challenge these regimes and Arab cynicism about American motives is for the United States to live up to its commitment to rebuild Iraq as a more humanistic and democratic country."

Another Kuwaiti reformer I spoke with, Shafeeq Ghabra, was also hopeful that the overthrow of Saddam and the emergence of a pluralistic Iraq could spark democratic reform in the Middle East. Ghabra was a professor of political science and the designated president of the new American University in Kuwait, which was scheduled to open its doors in 2004. A democratic Iraq, he told me, would expose even the most powerful Arab regimes to questions and criticisms they were unused to confronting.

"When an Arab summit breaks down in bickering and paralysis as the recent one just did, for instance, people might start to ask where is Egyptian leadership? Why is Syria still supporting Hezbollah? Why isn't Lebanon doing more to promote civil society? How far is Saudi Arabia planning on taking religion into its politics?" said Ghabra. "There are many regimes in the Middle East who are afraid of those questions, because they want to preserve the status quo, and thus they are hoping the United States fails in Iraq or gets involved in a quagmire."

If the United States were successful, on the other hand, Ghabra could imagine a democratic Iraq anchoring a growing bloc of reformist Arab states that would initially include the Gulf emirates and probably Jordan and Morocco. "At that point Arabs might start unifying behind goals such as modernity and capitalism and humanism and openness," said Ghabra. "Right now Arabs are unified only in their hatred of Israel, and that unity is defeatist. It has never led the Arab world anywhere."

Whether the violence of a war in Iraq would touch off a democratic revolution, begin a more stable liberalizing evolution, or ignite chaos and anarchy and mire America in a quagmire was the one question none of us could answer in early March 2003, yet on it everything hinged. Everyone in the region still remembered that after the Persian Gulf War of 1991 the United States helped incite a rebellion, and then stood aside as Saddam Hussein responded with a brutal counterstrike that killed thousands of Kurds and Shiites. Would the son of Bush follow through in the aftermath of a second Iraq war, my hosts wanted to know? Did America have the forbearance to see democratic reforms truly take root in Iraq? It was a question for which I had no confident answer.

"There is so much at stake now, not only for the Middle East but for America as well," Shafeeq Ghabra told me. "The United States has asked the Arabs to trust U.S. intentions, and it has challenged the rest of the world to help it undertake this major endeavor. If America doesn't follow through on its commitments this time to help rebuild a better Iraq, I fear this could be the confrontation that people will look back on one day and say, 'That was the beginning of the end.' This moment is that important," Ghabra emphasized. "It's either a new beginning, or the beginning of the end."

In those waning days while we waited to report to the desert and our respective embed units, Kuwait City was gripped by the strange elation known only to cities on the brink of war: London before the Blitz, Paris prior to the fall. We were all intoxicated on that giddy mixture of apprehension and the freedom that comes from living in the moment. Among the abundant offerings at the local shopping centers gas masks and chemical protection suits were on display. Nonessential embassy personnel had long since left the city, and the cover of *Kuwait This Month* magazine proclaimed "The Fear Issue," with an inside cover story on "Living in Fear." So by day we fired off copy and outfitted ourselves for war, and by night we dined on Kuwait's finest, substituting exotic fruit drinks for the highballs we all craved, and the expense accounts be damned.

On one such night we ate in an exclusive restaurant housed in a giant wooden *dhow*, one of the curvaceous Arab ships that still plowed the waters of the Persian Gulf. Besides Mike Kelly and myself there was mutual colleague and friend Steve Komarow of *USA Today*, along with another *USA Today* reporter and a Nairobi-based correspondent for "Voice of America" named Alicia Ryu. Over fresh local fish and steaks grilled to order, with the pungent aroma of fruit tobacco smoked in Arab hookah pipes as incense, we told war stories and tried to take our minds off what lay ahead.

Steve and Alicia talked about being shaken down by bandits in the mountains of Afghanistan while covering the U.S. war against the Taliban and Al Qaeda. As war zones go, Alicia volunteered that she much preferred Afghanistan, however, to the six civil wars in Africa she had covered from her bureau in Nairobi. Before even the year was out she would be covering the landing of U.S. Marines and international peacekeepers in Liberia. "There's nothing scarier than being shaken down by a twelve-year-old with a .50-caliber machine gun, and seeing in his eyes that the kid has absolutely no concept of consequences or mortality," she said.

Michael Kelly recounted his experiences in the Bosnian war, where he witnessed the riptides of ethnic cleansing as the Serbs torched the houses of Bosnian Muslims and Croats, who later returned the favor when the tides of war shifted. Kelly spent so many weeks in the trenches that he even caught a touch of that war's strange lunacy, belligerently arguing with security personnel for the flight home over his right—no, by God, his *duty*—to retain in his carry-on luggage the bayonet given to Michael as a parting gift by a Croat officer.

The war stories and place-names of global conflict piled up as the dinner wore on, the subtext to the entire conversation the realization that another violent chapter was about to be written. A casual observer overhearing that conversation of correspondents could be forgiven for concluding that at the beginning of the twenty-first century the United States was indeed engaged in something akin to a world war. Certainly that's what Michael Kelly and many of the neoconservatives felt, and you didn't have to wholly embrace the argument to find compelling the idea that there were common threads running through the tales of far-flung conflict recounted at our dinner table.

In a new forward to *Martyrs' Day*, Kelly described how he came to view the first Gulf War as only the opening salvo in a long struggle between "a wealthy, tolerant and relatively civilized Western culture, and a poor, relatively uncivilized and increasingly intolerant Eastern culture." The Gulf War was thus only an early chapter "in the war that will decide the things that a century of war not only did not decide, but kept from decision," he wrote. "Subsequent battles and subsequent tests have taken place, and in some cases are still taking place, in Somalia, Bosnia, Chechnya, Kosovo and Israel. The record of success in these tests has been mixed, and marked by a profound reluctance on the part of most American government policy makers to come to terms with the notion that what is involved here is not a series of disconnected, discrete crises . . . but rather chapters in a long struggle of the greatest importance. On September 11, 2001, that reluctance to face reality was forced to end."

On the drive home from dinner we passed one of the palaces of the emir, Sheikh Jaber a-Ahmed al-Sabah, whose family had ruled Kuwait as a relatively benign oligarchy for four decades. The white marble spires and fortresslike walls seemed to glow with their own pale light set off against the dark of a night sky and the sea beyond. The palace was built on the firm coastal beach of the Bay of Kuwait, but its true foundation, and the source of the al-Sabah's power, were the nearly one thousand wells of the nearby Burgan oil field, which pumped out 1.5 million barrels a day and stood atop proven reserves large enough to last into the twenty-second century. The Burgan was the second-largest oil field in the world.

Michael was unusually agitated that night. During the afternoon he had driven out to "Camp New York," where the Third Infantry Division was encamped, and had his first background interview with Third I.D. commander Maj. Gen. Buford Blount. In the original embed lottery, *Atlantic Monthly's* slot and Michael Kelly had been assigned to Coalition Forces Land Component Command (CFLCC), which had its headquarters not in Kuwait, but rather safely back in Qatar. Mike said he would as soon cover the war from Boston. The *Atlantic Monthly* had run a lengthy piece a year earlier on a Third I.D. peacekeeping rotation in Bosnia, however, and Kelly had used his contacts with the division to arrange an embed. That earlier *Atlantic Monthly* article on the Third Infantry Division had documented the frustrations of soldiers who joined the Army to fight wars and ended up yoked for over a decade to the plow horse of peacekeeping duty in the Balkans and elsewhere. Under present circumstances, I pointed out to Kelly the irony of the article's title: "Peace Is Hell." Mike laughed, but it had the edginess of all humor in those days. "Who knew?"

After talking with General Blount that day, however, the inevitability of war and the enormity of the operation ahead had sunk in for Kelly. "We're going all the way to Baghdad," Mike said with certainty, and even in the dark I could tell he was watching me for a reaction. In those early days of March there was still speculation in the press that Saddam Hussein would capitulate at the last moment and go into self-imposed exile to avoid another humiliating defeat at the hands of a Bush. Even under such a scenario, however, General Blount had apparently told Mike that one of the U.S. conditions would be for the Third I.D. to travel to the Iraqi capital and oversee the dismantling of Saddam's weapons programs. The only question, apparently, was whether U.S. troops would be fighting their way to Baghdad or not. Michael nodded his head when he saw that I grasped it. "We're going all the way to Baghdad, buddy!"

———

The afternoon before reporting to my embed unit in the desert, Michael Kelly, George Wilson, and I went on a final shopping spree at the Sultan Center shopping mall. The crowd in the still bustling mall was indicative of the straddle between modernity and tradition that Kuwait and the other Gulf emirates were attempting to make. Older women seemed to glide by, their bodies completely covered in traditional garb and only their inscrutable dark eyes showing beneath their robes. Middle Eastern mall rats were also in abundance, however, the young teenage girls sporting hip-hugging jeans and tight-fitting tops right out of a Britney Spears video. In the Sultan Center Michael Kelly pushed a shopping cart into which he, George Wilson, and I piled all manner of camping supplies and gear: rope, lanterns, flashlights, batteries, extra underwear, socks, a tent, trail mix, candy. I picked out the most imposing knife I could find, while for some reason Mike threw in packages and packages of baby wipes.

At one point we ducked inside a pharmacy where Mike asked the pharmacist to recommend a sunscreen for the desert. Learning that we were journalists, the woman, an Egyptian, confided that she had already purchased a one-way air ticket to Alexandria and was on the verge of fleeing the city. "As for you, I would recommend at least a SPF factor 20," she said to Mike with a wry smile. "Of course, the chemical weapons may add to your color."

On that last night before leaving for the desert, I stopped by Michael Kelly's room at the Sheraton to drop off some extra baggage that Hamouda was going to store for us. Mike was on the phone with his wife, but he ushered me into the room with a beckoning wave of his hand. His hotel room bore the clutter and spoke to the absentmindedness for which Kelly was deservedly renowned. Electronic cables and equipment and all manner of clothes and camping gear were strewn about. In one corner of the hotel room a laptop computer was set up, surrounded by books, magazines, and newspapers. In his copy of Stephen Ambrose's *D-Day: The Climactic Battle of World War II*, Mike had scribbled notes at the back of the book annotating a particular passage for further reflection. The passage Mike had underlined closed Ambrose's book and was drawn from the June 7, 1944, lead editorial in the *New York Times* on the D-Day invasion.

"We have come to the hour for which we were born. We go forth to meet the supreme test of our arms and our souls, the test of the maturity of our faith in ourselves and in mankind. . . . We pray for the boys we know and for millions of unknown boys. . . . We pray for our country . . . The cause prays for itself, for it is the cause of the God who created man equal and free."

While I made myself at home, Michael Kelly couldn't resist a little good-natured needling of my bachelor's ignorance, displayed at that afternoon's shopping spree, of the apparently great utility of baby wipes in the field. "Max," he told his wife Madelyn, the mother of his two young sons Tom and Jack, with typically infectious glee. "James didn't even know what they were made to wipe! I could tell! We should offer to *show* him!" We both laughed at that one, but there was something about sharing that moment of domestic intimacy that seemed to bring out a pang of homesickness in Mike that I hadn't noticed before.

On my way out of his room at the Sheraton that night, Michael offered a final handshake. "Be safe, and have a good adventure," he said. "I'll buy you a beer in Baghdad."

CHAPTER 10

Eve of Destruction

THE MEDIA CIRCUS was in full swing at Coalition Forces Land Component Command (CFLCC), which had established its media bureau for registering embedded journalists at the Kuwaiti Hilton resort, a squat, ugly complex of low mustard-colored buildings and bungalows by the shoreline on the outskirts of Kuwait City. You could easily see that the Hilton had been chosen for its gated seclusion, with its back hard against the blue waters of the Persian Gulf. All visitors had to approach from the front through a metal detector in a guardhouse by the gate, while their cars were searched by uniformed Kuwaitis using undercarriage mirrors and bomb-sniffing dogs.

After standing in line with a host of other journalists, I filed the requisite paperwork, provided proof of my vaccinations, and had my photo taken for a media badge. The uniformed men and women of CFLCC (pronounced "See Flick") who processed the journalists were friendly almost to a fault, cheerily asking what publication we worked for, where we came from back home, and had we yet received shots for anthrax and smallpox and filled out the next-of-kin paperwork? The whole scene had the feel of the first day of summer camp, and you could tell that with so much shared time ahead the counselors didn't want to spook the campers.

The presence of so many journalists was the result of a typically bold stroke by Defense Secretary Donald Rumsfeld, who decided that the best way to counter Saddam's well-oiled propaganda machine was to allow nearly six hundred journalists to embed with U.S. military units and witness the war firsthand. More so than ever before, America was thus going to have war beamed into its living rooms and splashed over its front pages in nearly real time, in all its attendant confusion and drama, with precious little time for military censorship or, for that matter, reasoned analysis. How that would affect the overall quality of the war coverage, or the public's understanding of what was actually happening, was still anybody's guess.

Before loading journalists onto busses for the ride out into the desert, CFLCC officials held an instructional on the tennis courts of the Kuwaiti Hilton in the art of rapidly donning a protection suit and gas mask under chemical attack. From their expressions it was impossible to gauge what the instructors made of the group of reporters hopping about breathlessly trying to fit into their suits and fumbling to draw the complex strapping of the rubber masks quickly over their heads, but in the event of an actual attack it was a pretty fair guess that the news business was in for a black day.

Inside, an Army doctor detailed the ravages that anthrax and small-pox visit on the human body, the better to convince reporters to opt for the vaccines. The slides of smallpox victims, in particular, were reminiscent of a high school hygiene class on advanced-stage venereal disease. After receiving our vaccinations, we gathered for a briefing by Captain Tom Bryant, a strapping and cheerfully gung-ho infantryman turned public affairs officer who gave each reporter his unit assignment. As a correspondent for an in-depth policy magazine like *National Journal*, I was assigned to the V Corps Headquarters itself, the better to get a bird's-eye view of the war from the headquarters commanding all Army maneuver forces in the invasion. Sitting next to me was a young reporter for the Talk Radio News Service named Gareth Schweitzer who had pulled duty with a combat engineer battalion. What did combat engineers do, he wanted to know?

"Don't worry, you'll be plenty close to the action," Captain Bryant assured him. "The combat engineers will likely be the first ones through the berm into Iraq, clearing a way through the minefields for the tanks."

Schweitzer muttered to no one in particular. "Oh, that's just great."

Outside, as we prepared to load our gear into a waiting bus, a handsome black sergeant by the name of Wilkins was trying to communicate with a Korean reporter who seemed to speak little if any English. Exasperated, Sergeant Wilkins broke into a spot-on Chris Tucker impersonation, the baffled Korean reporter substituting for Jackie Chan as a foil for the sergeant's bug-eyed antics. "Do you understand the words that are coming out of my mouth? I SAID, DO YOU *UNDERSTAND THE WORDS THAT ARE COMING OUT OF MY MOUTH!!?*" Later, after showing us pictures of his beautiful Thai girlfriend and young son, Sergeant Wilkins ushered us onto the bus with a final bit of advice. "You gotta maintain your sense of humor," he said. "Because there's gonna be shit out there in that desert that will suck the laughter right out of you."

Camp Virginia was a flat spot in a trackless desert given shape and contour only by the countless military vehicles, rows of tents, satellite dishes, portable toilets, and the fifteen thousand-plus U.S. Army troops that occupied it, with more of everything pouring in daily. The very presence of V Corps Headquarters out of Germany indicated the "task force" organization scheme that the U.S. military had improved upon over a decade of contingency deployments, whereby disparate forces from around the world are assembled in building block configurations tailored to specific operations. The spearheads for the planned invasion of Iraq were the Army's Third Infantry Division (Third I.D.) out of Ft. Stewart, Georgia, and the First Marine Expeditionary Force (First MEF) out of Camp Pendleton, California, reinforced by a British Royal Marine Brigade. The Third Infantry and First Marines were encamped nearby.

As the echelon above Third Infantry Division, V Corps Headquarters, commanded by three-star Lt. Gen. William "Scott" Wallace, would coordinate all U.S Army ground forces in theater, to include elements of the Eighty-second Airborne and 101st Air Mobile Divisions that were soon scheduled to arrive in Kuwait, and the Fourth Infantry Division, whose equipment was still sitting in ships in the Mediterranean Sea in the fading hope that Turkey might yet grant it permission to enter that country and establish a northern front in the war. Above V Corps was CFLCC, with responsibility for coordinating both U.S. Army and Marine maneuver forces, and in the command echelon above that Central Command, whose four-star commander Gen. Tommy Franks was responsible for coordinating all U.S. and allied land, air, and naval forces in theater.

Seeing that massive U.S. force gathering in the Kuwaiti desert, I was reminded of European officials' complaints that the rapid deployment of so much military power had overwhelmed the diplomacy on Iraq, imposing a military time line that had made war all but inevitable. The look and feel of Camp Virginia certainly reinforced the view that the operation was fast approaching its invisible tipping point, after which the amassment of so much deadly machinery and force would be difficult to reverse or stand down. When that pivot was reached, the path of least resistance would be violence and mayhem. It was the old adage of the streets, its incontrovertible logic expanded to strategic proportions: If you pull a gun, you had better be willing to use it.

The V Corps Media Operations Center, or "MOC" in military speak— essentially a tent two sizes too small that the public affairs unit had been forced to borrow when their own failed to arrive in theater—was headed by Lt. Col. Joe Richard, an intense military policeman from Maryland who retained the air of a small-town sheriff, competent and irascible. His deputy was Maj. Dean Thurmond, the resident cynic and iconoclast who seemed to believe the whole embed experiment was a conspiracy to make his life unbearable. Capt. Tom Bryant was an indefatigable Alabaman who kept a Crimson Tide banner above his workstation and managed to keep the MOC functioning on a daily basis with the good cheer of an infantryman in the field.

This was essentially the embed family for the only two reporters assigned to V Corps Headquarters, myself and Bernard Weinraub of the *New York Times*. Steve Komarow of *USA Today* was in and out of the MOC, having finagled the assignment of shadowing General Wallace throughout the war. Over many a dinner of mystery meat and mashed potatoes in the crowded mess tent, Weinraub entertained me with comparisons between our present surroundings and his usual routine of schmoozing movie and rock stars at Spago's as an entertainment reporter for the paper's Los Angeles bureau. The fact that Weinraub had been drafted into service in Kuwait based on his early experience covering the Vietnam War more than thirty years ago said something about how the unusual embed experiment was straining the personnel and resources of even the largest U.S. media organizations.

In that purgatory in the Kuwaiti desert, the most salient feature of life at Camp Virginia was long lines for virtually any human convenience. There were lines for chow and lines for the portable toilets, lines for the handful of showers and the morale-and-support tent, and endless lines around a desert block for the telephone tent and the Post Exchange (PX), a sort of 7-Eleven in the desert run by the Armed Forces Exchange Service (AAFES). During the intermittent air raid drills, the first soldiers to arrive crowded inside cramped concrete bunkers in bug-eyed gas masks that made every breath an effort; everyone else stood outside in long lines and patiently awaited their fate.

After more than a week of *Groundhog Day*-esque numbing sameness in the desert, I was drinking a cup of coffee outside the Media Operations tent and watching the line of soldiers outside the trailer that served as the PX. What on earth could they be selling in there, I asked a sergeant who was having a smoke nearby, that was worth waiting in line for hours under a desert sun?

"You wouldn't believe it," he told me. "Cigarettes and chewing tobacco. Warm Coke. Candy. A bunch of useless shit."

Then why do they wait?

He thought about that one for a while. "You know, some of those fellas have been out in this desert for months. Going in there, picking stuff off a shelf, laying down money for it. I guess it kind of reminds them of civilization."

We had a good laugh at that one, and some days later when there was a rare break in the line I went into the PX trailer to see what the excitement was all about. Half the shelves had been picked clean, and some of the others sported goods seemingly chosen as some sort of cruel joke. There were boxes of fabric softener sheets for making clothes "baby soft" in a clothes dryer. Another shelf bore stacked bags of barbecue coals. There was bottle upon bottle of salsa, but no chips to eat it with. Perhaps representing a deal that some local AAFES purchaser simply couldn't refuse, Muslim prayer rugs lay stacked in piles near the cash register.

On my way out after scouting the place I picked up a couple of cartons of American cigarettes as an afterthought, figuring they might come in handy as palm greasers in Iraq. On impulse I threw in some candy, a baseball cap with an "Enduring Freedom" emblem from the campaign in Afghanistan, and an extra T-shirt. After looking in vain for baby wipes, my supply of which was already running dangerously low, I added some disposable razors and a six-pack of nonalcoholic beer. As I waited in a long line at the cash register I grabbed an Elvis Presley CD off a rack and added it to the pile, even though my tastes of late were running more toward U-2 and Dave Mathews. I paid for it all in greenbacks and bagged my bounty. As I walked out of the shabby trailer it occurred to me that the sergeant was right: the sweet rhythms of commerce and the music of the cash registers worked like a narcotic, spiking my mood noticeably. That night when I got back to the tent, I noticed for the first time that my next-door bunk mate, a Marine reserve intelligence officer, had laid prayer rugs over the dusty floor beneath his cot in a configuration approximating wall-to-wall carpet.

Whatever personal reservations he might have had about the embed experiment, Col. Joe Richard left no doubt that he meant to fulfill its essential promise of allowing journalists an inside-the-dugout look at the U.S. military in wartime. On March 11, 2003, he thus accompanied me to an interview with Lt. Gen. Scott Wallace to get an overview of the planned operation that at that point had yet to even be given a name. General Wallace had apparently read my book *Prodigal Soldiers*, detailing the experiences of his generation of Vietnam-era officers, and was happy to talk.

In the top echelons of the U.S. military there are those who lead through the force of charisma and occasionally bombast, and others who rise through the ranks based more on their intellect and quiet determination. As I was to learn, Wallace fell into the latter category, though he shared the intensity common to all who attain senior command in the hypercompetitive ranks of the U.S. armed forces. He was a Kentucky boy, son of a salesman and World War II vet. As a young man Scott Wallace had answered the call of West Point, married his high school sweetheart, and somehow made a career of the military without ever really intending to. He just never turned down the next assignment or promotion. Like thousands of others in uniform he had sweated and toiled his entire adult life in relative obscurity, with expectation of little else beyond a ceremonial send-off and comfortable retirement. Now suddenly Lt. Gen. Scott Wallace was in command of an army on the eve of war at a decisive moment in his nation's history. Such was life in the U.S. military at the turn of the twenty-first century.

Wallace was also the last of a fading generation of officers whose formative years in uniform were spent in Vietnam. He could still remember the Christmas Eve call from the Red Cross in 1971, alerting him that his firstborn had arrived while Wallace was away serving as an adviser to South Vietnamese forces in Baclieu Province. The young Wallace had been so excited that he forgot to even ask whether it was a boy or a girl. As was the case with many of the Vietnam generation of officers, those early experiences with war also gave Wallace a sense of innate caution that was at odds with so much of what was happening in the Kuwaiti desert in late March of 2003.

Wallace had also spent much of his professional career, however, in cavalry regiments, totally self-contained and highly mobile units designed to probe ahead of main forces in order to engage and fix the enemy on the battlefield. Among Army officers, cavalry commanders were a special breed, with an independent nature and thirst for engagement that rarely went unrequited in wartime. As I was soon to learn, that made Scott Wallace a natural to execute an Iraqi invasion plan that was unlike any campaign plan in the war college textbooks.

In order to intellectually grasp the complexity of that battle plan and the challenges ahead, Wallace told me, it was useful to consider that there would essentially be five battles under way simultaneously in the war to come. The first battle was simply a continuous deployment of forces from points all around the globe, funneling them through the relative eye of a needle of Kuwait's Doha port. Notably, the lack of a western front from Saudi Arabia and a northern front from Turkey made the U.S. invasion route utterly predictable and necessitated extremely long lines of supply, or what the military called "lines of communication."

The requirement to funnel the entire force through the bottleneck of Kuwait, meanwhile, was partly behind Central Command's curious decision to launch the war, if it came, with a "rolling start," something not attempted by the U.S. military since D-Day. Rather than launch from a standing start with all of its formations stacked on top of each other in Kuwait, V Corps planned to have the Third Infantry Division fighting its way to Baghdad even as follow-on forces needed for the campaign continued to roll out of the holds of transport ships in Doha. Keeping frontline forces resupplied even while moving follow-on forces into the fray was the second battle in Wallace's construct.

"That's different from what we've done in the past, and it clearly poses challenges to the deploying forces," Wallace told me. "What guidance do you give to that commander who is just climbing off the boat, for instance, and who is still getting used to the time change and new environment? At the same time, I will have to be thinking about how we employ those new forces five, or six or seven days ahead when they link up with our forces already on the battlefield, because that commander needs to be thinking ahead about his mission. So that's an extraordinarily difficult transition to make."

The third battle was negotiating the radically different types of terrain that lay between the border of Kuwait and Baghdad. To the southwest lay one of the world's most inhospitable deserts, a flat, featureless expanse broken only by large troughs called *wadis*, and inhabited by nomadic Bedouins who had somehow scraped subsistence from its barren reaches for centuries. In the south the Euphrates and Tigris Rivers converged in a region of marshes that was home to an ancient people known as the Marsh Arabs. Saddam had persecuted the Marsh Arabs mercilessly, draining much of their native swampland after they joined the 1991 insurrection against his rule.

Between the two rivers was the green and fertile Mesopotamian Valley, which ran hundreds of miles down the middle of Iraq like a channel from Baghdad to the country's southern reaches, and which was crisscrossed by canals, irrigation ditches, rice paddies, and bridges. Much of that region, where the majority of Iraqis had lived for centuries, could be flooded and potentially made impassable if the Iraqi forces blew a couple of strategic dams.

"And only after you have solved the deployment, logistics, and terrain problems do you come to the actual fight with the enemy, and the problem of someone shooting at you," Wallace explained. "That's the fourth fight I spoke of, and in our best judgment the closer we get to Baghdad the more tenacious and determined the enemy is going to become." The fifth fight was the battle to maintain a tempo of operations such that the Iraqis were kept off balance at all times and unaware of significant vulnerabilities in the U.S. war plan. "That means doing as many things simultaneously to the enemy as you can, horizontally in terms of hitting him from multiple directions on the ground and vertically in terms of the joint fight with Air Force and Navy air power," said Wallace. "The point is to make this a multidimensional fight that overwhelms the enemy's command-and-control and keeps him off balance."

When he was finished, I pointed out to General Wallace that his five fights didn't even take into account the two that were of most concern to the American public and many defense experts: the potential for attack by chemical and/or biological weapons, and the likelihood of a very bloody urban battle for control of Baghdad.

"We have some of the best equipment money can buy in terms of protection against chemical and biological weapons, but I would be bullshitting you if I didn't tell you that there is a psychological toll involved with the use of those weapons," said Wallace. "Soldiers out here are anxious. They don't lack confidence, but there's a certain amount of anxiety. And the protective equipment does slow you down. It reduces your stamina both personally and organizationally."

In terms of the Battle of Baghdad, for which he would be in command of all Army and Marine Corps forces, Wallace said that he was determined to show patience in identifying those targets whose destruction with a combination of precision-guided munitions and hit-and-withdraw strikes by ground forces would unhinge Saddam's grasp of the city. "We need to go after those hard points without the intention of our forces spending long periods of time in bad neighborhoods."

When the interview was over, I mentioned in parting with Wallace that the plan to topple the regime in Baghdad and take control of Iraq seemed far more complex and risky than the last U.S. military campaign of similarly massive scope, the expulsion of Iraqi troops from Kuwait in 1991. "While it may not be obvious to a layman, this is dramatically different from Desert Storm," Wallace told me. "We're always accused of fighting the last war, but I can assure you this is not the last war. I repeat: *this is not the last war.*"

As I was to learn in the days that followed, the Iraq operation was designed by Defense Secretary Rumsfeld and his civilian team in the Pentagon to be the first transformational war on a truly grand scale. The prototype was Afghanistan, where Rumsfeld had similarly scrapped Central Command's original request for much larger conventional forces, opting instead to use small Special Forces detachments to marry U.S. air and space power to tribal forces that fought on horseback and used tactics little changed from those that chased the British from Afghanistan in the nineteenth century. The rapid toppling of the Taliban regime in the fall of 2001 had greatly emboldened Rumsfeld, who was pressuring Gen. Tommy Franks relentlessly to adopt his vision of transformational war by relatively small, highly mobile forces backed by precision-guided airpower and space-age surveillance and communications systems.

Only Iraq was not Afghanistan, and Afghanistan was not an altogether perfect model. A major with the 101st Airborne I spoke with in the Kuwaiti desert told me how the Pentagon's insistence that they forgo the standard artillery package in Afghanistan and rely on air support instead, led to his unit being pinned down and badly mauled by Taliban mortar fire in a particularly bad stretch of weather during the Battle of Anaconda. The lack of sufficient U.S. forces on the ground and reliance on local warlords as surrogates, also probably allowed Osama Bin Laden to escape capture during the Battle of Tora Bora, a setback of strategic proportions. Nor had the presence of relatively sparse U.S. forces kept the country from backsliding into feudal fiefdoms ruled by warlords in the war's aftermath. In the case of Afghanistan it could be plausibly argued, however, that the country's landlocked position and relative inaccessibility, combined with the urgency of the operation following 9/11, dictated a very unconventional approach.

In the case of Iraq, the United States would be invading a very populous country, with a large army and highly coveted resources, at the strategic crossroads of the Middle East. Not only would U.S. forces have to topple a regime whose seat of power was dead center in an ancient metropolis of more than five million citizens, but the Bush administration had also committed the United States to rebuilding Iraq as a functioning democracy in the aftermath of war. That meant limiting, to the degree possible, collateral damage and the destruction of Iraqi infrastructure, further complicating the military's task. The United States was totally in charge of the time line to war and possessed overwhelming military forces, and the stakes were higher than they had been in the lives of an entire generation of Americans. To choose to fight according to the still largely untested tenets of "transformational war" was audacious, and the willingness to do so rested on several key assumptions, and the acceptance of great risk.

The battle plan for Iraqi Freedom called for a small force, guided by space-based surveillance and communications systems and backed by precision airpower, to essentially rewrite the rules of warfare. Gone was the 3-to-1 attacker to defender advantage traditionally prescribed for offensive operations. Instead, a force of some one hundred thirty-seven thousand U.S. ground troops were to rapidly invade a populous country of more than twenty-five million and decisively defeat a potentially much larger foe fighting on his home turf and likely armed with chemical and biological weapons. At war's end, U.S. troops were then to rapidly transition from the kill-or-be-killed mind-set of high-intensity combat to the humanitarian posture of the peacekeeper and nation builder. The first truly large-scale war of the twenty-first century would thus pit the "shock and awe" of transformational warfare against much of the conventional wisdom on how wars should, and could, be fought.

That point was driven home during a classified briefing on the battle plan that I received along with Bernie Weinraub of the *New York Times*. Reading journalists into detailed war plans before the first shot was fired represented unprecedented journalistic access that would have been unthinkable before the embed experiment. Escorted into a chamber of the massive tent complex that was V Corps Headquarters, we were placed in front of a large map board that depicted with bold arrows the longest operational maneuver by a U.S. Army corps since Gen. George Patton ranged North Africa stalking the vaunted Afrika Korps of German Gen. Erwin Rommel, the "Desert Fox." The distances involved were also similar to those covered by General Eisenhower's forces as they drove toward the Rhine from the D-Day landings on Normandy. Both of those campaigns, however, took many months. V Corps hoped to have its forces encircling Baghdad in weeks if all went well.

Briefing us were Lt. Col. E. J. Degen and Maj. Kevin Marcus, both graduates of the Army's elite School of Advanced Military Studies (SAMS), a graduate school for strategic battle planners at Fort Leavenworth, Kansas. While any U.S. military campaign plan inevitably bears thousands of fingerprints, mid-career officers such as Degen and Marcus had done the intellectual spadework on what was to become the Iraqi Freedom battle plan, and both were obviously pleased at our slack-jawed reaction to its audacity and scope.

"I can remember when this plan started seventeen months ago as a 'What if?' drill over beers by a bunch of my classmates and me at SAMS," Degen later told me. "Recently we were told that a PowerPoint slide of what you've just seen ended up on President Bush's desk."

The map showed dual pincers representing a reinforced U.S. Army division and Marine Corps Expeditionary Force, backed by Air Force and Navy airpower, fighting up the Euphrates and Tigris River Valleys, respectively, all the way to Baghdad. The Third Infantry Division's Second Brigade and 3/7th Cavalry Regiment were to sweep left up Iraq's western desert in a swinging hook maneuver in order to bring the fight quickly to the Republican Guard Medina Division, which guarded the southern approaches to Baghdad. Though British forces attached to the Marines were to seize the southern oil fields and contain the key southern Shiite city of Basra, U.S. forces planned to simply bypass most other cities. The focus was on decisively destroying the Medina Division and quickly launching the Battle of Baghdad from four firebases encircling the city. The "what if" variables and "unknown unknowns" that are inevitable in any campaign plan must have been incalculable, I thought, in this one.

What stood out from the briefing was that the United States would be attempting to conquer another country with very lean forces—basically reinforced Army and Marine Corps divisions—without even a mobile reserve to act as reinforcement or secure long logistics lines. "The original battle plan envisioned a much larger U.S. force, so synchronization and tempo will be critical to the entire operation," conceded Marcus. "Everything must unfold fast so that the Iraqis don't know where they are being hit from, because it comes down to our advantage in mobility and firepower against the Iraqi advantage in terrain. Make no mistake, they are occupying defensible terrain."

As General Wallace later confided to me, the unusual rolling start to the war was probably unavoidable given the time lines involved and the fact that everything had to be threaded through the proverbial eye of the needle in Doha port. "It would simply take too long, and become too crowded, to mass all our forces in Kuwait before beginning operations. The question all along was how much force we would have available when the order came to start the war. The answer was, not a hell of a lot," Wallace said. "Traditional military thought holds that you need a mobile reserve in a campaign like this, in case something goes bad and you need to plug an unexpected hole, or something goes good and you want to exploit an unexpected opportunity. And we never had a reserve force. Never! So, yeah, I was somewhat concerned. I knew we would win the war because we were strong at the point of our spear, but we could still win it very ugly."

When I asked during the battle plan briefing what most concerned the war planners, Degen and Marcus exchanged meaningful looks and seemed to hesitate, and then pointed to a narrow spit of land roughly a hundred kilometers south of Baghdad that lay between the Euphrates River and a series of large lakes. "The Karbala Gap," said Degen emphatically. "That's a critical choke point for entering the Baghdad region from the south, because there are lakes and reservoirs to the west and a river valley to the east that is congested and difficult to maneuver in. We also think that if Saddam is going to use chemical weapons, the Karbala Gap and the Euphrates River crossing are the most likely targets."

There is a military adage that no battle plan survives the firing of the first shot, but after that initial briefing the Iraqi campaign plan rarely survived the dawning of the new day. The forces available for the fight, their arrival in theater, and their initial objectives kept shifting, as did the time lines involved. Senior officers told me this was a by-product of Rumsfeld's insistence that Central Command planning remain fluid and agile. After dramatically cutting Central Command's request for forces almost in half, Rumsfeld and the Office of the Secretary of Defense (OSD) had essentially told General Franks that he could have the forces he needed but only on an "as required" basis depending on how the situation unfolded.

Perhaps most significantly, Rumsfeld ordered Central Command to jettison the Time Phased Force Deployment Data Scheme, or "Tip Fid," by which commanders in the field normally identified forces needed for a specific campaign, and the armed services managed the deployment of those forces by order of first priority. The methodical nature such a deployment scheme ensured assaulted Rumsfeld's notions of transformational war. Instead Rumsfeld preached speed and agility, and he derided the Tip Fid as part of an "Industrial Age" mobilization process that was far too ponderous and slow. Rumsfeld was also determined to break the old paradigm of "overwhelming force" that the Tip Fid serviced. The idea of overwhelming force, of course, was a central tenet of the Powell doctrine, named after former Chairman of the Joint Staff Colin Powell, Rumsfeld's chief antagonist in the Bush administration's bureaucratic battles.

As senior Rumsfeld aides would later tell me, they had also drawn the lesson from Afghanistan that the U.S. military was at its most innovative when under the maximum amount of pressure, and they were happy to oblige. So in his inimitable fashion, Rumsfeld constantly cajoled Gen. Tommy Franks and the Joint Staff into abandoning the Tip Fid by constantly grilling them about why their deployment plan for Iraq was taking so long, why their assumptions about the war seemed so risk adverse and out of date, and why they really needed all those forces and support.

While it may have seemed logical to Rumsfeld and his senior staff inside the Pentagon, the decision to scuttle the time-tested deployment scheme gave the entire operation in Kuwait a dangerously ad hoc, back-of-the-envelope feel. Even as the days counted down to war, for instance, forces needed for the fight continued to pour off ships in Doha, and not necessarily in the order of first priority or with adequate equipment and supplies. The 101st was arriving in mid-March, for instance, but short of the support trucks needed to move them about the battlefield. The Corps Support Command that would be responsible for supplying the entire force, meanwhile, arrived with insufficient trucks and communications gear. At Rumsfeld's encouragement, Central Command also deployed combat forces with less than the usual complement of artillery, substituting instead more mobile and high-tech Apache helicopter gunships.

Brig. Gen. Daniel Hahn, the intense chief of staff for V Corps, explained to me the challenges of deploying for war without the carefully choreographed construct of a Tip Fid. His comments reminded me of an old military adage that amateurs and armchair generals talk grand strategy, while professionals talk about logistics. "Without a Tip Fid we're really practicing a 'just-in-time' buildup to war, which is certainly transformational in terms of allowing the political process to play itself out. With forces and equipment pouring off of ships and the battle plan changing every day we get closer to war, however, there's also a lot of tension. We're now talking about having to plug new forces almost immediately into the fight to come, and that scares me a little from a safety standpoint. In exercises and training we usually give units time to get their communications straightened out, and for guys to get used to the environment before they try and fly their Apaches one hundred feet off of the ground."

Privately, another general officer I spoke with was even more blunt about the uniformed military's tensions with Pentagon civilians over the scrapping of the Tip Fid. "Rumsfeld insists that the Tip Fid process is too ponderous and slow, and it may well be, but it's the only process we have for managing the flow of forces into a theater and matching them with needed lift and support. Since we've been ordered to abandon the Tip Fid, it would be really nice if those of us responsible for executing this campaign knew and understood what the hell is supposed to replace it. And we don't!"

No one felt the strains of Rumsfeld's transformational war plan, with its rolling start, ad hoc deployment, and lack of a clear deployment schedule more than a wiry and bespectacled man named Charles Fletcher, who had the intense air of an overstressed FedEx executive during Christmas rush. Instead, Brigadier General Fletcher commanded Third Corps Support Command, or COSCOM, which would be responsible for supplying all Army forces in the Iraqi theater. Fletcher would be "Mr. Logistics" for the war to come. When I met with him at COSCOM headquarters, he served up the first cold bottle of water I had in weeks and explained the challenge ahead in a set of daunting statistics.

An armored maneuver division such as the Third Infantry Division consumes roughly five hundred fifty thousand gallons of fuel a day on the move. When you added in V Corps support battalions and elements of the 101st and Eighty-second Airborne Divisions, COSCOM would have to supply maneuver forces with one million gallons of fuel each day, meaning it would have to have three million gallons in its pipeline of fuel trucks. Each of the over one hundred fifty thousand U.S. troops in Iraq, meanwhile, would consume an estimated 4.5 liters of water a day, which didn't include water that would be needed for decontamination if U.S. forces were attacked with chemical weapons. The harder those units and soldiers fought, the higher their ammunition, fuel, and water requirements would climb. The longer the logistics pipeline stretched—and it would need to stretch roughly three hundred miles to Baghdad—the greater the strain on the transportation system.

As a result of the drastic cut in forces and abandonment of the Tip Fid dictated by Rumsfeld and his staff, however, the support forces COSCOM had assembled in Kuwait were, according to Army doctrine, simply inadequate to the task. Key elements had simply been eliminated. "We basically spent a year building a force package that included very robust command-and-control for our support elements, for instance, but when the decision was made to only go with half our force we only had a very short time to adjust the shipping orders that would enable us to get the right forces to Kuwait," Fletcher told me. "So while that decision may have been smart from a strategic viewpoint, it has had a trickle-down impact on all our operations. I have never received my entire communications package, for instance, complicating secure communications over a supply line stretching hundreds of kilometers."

The Pentagon's decision not to call up many transportation units in the Reserves before Christmas had also created personnel shortages. COSCOM also had only roughly 150 heavy transport trucks in the theater on the eve of a war that Army planners estimated would require 700 trucks. "We're going to war not with what we need, but with what we have on the ground, so we threw away the doctrinal books on this operation a long time ago," Fletcher told me, noting that his transport units also had far less maintenance support than normal. "I believe we will make it all work, but I don't doubt that we face some hard choices in the coming days between supporting our soldiers forward with ammo, fuel, and equipment, and facilitating the continued offloading of ships in port and movement of forces forward."

Like the Army's combat units, Fletcher's COSCOM forces, which outnumbered any U.S. fighting division in the region, would attempt to compensate for lean forces on the ground with technology. For instance, Army doctrine called for support columns to travel in large formations with short communications lines, so most transport trucks had radios with only 30 km ranges and no GPS to pinpoint their positions. With logistics lines that would likely stretch hundreds of miles, COSCOM purchased four hundred commercial satellite trackers "off the shelf" so that headquarters could locate its highest priority vehicles, including fuel trucks, ambulances, and military police command vehicles that would provide convoy escort. Satellite phones were purchased for many drivers. High-priority cargo containers were labeled with radio-frequency tags designed to reveal location and contents at a simple query from headquarters.

The Army's Movement Tracking System, meanwhile, used technology similar to the "E-Z Pass" highway tollbooth cards to identify the position of critical cargo. Movement control teams would be dispatched with computer software that had analyzed optimum traffic flow and potential detours at every key crossroads and intersection on the road to Baghdad. The Army had even looked into the possibility of moving supplies to Baghdad on commandeered Iraqi railroad lines and on barges transiting the Tigris and Euphrates. As a final safeguard, plans were also in place to air-drop supplies to isolated units or those running dangerously low of critical supplies.

In characterizing the challenge COSCOM faced, Fletcher recounted the story of the "Red Ball Express" during World War II. On the recent fiftieth anniversary commemorating the Battle of the Bulge, Fletcher had bicycled over the route between Cherbourg and Bastogne in France that Gen. George Patton's Third Army had followed on its famous march to relieve surrounded Army forces caught in the Germans' last-ditch counteroffensive of December 1944. In a desperate attempt to keep Patton from outrunning his supply lines, the Army launched the Red Ball Express, a transportation bucket brigade that pushed supplies across France in the Third Army's wake of destruction. Fletcher saw strong similarities between that operation and his mission of resupplying the Third Infantry Division and other elements of V Corps.

"The Red Ball Express was a defining moment in the establishment of the transportation corps, because it was really the first attempt at resupplying a mobile armored force on a breakout offensive," said Fletcher. "This operation is similar, because we've never operated on these long lines of supply before."

For all its storied feats, however, I recalled that the Red Ball Express ultimately ended in every logistician's worst nightmare, with Patton's lead tank companies out of gas and stalled outside of Metz, France, where they became fodder for German Panzers. Only this time, I figured, it could be Third Infantry Division stalled at the end of a dry supply pipeline. Fletcher abruptly ended the historical analogy. "We've accepted some significant risks given the mission and our battle plan. That's all the more reason why we need to win this war quickly," Fletcher said. "But I can tell you this, I'm not going to let our forces run out of gas or ammo in the middle of a fight."

Shortly before the Iraqi Freedom campaign was launched, I was ushered into the "Black Hole," the most classified inner sanctum of V Corps Headquarters. Officially called the "Analytical Control Element," the Black Hole was where all of the varied streams of intelligence on Iraqi forces converged. The main tent consisted of a horseshoe-shaped bank of computers with the open end facing a large video-screen map. Around the horseshoe gathered liaison officers from the various intelligence agencies, including the Central Intelligence Agency, the National Reconnaissance Organization, the National Security Agency, the National Imaging and Mapping Agency, U.S. Space Command, and U.S. Special Forces Command.

"We call this room the 'targeting pit,' because when the war starts pandemonium will break out as people shout out targets and tracks, and it will look like the New York Stock Exchange," said Col. Steven Bolz, the chief of intelligence, or "G-2," for V Corps.

An intelligence officer gave a brief update. Sometime during the night a company of the Republican Guard Medina Division had repositioned and they had been unable to relocate it. Another company had moved to a tree line in order to hide from prying U.S. eyes in the sky, but they didn't expect it to try and fight from that position. A brigade of the Republican Guard Hammurabi Division west of Baghdad had also showed indications of repositioning south in the direction of one of V Corps' proposed staging areas for the Battle of Baghdad, which was a major concern. There were also human intelligence reports of clashes between Iraqi forces and Shiites celebrating a religious holiday in the southern city of Nasiriyah, leaving some thirty-five celebrants dead and indicating that Saddam was struggling to maintain internal control of Iraq.

In a side tent Colonel Bolz, a stocky man with a dark complexion and thoughtful demeanor, assessed the strategy driving Iraqi actions. "We think Saddam is focused on maintaining internal control, delaying our advance, and attriting our forces," he said. "In the north he's relying primarily on regular Army forces to hold against the Kurds. We see him pulling Republican Guard units closer to Baghdad in a 360-degree perimeter defense. In the south it's amazing to see how he's pushed paramilitary forces down to key southern cities in order to maintain his internal control and delay our advance. That really jumps out at you."

In terms of weapons of mass destruction, Bolz said there were as many opinions on whether Saddam would actually fire them as there were analysts in the Black Hole. "I've yet to see any hard evidence that he's preparing WMD, but if his main purpose is to delay our advance and he senses this is his last stand, I don't doubt that he will use them in desperation. We know he's used them in the past."

What stood out from the intelligence briefing was the degree to which the United States and Iraq really were preparing for the same war as if from different centuries. Colonel Bolz had his staff studying satellite-orbit tracks to determine how U.S. units on the move could maintain satellite communications linkages over distances that stretched hundreds of miles, a potential weak link in the battle plan. Planners in the Black Hole also talked about precision targeting for "maximum effect, and minimal collateral damage," in an attempt to produce the most humane military campaign in history.

Meanwhile, the Iraqis, out of necessity, had reverted back to almost prehistoric tools such as preparing oil fires in trenches and digging irrigation ditches to restrict U.S. maneuver forces to the roadways. To counter the U.S. technological advantage in satellite and robotic surveillance platforms, Iraqi commanders had made extensive use of low-tech camouflage and decoys, and intelligence indicated they would also try to burn the southern oil fields to create cover and slow the U.S. advance. The Iraqis had likewise placed significant military equipment near mosques and schools, knowing from long experience with the no-fly zones that U.S. aircraft would consider them outside the boundaries of engagement. Even the Iraqi chemical weapons that were the greatest U.S. fear were throwbacks to World War I trench warfare.

Not for the last time, I marveled at the clash of alien cultures, military and otherwise, that was at the center of this looming conflict. The wall-like berm out there in the desert delineating the Iraqi border represented a gulf in common experience and understanding as deep as time. Once it was breached, the secrets societies keep hidden even from themselves would be revealed to the world, written on a landscape of war.

CHAPTER 11

American Centurions

ON A MID-MARCH MORNING in nearby Camp New York where the Third Infantry Division was encamped, Michael Kelly came back from an intelligence briefing grinning ear to ear and looking for Ted Koppel. "You will not believe what just happened," Kelly told him, chuckling. "I just had a moment I've been waiting for all my life!"

Kelly recounted how the division's intelligence officer, a pale-looking woman in glasses who gave off the vibe of an uptight college professor, had tried to get him thrown out of the Third I.D. command post while she gave the commander a classified briefing. At first the woman tried to be subtle, rolling her eyes in Mike's direction and shaking her head. When that didn't work she asked outright that he be asked to leave.

"And General Blount just kept saying, no, he's *all right*. You can say anything you want in front of him," Mike recounted. "Can you *believe* that?"

In fact, neither the seasoned magazine writer nor the venerable ABC *Nightline* correspondent could quite fathom the unfettered access they had been granted into the inner sanctum of a wartime U.S. Army division, and they talked about it often. Though only acquainted for a matter of days, Kelly and Koppel were thrown together more by design than luck. Having read *Martyrs' Day*, Koppel instructed his executive producer in Kuwait to seek Kelly out as someone with a keen eye for detail and a historical perspective that might be useful for *Nightline*'s coverage. For his part, Kelly knew from past experience that network news crews packed the kind of resources and backup that could prove very useful to a lone war correspondent, especially one with a well-known penchant for leaving critical bits and pieces of his gear strewn behind him in a long trail of absentmindedness. That the two men hit it off immediately and became fast friends only added to their delight in what amounted to a marriage of convenience.

The Third Infantry Division's top two commanders, Maj. Gen. Buford

Blount and Brig. Gen. Lloyd Austin, had done their homework as well, and they decided to embrace the embed experiment and grant the two correspondents unprecedented access to their deliberations and plans. Both generals liked the moral certitude of Kelly's opinion columns arguing that the campaign to depose Saddam Hussein was a just war, and as a correspondent for the *Atlantic Monthly* they believed he might provide the definitive historical chronicle of the division's actions. Koppel was a widely respected journalist in the most important medium of the moment, network television. Privately, Koppel suspected that General Blount also enjoyed having at least one person around who was older, especially someone who had witnessed not a few wars firsthand, to confide in during tension-filled days.

So the two generals established a routine where one of them would brief both correspondents in tandem at the end of each day and answer whatever questions were on their minds. A tall and laconic southerner, Blount sometimes spoke so softly that a few reporters took to calling him "Mumbles," but one look in his eyes disavowed you of doing it within earshot. There were intelligence reports, Blount told Kelly and Koppel, that the Iraiqi Eleventh Division near the southern Iraqi city of Nasiriyah had taken to heart the message of all the air-dropped psychological operations flyers and might be ready to surrender. There were also reports that the Americans would be welcomed as liberators by the city fathers.

General Blount stressed that Saddam Hussein was the figurehead of the regime that needed toppling, however, and he exercised power from Baghdad. Baghdad remained the center of gravity for the campaign—not Nasiriyah, not Basra, not Najaf—and Blount intended to relentlessly drive the Third Infantry Division right to Baghdad, if need be over the dead bodies of the Republican Guard Medina Division and whatever other Iraqi units got in their way, the better to maximize the shock in Central Command's shock and awe strategy.

Early on in this period of waiting, General Austin sought Michael Kelly out and tried to explain the myriad ways the U.S. Army defied outdated Vietnam-era images or Beetle Bailey caricatures that the general felt too often defined them in the eyes of Americans who had no firsthand contact with the all-volunteer force. The gulf between a U.S. military that increasingly stressed policing the far-flung corners of an empire of global interests, and an American society that was supportive but somehow disengaged from the lives and sacrifices of its all-volunteer military, was a topic of much concern among senior military leaders. In large part that concern explained the military's embrace of the embed experiment, which senior officers like Austin saw as a way to reconnect American society with the lives of men and women in uniform who were fighting on its behalf. Austin, a tall black man with the distinct diction and dignified bearing of a Sydney Poitier, sensed in Michael Kelly a willing student of the modern U.S. Army.

While the Army's equipment may look the same as during the Desert Storm campaign that Kelly had covered a decade earlier, Austin explained, advances in information-age technologies and space-based command-and-control and surveillance systems had made them far more lethal. The U.S. military, he argued, had also learned how to fight much better as a joint team, largely putting aside the dysfunctional rivalries that in the past bedeviled combined operations by the Army, Air Force, Navy, and Marines.

"Take a hard look at all those things," Austin advised. "I also want you to get to know the people you are going to be with during this war, because many Americans have lost touch with their own military. Get to know the mid-level officers, most of whom have multiple graduate degrees. Talk to our senior non-coms who have college degrees. Watch how they lead from the front and set an example for our young soldiers."

For Americans who had little contact with the military, who still saw "military intelligence" as an oxymoron and expected generals to act like *Dr. Strangelove* parodies, what General Austin said next would truly be surprising. He paraphrased the British military historian John Keegan to the effect that Americans find warfare repulsive, but covet their freedom and have it only because they're best at war. "These American soldiers don't do it for fame, or fortune, or hope of reward," General Austin told Mike Kelly. "I want that true story of the Army told."

In the days that followed, Kelly could invariably be found in a corner of the Third Infantry Division's Command Post observing and scribbling furiously into his notepad. Whenever the division's headquarters staff of lieutenant colonels and majors changed shifts or had other moments of downtime, Mike Kelly would query them. Who developed the battle plan? What were your assumptions? Why did you decide to do it this particular way? How do the soldiers feel about the policy guiding this war, and will that affect the way they fight? So gentle was Kelly's questioning, interspersed as it was with jokes and stories about family, that many Third I.D. staff officers only realized much later that they had even been interviewed.

In one such conversation Mike Kelly confided in Lt. Col. Peter Bayer, the Third I.D. operations officer with whom Kelly would be riding on the long road to Baghdad, about his father's vehement opposition to the war to come, and the strains that disagreement had put on relations between father and son. That led to a discussion of the duty of professional soldiers to lay down their lives at the direction of political leaders they may or may not like, and policies they might or might not support. Maj. Mike Todd, the deputy operations officer, talked with Kelly about their respective upbringings, how it shaped their politics, and how they were about to witness politics played out by other, decidedly violent, means. Kelly compared photos of his children with Maj. Edward Bohemann, chief of plans for Third I.D., and talked about the Red Sox and sea-kayaking with Maj. Ross Koffman. He peppered them all with questions about how a battle plan that originally envisioned five divisions could possibly work with only a reinforced Army division and a Marine Expeditionary Force.

The driver of the Humvee he would ride into Baghdad was Sgt. Frederico Alzerreca. Mike Kelly and the young sergeant spent many hours discussing their close families, their favorite "MRE," or "Meal Ready to Eat"—Kelly's was the jambalaya—discussing almost anything, in fact, except their apprehension of what awaited them on the road ahead. Most of all they laughed and joked and laughed some more, Kelly privately confessing to Ted Koppel his utter amazement that every conversation with a twenty-year-old American soldier somehow turned out to be about beer and girls and sex. But mostly about sex.

In his lengthy conversations with generals and privates, and every stripe of U.S. officer and enlisted service member in between, Michael Kelly was putting a human face on America's modern-day centurions and fleshing out the myriad details of the Spartan world they inhabited. In truth, if you wanted to understand why early twenty-first-century America was not only the world's sole superpower, but also a nation whose military was more preeminent than any since the Roman legions, you could find few better microcosms to study than the U.S. Army's Third Infantry Division in March of 2003. Much to his excitement, Michael Kelly grasped that instinctively.

On paper, the Third Infantry Division looked similar to a division-sized unit in the armies of many nations. To the casual observer it appeared almost identical to the same U.S. Army division of ten or even twenty years earlier. There were the same 250-odd Abrams M-1 tanks practicing maneuvers in the desert, their tracks pawing the sand and their deadly 120 mm snouts wagging in the wind. Overhead, the same Apache helicopter gunships, and Air Force F-16 and Navy F-18 fighters that Michael Kelly had seen during Desert Storm were once again rehearsing midair maneuvers in a brilliant blue sky over Kuwait. In the distance, formations of Marine Corps CH-46 "Sea Knight" helicopters could be seen each day ferrying equipment from the so-called Gator Navy's amphibious ships sailing in the nearby Persian Gulf to the Marine Expeditionary Force encamped on the Third Infantry Division's right flank. Certainly the tents, trucks, bulldozers, cargo containers, forklifts, portable toilets, and other universal trappings of a modern army encampment looked the same as a decade or more ago, as did the ubiquitous U.S. Army soldiers in their chocolate-chip, desert-camouflage fatigues. All appeared just as it had been, once upon an earlier war with Iraq.

Yet even if the U.S. military of March of 2003 looked indistinguishable to the layman from the reflections of its predecessors, in reality it was an altogether different force. Despite the fact that the major weapons platforms appeared identical for the most part, those weapons' electronic eyes, ears, and precision-guided munitions, and the invisible levers that guided and coordinated their actions through electronic streams of information stretching deep to the rear and even into space, had all undergone a quiet revolution over the past decade. That technological revolution lay at the heart of Defense Secretary Donald Rumsfeld's faith in transformational warfare.

As just one indication of that change, during Desert Storm only one in twenty U.S. bombs were laser guided, and only one in five U.S. fighters were capable of employing laser-guided bombs. By 2003, three out of five bombs dropped during Operation Iraqi Freedom would be precision guided, every U.S. fighter aircraft in the Iraqi theater could guide precision weapons, and intelligence gathered from space-based satellites could at times be relayed directly into their cockpits even while in flight.

Maj. Mark Shaaber, an information officer in Kuwait who specialized in "C4ISR," or command, control, communications, computers, intelligence, surveillance, and reconnaissance, tried to explain that technological revolution. The Army's own doctrine and tactics, he conceded, had yet to fully catch up with the advancements in technology realized over the past decade. "Our tanks and trucks don't drive any faster today than a decade ago, nor do our aircraft fly any faster. Our soldiers still have to eat, drink water, and be supplied from the rear by the same logistics line. What has changed dramatically, however, is our ability to gain better situational awareness of the battlefield so that we can position our weapons and forces better, make decisions faster, and transmit orders rapidly to units on the move who can implement them with less hesitation and probing of the enemy. In the larger scheme, that has made us a much quicker-reacting force than even ten years ago."

For Michael Kelly, signs of that technological revolution were everywhere inside the main headquarters tent for Third I.D., where he spent countless hours prior to the war watching and asking questions. The central focus of the command post was not a traditional acetate map board marked by grease pencil, but rather a living map projected onto oversized video screens and fronted by staff officers working on laptop computers around a horseshoe-shaped desk, each station demarking a war-fighting specialty and area of responsibility: operations, intelligence, logistics, fire support, air defense, engineers. The screens glowed with maps of the Iraqi area of operations drawn from classified imaging satellites, meticulously detailing the positions of friendly and suspected enemy forces. Concentric circles dotted the map, representing coverage radiuses for advanced Patriot-3 antimissile batteries, and streaming video showed real-time images of enemy territory and formations relayed from robotic surveillance aircraft, or UAVs (unmanned aerial vehicles).

Friendly forces on the map display were clearly identified in blue using a satellite tracking system that monitored electronic emitters broadcasting from every U.S. unit. The Blue Force Tracker system was originally designed to avoid the tragic accidental targeting of friendly forces by allied aircraft during Desert Storm, but its most remarkable contribution to operations was to increase vital situational awareness of the position of U.S. forces. Meanwhile, where Desert Storm commanders had complained about the stinginess of the national intelligence community in releasing satellite imagery and strategic signals intelligence, both sets of information streamed through V Corps and into the Third I.D. command post, as did information from U-2 spy planes and Joint Stars ground-surveillance aircraft, as well as updates from Special Forces units and Army scouts on the ground in Iraq. Liaison units from U.S. Space Command in Colorado Springs, Colorado, were on hand to help tactical commanders access the entire panoply of space-based intelligence. All of that information in turn was crunched and fused by high-speed computers using a special computer algorithm that could handle one thousand data inputs an hour, automatically updating without human prodding the suspected positions and movements of Iraqi units, which appeared on the map display in red.

Because it recognized no artificial boundaries between services or individual systems, between space-based or human intelligence, that technological fusion had forced upon the separate services a degree of cooperation in combined operations that would have been unthinkable even a decade ago. During Desert Storm, for instance, the senior Navy component commander on his ship in the Persian Gulf did not even have electronic access to the "air tasking order," or the daily bombing schedule, because of incompatible communications systems between the Navy and Air Force. The paper order had to be hand-delivered out to his ship each day.

Even if the national intelligence community had been willing to part with the most sensitive space-based intelligence in 1991, processes and technology of that time would have prevented them from getting it into the hands of commanders in the theater quick enough to be of use. By contrast, in 2003 the numerous major echelons of U.S. military commands in theater all shared the common tactical picture of the battlefield that was projected on the Third I.D.'s electronic display. It wasn't a perfect picture by any means. There was still an opaque overlay of subjective guesses and technological glitches and "unknown unknowns," but that common picture pierced a critical veil in the ever-present fog of war and provided a level of situational awareness unprecedented in modern warfare.

Especially for journalists who had limited exposure to the U.S. military, the American soldiers and Marines operating all of that complicated technology and lethal machinery initially seemed throwbacks to an earlier time. The humorist and author P. J. O'Rourke, who was in Kuwait and in frequent touch with his friend Mike Kelly, said after a visit that the mid-level officers reminded him of an idealized version of a squeaky clean America that may or may not have existed sometime around the 1950s. "The lieutenant colonels and majors all look like dads in that 'Suddenly it's 1960!' Chrysler commercial," he observed. "A few of them even smoke pipes! The captains are all presidents of the Sigma Xi House circa 1962. And the lieutenants and corporals all look like they're twelve years old!"

Embedded journalists like Michael Kelly peered longer into the face of the U.S. military. He got to know the people behind that clean-cut image and came to realize that, underneath the short haircuts, the American soldiers of 2003 were far different from their draft-era counterparts and unlike any U.S. force the nation had ever fielded. As professional soldiers they were on average older, better educated, more likely to be married, and more likely to be minorities than their forebears. Among them were far more gun-slinging, rifle-toting female soldiers, who followed in the footsteps of the forty-one thousand women deployed during Desert Storm. A milestone of shared sacrifice, Desert Storm led to the opening of many combat and combat-support posts to women during the 1990s, including jobs on warships, in the cockpits of combat aircraft, and in Army air-defense brigades. In fact, the commander of the Thirty-first Air Defense "Patriot" brigade attached to Third I.D. in Kuwait was Col. Heidi Brown, from Ft. Bliss, Texas.

There was also more gray at the temples of many of the soldiers deployed to the Kuwaiti desert, a telltale sign of the increasing integration of "citizen soldier" Reservists into the close-knit fabric of the all-volunteer force as it stretched to cover the global commitments of a superpower. During nearly four decades of the Cold War there had been only two presidential activations of the National Guard and Reserves, while there had been five presidential call-ups just since the fall of the Berlin Wall: Desert Storm, the Balkans, patrolling the northern and southern no-fly zones over Iraq, Afghanistan, and once again Iraq.

That record pointed to another critical way that America's modern-day centurions were different from their predecessors of even a decade before—real-world experience. The rank and file of the force that prevailed in Desert Storm were soldiers who had never seen combat during the Cold War, led by combat veterans who had known bitter defeat in Vietnam. With the Vietnam generation of officers now fading almost entirely from the scene, the U.S. military that was gathered in Kuwait in March of 2003 was filled with professional soldiers seasoned by a decade's worth of war and contingency operations—Panama, Iraq, Somalia, Haiti, Bosnia, Kosovo, Afghanistan—led by officers who had known mainly victory. That seasoning gave the U.S. military a brashness and deep reservoir of confidence. It also saddled them with great expectations.

Especially for journalists from national media in Washington, New York, and Boston, there was one final characteristic of the U.S. military that was striking. Almost none of the sons and daughters of America's political, cultural, and business elite were present in their ranks. Few of the youngsters who lined up for hours to call home before crossing into Iraq were phoning Congressmen or cabinet secretaries or corporate presidents. The more you talked with them the more you realized that these were the progeny of police officers and firemen, of schoolteachers and farmers, and of former career military men. They were the graduates of small-town colleges and state universities and the service academies. Even in a time of global war, the United States had become comfortable relying on a permanent warrior class drawn almost exclusively from the ranks of America's middle and working classes to defend the far reaches of its empire and do its fighting and dying. For the first time since Vietnam, those U.S. soldiers were about to enter a war on which the nation itself was deeply divided, making the gap between the elites who decide on war in Washington and this broad swath of working-class America sent to fight it all the more striking.

In those waning days before war the homesickness that had been kept at bay by eighteen-hour days and adrenaline began to sweep through the ranks like a fever, and everyone who could find the time and the means phoned home. Michael Kelly was on one such call with his young son Tom when General Austin found him. At Kelly's urging Austin spoke briefly with the boy, who was excited to talk with the deep-voiced general over a satellite phone. Later, Tom told his father that he had the Army figured out.

"There's probably a general just in charge of fixing tanks," said Tom. "And another general just in charge of getting food."

"Yes," Mike Kelly told his son. "They're called sergeants."

At one point during those final days of waiting, Mike Kelly and Lt. Col. Peter Bayer, the Operations Officer for the division, were having one of their heart-to-hearts. Bayer, a tall and ramrod-straight soldier with piercing eyes, confided to Kelly that he had a nightmare the night before that they had been hit by chemical weapons, the entire division disappearing in his dream into a poison cloud. Michael Kelly recounted his own recent nightmare, one that had recurred throughout his entire career. "It's always the same," said Kelly. "I wake up to find that somehow I missed the big story."

The weather began to kick up in mid-March, with seasonal storms of increasing intensity suggesting a sixth battle that had failed to make General Wallace's top-five list: sandstorms that swept across the desert like hurricanes over the open ocean, gathering in strength and intensity until they blotted out the sun and stars in a giant wave. One such storm descended at dusk while Bernie Weinraub and I were trying to file stories, blocking the signal of our satellite phones. We tied handkerchiefs around our faces and donned goggles, but by the time we exited the media tent to try and find our fifty-man sleeping tent the night was pitch dark and howling. The beams of our flashlights penetrated only a few feet into the murk.

By the time we finally found our tent, a walk that usually took ten minutes had consumed well over an hour, and at times we had come perilously close to stumbling blind into razor-sharp concertina wire. Both of us were as covered in grime as coal miners. Dust was caked in our nostrils and scratched at the back of our throats; it hung in a viscous brown cloud inside a tent illuminated by crazily swinging lightbulbs, where row upon row of huddled forms were trying to ride the storm out inside their sleeping bags. The only sound was the whipsaw flapping of the tent and the shriek of the wind outside. God help us all, I thought, if we get caught in something like this in the middle of a war.

The next morning the storm had passed and soldiers climbed out of sleeping bags that were covered with a thick layer of sand. The tent filled with the sounds of hacking coughs, and there was none of the normal jaunty bravado. Everyone seemed out of sorts. "It happens after every sandstorm," a sergeant told me as we used bottled water to try and scrub the grime off. "Something about the drop in barometric pressure puts people on edge."

Lt. Col. Joe Richard was certainly no exception. As we walked down the long line of soldiers waiting at the entrance to the mess tent that morning I could hear him muttering under his breath. As we ate, the primary cause of his irritation became clear. Word had come down that the war would start within days, and Turkey had definitely denied use of its territory for the Fourth Infantry Division to open a northern front. On hearing the news, some of Richard's foul mood began to wear off on me.

Of course I had closely covered from Washington, D.C., the diplomatic debacle in the run-up to war, but out in the desert the dimensions of that failure seemed both larger and more personal. For soldiers waiting on the eve of war in the Kuwaiti desert, Turkey's decision seemed the last in a long series of insulting slaps from supposed friends such as the French and Germans. Even the Saudi Arabians had refused to let the United States launch a front from territory that U.S. forces had fought and died defending from Iraq a decade earlier. Without a northern front launched from Turkey, two Republican Guard divisions positioned north of Baghdad would now be free to reposition themselves to confront us as U.S. forces closed from the south along stretched-thin logistics lines. Instead of feeling part of a grand coalition as in 1991, U.S. and British forces in the Kuwaiti desert in March of 2003 felt they were in an "us against the world" fight.

"I hope Saddam attacks Israel again, only this time they just nuke him in return," said Joe Richard. "Save us all a lot of trouble and heartache. Just look around you. I guarantee you some of these boys won't be going home."

With the clock ticking down, I broached a sensitive subject. Plans didn't call for the V Corps Headquarters to move into Iraq until day three or four of the war, and I didn't want to cover a war in Iraq from the Kuwaiti desert. Somewhat to my surprise, Joe Richard was sympathetic. After clearing it with General Wallace he reattached me to the V Corps Tactical Operations Center or "TAC," which would follow directly behind lead elements of the Third Infantry Division sweeping through the western Iraqi desert, and serve as General Wallace's forward command post during the war. I was to be the only journalist embedded with the V Corps TAC. Dropping me off at my new assignment, Joe Richard shook my hand and said good-bye in a way that suggested in the future being more careful what I wished for. "Good luck, James," Richard said. "You're going to be in the shit now."

CHAPTER 12

March Madness

THE SOUND CAME with such suddenness and ferocity that all heads craned skyward as if in supplication. Somewhere overhead an Iraqi ballistic missile was boring back through the atmosphere at terminal velocity. Just to the right of our 110-vehicle convoy, a Patriot antimissile battery answered, the sparkling contrails of two missiles clearly visible as they soared toward an impact point nearly six miles overhead. Vehicles lurched to a stop on the shoulder of the blacktop and hundreds of soldiers scrambled out in a fire drill of flailing arms and legs as they donned chemical protection suits and gas masks. A multi-wheeled Fox detection vehicle drove down the length of the column, "sniffing" for chemical or biological agents. Within minutes the Patriot battery reported a successful intercept, confirming that the Scud's projected impact point was less than a third of a mile directly in front of the convoy.

The war the United States unleashed early that morning of March 20, 2003, was officially joined.

In one of the command vehicles shepherding the V Corps Tactical Headquarters toward Iraq, where it would command the Army's invasion and direct the battle for Baghdad, Lt. Col. Rick Nohmer turned around to check on his charges, which included a reporter for *National Journal* magazine. A tightly wound Army Ranger and West Pointer, Nohmer had the infantryman's knack for growing more calm even as situations became more tense.

"Well, I guess that will get everyone's head in the game," he said.

Even after the interminable months of anticipation and buildup, the Iraq war had begun as wars so often did, unexpectedly. Sometime in the previous night the United States had fired cruise missiles at a structure in downtown Baghdad in a surprise strike at Saddam Hussein, jumping the scheduled start of the war up by twenty-four hours. Because the air tasking order could not be adjusted fast enough to compensate, the last minute change meant that the Third Infantry Division would initially cross into Iraq with little close air support or the deep air strikes against Iraqi forces that had been anticipated. That morning over coffee I had asked an intelligence officer what gives.

"We almost got the bastard," he said. "Some idiot in his inner circle used his cell phone."

As our convoy crested a ridge at dusk on March 20, near the border between Kuwait and Iraq, the vista brought home the enormity of the endeavor ahead. Spread out on the high-desert bluff before us, on the far western flank of the U.S. forces poised in the Kuwaiti desert, were the three hundred-plus vehicles of the main command headquarters of the Third Infantry Division, which would spearhead the invasion. Clearly visible in attack position on the desert floor beyond was the "heavy metal"—the M-1 Abrams tanks and Bradley Fighting Vehicles of the division's Second Brigade Combat team—which would clear our path through Iraq.

The Third I.D.'s other two brigade combat teams were assigned the objectives nearest to Kuwait in southeastern Iraq. In a separate pincer-like column, a Marine Expeditionary Force accompanied by British forces would seize the strategic southern town of Basra and attack toward Baghdad on the Army's right flank. While it was anticipated that those other forces would encounter the most fighting in the first days of what was now being called Operation Iraqi Freedom, the secret battle plan envisioned this flanking force as the main effort in setting the stage for the assault on Baghdad. It was to conduct a three-day surprise march up the desert wastelands of western Iraq in order to bring the fight early and decisively to the Republican Guard Medina Division guarding the southern approaches to the Iraqi capital. If the Medina chose to stand and fight, U.S. commanders meant not just to defeat it, but to visit upon it such utter destruction that the blow would knock the will to fight out of the entire Republican Guard.

Once the Tactical Headquarters convoy was arranged in a box formation, with military police Humvees with mounted M-40 grenade launchers posted as perimeter security, soldiers scrambled to set up their cots in the dying light. The late afternoon haze hung like a dark curtain on the horizon that the sun burned through only as a white orb. As I sat taking in the otherworldly landscape, a large black scorpion made a line directly for me as if relaying a personal message. Just before it reached my feet, the scorpion disappeared beneath the boot of Sgt. 1st Class David Bell, my Humvee driver and a good argument for why the noncommissioned officer corps is considered the backbone of the U.S. Army.

"Sergeant Bell, shame on you! We're not supposed to disturb the local wildlife," said Rick Nohmer, before shouting out a warning. "Listen up people, better check before putting your boots on in the morning! A creepy crawler already nearly got our journalist!"

"Don't mind Colonel Nohmer," Bell told me quietly. "He's just a little crazy."

If so, then I figured Nohmer was well in tune with the tenor of the times. The day before General Wallace had visited his forward command post to wish us Godspeed in the critical days ahead, confirming that the decision to launch Operation Iraqi Freedom had finally been made. Wallace would be traveling in two experimental tracked command vehicles with more communications and computer power than an entire division headquarters during Vietnam, another indication of the transformational technology on which so much now depended. If all went well, his mobile command post would meet up with our tactical headquarters sometime in the next three to five days at Objective Rams on the outskirts of Najaf and within a hundred miles of Baghdad.

"Last night in a speech, President Bush gave Saddam Hussein one final chance to leave Iraq. The President said that if Saddam doesn't leave Iraq on his own, then we will do it for him, and we are going to, because that's the right thing to do. It's time for Saddam to go," Wallace told the assembled troops, standing on the runner of a five-ton truck and surveying his tactical headquarters staff. Recounting the wars Saddam had waged on his neighbors, and the gassing of his own people and others with chemical weapons, the usually soft-spoken Wallace cast the war ahead in terms instinctively grasped by American soldiers.

"This war is not about religion, or occupation, or oil. It's about liberation," said Wallace. "This is an opportunity for us to give back to the Iraqi people that which is theirs—their country and their way of life. It's also a chance for us to give back to our own country a sense of security they haven't felt since September 11. Since then our families and friends have been living in the shadow of fear—fear that weapons of mass destruction will fall into the hands of the terrorists. I believe, and I hope you believe, that Saddam and members of his regime are perfectly capable of giving such weapons to the terrorists. I don't know about you, but I want my family and friends to live in a world where they don't worry about leaving their homes. I want my grandchildren to grow up in a world where they don't fear getting on an airplane. *That's* what this war is about!"

"HOO-AHH!" The Army's all-purpose retort had barked from two hundred-odd throats that morning. Less than forty-eight hours after the pep rally the soldiers of V Corps Tactical Headquarters had shaken off the repercussion of an Iraqi missile attack, their heads very much in the game.

Shortly after nightfall on that first day of the war, the officers and senior sergeants of V Corps TAC gathered on the bluff to witness the Third

Infantry Division's scheduled artillery barrage of Iraqi border posts. The very fact that the tactical headquarters of an entire Corps was exposing itself so close to the front line was a clear indication of the primacy put on tempo and synchronization in the campaign. Whereas the Desert Storm ground campaign of 1991 was preceded by thirty-eight days of aerial bombardment, U.S. commanders would launch Iraqi Freedom with nearly simultaneous air and ground assaults, hoping in blitzkrieg fashion to overwhelm Iraqi command-and-control capabilities and hopefully convince the enemy to quickly quit the fight. They also reasoned that Iraqi forces reeling from a simultaneous, coordinated onslaught would be less able to mount an attack with chemical or biological weapons, to set fire to southern oil wells, or deduce the vulnerabilities inherent in the transformational U.S. battle plan.

Standing next to me on the bluff was Lt. Col. Rob Baker, field commander of the V Corps Tactical Headquarters convoy and V Corps' deputy operations officer. In the coming days Baker would be responsible for guiding our convoy through the desert and whatever it held, and to help serve as General Wallace's designated eyes and ears for the battle to come.

In the field you can generally tell the good officers by how they handled the stress and fatigue, and as I was soon to discover Baker was among the best. A man in his early forties, with an athlete's bearing and the quiet air of natural command, Baker had been an academic and athletic standout in high school and had hoped to land a full athletic scholarship to college. When one didn't materialize Baker went to West Point to play football and save his parents the burden of paying for college. There on the U.S. Military Academy's tree-shaded campus overlooking the Hudson River, Baker had listened to instructors and mentors, to men he admired, talk unself-consciously of a duty to serve others, of the honor in discipline and self-sacrifice, of a greater good in service to country. Duty, honor, country. Like so many of the officers now poised to lead the United States into battle, Baker had found that call to duty resonating deep within. So while high school friends like Cal Ripkin had gone on to sports fame, and other friends had made fortunes in business, Baker had lived the vagabond life of the Army officer and uprooted his family countless times in order that one day he might stand on a bluff like this, poised to lead soldiers into battle.

Standing on that bluff, I asked Baker what were his greatest concerns. Simply getting the tactical headquarters and his people and equipment to the secret staging area near Najaf, nearly three hundred miles away, was as far ahead as he cared to think. "The move we're about to make will be unprecedented in terms of the pace of our operations and the distances covered," Baker told me. "We'll be moving in a matter of days forces that would have taken months to advance during World War II. That's why it's so important that we keep the pressure on the Iraqi army nonstop with deep attacks, with Air Force close air support, and with our maneuver ground forces. We know we're superior technologically to the Iraqi army. The place we'll be taking risks is in stretching our logistics lines hundreds of miles through territory that may not be secure once our lead elements have passed by."

When I asked what gave the Army confidence that it could advance on such aggressive time lines, Baker recalled his experience as an infantry platoon commander during the 1983 invasion of Grenada. At that time U.S. forces were operating on dated *National Geographic* maps, and at one point they very nearly bombed the American students they were sent to rescue as a result. Communications systems were so incompatible between the separate services that Army commanders on the island had to use AT&T calling cards to route through the United States requests for close air support from Navy ships visible just off shore. By contrast, Baker pointed out that V Corps TAC would be guided in the journey to come by satellite imaging maps, precise GPS locators, and satellite communications. They had maps of Baghdad that numbered every single building in the city and showed their contours down to one meter of resolution, and thought nothing of it.

So technology really had so dramatically changed the nature of warfare?

Baker thought about that one a while. "You know, until you see the physical carnage of battle—the dead and bloated bodies, the rot—the reality doesn't fully sink in of what this business is really all about. Once we see that it will become real."

Right on time at 1700 "Zulu," or Greenwich mean time, the big guns of the Third Infantry Division artillery brigade opened up on Iraqi border posts. Muzzle flashes flickered across the dark desert floor below us like lightning squalls, the distant thunder of their impact sounding the approach of an angry giant. For soldiers on the precipice, the group was generally subdued and quiet. Everyone understood without saying so or seeing it yet that somewhere out there real people were really dying. I doubted very much that the poor souls left for fodder out there in isolated border posts cared much for the regime they were being sacrificed for. At that moment we all understood that there was no going back. After standing uneasily at the crossroads for so many months, America had chosen war.

By midmorning on March 21 our convoy was trailing the heavy metal of Second Brigade across the border at Al Abraq, a lonely and deserted police station on the Kuwaiti side of the line. A buffer zone of electric fences had already been breached and mangled by the passing of many tracked vehicles. After we drove past one of the border posts destroyed in last night's barrage, Rick Nohmer checked the coordinates on his GPS receiver and confirmed that we were officially in Iraq. Maj. Joe Samek, an engineer attached to V Corps TAC, gazed out the window of our Humvee at the destruction. "You know, this is the first time I've been in a foreign country uninvited."

Sometime later in midmorning the convoy left the blacktop and steered westward into the Sabra al Hijarah, a flat and featureless desert primarily inhabited by scattered Bedouins and members of the poisonous sack family—lizards, snakes, and scorpions. "Say good-bye to the hardball," Sergeant Bell said, turning off the two-lane roadway that all of us would soon miss.

Riding herd on a convoy of massive machinery broken into three separate "cells" and stretching eight miles over broken terrain requires surprisingly intricate orchestration. Ours was but one of scores of support columns consisting of thousands of vehicles, all jockeying for position on what amounted to goat trails in the Sabra al Hijarah. Colonel Nohmer was constantly on one of the command vehicle's three tactical radios, trying to maintain the integrity of his column in an ever-present dust cloud. Vehicles that broke down were either quickly repaired by the maintenance crew or strapped to giant tow trucks called HEMMITs (heavy expanded mobility tactical truck), lest a delay break up the column. After a certain point, breakdowns became more or less constant and later we even passed one HEMMIT being towed by another.

"Talk about your monkey fucking a football," Sergeant Bell said with a whistle. "Yep," said Nohmer. "Murphy is with us today."

In the middle of the night, the convoys converged at a set of GPS coordinates on the first of three refuel-on-the-move sites in a patch of otherwise featureless desert. Soldiers acting as refuelers appeared asleep on their feet, standing under arc lights in a cold rain as they topped off endless lines of vehicles from fuel trucks for the next leg of the trip north. Over the next eighteen hours, those refuelers would service more than fifteen hundred vehicles, yet before the nearly fifty-hour road march was done some of the lead convoys would nevertheless stall in place for lack of fuel. At one point a cruise missile heading for Baghdad passed low overhead, its unearthly whine receding slowly into the dark like a banshee wail. In the first twenty-four hours of the war Navy ships in the Persian Gulf would fire thirty-six Tomahawk cruise missiles at command-and-control targets in Baghdad.

After a sleepless night and morning of travel, we had yet to encounter any sign of indigenous life save for a lone camel on the horizon. Our only connection with the rest of the war was BBC World Service coming in over a shortwave radio. There were also reports of oil fields burning outside Basra and the downing of a helicopter ferrying British troops that resulted in high casualties. "Sergeant Bell, see if you can pick up March Madness on AFN," Major Samek said, referring to Armed Forces Network and the NCAA basketball tournament. Then he thought better of it. "I guess we're having our own March Madness out here."

By midafternoon on March 22 the scenery began to change. The flat, barren expanses of the Sabra al Hijarah gave way to a high desert landscape of elevated bluffs and plateaus, dotted with scrub brush and even a few scattered palm trees. After picking up a two-lane blacktop, the convoy turned from the western desert east toward the Euphrates, passing through the oasis town of Al Salman. An old fortress stood on a hill overlooking palm groves that constituted the first available shade we had seen in a hundred-mile radius. The roadside of the Shiite town was dotted with Arab men in traditional robes and young children, flashing the victory sign, some putting their hands over their hearts in Arab salute, others shouting "America, we love you." A young, olive-skinned girl in a bright red dress waved a miniature American flag. Al Salman was the first taste of liberation that any of us had experienced, and it had a sweetness that none of us would ever forget.

By late afternoon of the second day, synchronicity ground to a halt as multiple conveys converged on congested two-lane roads. Senior officers from different units could be seen shouting and gesturing at one another at various crossroads marked "Route Hurricane" and "Route Tornado" in crude, hand-painted signs placed there by advanced scouts. Everyone was trying to keep their convoy intact and gain a precious few hours on the march northward. The treacherous wadis and the axle-deep sands of the western Iraqi desert had proved far worse than analysts had anticipated based on satellite photos. In particular, dust the consistency of talcum powder had slowed the anticipated rate of advance to roughly half that expected. At various points Humvees would disappear in pools of dust that cascaded over their windshields in blinding waves.

After more than thirty hours in a straight desert march, tempers grew short and reflexes dulled, and the accidents came in clusters. At each pause the heads of many drivers drooped to their chests, and glassy-eyed commanders struggled even to remember their own radio call signs. All along the route, overturned cargo vehicles, fuel trucks, and broken Humvees littered the landscape. I counted at least five disabled bridging vehicles—old M-60 battle tanks retrofitted to carry giant bridge spans—which could spell trouble if the Iraqis were successful in destroying key bridges across the Euphrates. Before even attempting a contested river crossing, Third Infantry Division would lose 70 percent of its mobile bridging equipment due to mechanical failure.

After a second refueling stop, a V Corps truck driver fell asleep at the wheel of a five-ton transport truck, rear-ending a Humvee and trailer, destroying a generator, and in turn being rear-ended by a tow truck whose radiator was smashed. Colonel Baker decided to halt the convoy and let its weary drivers snatch a few hours sleep. Pulling the convoy into a "box formation" reminiscent of settlers circling the wagons in Indian territory, Baker placed the MP escorts on the perimeter and gave his soldiers a few hours of much-needed rest. The maintenance pit crew worked through much of the night, however, cannibalizing parts and patching together broken vehicles for tomorrow's march. Under a brilliant, star-studded sky the lights of similar encampments were visible stretched across the flatlands, and the unmistakable clanking and gnashing of tanks and heavy-tracked vehicles echoed in the night.

In a nearby tent, Baker and his deputy, Lt. Col. Eric Wagenaar, had set up a temporary "hot" TAC, monitoring the tactical radio net of lead elements of the Third Infantry Division just ahead, and relaying information via secure satellite communications back to V Corps Headquarters at Camp Virginia, Kuwait. Until it could fully set up operations at Objective Rams, acting as a communications relay was one of the major functions of the V Corps TAC. Already the strains that the Pentagon's transformational war plan was putting on equipment designed around more traditional doctrine were evident. The mainstay FM radios in Army formations only had a fifteen- to twenty-mile range, barely enough to keep a single convoy in sync during such a rapid and deep advance. Meanwhile, the mobile subscriber equipment (MSE) radios, the Army's primary means of data transmission over long distances, could only operate from a stationary position, hardly suitable for a nonstop road march. That left Third I.D. advance formations to rely on the V Corps TAC as a relay for satellite communications, along with the relatively few tactical satellite radios and iridium satellite phones they possessed.

According to the message traffic that came that second night, Iraqi Freedom had unfolded pretty much as planned in its initial days. After capturing the Talil Air Base near Nasiriyah, the Third Division's First and Third Brigade Combat Teams were conducting the "capture and pass" hopscotch of a combat division on the offensive, moving up Highway 1 from the south and closing on the nearby town of Samawah. Just ahead of us, 3/7th Cavalry Regiment had captured key bridges just to the west of Samawah, but had immediately been engaged by mortars, small-arms fire and rocket-propelled grenades (RPG). In addition to regular Iraqi troops, the 3/7th Cav commander reported repelling fierce attacks by paramilitary irregulars driving light pickup trucks mounted with .50-caliber machine guns. Tomorrow looked to be an eventful day.

As I lay on my cot staring at the night sky, Sergeant Ball pointed out the belt of Orion. Inside the vehicle the shortwave radio was broadcasting BBC war reports. News of the first American soldiers and Marines killed in action came to us over the airwaves. "You know, this whole operation is so similar to how we train that in a way it's hard to grasp that it's real this time," said Ball. "Hearing about those KIAs and casualties, though, kind of makes it hit home."

Early the next morning soldiers of the V Corps TAC were pulled reluctantly out of their sleeping bags by shouts in the dark, and everyone was told to pack up and be ready to shove off two hours earlier than expected. The Second Brigade Combat Team had run into heavy resistance in trying to clear Objective Rams, a desolate spot just west of the Shiite holy city of An Najaf that V Corps battle planners had chosen as the staging area for the fight with the Medina Division. The V Corps TAC was needed to help coordinate close air support for Second Brigade, and to launch a deep strike by Apaches against elements of the Republican Guard Medina Division that night, before anticipated bad weather blew in.

In fact, the Air Tasking Order still had yet to adjust to the campaign kicking off twenty-four hours early, and there had been very little air support for lead maneuver elements or deep attacks to keep pressure on the Medina and other Republican Guard forces south of Baghdad. The convoy's MP detachment was told to test fire their weapons, and every soldier in the convoy locked fresh magazines into their M-16 rifles and sidearms.

As the convoy approached Objective Rams late in the afternoon of March 23, the sights and sounds of nearby combat were everywhere. Broken down M-1 tanks blocked a shoulder of the road and an overturned fuel tanker lay on its side beside a bridge. Three thick plumes of black smoke snaked from the near horizon. Over the tactical radio network, lead elements of the Second Brigade could be heard fighting just ahead, the urgency of combat unmistakable in their voices. To the continued surprise of U.S. commanders, outgunned Iraqi irregulars were standing their ground and fighting to the death at Objective Rams, and before the battle was over the bodies of an estimated 350 paramilitary fighters would litter the area. Adding to the surreal scene were dust devils that skirted across the broken landscape and bottled the light of a late afternoon sun in swirling vortexes.

By nightfall on March 23, roughly four days into the war, V Corps TAC was launching Apache attack helicopters from the Eleventh Aviation Brigade directly against elements of the Republican Guard Medina Division in the area around Karbala. Standing outside the tent that night, Lt. Col. Eric Wagenaar and I watched as the Apaches roared overhead one by one, and then became dark silhouettes against the twinkling lights of nearby Najaf.

Up to that moment, the Iraqi Freedom campaign had largely lived up to its transformational billing. In just over fifty hours a corps-sized U.S. Army combat force had traveled nearly two hundred miles over difficult and dangerous terrain, guided by a constellation of surveillance satellites and airborne drones, and was launching a deep strike at the enemy's center of gravity with Apache gunships. Among the dog-tired troops who made the journey, the knowledge that no other army in history had traveled so far on such tight time lines was a point of considerable pride. Meanwhile, in northern Iraq, company-sized detachments of Special Operations Forces were working with local Kurdish forces, employing hit-and-run tactics and acting as laser-wielding human sensors to bring in devastating U.S. airpower, tying down a number of regular Iraqi army divisions.

"You know, if you can't get a rise out of seeing those Apaches launch out into the night, then something is wrong with you," Wagenaar said, his voice rising to be heard above the backwash of the helicopter rotors. The deputy officer in charge of the V Corps TAC, Wagenaar was the likable offspring of Dutch immigrants whose love of their adopted country inspired all three sons to join the U.S. Army. At that moment, he expressed a sense of awe as well as anxiety about what the U.S. military was about to undertake. "I worry about those pilots," he said. "We're sending them against some really tough targets tonight."

Inside the bubble of an AH-64 Apache cockpit at night, the world seems weightless and liquid and as benign as a dark womb, but Lt. Col. Mike Barbee knew better. Commander of the Sixth Squadron of the Eleventh Attack Helicopter Regiment, Barbee was leading his "troop" of Apaches north on the night of March 23 to take the fight directly to the Medina Division for the first time in the war. Because the launch of the war was jumped up a day and the air tasking had yet to fully adjust, the Medina remained unscathed and the armor and artillery of its Fourteen, Second, and Tenth Brigades were sitting astride the Third Infantry Division's path of advance just to the north of Karbala. If Iraqi intelligence got wind of our position, the Medina Division also posed a potential threat to the key Logistics Staging Area being assembled at Objective Rams.

In truth, the decision to even launch the Apaches that night was controversial, and indicative of the significant risks inherent in Central Command's transformational battle plan. The race to Objective Rams had left the Apache regiment short of the fuel, communications equipment, and base security called for in Army doctrine. The lack of fuel in turn forced planners to plot fairly direct south to north attack routes that would take the Apaches near several major towns and cities. Meanwhile, intelligence on the exact whereabouts of the Medina brigades was also somewhat sketchy, with Eleventh AHR intelligence officers plotting target grids with about a 75 percent certainty they actually contained enemy forces. As if that wasn't enough, the staging area chosen for the Apaches was covered in the same loose "moon dust" that had bedeviled the advancing U.S. forces virtually from the start.

Given the small size of the U.S. invasion force, however, the Eleventh AHR represented a major portion of V Corps' firepower. In a nod to Secretary of Defense Rumsfeld's insistence that it focus on agility and high technology rather than on more conventional force packages, U.S. Central Command had gone heavy on the deployment of Apaches, specifically in lieu of a more traditional mix of heavier and slower artillery systems. Commanders were thus anxious to get the Apaches into the fight before anticipated bad weather grounded them, possibly for days. Tellingly, at the final "Go/No Go" decision brief, not one commander had dissented from the decision to launch the Apaches.

Yet from the very beginning the Apache mission was bedeviled by surprises. One of the attack helicopters crashed on takeoff, its pilots blinded and disoriented by the impenetrable cloud of dust kicked up by its heavy rotors. Meanwhile, the story relayed to Colonel Barbee and his pilots by their infrared night-vision optics deviated from the prepared script in bothersome ways. The computerized *FalconView* route planning and mission rehearsal system that the Apache pilots had used to plot and practice the attack on Medina elements around Karbala indicated that the ingress route passed primarily over rural areas. Instead of the comfortable terrain of dark patches that Barbee had expected to see below, however, was an electric spiderweb of lights that clearly indicated towns and cities and nearly uninterrupted urban sprawl. Everyone understood cities spelled trouble.

Even using Apache helicopter gunships as a deep-strike weapon was a departure from their more traditional role scouting out ahead or flying over the shoulder of U.S. ground forces. A troop of Apaches from the 101st Airborne Division had actually begun the 1991 Persian Gulf War with a one thousand-plus-mile mission to take out early warning radar sites in western Iraq, confirming the destruction with their gun cameras. But that mission had been flown over open desert, where there was no danger the black aircraft could be silhouetted against city lights.

Colonel Barbee and the rest of the Apache pilots and gunners drew confidence from the powerful "Iron Birds" that reared and bucked beneath their fingertips. The Apaches were armored and bristling with lethal weaponry, including Hellfire laser-guided missiles, 70 mm Hydra rockets, and a 30 mm chain gun that swiveled in unison with the opera-tor's head movements. Flying low and relatively slow at night, however, they could also be ranged by virtually any weapon in the enemy arsenal, from shoulder-fired SA-7 missiles and the truck-mounted antiaircraft guns much favored by Iraqi forces, to a standard AK-47 rifle.

As Barbee would recount to me days later in an interview, just as his Apache troop was approaching the target objective, a very queer thing happened. The lights around Karbala extinguished as if tripped by a cir-cuit breaker. It was almost like a signal of some kind. Before the Apache pilots could even guess at the source of the blackout or its possible mean-ing, the lights came back on in a blinding flash. And with them a wither-ing barrage of antiaircraft fire from virtually every direction, licking skyward with deadly tongues of tracer fire. After nearly a decade of play-ing a deadly game of cat-and-mouse with U.S. pilots enforcing no-fly zones over Iraq, Iraqi air-defense troops had devised a decidedly low-tech but effective early warning system. And the Apache pilots had just flown into their trap.

Colonel Barbee and his pilots initially tried to continue locating the Medina Division targets even as their aircraft were pinged by small-arms fire, but repeated hits quickly indicated that enemy gunners were draw-ing a dangerously accurate bead and there were airbursts and explosions from rocket-propelled grenades or antiaircraft artillery. Barbee and his troop broke off the main attack and swung their chain guns around to suppress the murderous fire, their heads on a swivel and the chattering recoil of the 30 mm cannons shuddering through the airframe and adding to the confusing din of battle. Looking around, Barbee realized his pilots were holding back their suppression fire out of fear of causing collateral damage, a concern that had been repeatedly drummed into them in plan-ning for a military campaign billed as the most humane in history. As numerous tracer streams continued to probe the night sky with lethal flame, blinding Apache gunners peering through light-sensitive thermal goggles, Barbee failed to see the humanity in it all. If they lived through this ambush, he vowed to never again let his soldiers show hesitancy to engage someone who was trying to kill them.

The scene for the Second and Third Apache troops enroute to the target was equally chaotic. The ingress routes they had plotted for the sequential attacks were clearly too close together and had been compro-mised, and the follow-on attackers were sustaining heavy triple-A fire all the way to the target. Virtually every Apache crew endured the sickening sound of bullet impacts chewing off pieces of their helicopters, in many cases shattering their sensitive night-vision optics. Barbee and the other commanders also quickly realized they had made another mistake in not establishing more varied egress routes. Attempting to exit the kill sack, the Apaches flew down what had become a gauntlet of increasingly well-coordinated fire. Even before the first gunships had broken contact and were in the clear, a frantic mayday came over the tactical radio net. An Apache was going down.

The mood in V Corps Tactical Headquarters on the morning of March 24 was sour and worsening by the hour. A total of thirty of thirty-one Apaches of the Eleventh Attack Helicopter Regiment sent against the Medina Division the night before had been hit by enemy fire. One crash-landed and another was shot down, its crew captured by Iraqi forces. As soon as confirmation came of the crews' capture, U.S. commanders called in a strike to destroy the downed helicopter, but not before Iraqi television recorded pictures of Iraqis dancing and joyfully cheering atop its crippled carcass, a public relations coup. As many as half of the Apaches were so badly damaged that it was doubtful they could reenter the fight to come, significantly degrading V Corps combat power even before the battle with the Medina and other Republican Guard elements had begun. More worrisome to V Corps commanders, in one of their first encounters with sustained resistance, the Iraqis had achieved tactical surprise and a measure of success in repelling the U.S. attack.

The greatest cause of tension in the V Corps TAC, and the biggest surprise of the Iraqi Freedom campaign to date, was the actions of fanatical Saddam fedayeen paramilitary forces. Using tactics that U.S. frontline commanders described as suicidal, Iraqi paramilitaries and the irregulars they drove before them were repeatedly assaulting U.S. armored forces and convoys on foot or in the back of the "technical vehicles," jury-rigged pickup trucks with machine guns mounted in the rear.

Initially considered a nuisance, albeit an unnerving one for many U.S. troops, the fedayeen were quickly developing into a strategic dilemma. The transformational battle plan for Iraqi Freedom had always relied heavily on the speed and tempo of U.S. maneuver forces to keep the enemy off balance, and to mask the vulnerabilities inherent in the U.S. plan: lean forces and a long and exposed lifeline of supplies and reinforcements. Much to the surprise of U.S. commanders and intelligence analysts, the thousands of fedayeen loyalists Saddam had sent to Iraq's southern cities before the war had inspired such fear among the local populace that the cities had failed to fall in the face of U.S. liberation as anticipated. Key cities along V Corps' line of advance—Nasiriya, Samawah, Najaf, Karbala—thus stayed stubbornly in the grip of Saddam loyalists who were coming out at night to attack and harass the exposed U.S. supply lines. The havoc that could wreak on U.S. plans had become clear just the day before, when a convoy of the 507th Maintenance

Company had been ambushed. Initial reports indicated that eleven soldiers had been killed, nine wounded, and seven were missing and possibly captured.

"I'm very concerned about our convoy security. We have to get that straightened out before the fedayeen realize just how vulnerable our lines of communication are," General Wallace—radio call sign 'victory 6'—told his commanders during the March 24 morning commanders briefing. "We have to take this very seriously. We have a very, very vulnerable situation here. People are tired. They've traveled a long distance, and they are not as alert as they should be. Just looking around at our command post area, it's clear to me that we are not up to speed yet on security. Victory 6, over."

In truth, the situation was even worse than General Wallace described. Air Force weather satellites revealed the approach of a massive sandstorm that was due to hit the area sometime in the late afternoon. His intelligence and logistics officers estimated that the storm could delay resupply convoys for days. That meant that the logistics calculus no longer squared. The Third Infantry Division had crossed into Iraq with five days of supplies in terms of water, food, and ammunition. The storm was due to hit on the afternoon of the fifth day. If convoys carrying two days' worth of resupply were delayed by days, then his lead elements were in danger of "outrunning their own headlights," in the words of V Corps Operations Officer Col. Steven Hicks.

Yet pausing at Objective Rams indefinitely while forward elements were resupplied carried its own severe risks. V Corps intelligence indicated that Iraqi artillery battalions in the region of Najaf and Karbala could potentially reach lead U.S. Army elements, including V Corps Tactical Headquarters, possibly with the same type of chemical and nerve gas shells that Saddam had used to devastating effect in the Iran-Iraq war. The longer major Army formations paused in the region of Objective Rams, the greater the chance that the Iraqis would draw a bead on them. The speed and tempo of the U.S. advance had always been the best protection against attack by chemical weapons. Now both were threatened as the forward advance ground temporarily to a halt.

General Wallace faced another urgent decision on March 24. Maj. Gen. Buford Blount, the aggressive commander of the Third Infantry Division, wanted to send part of the 3/7th Cavalry in a feint across the Euphrates River just south of nearby Najaf in order to distract and pressure the Medina brigades positioned in the region. The feint would hopefully draw the attention of Iraqi commanders east to the region between the Euphrates and Tigris Rivers, and away from the Karbala Gap to the west, the intended breaching point for the next phase of the advance on Baghdad.

"With this weather coming in, it's possible the 3/7th could get across the river and then not have any close air support to back them up," Wallace said, clearly worried.

"Yes sir, that's possible," said Colonel Hicks. "But General Blount doesn't want to let up on these guys. He wants to give them something else to think about."

As the weather began to kick up in midafternoon, bad news continued to pour in to the V Corps TAC. A U.S. F-16 had mistakenly fired a HARM antiradar missile at the Patriot antimissile battery providing cover to the TAC, leaving General Wallace and the headquarters defenseless against missile attack. There were also intelligence reports of a force of thirty Iraqi tanks and tracked vehicles on the move in the vicinity and possibly heading for the TAC. At one point it almost seemed as if there were not enough senior officers to cope with all the bad news in what came to be known in V Corps as "the darkest day."

"Listen up people! We have five colonels up here issuing guidance, and that's too goddam many!" Colonel Wagenaar shouted at one point from the top of the horseshoe-shaped command center.

"You may recall that we had contingency plans for a possible capitulation of Republican Guard forces," shouted Colonel Hicks, the operations chief. "Well, I have a news flash for you people. They aren't quitting!"

From his seat just in front of my computer, Lt. Col. Gary Luck, the Third Infantry Division liaison at the V Corps TAC, hung up the phone and turned to me. "I didn't think things would get this tense so early. The main fight hasn't even started yet," said Luck, an unassuming military brat whose Army career had so far unfolded in the shadow of his father, a former four-star general and commander in chief of the Eighteenth Airborne Corps. We both agreed that three-plus days of sleep deprivation were taking their toll. "Last night I visited the G-3 [operations officer] of my *own division*, and he looked at me like I was a *mujaheddin*!"

That afternoon Third Infantry commanders reported another disturbing phenomenon of the war. Family members of the hundreds of Saddam fedayeen irregulars killed in recent battles around Objective Rams were approaching U.S. security lines to collect their dead from the battlefield. According to U.S. soldiers who escorted the relatives, many of the Iraqis stood over the mangled bodies of their loved ones and cursed them to Allah for dying in the name of Saddam Hussein. But they cursed the Americans too.

After lead elements of 3/7th Cavalry crossed the Euphrates River south of An Najaf and seized a key bridge in preparation for the first probing by U.S. maneuver forces of the Medina Division, the freakish storm blew into the region. Inside the V Corps tent a small group of officers had gathered around Colonel Luck, who was monitoring the tactical radio net for the Third I.D. The 3/7th Cav had clearly stumbled into a major fight on the other side of the Euphrates, the intensity of the combat evident in the high pitch of the disembodied voices that came floating over the radio waves. There were reports of dismounted Iraqi infantry swarming the U.S. column, of swirling sand blinding night-vision optics, and one M-1 tank crew reported being hit from the rear and disabled, the voice of its commander gaining a frantic edge. Then another tank reported being hit, and yet another, and the storm of March 24 had only just begun.

Outside I tried to conduct a radio interview over my satellite phone. The host was nattering on about divided support for the war back home, but I could barely hear him over the howl of the wind and the flapping of the headquarters tent. Above me the rays of a late-day sun were trapped in a swirling cloud of dust and sand, turning that entire, strange landscape into an unworldly shade of burnt red. No one I talked to later who witnessed that eclipse of the sun could recall ever seeing its like. Under the circumstances, with U.S. and Iraqi forces involved in a desperate firefight literally at the gates of ancient Babylon, the storm seemed biblical and full of portent, though its meaning was any soldier's guess.

CHAPTER 13

Gates of Babylon

F OR IRAQI COMMANDERS the sandstorm must have seemed a sign of divine providence. For nearly a week Iraqi forces laying in wait around Najaf had been unable to move without detection by the unblinking eye of U.S. satellites and airborne drones. Now a storm the like of which even the Iraqis had rarely seen descended like a sign from Allah. The American forces had crossed the Euphrates and entered into the ancient land of Babylon, advancing north up a series of towns and villages separated by marshy rice paddies and crisscrossed by canals and irrigation ditches. Without the benefit of their eyes in the sky, the Americans were marching blind into terrain known to many of the Iraqis since birth, land that largely negated U.S. advantages in weapons range and maneuverability. An Iraqi commander ordered a tank unit north of Najaf south to intercept the U.S. forces, and the Saddam fedayeen threw everything they had at the Americans. This was the fight the Iraqis had always wanted.

As they fought their way up the road east of Najaf at night in swirling rain and dirt, 3/7th Cavalry tank commanders realized that they were stumbling into a series of L-shaped ambushes in what came to be known simply as "Ambush Alley." The storm had grounded the armed OH-58 "Kiowa Warrior" helicopters the 3/7th Cav normally relied upon as its forward scouts, and the swirling mud spray of the storm was producing "negative illumination"—blinding night-vision scopes, thermal optics, even standard goggles.

Out of that stormy murk fedayeen fighters appeared like wraiths, swarming U.S. tanks and armored vehicles, their traditional robes tossing wildly in the wind. U.S. soldiers responded with suppression fire from the M-1 Abrams' 7.62 coaxial machine gun. Hatches were flung open so soldiers could fire with their M-16s and even 9 mm Beretta pistols in a desperate attempt to keep the enemy infantry at bay. By the third ambush, lead elements of the 3/7th were running out of small-arms ammunition, and in some cases were fighting with AK-47s taken off dead fedayeen. The entire advance ground nearly to a halt after dismounted Iraqi fighters blindsided and disabled two M-1 tanks and a Bradley Fighting Vehicle with RPGs fired at close range. The 3/7th Cav was in a knife fight and the enemy had found a critical weakness to exploit, swarming U.S. armor from behind with infantry. And still the Iraqi tank forces continued to close from the north.

Sixty-five thousand feet above that desperate fray in the thin air and vacuum-quiet of near space, a U.S. Air Force "Global Hawk" unmanned drone was sending probes through the sandstorm like a screeching bat, locating its prey with radar echo. That radio-wave data was beamed to a U.S. satellite, relayed to Beale Air Base in northern California, and sent by computer to photo interpreters at an Air National Guard center in Reno, Nevada. The picture that emerged on their computer consoles was of Iraqi tank and armor formations on the move and closing with U.S. forces.

Target coordinates developed by the airmen soon streamed via satellite into Central Command's Air Operations Center at Prince Sultan Air Base in Saudi Arabia, which radioed them to a B-1 bomber crew flying high above the storm. That globe-spanning cycle of surveillance, analysis, and retargeting for aircraft already in the air represented a capability that Air Force air controllers could only have dreamed about a decade earlier during Desert Storm. Literally within minutes of first detection, a lethal fusillade of 2,000 lb JDAM (Joint Direct Attack Munitions) bombs were hurtling through the night, each guided by GPS to a designated target coordinate and carrying a deadly message about the unprecedented reach of transformational warfare. The Iraqi armored formation below would never have time to ponder how it had been so mercilessly exposed beneath the cover of a seemingly impenetrable storm at night.

On March 27, Lt. Col. Earnest "Rock" Marcone, commander of 3-69 Armor Battalion, First Brigade, Third Infantry Division, was inspecting a damaged bridge across the Euphrates just north of Najaf along with his combat engineers, and wondering how the hell he was going to get U.S. tanks safely back across the river. Showing some tactical acumen, the Iraqis had waited until three of the battalion's M-1 tanks had crossed the bridge before detonating hidden explosives, dropping a section of the bridge in pancake fashion and rendering it questionable for crossing. Marcone's boss was worried that they were facing a *Black Hawk Down* scenario similar to Mogadishu, with American soldiers trapped in a firefight and outside the reach of reinforcements. Meanwhile, the sound of fighting across the river in the nearby village of Al Kifl was thunderous.

With the sandstorm raging well into its second full day, fedayeen and other Iraqi paramilitaries continued to fight fanatically from their bases in Najaf and the surrounding towns and villages. A hasty order had thus come for the Third Infantry Division to essentially surround the holy city from all sides and protect the nearby logistics staging area at Objective Rams, just west and slightly south of the city, at least until the storm had abated. The damaged bridge that Rock Marcone was inspecting at Objective Jenkins was critical to drawing the noose around Najaf and isolating the city from reinforcements that were pouring down from the north in the direction of Baghdad and Al Kut.

An Italian American who wore a large belt buckle emblazoned with the motto of the Third Infantry Division—"Speed and Power"—Marcone was a flamboyant yet thoughtful commander much admired by his troops. His real name was Ernest, but few of his own men could have told you that. What mattered to them was that Marcone backed up his swagger with a combat veteran's confidence and grit under fire. A veteran of Desert Storm, Marcone had also participated in seventeen "Blue Force" engagements with the vaunted opposing force at the Army's National Training Center. And right at that moment, nearly all of Marcone's experience as an armor commander suggested that the Battle of Objective Jenkins was skewing dangerously off kilter.

This was not a fight they had planned for or rehearsed, and if the Jenkins Bridge proved impassable Marcone realized they were not organized or well prepared to conduct a rapid-assault bridge crossing using mobile bridging equipment. Yet somehow he had to extricate his tanks that had already crossed the bridge before the Iraqis attempted to blow it. Moreover, some units had been attached to his task force at the last moment for this mission, and Marcone sensed from communications traffic that they had failed to grasp the critical "commander's intent" behind his orders. The battle for the Jenkins Bridge and Al Kifl was thus turning into one of the unanticipated "engagements in place" that he had practiced at the National Training Center, and Marcone sensed that mistakes were being made. As Marcone would explain to me days later, those mistakes were potentially matters of life and death.

At the outskirts of nearby Al Kifl, a small town consisting of a main street and four or five blocks of low-slung, cement buildings fronted by shops and restaurants, U.S. tanks were taking fire from virtually every doorway and rooftop. The hastily constructed plan had been to secure the town in order to block any Iraqi forces from reinforcing Najaf from the north or retaking the strategic Jenkins Bridge. The Iraqi defenders in Al Kifl were fighting so ferociously, however, that U.S. commanders wondered whether the town might harbor a chemical weapons factory or weapons storage facility.

Through the swirling dust of the sandstorm the muzzle fire of the Iraqi weapons winked and flashed from every direction, and the explosions of RPGs rocked U.S. tanks. Once again U.S. forces were in an eyeball-to-eyeball slugfest where the main advantage was their training and the thickness of their armor. Most of the killing in Al Kifl was done with machine guns and automatic rifles at less than thirty meters. The narrow main street was barely wide enough for an M-1 Abrams tank to swing its 120 mm muzzle fully around. As Capt. Carter Price, commander of C Company, 2-69 Armor, would recall in an interview days later, when he opened fire with his main gun on a building where enemy fire seemed to be concentrated, the effect in Al Kifl's narrow main street was shocking. The back-blast of the powerful 120 mm cannon literally sucked Iraqi fighters out of windows and doorways, sprawling them onto the street. The U.S. troops opened up on them with automatic weapons.

Still on the far side of the Jenkins Bridge, Rock Marcone ran down the stairs beside the bridge to assess the damage of the Iraqi demolition. To his relief it seemed as if the Iraqi demolition experts had botched the job, succeeding only in dropping part of the bridge that was still over the far bank. Though the bridge was sinking, Marcone estimated that it could still support a seventy-ton M-1 tank. Walking out to the midpoint of the bridge, Marcone ordered his own tank to cross. Expecting the tank to stop midway and pick him up, Marcone watched bemused as his crew tore across the bridge before the damaged span could give way and drop them into the river. Another M-1 and a Bradley crossed in quick succession to reinforce the tanks stranded on the east bank.

After withdrawing the U.S. tanks from Al Kifl and back across the Euphrates where they could offer supporting fire, Marcone reinforced the far side of the river with much lighter Bradley Fighting Vehicles. Along with dismounted infantry, Marcone arranged the Bradleys into ambushes with interlocking fields of fire guarding all approaches to the strategic road intersection at Objective Jenkins. The key northern approach to An Najaf was now secured. Then the task force hunkered down in the sandstorm and waited for the Iraqis to come to them and try to recapture the bridge. They would not have to wait for long.

Maj. Jon Segars was one of the first to see the trucks coming toward the intersection from the north road leading from Al Hillah, near the site of the ancient fortress of Babylon. As the lead truck approached threatening range, Segars ordered a gunner to take the vehicle out with a high-explosive round. The explosion engulfed the truck, which careened off the side of the road. What shocked Segars and his troops was that an Iraqi carrying an AK-47 barreled out of the wreckage and charged on foot straight at them. A gunner hit the man multiple times, and still he kept coming. "Basically, we had to cut his head off with the machine gun to get him to stop," Segars later recalled.

Every ten or fifteen minutes the bizarre and unnerving scene was repeated. Ignoring the smoldering wreckage on both sides of the road, Iraqi "technical vehicles" would barrel toward the U.S. positions with machine guns blazing. In some cases, when the Iraqi trucks were not firing, U.S. troops would try and dissuade them by firing warning shots over the driver's head. And still they drove into the teeth of the American ambush until blasted into burning shrapnel and gore.

At one point First Brigade Commander Col. William Grimsley, an intense man who bore a close resemblance to the actor Richard Dreyfuss, joined Marcone near the Jenkins Road intersection. Both men watched incredulously as the suicide attacks were repeated five or six times in the space of half an hour. "I freaking cannot believe this is happening," Grimsley said, shaking his head. "These people have to be out of their minds."

Spotting a U.S. soldier treating one of the Iraqi wounded, Grimsley grabbed an interpreter and walked over. Despite having a rifle wound in his leg, the Iraqi was grinning at the Americans as if he had just won the lottery. After bandaging him up and offering him water, Grimsley asked some questions through the interpreter. No one wanted to really think about the tragic implication of the man's story, which Marcone confirmed was similar to those told by other Iraqi fighters who lived to tell it. Fedayeen had come into Al Hillah and various other towns days before and handed out rifles to all the men, the man said, taking their families hostage with them on their way out of town. Go and fight the Americans, the fedayeen ordered, or we will kill your families.

Numerous times in the next thirty-six hours Iraqi paramilitaries tried valiantly, yet in vain, to recapture and destroy the Jenkins Bridge. At one point it became a matter of hand-to-hand combat. After shooting and capturing one wounded paramilitary fighter, Marcone was confronted by a man who sprang from behind a low wall brandishing an AK-47 rifle. For a moment both men seemed paralyzed by finding the other in his face, and before the Iraqi could react Marcone wrestled his weapon away and struck the man to the ground with the rifle butt. Eventually U.S. medics carted both Iraqis away. At another point an Iraqi mortar round exploded so close that Marcone was knocked unconscious for nearly an hour. But 3-69 held the bridge.

When the sandstorm broke on March 28, with the noose around Najaf nearly complete and gradually tightening, Lt. Gen. Scott Wallace of V Corps met with Maj. Gen. Buford Blount of Third I.D., and together they inspected the battle scene at Al Kifl. They were accompanied by a few embedded reporters, including Michael Kelly and Ted Koppel. That the Army's two most senior commanders in Iraq positioned themselves so close to the fighting was indicative of the Army's lead-from-the-front ethos, and commanders routinely conducted such after-action reviews to quickly distill the lessons of battle while memories were still fresh. On viewing the carnage and destruction at Al Kifl, both the generals and the reporters were equally sobered by the oldest lesson of war there is.

The burnt husks of trucks, cars, and buses by the score lined the dusty main street leading through Al Kifl, and mangled bodies still lay everywhere in obscene poses of death. As Colonels Grimsley and Marcone walked the group through the battle, U.S. soldiers followed close behind tossing body bags into the back of a 2.5-ton truck whose large bed was rapidly filling to capacity. When Capt. Carter Price was asked by General Wallace about the morale of his troops after the battle of Al Kifl, he stared for a moment into the middle distance. "Sir, the day my guys saw their first dead body was a pretty significant event. The day they killed someone for the first time was another significant event. Mostly everyone's focus now is on getting the job done and then going home to see the wife and kids again."

General Blount walked up to a small group of middle-aged Iraqis, and asked through an interpreter what they wanted. One of the men was looking for his son, the interpreter said, who had been sent to fight the Americans under threat of death for his entire family. The return of the families held hostage was the first solid indication that such stories were really true, and that many of the fedayeen had at least temporarily fled the area. No one wanted to think about the likelihood that the man's son was on the back of the funeral truck slowly making its way through Al Kifl.

Someone called the group over to a small barbershop on the main street whose plate glass window had been shattered during the fighting. Stepping gingerly over the broken glass and checking for booby traps, Mike Kelly, Ted Koppel, and Generals Wallace and Blount all looked to the back of the shop at a strange sight. Across the entire back wall, someone had painted a stylized mural of the New York City skyline, complete with the Twin Towers of the World Trade Center still intact. Instead of the Hudson River in the foreground, however, the Euphrates was depicted, lined by date palms. It was easy to imagine that the owner of the mural had once lived in New York and apparently missed it a lot. Indeed, it seemed likely that the proud barber who once lived and worked in that shop in Al Kifl before the coming of the fedayeen had loved New York.

As they finished their tour of the town each one of the group, the generals as well as the chroniclers, were lost in their own thoughts. Everyone understood that the "most humane war in history" had gotten a lot less so at Al Kifl. That was no fault of the American soldiers, it was the way of war. After Al Kifl, there was just no kidding yourself anymore that this war would prove any different than all the rest. Later, Scott Wallace confided to me that he worried about the effect of so much close-in killing on the psyches of his young soldiers.

For General Wallace, the scene of fierce fighting and determined opposition by the fedayeen in Al Kifl would reinforce his most fateful decision of the Iraqi Freedom campaign; to consolidate his forces and support at Objective Rams rather than push immediately ahead to Baghdad and leave his logistics trail exposed to such a fanatical enemy. But there was more to it than that. Seeing the carnage, Wallace made a point to seek out Matt Garrett, a young platoon leader in the 3/7th Cavalry whose unit had also been heavily engaged in the sandstorm fight. Wallace had an e-mail message from the young man's father conveying just how proud he was of Matt and how much he loved his son. Tom Garrett had been Scott Wallace's West Point roommate and best friend in the Army. Delivering that message to Matt Garrett suddenly seemed very important, and it was a bright spot in an otherwise grim day.

As for General Blount, the scene at Al Kifl only seemed to increase his desire to restart the offensive on Baghdad as soon as possible lest they become bogged down in a series of similar lesser battles. As he had stressed all along, the center of gravity in this war was Baghdad, and Blount was anxious to start the final march. His determination to get going again would create significant tension between the two generals over how quickly to relaunch the offensive, but such tensions were the backstory to every military campaign.

The carnage and desperate fighting at Al Kifl also highlighted a paradox that both Michael Kelly and Ted Koppel had been grappling with since the beginning of the campaign. As long as they stayed close to General Blount at Third I.D. headquarters, both reporters had a bird's-eye view of how the entire campaign was unfolding. Seeing Al Kifl convinced both reporters, however, that they were missing an important element of the story. Shortly after the tour, both Koppel and Kelly spoke with Col. Will Grimsley about leaving headquarters and embedding into his brigade for the coming assault on Baghdad. By the end of their talk, Grimsley agreed to bring them onboard.

Back at Third Infantry Division's headquarters Mike Kelly took his leave of his Humvee companions, Lt. Col. Peter Bayer and his driver Sergeant Alzerreca. Bayer understood immediately that Kelly wanted to be closer to the soldiers doing the actual fighting. Before saying good-bye Bayer asked about Mike Kelly's father.

"You know, I talked to him on the sat phone recently, and he's changed his mind about this war," said Kelly. The Irish son in Mike was obviously buoyed by his father's change of heart and the thought that Tom Kelly now understood the justification for a war to depose a dictator like Saddam Hussein. Kelly had also spoken with his mother, enlisting

Sergeant Alzerreca to assure her that everything was fine and that Kelly was in good hands. Thinking back on that conversation, Sergeant Alzerreca tried to talk Mike out of leaving. "Why would you want to go to the front lines when you have everything you need right here?" Sergeant Alzerreca asked. Kelly tried to explain that the more he saw of this war, the easier it would be to write the book that was already growing within him.

When Mike Kelly left, Sergeant Alzerreca spoke with Colonel Bayer about the work ethic and devotion of the hard-driving reporter who seemed oblivious to the dangers of his assignment. Kelly had a job to do, and he was proud of it. That was an epiphany occurring to a number of soldiers and scribes who recognized somewhat kindred souls in those days of the embed experiment. "And Mr. Kelly never complained about a damn thing," said Sergeant Alzerreca, as both men nodded in agreement at the common fitness report that was shaping up in their minds. "You know, sir, I think he'd make a damn good soldier."

CHAPTER 14

The Enemy Votes

A DISTANT SHOUT came out of the dark of early morning. It could mean just another soldier waking from a nightmare. No reason to jump to conclusions or out of a warm sleeping bag. Yet the shout spread through the camp and grew nearer in an unmistakable sign of urgency. The tent barracks suddenly sprang to life amid the frenzied buzz of sleeping bag zippers and a wild light show of careening flashlight beams, as outside a chorus grew throughout the base camp.

"Gas! Gas! Gas!"

In the period during and just after the sandstorm that would become known simply as "the pause," the V Corps Tactical Headquarters at Objective Rams bolstered its reputation as a Scud magnet. Just the day before, a nearby Patriot battery intercepted an Al Samoud missile nearly overhead, with the shock wave of the aerial impact providing all the warning anyone needed to reach for the protective gear on his or her hip in a well-practiced draw. After this latest attack, when three missiles fell near the base camp, each as inaccurate yet potentially lethal as the previous, the V Corps soldiers and I simply lay back down in the dark in our cots in full chemical-protection outfits, patiently awaiting either the all-clear signal or the first telltale signs of nerve gas attack. These latter were said to include a dance called the "broken chicken" that would be performed by anyone with a faulty seal in their gas mask. To the dismay of fellow travelers, several soldiers proved the rumor that you can actually snore through a gas mask.

Unable to sleep, I walked to the V Corps Tactical Headquarters tent. The scene inside was surreal. Everyone could read the wall-sized map board and see that we were perilously close to the "Red Zone" surrounding Baghdad that intelligence identified as the likely tripwire for Saddam's suspected arsenal of nerve gas and chemical weapons. Such proximity cleared the mind wonderfully, putting to rest academic arguments about whether Iraq possessed and would dare use weapons of mass destruction. Saddam had used them to devastating effect in the

Iraq-Iran war, and once cornered it seemed a fair bet to those of us approaching the red line that he might use them again. Inside the headquarters tent, row upon row of staff officers peered at laptop computers through bug-eyed masks like a race of mutant insects.

The issue of the headquarters' vulnerability to ballistic missiles such as Iraq's Al Samouds, Ababil 100s, and the infamous Scuds—essentially Iraq's only deep-strike weapons capable of delivering chemical warheads—remained contentious. No sooner had we set up at Objective Rams, for instance, than word came that a U.S. F-16 jet had mistakenly taken out the radar of our Patriot battery. Stressed to near the breaking point just by supplying food, ammo, and fuel to forward forces, the logisticians of Corps Support Command were failing miserably in supplying replacement parts for fixing such equipment needed by forward forces.

"Where in the *hell* is our goddam Patriot coverage?" a lieutenant colonel and shift leader had shouted at one point at two junior air-defense officers assigned to V Corps.

"Hey! Lay off my troops!" came the reply from the back of the tent, causing all heads to turn. In the high-octane testosterone swamp of a combat headquarters in wartime, the sound of a woman barking back at the big dogs was a novelty. When it was determined that the woman in question was wearing the wings of a full-bird colonel, the tent quieted down noticeably and everyone went back to their work.

As the first female in the Army ever to command a combat brigade in wartime, Col. Heidi Brown was at the vanguard of a woman's movement that began with the establishment of the all-volunteer force in 1973, and accelerated greatly after numerous combat slots were opened to women following the 1991 Persian Gulf War. Brown herself was a 1981 graduate of the U.S. Military Academy, only the second West Point class to accept women. In an interview, Brown told me she found in the crucible of West Point the inner strength that allowed her not only to advance, but also to thrive in what had been an all-male bastion. Over the next twenty-two years, the Army repaid her dedication by providing every opportunity to advance and satisfy her career goals: two master's degrees; a stint as a West Point deputy commander; assignment to the Joint Staff; battalion command.

"And I prayed for the opportunity to be one of the few officers who gets to command a brigade, and here I am, living the dream," Brown told me. "I had no earthly idea that I would take that brigade to war, but here I am."

In times of war, however, the Army has ways of calling in its debts of duty in unpredictable ways. While the improved PAC-2 and PAC-3 Patriots were already credited with intercepting eight of the twelve Iraqi missiles fired thus far in the war—including one bearing down on the V

Corps TAC convoy on the first day of the campaign—on March 23 a Patriot battery had tragically misidentified and destroyed a British Tornado fighter-bomber, killing its two-man crew. Soon, the military would be investigating the likelihood that another Patriot battery shot down a Navy F/A-18 fighter.

Worst of all, a supply convoy of Brown's Thirty-first Air Defense Brigade was ambushed near Nasiriya on March 24. About three dozen members of the 507th Maintenance Company came under attack. At least two were killed, five others became the first prisoners of war in Iraqi Freedom, and eight were listed as missing, including Pfc. Jessica Lynch. When I asked about news reports that the 507th had taken a wrong turn and gotten lost before it was ambushed, Brown had to cover her face a moment to collect herself.

"My soldiers in that convoy, they did everything right," Brown said with glistening eyes and a clenched jaw. "The soldiers who gave their lives in the firefight, the ones who later succumbed to their wounds, the soldiers who were taken prisoner—they all did everything right, and they did it bravely."

After learning that Brown had not been able to contact her parents since the beginning of the war, I lent her my satellite phone and watched as she walked out of the tent and called her parents. Her father had served in both World War II and Korea, and had instilled in his six children a sense of duty such that four of Heidi Brown's five siblings—her twin brothers and two of her three sisters—had likewise served long military careers.

Watching her talk about her troops, the pain of answered prayers written all over her face, it occurred to me that Heidi Brown was all that she had dreamed of being: just another brigade commander, confronted by the awful truth that you can do your job and love your troops, but you can never avoid sending them into harm's way.

In the days after the sandstorm of March 25–27, Gen. Scott Wallace was a taciturn presence in the V Corps Tactical Headquarters tent. Each day he would stop by for a few hours and confer with Col. Steve Hicks, the V Corps "G-3" or operations officer. The two men would confer quietly with a few close aides, their laser pointers dancing over the map screen. After Wallace left, Hicks would sit before the map board alone, run his fingers through close-cropped gray hair in a motion that was more tic than grooming, and stare some more. Occasionally he would bark an order, indulge in an outburst of temper, and then return to a lonely vigil that he maintained for days, broken only by a few hours' sleep snatched on a cot in the back.

For his part, General Wallace spoke little in those days, especially when a reporter was around. In truth, Scott Wallace was enduring the low point of his long career as an Army officer. In everything he did was the realization that Wallace's signature moment of command was balanced precariously on the edge of a precipice.

V Corps commanders were well aware that the lack of obvious forward progress in the campaign had provoked a storm of criticism in Washington, D.C. Everyone in the TAC knew that General Wallace's offhand comments to a *Washington Post* reporter—to the effect that U.S. forces had been surprised by the intensity of the Saddam fedayeen, that they were not the enemy U.S. forces had war-gamed against, and that the war might take longer than originally anticipated—had caused a major controversy at the Pentagon, where Secretary of Defense Donald Rumsfeld characteristically denied any surprises or slippages in the schedule.

The Pentagon had quickly sent word of its displeasure. CFLCC Commander Lt. Gen. David McKiernan called Wallace with a warning that his comments to the press had caused extreme consternation at the highest levels of the U.S. government, and that he was to shut up around reporters. Wallace was suddenly at the center of a very public controversy and apparently on Rumsfeld's personal shit list, a private ledger from which few U.S. Army generals escaped with their careers intact. Somehow Wallace had to put all that out of his mind and not let it affect the most important tactical decision he would ever make.

The controversy was vintage Rumsfeld. After hamstringing his field commander's ability to cope with unforeseen surprises by insisting both on a transformational war plan and a very lean force, the brash Defense Secretary simply refused to admit that surprises had occurred. At the front, however, the truth behind Wallace's comments were self-evident. For commanders in the field, a determined enemy is an occupational hazard, and tactical surprises are not to be apologized for, but rather counted upon. The only cardinal sin is failing to correct for them—the resulting penalty being a potential military debacle. The intense consultations between Wallace and Hicks were about trying to adjust to a tactical situation very different from what they had planned and war-gamed.

From the beginning, Wallace was convinced that three conditions must be met before he could in good conscience order the final assault on Baghdad. First, there could be no pausing once they crossed into Saddam's Red Zone surrounding Baghdad that stretched as far south as Karbala, within which U.S. forces would be in range of virtually every weapon in the Iraqi arsenal, including weapons of mass destruction. Wallace thus wanted adequate supplies stockpiled at Objective Rams for his lead forces to make it all the way to the capital without resupply. They simply could not afford to have units run out of fuel or ammo somewhere within the Red Zone, vulnerable to WMD and Iraqi counterattack, and dependent on resupply convoys stretching all the way back to Kuwait.

Secondly, Wallace felt he needed to know with reasonable clarity the disposition of the Republican Guard Medina Division and supporting elements guarding the southern approaches to Baghdad before he sent the Third Infantry Division against them. Finally, the Third Infantry Division itself needed to be consolidated in the area around Najaf and Karbala, with all three of its maneuver brigades postured in echelon fashion for the hopscotch, seize-and-pass maneuver of a combat division on the offensive.

The problem confounding Gen. Scott Wallace and Col. Steve Hicks was that when the sandstorm finally broke on March 27, none of those three critical preconditions existed.

The sandstorm itself had delayed by days supply convoys headed for Objective Rams and the nearby Logistics Staging Area (LSA) Bushmaster, with numerous convoys still wandering lost or severely off course in the Iraqi desert. While V Corps intelligence officers knew the Medina Division was positioned somewhere in the dense terrain east of Karbala, they could not pinpoint the precise location of its brigades and battalions, a number of which had repositioned and gone to ground during the sandstorm. Worse, during the fighting around Najaf, U.S. commanders were unpleasantly surprised to find that elements of the Republican Guard Nebuchadnezzar Division had moved down from the north to reinforce the Medina and backstop Baghdad's southern defenses. There were also intelligence reports that two brigades of the Adnan Republican Guard Division had repositioned from the north during the sandstorm into the Karbala Gap and astride Highway 6 southeast of Baghdad, directly into the path of the intended U.S. advance.

For all the United States' vaunted space- and air-based surveillance capability, it was also becoming obvious to General Wallace that bomb damage assessments were lagging air strikes by forty-eight hours or more, making it impossible for V Corps commanders to determine the degree to which strikes by coalition aircraft were degrading enemy forces in their path.

Finally, far from consolidating for the final push to Baghdad, the Third Infantry Division, the spearhead of the U.S. Army attack, was spread all over hell's half acre, battling Saddam fedayeen and protecting U.S. supply lines and logistics staging areas. With no mobile reserve, the spearhead of the Iraqi Freedom campaign had one brigade containing Samawah in the south, another encircling Najaf to the north, while a third was protecting Objective Rams from a position near an escarpment just south of Karbala. All of which brought Wallace and Hicks back to the most unpleasant surprise of all: Saddam's fanatical fedayeen loyalists.

Once again they were back to the primary conundrum: the transformational battle plan for Operation Iraqi Freedom had always relied heavily on the speed and agility of U.S. maneuver forces to keep the enemy off balance, and to mask the vulnerabilities inherent in the U.S. plan: lean forces and a long and exposed lifeline of supplies and reinforcements. Those vulnerabilities were exacerbated by the demands of the initial, two-hundred-mile march and the surprisingly fierce sandstorm. Meanwhile, instead of falling in the face of the U.S. onslaught and to liberation as anticipated, key cities along the V Corps path of advance—Nasiriya, Samawah, Najaf, Karbala—had stayed stubbornly in the grip of the fedayeen loyalists, many of whom still came out at night to harass the soft underbelly of U.S. supply lines. General Wallace had continually cautioned his officers that the Iraqi enemy would have a vote in the course of the war. As the reports and after-action reviews of U.S. engagements with the enemy poured into V Corps Tactical Headquarters after the sandstorm, the inescapable conclusion was that the Iraqis may have identified a potential Achilles' heel in the transformational U.S. battle plan.

Lt. Col. Kenna McCurry was the V Corps TAC's wiry intelligence officer. "We knew the fedayeen would be a problem, but we underestimated the intensity and fanaticism with which they'd fight," he told me at the time. Military analysts estimated that Saddam had pushed between two thousand and four thousand fedayeen fighters into each of the southern cities along the U.S. path of advance, with as many as thirty thousand or more in reserve. Despite Pentagon statements to the contrary, the question of why the fedayeen and other Iraqi paramilitaries fought so ferociously was the central mystery of the first week of the war. Theories ricocheted through the V Corps Tactical Headquarters. Some were based on intelligence and others on soldierly conjecture: the fedayeen were hopped up on drugs; they had been reinforced by busloads of Palestinian martyrs; they were raised since childhood under the tutelage of Uday Hussein into a cult of Saddam worship. "For them to repeatedly rush tanks and armor as dismounted infantry is reminiscent of the Japanese kamikaze pilots of World War II," McCurry told me.

Listening to everything that U.S. Army intelligence did not understand about the fedayeen, I felt a sense of uneasiness grow in those tense days. The Bush administration and Pentagon civilians were convinced that Saddam invoked fear but little loyalty in his armed forces, and that Iraqi resistance would thus crumble quickly in the face of U.S. military superiority. If an assumption so fundamental not only to the Iraqi campaign but also to its aftermath was so clearly wrong, you had to wonder what other ugly surprises awaited U.S. forces in this strange culture.

Certainly credible reports of the Saddam loyalists' depravity abounded. "Fallah" was a deserter from the regular army that I interviewed through an interpreter just after the sandstorm broke in March 2003. He was a weather-beaten first sergeant who claimed to be forty-two years old, but looked a decade older. Crouched on his haunches amid a group of fellow deserters at a U.S. checkpoint outside Najaf, Fallah told a story that was typical of the Iraqi army stragglers who walked great distances to surrender to U.S. forces.

The regular Iraqi army, Fallah said, was tired and hungry. Many soldiers from Najaf, a Shiite holy town with little natural affinity for Saddam or his Sunni Baath Party, had hoped to surrender to U.S. forces. Then, apparently in the middle of the night, came a knock on their doors by men wearing black robes, with only their eyes visible through the folds. When I asked who the men were, Fallah became agitated, pronouncing the name like a curse.

"Fed-a-YEEN!"

Fallah also insisted that the Saddam loyalists had taken the families of Iraqi soldiers hostage, and threatened to kill them unless their men went out to fight the American invaders. Any deserters were summarily shot by fedayeen overseers who, Fallah said, were high on a drug that made them both fanatical and obedient. Though none of it could be independently verified, there was plenty of empirical evidence of fedayeen cruelty. An intelligence dispatch posted on the bulletin board in the headquarters tent reported that fedayeen had gouged out the eyes of a young Iraqi deserter, then driven him around Baghdad on display as a warning to others. Some of the Republican Guard units had also adopted fedayeen tactics, using women and children as human shields.

Though their tactics were barbaric and tactically suicidal, the fedayeen created a strategic dilemma that was pushing General Wallace to his fateful decision. The center of gravity in the campaign's early stages had shifted, he determined, from Baghdad to first solving the riddle of the Saddam fedayeen. Because Najaf in particular was a hub of fedayeen activity and sat adjacent to their key logistics staging area, the encirclement of the holy city and neutralization of its fedayeen fighters there would become a dress rehearsal for the Battle of Baghdad.

Rather than push ahead immediately to Baghdad when the weather broke, Wallace thus decided instead to pause the U.S. forward advance to allow supplies to accumulate at LSA Bushmaster, and to consolidate the Third Infantry Division for the final thrust to Baghdad. To accomplish that Wallace ordered lead elements of the 101st Airborne Division, which was originally slated to assist in the encirclement of Baghdad, to instead relieve the Third Infantry Division units containing Najaf. However, because the Pentagon had jettisoned the Tip Fid to accommodate Rumsfeld's transformational war-fighting concepts, the 101st had arrived without its proscribed allotment of support trucks, raising concerns about how fast it could conduct the "relief in place," or RIF.

With no mobile reserve on which to rely, Wallace likewise requested permission from CFLCC to employ the Second Brigade of the storied Eighty-second Airborne Division, which had been held as a strategic reserve back in Kuwait ready to fly directly to Baghdad in case Saddam capitulated early. General McKiernan fully endorsed Wallace's decision to instead have the Eighty-second relieve the Third Infantry Division at Samawah.

With political pressure to restart the offensive mounting back in Washington, D.C., and the Third Infantry Division commander General Blount champing at the bit, Wallace was under intense pressure. He needed for the relief in place of the Third I.D. at Samawah and Najaf to go quickly and without a hitch. His fragmentation order, or "Frago," to Eighty-second commander Maj. Gen. Charles "Chuck" Swannack Jr., dated March 26, 2003, was thus the epitome of a commander making his intent clear.

"Message from Gen. Wallace for Maj. Gen. Swannack: Get your ass up here."

———

Between March 28 and 30, the 101st Air Mobile and Eighty-second Airborne elements conducted their relief in place at Najaf and Samawah, the Army's two most storied airborne divisions happy to get into the action. In one of the field latrines an Eighty-second paratrooper had written about his helicopter-borne compatriots: "101st Air Mobile: Too lazy to walk, too scared to jump." As the 101st began relieving the Third Infantry and isolating Najaf, a 101st Airborne liaison in the TAC proudly pronounced "Let it be officially noted that the 101st is one hundred kilometers ahead of the Eighty-second Airborne!"

To which an observant officer added to much laughter, "Yeah, and you're both behind the Corps TAC."

As U.S. forces tightened their grip on Najaf, Delta Force and Special Forces commandos from Task Force 20 became a regular presence in the V Corps TAC. Since before the war they had been scouring the desert to our west in specially outfitted ATVs (all-terrain vehicles) and pickup trucks with mounted machine guns, looking for any mobile Scuds that might try and target Israel. Besides conducting such traditional long-range surveillance operations, Special Forces in northern Iraq were serving as critical force-multipliers. Operating with the support of the 173rd Airborne Brigade out of Vicenza, Italy, and about ten thousand Kurdish fighters, the Tenth Special Forces Group in northern Iraq was tying down elements of thirteen Iraqi divisions.

Based largely on the positive experience in Afghanistan, and on Secretary of Defense Rumsfeld's well-known admiration for the Special Forces ethos of agility and flexibility, the transformational war plan for Iraqi Freedom had the Army relying more heavily on Special Operations Forces (SOF) than at any time since Vietnam. Compared to Desert Storm, for instance, when thirty SOF detachments operated largely independent of conventional forces, the Iraqi Freedom campaign utilized more than one hundred SOF detachments, many of which were closely integrated into the operations of conventional forces.

None were more closely integrated than those helping General Wallace and V Corps solve the critical riddle of the fedayeen in Najaf. Like previous commanders involved in what was essentially counterinsurgency warfare, Wallace was finding that the U.S. ability to collect intelligence on the enemy through electronic intercepts or overhead surveillance was largely negated by fedayeen tactics. The Iraqi irregulars didn't wear uniforms nor use standard field radios to communicate, and an unmanned aerial drone flying at twenty-thousand feet couldn't filter out fedayeen fighters from everyday Iraqi civilians.

So each day Wallace met face-to-face with the commander of the SOF detachment that had infiltrated commandos into Najaf just before the sandstorm in order to establish contact with Shiite clerics and tribal leaders, and to gauge the attitude of the citizens of Najaf. "Sir, the tribal leaders are more scared of the fedayeen than they are of us, and until we make it clear that U.S. troops are here to stay, they are going to sit on their hands," said the SOF leader.

Wallace told the Special Ops commander that he needed the ten-digit GPS coordinates of both the fedayeen and Baath Party headquarters. Within days, those ten-digit spots on the electronic map board in the V Corps TAC were marked on the near horizon by a dark plume of smoke. The process of putting the fear of U.S. airpower into the paramilitaries holding Najaf, and convincing the locals that the U.S. military was here to stay, had begun.

With their soft caps and mustaches, exotic weaponry and signature swagger, the Special Ops commandos always cut a badass figure around V Corps TAC, and why not? They were impossible to miss, however, and in general wanted nothing to do with embedded reporters. One exception was a Southern good ol' boy who realized that the journalists could access Internet sports sites on our computers via satellite. He would scroll through the scores and we would idly chat, the only unspoken rule being that nothing much was said.

Alicia Ryu, the attractive Korean reporter for "Voice of America" that Mike Kelly and I had dined with in Kuwait, had by this time hitched a ride on a Chinook helicopter and shown up at the V Corps TAC, her reputation for fearlessness apparently well deserved. Alicia asked the good ol' boy where he had acquired the traditional Arab head covering that all of the commandos generally wore as neck scarves.

"Oh that. I got that from a local," said the Special Forces trooper.

"You've had time for shopping?" Alicia asked with a laugh.

"Well, let's just say that I knew he wouldn't be needing it anymore."

Afterward, Alicia confided to me that Americans were beginning to freak her out. "You all seem so easygoing and ready with a joke," she said. "Yet I get the distinct feeling you could just as easily slit my throat as talk to me, and then think nothing of it later."

I knew what Alicia meant. The Special Forces commandos reminded me of a group of scouts I had sat next to in the mess tent one night back in Camp Virginia. I had immediately sensed that they were different from the rear area troops. Instead of the standard issue M-16s, they carried the stubbier M-4 assault rifles favored by Special Forces, and they had extra clips of ammo taped to their gun stocks and bulging from the pockets of grimy desert camouflage uniforms. They also seemed somehow closer-knit than the soldiers I had become accustomed to, as if they could finish each other's sentences with a knowing glance. We had struck up a polite conversation and I told them I was an embedded journalist, and asked what they did. "We're scouts," one of them said, and I immediately understood. They were a long-range reconnaissance patrol, one of the scout teams I knew were crawling all over Iraq in preparation for the war to come.

So if they told me what they'd been up to, I joked, I guess they'd have to kill me, huh? The scouts smiled at each other and laughed, and then laughed some more with those knowing looks, until somehow it wasn't funny anymore. After that, I quickly finished my dinner in silence and took my leave.

CHAPTER 15

Fuel Masters, Water Dogs, and Gorilla Snot

AS THIRD INFANTRY DIVISION began to consolidate its brigades between Najaf and Karbala on March 29–30 in preparation for the final push to Baghdad, I toured the nearby LSA Bushmaster with V Corps Sgt. Maj. Kenneth Preston, the senior noncommissioned officer for the entire Corps. Preston was a quiet and steadfast "soldier's soldier," and he was determined to show me a side of the U.S. Army that rarely made the nightly news or appeared in newspaper headlines.

Witnessing firsthand the buildup of support that had been accomplished in just a matter of days around Objective Rams, I was struck by how much transformational warfare still depended on familiar pillars of U.S. military strength, including the innate talent and appetite for organizing the "Big Project." Whether that entailed digging a canal across Panama, launching an invasion force across the English Channel, or moving an army half the length of a disputed country in little over a week, it seemed not to matter. Throughout the sandstorm and in the days after, the U.S. Army's unheralded support, supply, and engineering battalions had worked tirelessly doing what no other force in the world could do: moving a logistical mountain of supplies so far and so high that already by the end of March, V Corps could very nearly glimpse Baghdad in the distance.

At a nearby clay quarry that had been scouted long before the war began, bulldozers and dump trucks requisitioned from an Iraqi cement factory were digging and transporting clay to an airstrip under construction by the Ninety-fourth Engineering Battalion. At the airstrip, Capt. Alex Deraney and his troops of the 535th Combat Support Company mixed the clay with a quick-drying composite lovingly referred to as "gorilla snot," laying it down in a thirty-five-hundred-foot runway that was nearly complete and ready to accept C-130 transport aircraft. Caked with dust and sporting a week's stubble of beard, Deraney had the thousand-yard stare and slurred speech of the chronically sleep deprived. When I asked how his war had gone so far, he had to think for a long moment.

"We were the first clearing a way through the berm on the Kuwait–Iraq border. Helped establish the airfield at Talil. Did an assault bridge crossing of the Euphrates near Nasiriyah. Built this airfield in less than a week," said Deraney. When I asked when he had last had a night's sleep, Deraney couldn't remember for sure. "Four or five nights ago, I think."

Nearby we visited a small oasis where Sgt. 1st Class Avery Wood and the other "Water Dogs" of the 226 Quartermaster Water Purification Company were pumping nearly sixty thousand gallons a day of potable water from three "reverse osmosis" purification pumps, critical support for the thousands of thirsty U.S. troops who kept arriving in a seemingly endless convoy from the south. A scant few miles away, the "Fuel Masters" of Corps Support Command gave us a tour of a massive fuel farm. Like everyone else at LSA Bushmaster, 1st Sgt. George Hosster and his troops had worked through the sandstorm and the days after with little sleep or rest. The result were giant bags of JP8 fuel, some as large as 210,000 gallons, cradled in sand berms and lined up side by side for more than a hundred yards, ready to quench the voracious thirst of a combat division on the offensive.

"We don't get much respect from the helicopter pilots and tank drivers," Hosster told me. "But I tell them all the time, 'Without us, you're just dismounted infantry carrying pistols, or soldiers manning a pillbox.'"

While visiting the Fuel Masters we ran into a friendly Army chaplain, Maj. Larry Holland. It was obvious that he and Sergeant Preston went way back. As an instructor at the U.S. Army's chaplain school at Ft. Jackson, South Carolina, Holland was supposed to be in a classroom. Because the Army was short on chaplains, however, he had volunteered to deploy to Iraq. "I wasn't going to let the Army send a battalion to war without a chaplain," explained Holland, who had conducted seven services in the past three days alone. "This is actually a very good ministry, because faith just explodes out here. Back in garrison I might have a service and only a few people show up. Out here they come by the hundreds to every service. Everyone confronts their faith in a war."

What enlightenment could a man of God bring to such a seemingly forsaken place, I wondered. "Soldiers ask me all the time how I can be part of war, and still be a faithful chaplain," said Holland. "What I tell them is that it comes down to good and evil. I wouldn't be out here if I didn't believe that. So I tell the soldiers that what we have to do is just lean on one another. Because out here we're all the family each of us has."

At a checkpoint on the outskirts of Najaf that was manned by newly arrived soldiers of the 101st Airborne, we got a foretaste of the ominous ambiguities in store as the mission transitioned from high-intensity combat at the front to something between low-intensity combat and stability operations. In that phase, U.S. soldiers and Iraqis would inevitably rub up closer against each other, with all the cultural frictions and danger that entailed. Days earlier, for instance, a car bomb had killed four U.S. soldiers at a similar checkpoint. That escalation in tensions, in turn, led to one of the most grisly incidents of the war thus far. Due to a misunderstanding, U.S. troops at another checkpoint had opened fire on an Iraqi van. When the shooting finally stopped and the soldiers approached the van, they were horrified to find the bloody remains of seven women and children. Ever since, checkpoints had become an increasingly tense point of interaction between U.S. troops and local Iraqis.

At the 101st checkpoint we watched two soldiers stop a vehicle and search its passengers, two men and a woman in traditional Islamic garb and veil. In a gesture of intended respect, a young U.S. soldier declined to pat the woman down, signaling instead to the man to have his wife simply shake her arms so it would be clear the woman was not concealing a bomb beneath her robes. The more uncomprehending the Iraqi's expression became, however, the louder the U.S. soldier spoke and the harder he flapped his arms, looking every bit the "Screaming Eagle" of his division's namesake.

What the Iraqis and the Americans surmised from their first encounter with one another was impossible to read behind expressions of bewilderment on both sides. With its confusing and tragicomic interplay between alien cultures, and its potentially lethal undertones, the scene at the checkpoint that day seemed to me an apt metaphor for the Iraq war: a clash between two uncomprehending peoples that was destined to change both in ways no one could predict. In the distance behind the checkpoint, two 101st helicopters were clearly visible, swooping and banking like black bats around the Golden Dome of the Mosque of Ali, resting place of the prophet Mohammed's son-in-law and the founder of the Shiite sect.

"Attention in the TAC! Fire Mission! Clear a grid!" On the morning of March 31, V Corps had launched five simultaneous, limited-objective attacks south of Karbala in preparation for the final push to Baghdad. To deceive Iraqi commanders that the main attack and key crossing of the Euphrates River was coming south of Karbala, the Second Brigade of the Third Infantry and 101st Airborne divisions made feints toward the towns of Hindiyah and Al Hillah, in both instances becoming involved in intense combat west of Karbala. Meanwhile, attack aviation elements of the 101st made an armed reconnaissance and established a forward operating base just south of the Bahr al-Milh Lake and west of Karbala, protecting the Corps' left flank for the maneuver to come. Finally, the 101st and Eighty-second began operations to "isolate and clear" fedayeen elements in Najaf and Samawah.

The Iraqis fell for the deception. As captured maps from the Medina Division's Tenth Brigade later confirmed, Iraqi commanders were convinced by the feints that the main U.S. effort was coming up Highways 8 and 9 east of Karbala, and they began repositioning their forces to interdict that advance. By the late afternoon of March 31, U.S. reconnaissance was picking up Iraqi vehicles, artillery pieces and tanks on heavy-equipment transporters repositioning east of Karbala, in broad daylight and within clear view of U.S. Air Force, Navy, and coalition aircraft. The scene inside V Corps TAC was frantic as commanders took advantage of the target-rich environment, calling out fire missions on the exposed Iraqi forces with air strikes and long-range artillery.

General Wallace was clearly relieved to be back on the offensive and seizing the initiative after the nearly five-day pause. The situation in Najaf in particular, however, continued to concern him greatly. Of all the cities he had hoped to avoid fighting in, Najaf topped the list due to its religious significance as site to some of the holiest Shiite shrines. Wallace spoke daily with Maj. Gen. David Petraeus about his desire that U.S. forces not get "stuck in the city." After one such meeting at the V Corps TAC, I asked Petraeus about his plans for Najaf. "I don't know if we'll have to take the city neighborhood by neighborhood or not. But I do know that these people need to see us and believe we're willing to stay."

On March 31, the 101st efforts to isolate Najaf morphed into a full-fledged attack to clear the city of the fedayeen and paramilitaries. After bringing in precision air strikes on fedayeen headquarters and other targets, Col. Ben Hodges of the First Brigade launched a combined arms "thunder run" that brought U.S. forces all the way to the center of town and the Mosque of Ali. Along with another armored hit-and-withdraw operation through the eastern side of the city the next day, the two raids seemed to break the back of the resistance.

When General Wallace first heard of Colonel Hodges's thunder run with tracked M-1 tanks and Bradleys driving into central Najaf, he was upset. Not only did such a heavy incursion seem to risk sparking a backlash among the city's Shiites, but using heavy armor in an urban setting unsupported by light infantry violated Army doctrine. After reflecting on the rapid success of an operation that integrated precision air strikes, armored raids, and then light forces, however, Wallace decided that Maj. Gen. Dave Petraeus and Colonel Hodges had made an invaluable contribution to the Iraqi Freedom campaign: they had given V Corps and the

Third Infantry Division not only a blueprint, but a dress rehearsal for the Battle of Baghdad. With each lopsided fight between U.S. forces and Iraqi paramilitaries and irregulars, U.S. troops gained confidence and the Iraqis lost hundreds of fighters. When I asked General Wallace why the fedayeen and Iraqi paramilitaries never seemed to adjust their suicidal tactics, he confessed that V Corps commanders had wondered about the same thing. "We don't think enough of them are surviving these fights to learn from them."

As V Corps TAC struggled to manage and track five simultaneous attacks on March 31, Operations Chief Steve Hicks resumed his constant vigil before the electronic map board, his gaze fixed on a single point. The subject of his intense interest was a sliver of land between a large body of water known as the Bahr al-Milh, or "Sea of Salt," and the Iraqi town of Karbala. In essence, all of the fighting then under way was designed to mask the importance U.S. planners had always placed on that milewide sliver of land known as the Karbala Gap.

The area east of Karbala and the Euphrates River where U.S. forces were feinting was a river valley dotted with cities and towns and crisscrossed by canals, irrigation ditches, and small bridges. As U.S. commanders were even then discovering, that kind of congested terrain and urban sprawl largely negated U.S. advantages in weapons range and speed of maneuver.

"The area occupied by the Medina east of Karbala, between the Euphrates and Tigris Rivers, is very complex and restrictive terrain where we think the Iraqis want to draw us into a close urban fight," Hicks told me. On the other hand, just north of Karbala was a wide-open swath of territory bordering the eastern shore of Bahr al-Milh and flanking the Medina Division and the southern approaches to Baghdad. This territory just north of Karbala was tailor-made for U.S. maneuver forces. "That's why I've always felt the passing and holding of the Karbala Gap was critical to this campaign," said Hicks. "It will open up the flank of the Medina Division and the southern approaches to Baghdad, and once Saddam's best division is defeated it will be very hard for the Iraqis to contest this war with conventional forces."

The problem was the Karbala Gap itself. A natural chokepoint less than eighteen hundred meters wide at some points, the gap included marshy agriculture land and rock quarries, with only two or three little roads winding through. On one side was the contested town of Karbala, which was still in the grip of Saddam fedayeen, and on the other a dam that if sabotaged could deluge U.S. forces with the waters of the Bahr al-Milh. The gap offered good fields of fire for defenders, and U.S. intelligence suggested that Iraqi artillery and rocket forces had positioned themselves to form a "kill box" in the gap. And then there was the matter of chemical weapons.

"The Karbala Gap is very near the red line that we expect will trip the use of chemical weapons. If the Iraqis are ever going to use chemicals, that's where you'd expect them," Hicks told me on the afternoon of April 1. That night the Third Infantry Division was scheduled to shoot the gap. Although a persistent chemical agent dropped in the gap would not stop U.S. armored forces driving pressurized tanks and armored vehicles, Hicks said, it could cut their critical supply lines.

"I'll tell you the truth," said Colonel Hicks, a man whose lack of even prudent fear was renowned within V Corps. "The Karbala Gap is scary to me."

CHAPTER 16

Baghdad Calling

THE MOON was only a sliver in the early morning hours of April 2, and the Karbala Gap was a dark and deeply eerie place. The tight confines of the gap seemed to amplify the percussive sounds of nearby battle and the clanking of First Brigade's armor as it lurched over the broken terrain. Less than a mile to the east Lt. Col. Rock Marcone's Task Force 3-69 Armor Battalion was screening the town of Karbala, repelling a slew of determined but mostly unorganized Iraqi assault teams and destroying the odd Iraqi tank, while the rest of First Brigade felt its way across the pitted and uneven terrain to two earthen bridges. Everyone was tensed for the batten-down alert signaling that the incoming artillery carried chemical weapons or nerve gas. As if that wasn't enough to worry about, intelligence or rumor, and in a war zone they often seemed inextricable, indicated that the Iraqis might blow the dam that bordered the gap from the west, sending the black waters of the Bahr al-Milh cascading down to sweep away the foreign invaders.

A First Brigade Bradley Fighting Vehicle crested a rise, its commander scanning the terrain ahead with night-vision optics. He spotted an Iraqi T-72 tank and a soldier standing beside it. Quickly, before the tank crew could react, the Bradley commander swung his turret and fired a volley from his powerful 30 mm chain gun, striking the tank and eviscerating the soldier. The tank's turret never even moved. As the Bradley approached the T-72 there were shouts in English and a commotion, U.S. soldiers were running toward the tank, and the Bradley commander leaped out and approached the dead soldier. Only laying on the ground was the mangled body of his own dead captain, who had stopped to check the already disabled Iraqi tank for maps or intelligence. Another U.S. soldier had been swept up in war's riptide of horror and regret.

Despite sporadic Iraqi rocket and artillery fire, First Brigade made it through the Karbala Gap meeting only light resistance. The Medina and Adnan Division elements they expected had apparently taken the bait of the previous day's feints, repositioning to the east of the city. Around 6:30

A.M. the next morning, Col. William Grimsley halted First Brigade Combat Team to refuel. The passage through the feared Karbala Gap that they had anticipated would require as much as twenty-four hours of fighting had been accomplished in less than five. After Third I.D. Assistant Commander Gen. Lloyd Austin issued the order to maintain momentum and immediately continue the attack to secure the crucial bridge crossing the Euphrates at Objective Peach, Grimsley conferred with Lt. Col. Rock Marcone. Once again Marcone's 3-69 Armor Battalion was chosen to spearhead the attack.

Grimsley and Marcone had anticipated that the Iraqis would defend heavily either at the Karbala Gap or at the Euphrates River at Objective Peach which, along with all of Third I.D.'s objectives, was named for a county in their home state of Georgia. The relatively easy passage of Karbala meant that their crossing of the Euphrates would likely be hotly contested.

After the battle for the bridge at Objective Jenkins, however, both Grimsley and Marcone had thought long and hard about the mistakes that were made and how to correct them. They assumed that once again the bridge would be rigged for demolition, and they talked about what to do about it. At Jenkins the Iraqis had used German-made demolition firing mechanisms, and after closely analyzing the gear, ranges, and map coordinates around Objective Peach, Marcone and his officers anticipated the most likely positions for Iraqi trigger teams on the far side of the Euphrates. He intended to bring artillery and Air Force precision-guided weapons down on their heads.

Reconnaissance teams were sent ahead and combat engineers backed by boats and mobile bridging equipment were placed just behind lead armor elements in the attack echelon. Apache gunships would fly over their shoulder and provide long-range suppression in a combined air-land assault designed to quickly seize the bridge before the Iraqis could blow it or call in reinforcements to contest the crossing. The two U.S. Army officers had gone to school on the Iraqis, and it revealed perhaps the most transformational characteristic of the U.S. military: a learning organization that emphasized centralized command and decentralized operations, and empowered individual commanders to seize the initiative with intellect and daring.

Reconnaissance indicated that the Peach Bridge was held by at least one dug-in Iraqi reconnaissance company. Colonel Marcone called in Apaches and close air support, and placed his tanks on high ground to provide suppression fire, but the Iraqis successfully blew a hole in the bridge with rigged explosives and they kept U.S. troops at bay with tank and mortar fire while attempting to finish the job. Desperate to save the bridge, at that moment Marcone gave an order not heard from a U.S.

Army officer since World War II: He called for an assault-boat crossing of a river under heavy enemy fire.

With artillery-borne smoke charges providing cover, First Brigade infantry and combat engineers launched their boats into the enveloping fog over the Euphrates. Forty-five minutes of intense fighting ensued that included virtually every form of fire detailed in the Army's war-fighting manual, from direct to indirect and virtually everything in between—rockets, tank fire, mortars, missiles, artillery, small-arms and machine-gun fire. The precision of U.S. fire was on terrifying display, as U.S. gunners put tank rounds literally through the windows of a house on the far side occupied by Iraqi defenders. A few M-1s were hit by mortar rounds, but once again the U.S. Army's main battle tank proved impervious to most Iraqi weapons.

In the midst of the battle the Euphrates Bridge seemed to float just above the fog, literally hanging in the balance. Beneath the mists, however, combat engineers in rafts or standing in water up to their shoulders were frantically cutting wires and disabling Iraqi demolition charges. Finally the order was given for 3-69's M-1 tanks and Bradleys to cross the damaged bridge and secure the far side. By sunset, the last seriously contested gate on the road to Baghdad was flung wide open.

As 3-69's armor secured the far side of the Euphrates, its support convoy poured over the damaged Peach Bridge, carrying a number of embedded reporters, including Michael Kelly, Ted Koppel, and a CBS camera crew led by Mario Decalvalho, a legendary cameraman who had covered ten wars. "Eleven if you count Angola," Mario said, referring to a war he fought in as a former Portuguese commando. Decalvalho and Kelly were especially happy to see each other, as their friendship went as far back as the presidential campaign of Michael Dukakis that they both had covered.

The veteran correspondents all shared a dinner whose main menu item was euphoria. Everyone had been nervous about passing through the Karbala Gap and crossing the Euphrates. With those two obstacles safely breached it seemed likely that the war was coming to a head, though the battle for Baghdad still loomed. Even before the meal was over, however, sounds of nearby fighting erupted as the Iraqis launched a furious counterattack to try and retake the bridge over the Euphrates.

Only this time Lt. Col. Rock Marcone and 3-69 were prepared. Captured documents had tipped them that an Iraqi Republican Guard commando battalion and the Tenth Armored Brigade of the Medina Division would likely try and counterattack in the night. Once again Marcone had drawn on his experience from the fight for the Jenkins Bridge near Al Kifl, setting up defensive positions with wide fields of fire and establishing a kill box. After intermittent shelling from Iraqi artillery and mortar positions, the main attack came around 3:00 A.M., with the Republican Guard commandos coming on foot from the north, and the Tenth Armored Brigade advancing from the south, led by a tank company and as many as fifty armored personnel carriers.

Over the next few hours Task Force 3-69 repelled the counterattack, destroying fifteen T-72 tanks, thirty Iraqi armored personnel carriers, and killing the commander of Medina's Tenth Armored Brigade. Inside the Iraqi commander's tank, Marcone found a map that indicated that their feints of a few days before had worked: The map clearly anticipated the U.S. main effort coming from the south and east of Karbala, explaining the relatively light defenses at the Karbala Gap and Objective Peach.

During the night of the Iraqi counterattack at Peach, the correspondents got little sleep. Iraqi mortar and artillery rounds fell intermittently near the U.S. bridgehead. At one point, the scream of a round grew sickeningly shrill until someone in the tent shouted "Incoming!" and Ted Koppel, Mike Kelly, Mario Decalvalho and the others dove to the ground. After the nearby explosion, the correspondents pulled their noses out of the dirt and brushed themselves off, including CBS executive producer Leroy Severs, who stood six foot five and weighed nearly 260 lbs.

"You know something," Michael Kelly said with a twinkle in his eye and his best Art Carney-to-Jackie Gleason inflection, "You move pretty fast for a big guy."

Early the next morning of April 3, First Brigade began screening the passage of the Second Brigade Combat Team so that it could continue in hopscotch fashion to push to a key highway interchange just south of Baghdad designated Objective Saints, all Corps objectives having been named after NFL football teams. The experience of the Second Brigade the previous night revealed just how critical it was that First Brigade captured the Euphrates Bridge. In an attempt to relieve congestion in the Karbala Gap, two of the Brigade's battalions had been sent east around the other side of Karbala into the area where Iraqi forces were led to believe U.S. forces would come all along. Both battalions had quickly become so bogged down in the marshy terrain that they turned around and headed for the gap after all. Early that morning, Second Brigade Commander Col. Dave Perkins had decided to press the attack to Saints with a single battalion rather than wait for the other battalions to catch up. The Third I.D. was finally on the move, and General Blount was not about to let up on the accelerator.

In the meantime, First Brigade commander Col. Will Grimsley called a meeting of his battalion and task force commanders to discuss the mission to seize Objective Lions, the queen of the Iraqi Freedom chessboard: the Saddam Hussein International Airport on the western outskirts of

Baghdad. During the meeting, an obviously excited General Blount arrived with his operations officer, Lt. Col. Peter Bayer. The plan had been for the First Brigade to attack the airport the next morning, but Blount clearly wanted to push the schedule up.

"How soon can you move on the airport?" Blount asked.

"Well sir, I could probably go this afternoon if you need me to," Grimsley replied without much enthusiasm. "But what I really don't want to do is attack the airport at night. As you know, the terrain around there is very rugged and difficult. There are lots of canals and other obstacles."

"Okay, but if you're going to get up there before dark you need to be ready to leave by 1400," said Blount, indicating that First Brigade needed to be ready to move by 2:00 P.M.

Though he didn't let on, Blount was churning inside. After champing at the bit for days during the pause, the Third Infantry Division had finally been given its rein and Blount was determined to press ahead relentlessly to keep the pressure on the Iraqis. As only a commander at the front can, Blount sensed that the Iraqi forces were reacting too slowly to their advance through Karbala and across the Euphrates to reposition and effectively counter the U.S. thrust. Lead elements of the Second Brigade were already reporting finding frontline T-72 tanks near Objective Saints, the key highway interchange just south of Baghdad, with their engines still running and their barrels pointing south. The Iraqi crews were apparently unaware until the last minute that they had been flanked from the west. If he acted decisively now, Blount believed he could cut off and envelop the Medina Division at Objective Saints, and establish the key staging area for the assault on Baghdad at Objective Lions. The last thing he wanted to do was give Saddam an extra few days to reposition Republican Guard forces south of Baghdad into their path.

After meeting with Colonel Grimsley, Blount thus called his boss, V Corps commander General Wallace, and asked for permission to initiate an attack on the airport immediately. He knew that the V Corps staff was still debating several options for taking the airport, including a possible air assault by the 101st Air Mobile Division in order to avoid possible heavy losses to tanks and support vehicles in such dense terrain. Blount insisted, however, that the Third Infantry Division was the better choice.

"Sir, we trained for this," Blount told Wallace. "We're prepared for this. We're ready for this. We need to go now."

There was a pregnant pause on the radio channel, and a hush in both headquarters as the staffs waited anxiously to hear the corps commander's decision. For his part, Gen. Scott Wallace knew that he had come to another fateful decision in the campaign. On the downside, the intelligence on the size and disposition of Iraqi defenders at the airport was sketchy. While the GPS-assisted Blue Force Tracker gave an unprecedented, if slightly delayed, picture of the relative positions of U.S. and coalition forces, Wallace had learned by that time to essentially discount its depiction of "red" or enemy forces. These were plotted in large part based on conjecture, and reliant on bomb damage assessments that lagged events by as much as two days. That was far too slow for warfare conducted at such speed.

Wallace and his staff suspected that roughly a brigade of Special Republican Guards were in defensive positions at the airport itself, with the Seventeenth Brigade of the Hammurabi Division available to defend the roads leading from the airport to the city. An additional Special Republican Guard battalion and two brigades of light infantry were thought to be available to defend Baghdad proper, along with as many as 15,000 paramilitary forces.

Additionally, pushing up the schedule for the airport attack could wreak havoc on the careful sequencing of the advance, and risked committing lead elements of the division piecemeal to a blind "movement to contact," rather than a more deliberate attack based on reliable intelligence.

"Sir, I'm afraid this guy will drive all the way to downtown Baghdad if we don't rein him in," said Col. Steve Hicks, V Corps operations chief, referring to General Blount.

On the other hand, Wallace had the same sense as Blount that the Iraqis were on the ropes. It seemed to take the Iraqi command-and-control system roughly twenty-four hours to react to U.S. moves and filter orders from Baghdad down to forward troops. The speed of the Third Infantry Division's advance had gotten inside that Iraqi decision-making loop, with devastating results for frontline Iraqi forces. With the successful seizing of the Euphrates River crossing, Wallace decided, U.S. forces had Saddam Hussein by the balls.

"Have a good fight," Wallace told Blount over the radio, falling back on the instincts inculcated in all U.S. Army leaders to give field commanders great sway in determining, in the heat of combat, how best to exploit a reeling enemy. "Victory 6, out."

CHAPTER 17

Brothers in Arms

ON THE EVENING of April 3, with Task Force 3–69 literally battering down the walls to Saddam International Airport and the Third Infantry Division's juggernaut in full fury, the picture of the resultant carnage was on vivid display inside V Corps Tactical Headquarters. Live and on video, Iraqi soldiers were dying by the hundreds. The continuous charge of the Third Infantry Division through the Karbala Gap, over the Euphrates and to the very outskirts of Baghdad had, in the words of a senior officer, "kicked the anthill." Finally sensing that they had been outflanked and were in danger of being cut off, major remnants of the Medina and other Republican Guard units to the south were scurrying north up Highways 10 and 8 and associated tributaries, trying under the cover of night to retreat into Baghdad with their tanks, towed artillery, and missile launchers, possibly for a final stand. Only they were being followed.

Unseen overhead, an unmanned drone would zero in on a military vehicle or enemy emplacement and linger, its images broadcast in real time on the tactical headquarters' electronic display. As opposed to Desert Storm just over a decade earlier, when U.S. forces relied on a single unmanned aerial vehicle (UAV) model in their arsenal, in Operation Iraqi Freedom ten different types of unmanned drones were tracking the movement of Iraqi forces from above, from continent-spanning Global Hawks flying in near space, to tiny Dragon Eyes that could be hand-launched by a forward squad. These were in addition to a fleet of fourteen manned U.S. Air Force Joint Stars ground surveillance aircraft in theater, enough to provide twenty-four-hour coverage of parts of the Iraqi battlefield. There were still not nearly enough drones to suit U.S. commanders, but their prominent role in the Iraqi Freedom campaign was an inescapable example of how technology was reshaping the modern battlefield.

After V Corps' Hunter drone transmitted the coordinates of an Iraqi vehicle, the operations chief of the TAC would relay the GPS grid to an Air Force liaison officer (ALO). Then the entire headquarters would wait and watch until the death sentence was carried out with a precision-guided bomb. For disquieting minutes, we all knew what the figures clearly visible on the ground could never guess as they went about their soldierly duties supposedly under the cloak of darkness, refueling a tank or smoking cigarettes around an artillery tube: They were condemned men.

Watching that annihilation, General Wallace sensed that he was truly witnessing something transformational in the nature of modern warfare. In a joint, combined-arms operation, maneuver forces were flanking and flushing out an enemy at risk of being overrun until they were forced to reposition, at which point they became easy prey for precision U.S. air-power. In just the twenty-four-hour period following the Third Infantry Division's breach of the Karbala Gap, the U.S. Air Force would destroy 25 percent of all the enemy targets it hit during the entire war up to that point.

The electronic map board in the TAC also displayed a nonlinear bat-tlefield, over which brigade and even smaller battalion-sized U.S. forces roamed and fought largely independently, calling in devastating preci-sion strikes with growing alacrity wherever the enemy massed to contest their passing, or fled to avoid their fury. At times the Third Infantry Divi-sion advanced so fast, and in so many different directions, that its lead elements were in danger of crossing the demarcated "forward edge of advance," possibly risking fratricide from Air Force and coalition pilots who had a free hand to bomb beyond that line. Those boundaries had simply been drawn up under a doctrine that did not anticipate such rapid speeds of advance. At one point Third Infantry Division was spread out over a 16,000-square-kilometer battle space that was 230 kilometers deep and 70 kilometers wide. The era of massed formations fighting in neat echelons, with an easily discernible front line and secure rear area, might well have been passing before General Wallace's eyes.

Meanwhile, the deadly hail raining down on the Iraqis from a pitch-black night sky included the full panoply of U.S. armament, from individ-ually targeted JDAM bombs dropped from B-1 bombers flying at more than fifteen thousand feet, to the devastating fusillade of bullets spit from the Gatling guns of an AC-130 Hercules known as "Spooky." That merci-less firing squad also included 500 lb antitank "cluster bombs" that frag-mented before impact into hundreds of mini-bomblets, each crammed with high explosive. Just before hitting the ground those bomblets ignited into a vapor burst of razorlike shards screeching through the air at four thousand feet per second, each capable of penetrating six inches of steel armor. What they did to a human body was unforgettable, no matter how hard you tried.

The UAV images on display in the V Corps TAC were not the sanitized versions shown at U.S. Central Command press briefings of bombs flying through the windows of buildings. On real-time Hunter video, people were clearly visible at night in the reverse highlights of the drone's thermal camera, their figures blown like scarecrows by the percussive blast of a nearby bomb. After one such strike on an Iraqi crew manning an artillery position near Objective Saints, Lt. Col. Eric Wagenaar, the operations officer in charge, was asked about movement in the corner of the image. He waited until the drone focused in and answered the question all on its own.

"That's a wounded Iraqi soldier, trying to crawl away," said Wagenaar, stating the all too obvious.

America chooses among its finest men and women to form an elite warrior class, and then it places them in kill-or-be-killed situations. Shame on anyone who would fault them for being good at killing. After the unmanned drone displayed yet another successful strike against an Iraqi mobile rocket launcher, its driver standing under a palm grove smoking a cigarette one moment and then eviscerated in a dirty cloud the next, prompting a cheer to erupt inside the TAC, I remarked that it was a passing strange business they were in just the same.

Both Wagenaar and Lt. Col. Rob Baker, two thoughtful U.S. officers if ever there were any, nodded in agreement. Under the circumstances neither cared to argue the point.

"It's one helluva thing, watching people die," said Rob Baker.

While no accurate tally of Iraqis killed in the war existed, those images of the final rout before the Battle of Baghdad suggested that the dead must surely number in the thousands upon thousands. Someday the sad tableau of their lives would have to be translated from the Arabic, I thought, the better to understand what happened here. How came these soldiers to be ensnared by the tyrant Saddam Hussein, and what strange twists of history led them twice into disastrous confrontations with the U.S. military? What penance would America have to serve, I wondered, for this terrible power we possessed?

By the break of dawn the next morning, the mood in the TAC was considerably more somber. "Yesterday was a bad day," Col. Steve Hicks, V Corps operations chief, explained as I stopped by for a quick update after a few hours of sleep. Task Force 3–69 was still fighting a pitched battle with Special Republican Guards, he explained, who at first light had counterattacked out of a hidden bunker complex that laced Saddam International Airport.

The night before, there was the Army captain who had been killed in the Karbala Gap by friendly fire while searching a destroyed Iraqi tank for maps and intelligence. A Third Infantry Division engineer, meanwhile, had suffered a gunshot wound to the head. Another Army squad suffered three reported casualties from what was believed to be a RPG attack, although the Army was investigating whether that could also be a case of blue-on-blue fire from a U.S. F-15 aircraft. One of Third Infantry Division's Humvees had been hit by an Iraqi RPG at the airport, and another had turned over into a canal while evading enemy fire. Both incidents had resulted in casualties. A division Black Hawk helicopter had also crashed near Karbala.

As Colonel Hicks reviewed the grim tally of the previous thirty-six hours, the radio on the tactical headquarters command desk crackled angrily to life. For the second time, Third Division Headquarters wanted confirmation of the casualties from the Humvee that had fallen into the canal. One of its occupants was apparently a reporter, and HQ wanted to know from its frontline unit who was killed.

Except the name Lt. Col. Rick Nohmer was scribbling on his pad had to be a mistake. Something in my expression made Nohmer, my Humvee companion during the long drive through Iraq, stop what he was doing.

"Mike Kelly," he said. "Did you know him?"

The road to Baghdad was scorched black, the burned husks of tanks and trucks mounted with antiaircraft guns littering the deserted roadside for miles, each dark smudge of ash and charred detritus along the way bespeaking human drama with a violent end. The stench of rotting flesh rose from various wreckage, and occasionally Bedouin tribesmen would raise their heads from the skeleton cab of a truck long enough to smile and wave, before returning to their macabre scavenging. At random intervals the guardrail along the highway was crumpled as if from the blows of a massive fist.

At Objective Saints, where Highways 8 and 10 intersected just south of Baghdad, the mangled remains of an M-1 tank blocked one side of the highway, and U.S. troops worked to clear an area blasted by an Iraqi rocket the day before, April 7, killing three U.S. soldiers and two journalists. My journey to find Task Force 3–69 and learn the details of my friend's death was mostly a matter of tracing the path of destruction left in the Third Infantry Division's wake on its way to Baghdad. Twenty minutes into the trip, I was seized by a premonition of death so strong that I had to bite my clenched fist almost until it bled to stifle a nauseating wave of fear.

My fear was not altogether irrational, not that it mattered. Everyone had lived with varying degrees of anxiety ever since Kuwait; it was as inevitable in a war zone as lack of sleep or the monkey stench that comes from not showering properly for weeks. No one was in control of the trig-gers that could in an instant spike that general anxiety into something deeply malevolent and personal. In my own case the primary trigger was the death of Michael Kelly. Hell, we all loved Mike, and losing someone you love has a way of turning the general awfulness of war into a specific kind of horror. Nor did it help that I was traveling through a war zone in a soft-skinned Humvee without so much as a helmet or a flak jacket, and coming to realize along the way that my companion was quite possibly insane.

When Col. Steve Hicks had offered to take me along on an im-promptu trip to the airport to try and find Task Force 3–69, I only had minutes to get ready. Sergeant Ball had moved the Humvee I had traveled in, which contained both my flak jacket and helmet, and it was nowhere to be found. Everyone was as superstitious as a witch by that time, and the disappearance of my gear seemed a bad omen. After we left the gate of V Corps TAC's hastily secured camp at an abandoned Iraqi airfield, I also realized that instead of a convoy with proper escort, we would make the journey through still-contested battle space in a soft-skinned Humvee, with only one other armored Humvee trailing as security backup. Even the U.S. sentries at various checkpoints we passed along the way, all of them bristling with M-1 tanks and Bradleys, looked at us with a combina-tion of surprise and disbelief. Some shook their heads at the crazy-assed colonel out for a drive through the countryside.

Each time we approached an Iraqi vehicle on the mostly empty roads, a number of them the same style Toyota trucks favored by the Saddam fedayeen, Colonel Hicks and his driver would unholster their pistols and wave at the Iraqis to turn around. Tense moments ensued as the Iraqis decided what to do in the equivalent of a Mexican standoff. When I asked Colonel Hicks if he was worried about driving into a fedayeen ambush, he guessed that most of the paramilitaries had retreated into Baghdad for the big fight. His driver, a cheerful young black trooper whose name I missed in all the excitement, began to regale me with the exploits of Colo-nel Hicks the fearless, which unbeknownst to me were apparently re-nowned within V Corps. At that precise moment I hated them both.

At Saddam International Airport the signs of recent battle were every-where. A large airliner lay in a still-smoldering heap near one terminal, its giant tailfin proclaiming the demise of Iraqi Airlines. A massive smoke plume rose on the near horizon. Third Infantry units informed us that Task Force 3–69 had left the airport complex and was expanding the cor-don of Baghdad just to the north, where block-to-block fighting was under way. We crossed the runways in the northern part of the complex looking for a way out.

"Watch out!" Colonel Hicks yelled, jerking the arm of his driver and causing the Humvee to swerve violently. Then to me, "We almost ran over a mine."

Just outside the north side of the airport, through a row of palm trees, there were signs of very recent fighting. Blackened earth still smoldered as if from a flame-thrower blast, revealing the position of a bunker complex. Before I understood what was happening, Colonel Hicks had jumped out of the cab, drawn his 9 mm pistol, and was peering into the depths of a recently occupied bunker, perhaps hoping to confront any stragglers. His security detail scrambled wildly to catch up. When Hicks returned to the Humvee, I half-expected him to start waxing eloquent about the smell of napalm in the morning.

We crossed a nearby bridge overpass occupied by a U.S. squad that was hunkered down behind the railing with Javelin antitank weapons. They didn't know where 3–69 Tactical Operations Center (TOC) was located, but we were welcome to check under the bridge where their own TOC was positioned. Inside the tent, a map board showed a building-by-building lay-down of the surrounding area. The TOC we were in was indicated by a blue pin on the map. It was surrounded on three sides by red pins. Nearby we could hear the impact of mortar fire.

"Colonel Hicks, I think maybe we should head back," I said outside the tent, my premonitions getting stronger and my shit weaker by the moment. "It's not important enough to risk getting killed just to find 3–69."

"Oh, I've got too much to live for, don't worry," Hicks replied, nonplussed. "Anyway, I won't get lost."

Colonel Hicks instructed his driver to turn down a side street, and then follow another lone Humvee for a ways, and just like that we were lost. After striking a dead end in an abandoned ammo dump, we retraced our route, took another turn down a dirt road, and drove past a bullet-pocked empty guard tower and through a breach blasted in a stone wall east of the airport. RPG launchers, their bulbous warheads looking misshapen and out of scale with their riflelike stocks, were stacked on the side of the road like so many cords of wood.

Soon the road spilled into one of Saddam's expansive palace complexes, and we began to see vehicles with the insignia of the 3–69 Armored Battalion. M-1 tanks and Bradley Fighting Vehicles were parked around the palatial residences and guesthouses, every building and balcony opening onto the cool, green expanse of a man-made lagoon. The seasoned combat veterans of Task Force 3–69 were milling about, taking no more notice of the intermittent "BAWUMPH!" of a nearby mortar impact than they would of a car horn.

Inside a company tactical operations tent, we watched a young captain and his lieutenant brief on the battle under way to secure the area northeast of the airport. The first thing that leaped out at someone accustomed to a rear-echelon headquarters was how improbably young all the soldiers seem at the tip of the U.S. spear, these all-American boys with their down-home accents and immigrant names. The only sign of their rapidly vanishing innocence was a certain wariness about their eyes that no amount of rest would soon erase.

In the meantime, however, the GIs of the 3–69 had the keys to the palace, and many were partaking of all the comforts of the kingdom, including an indoor swimming pool. The former occupants, apparently Uday the torturer and his twin spawn Usay Hussein, were nowhere to be found. Outside in a stone courtyard once reserved for courtiers and supplicants to the regime, I saw that someone had strung a clothesline and proudly unfurled the green-and-black colors of Army-issue underwear. Mike had come so close, I thought, and he would so have loved the view.

Inside the marbled expanse of one of the palaces, the officers of 3–69 were gathered around a mahogany conference table, planning a thunder run into downtown Baghdad the next day, looking for a fight or surrender, whatever the remnants of Saddam's regime preferred. After the officers' brief was finished, Colonel Hicks introduced me to a dark-featured lieutenant colonel with a sharp gaze. The two men obviously had served together in the tight-knit club that is the U.S. Army officer corps, and Hicks explained why we had come.

"I want Mike Kelly's kids to know that I think their dad was a hero, and very brave," was the first thing out of Rock Marcone's mouth. Sitting us down in his temporary palace office, Marcone explained how the two, soldier and reporter, had become friends in short order. The First Brigade had adopted Kelly as one of their own, he said, and somehow I felt better knowing that Mike had been among friends up to the last.

Marcone recounted 3–69's final approach to Baghdad and the battle to seize the airport. After they had crossed the Euphrates, Marcone said, the landscape had changed from desert to a verdant valley of palm groves, rice paddies, and irrigation canals. Two of his tanks got quickly mired up to their armored skirts in that marshy ground, and the rest were forced to stick to paved two-lane roads that led through numerous small towns and villages. About ten miles south of Highway 1 leading to the airport, the column began receiving Iraqi mortar fire and fighting its way through machine-gun and RPG ambushes. At dusk, lead elements finally moved onto Highway 1 and began laying down preparatory artillery and rocket fire on the airport.

By the time Task Force 3–69's lead tanks left the Highway 1 interchange less than two miles from the airport, Rock Marcone said the unit was confronting exactly what he didn't want—a night attack against uncertain opposition with zero illumination. There were not even many stars visible, much less a discernible moon. The only light was an unearthly glow coming from the airport complex itself, a bonfire left in the wake of U.S. artillery strikes. As if the airport grounds were not eerie enough, during the assault all of the lights in nearby Baghdad mysteriously went dark, suggesting to some a last, desperate signal of some kind from Saddam Hussein.

A more immediate surprise for Marcone and his troops was the dense patchwork of marshes and canals that lay between the highway exit and the airport. They hadn't had time to conduct a proper reconnaissance of the terrain, and it was far worse than their aerial maps had indicated. What looked like a two-lane hardtop from a satellite photo was really little more than a raised path with canals on either side. In some places the M-1 tanks and Bradleys literally hung over the elevated roads. The second surprise was an absolute maze of fifteen-foot walls surrounding the airport complex itself, with no obvious gates in sight. Marcone shot a heat round at one wall in an effort to punch a hole through it, but the explosion barely made a dent in the massive, steel-reinforced structure. In desperation, Marcone ordered an M-60 bridge vehicle to drive into the wall like a battering ram to knock it down. Once on the airport grounds Task Force 3–69, split into two pincers for a tandem assault, fought a pitched battle through the night and into the next morning with commandos from Saddam's elite Special Republican Guards.

In the midst of that fight, Marcone heard on the radio that the convoy carrying his tactical operations center just to his rear was taking direct fire. *Oh, my God,* he thought, *in our hurry to get onto the airport we've driven our support columns into an ambush.* The radio had crackled as numerous vehicles reported that Iraqi infantry were coming out of hidden bunkers and firing on 3–69's soft-skinned supply train. Two scouts in a Humvee were hit by RPG fire, and needed immediate medical evacuation. Then a report came that another Humvee taking evasive action had flipped over into a canal in the pitch dark, its occupants trapped in the murky waters. Michael Kelly and the staff sergeant in charge of the 3–69 maintenance pool drowned in that canal.

"I can tell you that when you fight three battles with somebody, you get pretty close," said Rock Marcone, who counted Kelly among First Brigade's fourteen killed in action up to that point. "Michael Kelly was just a prince of a man."

As we sped the twenty or so miles back to camp at dusk over deserted roads, even Colonel Hick's jovial driver grew silent and tense. Driving through the verdant countryside, we saw Iraqis in robes and bare feet coming out of the gates of large mansions we assumed to be affiliated with Saddam's hated Baath Party, pushing wheelbarrows stacked high with pilfered goods. Most would stop long enough to smile and wave at the passing Americans, and then carry on with their cheerful looting. With darkness setting in, Hicks asked his driver to slow down.

"Sir, it's my job to get you back to camp alive," the driver replied. "I figure at this speed we make a tougher target."

Back at the camp the day's pent-up tension and fear and all the rest of it left me, and I was weary as never before. Before retreating to my computer to try and write it up, I tried to thank Colonel Hicks. He just shrugged it off. Then the crazy-assed, hard-charging colonel set me straight, revealing the journey as a gesture of such tenderness that for the moment I was speechless. The soldiers inevitably did that. They looked out for you in ways you didn't anticipate, and covered your back even before you realized it was exposed. It is why war stories are the best and worst stories any of us will ever remember.

"I just thought you needed some closure," Steve Hicks told me.

The sergeant who died in the canal with Michael Kelly when their Humvee overturned was Staff Sgt. Wilbert Davis, and he too had a wife and two young sons. As the head of 3–69 Armored Battalion's maintenance unit, Davis would never let a piece of equipment out of his care unless it was in top shape and ready for whatever the soldiers operating it might confront. If that meant that he and his troops had to work late shifts in what is largely a thankless task, so be it. His job and dedication were points of pride to Davis. Whenever one of his soldiers felt the world crashing down on his shoulders, as soldiers sometimes will, Davis would sit the soldier down to talk and not get up again until he had somehow elicited a grin and a laugh. He and Mike Kelly must have gotten along just fine.

Edward Korn was the Third Infantry Division captain killed in the Karbala Gap while searching an Iraqi T-72 for possible intelligence documents in a case of blue-on-blue fratricide—let "friendly fire" forever vanish from the lexicon. Sgt. 1st Class Paul Smith, the platoon sergeant with the Eleventh engineers who was shot in the head the same day, later succumbed to the wound. But not before dragging his wounded men out of harm's way under fire, and then holding as many as one hundred Iraqi Special Republican Guards at bay with a .50 caliber machine gun. Paul Smith's actions allowed his unit to regroup and organize a counterattack that ultimately stopped the Iraqi commandos. Sergeant Smith was later awarded the Congressional Medal of Honor, the nation's highest award for valor.

The three artillerymen who died as the result of a likely RPG attack were Todd Robbins, Randy Rehn, and Donald Oaks. The RPG that hit a

Humvee killed Tristan Aitken, a captain. The crew members of the downed Black Hawk were Capt. James Adamouski; Sgt. Michael Pedersen; Specialist Mathew Boule; and Chief Warrant Officers Eric Halvorsen, Eric Smith, and Scott Jamar. All perished in the crash.

Say the names aloud, each a distinctive voice in its own right, and all entrusted with the love and secret histories of their brothers in arms, of families and friends, of whole circles of family and friendship beyond that. Each one a voice now stilled. The awful silence at the center of that void continues to spread in concentric shock waves of grief in America. Assurances that the United States was on the verge of "transforming" not only the region but the nature of warfare itself, that it could achieve a "low cost" victory in Iraq while fighting a "humanitarian war," that the fallen have the thanks of a grateful nation—all those comforting words are beyond hearing in that mute realm of sorrow. The stricken are lost in the deafening silence of one bad day. I had no doubt that there would be many other bad days to come in Iraq, for soldiers, for journalists, and not least of all for the Iraqis themselves.

CHAPTER 18

Iraq and a Hard Place

ON APRIL 11 the V Corps Tactical Operations convoy prepared to reposition to the newly named Baghdad International Airport. Everyone packed up their gear as teams of soldiers broke down the massive headquarters tent and lit bonfires to burn our garbage. Around one of the fires I struck up a conversation with a young sergeant who was eating a prepackaged Meal Ready to Eat (MRE). Rating the various MREs on a gastronomic scale from surprisingly not bad to really quite atrocious was a staple of conversation, and I asked the troop which one he was eating. He squinted at the package.

"Country Captain Chicken," said the sergeant.

"That's a new one on me. Any good?"

"I blame it on the goddamn Clinton era, when instead of buying us new weapons they did things like add curried chicken to the MRE menu," he explained. "Only they knew most Joes would find Indian curry too foreign, so they concocted the most all-American name imaginable for it—'Country Captain Chicken.' Just to fool us ignorant grunts."

"So I guess you hate the Country Captain Chicken, huh?"

The sergeant took another bite while he thought about it. "I absolutely love this stuff," he said. "I truly do."

About twenty kilometers south of Baghdad the V Corps Headquarters convoy hit the outskirts of Mahmudiyah. As traffic slowed to a stop we came abreast of several crowded buses heading in the opposite direction. On closer inspection the buses were filled to capacity with military-age Iraqi men with close-cropped hair and lean physiques, all of them glowering at our passing convoy. U.S. commanders had expected most Iraqi army forces to eventually lay down their arms, and then to pick them back up in service of whatever interim government was established to maintain control. Instead it looked like the Iraqi army was melting away into the countryside.

"Look at them," Lt. Col. Rick Nohmer said from the front seat of our Humvee, pointing at the buses. "I would wager a year's salary that's the remnants of the Republican Guard."

On the narrow main street of Mahmudiyah the convoy slowed as it snaked around the charred remains of an Iraqi T-72 tank that was blocking half the road, and then stalled altogether as the townspeople swarmed around our vehicles like a warm embrace. Children by the hundreds shouted and waved, flashing the thumbs-up sign. Hoping for candy or even a friendly wave, they were drawn irresistibly to the open windows of our Humvees and trucks. Men and women in traditional garb jammed the sidewalks, jostling for a closer view of this strange army that seemed to appear out of nowhere. In a doorway, an old man in robes, his white beard framing a weather-beaten face, returned my wave with an inscrutable half smile.

Even as the Iraqi throng gathered closer, and as U.S. soldiers snapped photos of this long-anticipated moment of liberation, an unseen voice from somewhere in the crowd cut through the euphoria like a knife.

"Fuck you!"

Suddenly vigilant again, U.S. troops scanned the crowd anew. One American soldier noticed a sullen young man on a balcony, making a pistol with his bare hand and aiming it at the Americans in a universal gesture that needed no translation. Another local was seen talking rapidly into a cell phone and scanning the length of our convoy, as if counting its numbers. Another soldier saw an Iraqi man kick a child in the head as punishment for cheering the foreign troops.

In the cab of one of our convoy's lead trucks, Master Sgt. Timothy Westbrook's grim expression reflected an increasingly common realization among U.S. troops, as one more soldier came to understand how a warm welcome could turn threatening in a Baghdad minute. Unseen beneath his truck window, Westbrook, a friendly but no-nonsense military brat from Jacksonville, Florida, readied a SAW (squad automatic weapon) machine gun in one hand, and freed his 9 mm handgun with the other.

"I can assure you," Westbrook told me, "I wasn't taking any damn pictures."

Capt. David Waldron, a company commander with Third I.D.'s Third Brigade, who I talked with a few days later, almost paid dearly for his own similar epiphany. Riding at the head of a column of M-1 tanks entering Baghdad, Waldron was waving to a smiling crowd of Iraqis who greeted his unit as liberators. "Then out of nowhere a rocket-propelled grenade hit us from the rear," said Waldron, sporting shrapnel wounds and a bandaged hand. "That's sort of a microcosm of the situation we find ourselves in right now."

After we exited the town without incident, the whole bad vibe might have been written off as a case of missed cultural cues and frayed nerves. Except that the next day, nineteen U.S. soldiers of the 101st Airborne Division were wounded—and six hospitalized—in a grenade attack while passing through Mahmudiyah.

On April 11 I ran into General Wallace on the tarmac of the Baghdad International Airport, off by himself smoking a cigarette near the two tracked vehicles that had served as his mobile command center throughout the war. Ever since the breaching of the Karbala Gap, Wallace's demeanor and spirits had picked up noticeably, and I struck up a conversation about the remaining resistance in Baghdad.

"You heard it here first," Wallace told me. "The Iraqi regime is finished, and the Iraqi army has disappeared."

In retrospect, the "shock and awe" of the Iraqi Freedom campaign was finally delivered with two daring thunder runs that the Third Infantry Division unleashed straight into the solar plexus of the Iraqi regime on April 5 and 7. Characteristically determined to "pile on" and keep pressure on Iraqi forces holding the city, Gen. Blount was also provoked mightily by Iraqi information minister Mohammed Saaed al-Sahaf (aka "Baghdad Bob"). On April 5 he thus ordered an armored strike into the city. Twenty-nine M-1 tanks, fourteen Bradleys, and numerous M-113 armored personnel carriers from his Second Brigade conducted an "armed reconnaissance" from Objective Saints south of Baghdad, through the city, and out west to the airport.

"I felt like I had the Iraqis on the ropes, and I didn't want to give them a chance to collect themselves," General Blount told me in an interview days later. The Iraqi forces still had plenty of artillery and rockets that could target U.S. forces, he said, pointing to the devastating Iraqi missile strike on April 7 that took out a battalion tactical operations center at Objective Saints, killing three soldiers and two embedded journalists, and wounding seventeen others. "I wasn't willing to just sit at the airport for three or four days and give them that chance to target us at will. With the Iraqi information minister insisting that we were nowhere in the area, I also wanted to make the point that U.S. tanks were in Baghdad. I don't think they were expecting that."

Blount knew that launching an armored raid deep into urban and hostile territory, unsupported by supply convoys or U.S. infantry that could keep Iraqi dismounts at bay, went directly against Army doctrine. U.S. forces had learned in the Battle of Najaf, however, that if properly deployed, armor could have a devastating impact in urban warfare, both as psychological weapons and as killing machines. U.S. tanks and Bradleys had also proven themselves remarkably survivable against most Iraqi weapons. The laconic general was more than willing to rewrite the doctrinal field manuals if that's what it took to topple Saddam from his Baghdad pedestal. Indeed, that ability of U.S. forces to quickly learn and adapt, and to rewrite doctrine on the fly based on analysis of a rapidly changing intelligence picture, would later be judged as perhaps the most transformational aspect of the entire Iraqi Freedom campaign.

The chain of command was concerned, however, that the armored columns would become snarled in tight streets and down dead-end alleys, where they would become fodder for Iraqi dismounts or cut off from resupply. Third Infantry Division staff had thought through the thunder runs carefully, however, and the sweeping right-hook route they chose from Objective Saints, through Baghdad and out to the airport, consisted of four- and six-lane highways and boulevards. General Blount and his staff knew they were sending the Second Brigade "Spartans" down a gauntlet, but they were convinced that as long as the armored recon force kept moving it could both survive and decisively probe the extent of Baghdad's defenses.

The two-and-one-half-hour operation turned into one of the most harrowing battles of the Iraqi Freedom campaign. Iraqi forces placed numerous barricades, supported by ambushes, across the Spartans' chosen path. At one point an M-1 was disabled by a recoilless-rifle strike in its rear section. While the Spartans halted in an attempt to rescue the stranded crew, as many as 250 Iraqi paramilitaries and Special Republican Guards swarmed the area. As two members of the tank crew were evacuated into an M-113 they were shot, one in the eye and the other in the shoulder. Another M-1 tank and a Bradley caught fire. Staff Sgt. Stevon Booker, a tank commander, was killed by Iraqi fire while engaging the enemy from the turret with his M-4 carbine.

Once again most of the fighting and killing during the thunder run was accomplished at close range with machine guns and M-16 automatic rifles. Col. David Perkins, the gutsy commander of Second Brigade who led the raid, fought off Iraqis point-blank with his 9 mm pistol during the fight. After breaching a final roadblock and arriving at the airport, the Second Brigade Spartans evacuated their wounded and the body of Sergeant Booker, extinguished fires in a number of vehicles, and swept out the brass casings of spent rounds that literally covered the floors of the armored personnel carriers. Though generally reticent in calculating enemy dead during the campaign, Third Infantry Division estimated as many as two thousand Iraqi troops had been killed in the operation.

Surprisingly, even the appearance of U.S. armored forces on Baghdad streets, and the horrific death toll from the April 5 thunder run, failed to silence the loquacious Baghdad Bob. As the Iraqi information minister made absurdly clear, the tyrant's world was premised on repeating the "Big Lie" long enough, and loudly enough, until people willfully deceive themselves. Perhaps none of Saddam Hussein's lies was crueler than his insistence until the very end that Iraqi forces still had a fighting chance in the war. As one senior U.S. officer told me, "Perhaps the most effective propaganda tool we could have used in convincing the Iraqis to give up this fight earlier would have been to send them a demonstration tape of the M-1 Abrams battle tank in action."

With no demo tapes available, Col. David Perkins decided on April 7 to send the actual article itself into the very heart of Saddam's regime. This time he meant to convey an unmistakable message to any defenders taking heart from Baghdad Bob's propaganda. So despite the thunder run having only limited objectives on the outskirts of town, halfway into the operation Colonel Perkins ordered his all-armored strike force to turn east into the center of the city.

On the way downtown the Second Brigade task force met sometimes intense but mostly unorganized resistance, and fought their way through numerous ambushes and hastily constructed mine fields without stopping. Soldiers marveled as they rumbled under the giant crossed swords and passed the VIP stands on Saddam's parade complex, then established a blocking position at a key intersection next to the Al Rasheed Hotel and across from Saddam's Tomb of the Unknowns. Soon they were in control of Saddam's main palace complex, and the television cameras were rolling as Colonel Perkins and his men toured the ornate grounds. As Colonel Perkins discovered to his delight, the grassy parks, open plazas, and wide boulevards of downtown Baghdad offered the interlopers excellent fields of fire. At that point, Colonel Perkins radioed General Blount with an unusual request. He told the general that if the task force could hold out through the night in Saddam's palace complex, the war would be over. Though an uninvited guest, Dave Perkins wanted to stay the night.

Watching the thunder run progress from his mobile command post, General Wallace first became aware that the plan had changed only when the blue icons on his Blue Force Tracker turned right off Highway 8, heading downtown. At that point Wallace began eavesdropping on the Third Infantry Division command net, listening to the running commentary between David Perkins, and Generals Blount and Austin as they discussed the risks and potential rewards of remaining in downtown Baghdad through the night. Even standing still, the Spartans' M-1 tanks were burning fuel at a rate of fifty-six gallons *an hour*, and they had already been running for more than three hours straight. If they couldn't be resupplied sometime in the night, Colonel Perkins and his task force would run out of fuel and most likely ammo. Wallace knew he had another critical decision to make.

When General Blount called and told him directly that Colonel Perkins wanted to stay downtown, Wallace voiced his concerns in a series of probing questions. He understood that Perkins was holding defensible terrain, but it would be difficult to resupply him and virtually impossible to quickly evacuate any casualties his task force incurred in the likely counterattack to come. Each commander understood that there were heavy risks involved, but both also sensed a potential checkmate of the Saddam regime. In the end, Wallace concurred that Second Brigade's armored task force would hold the main palace complex through the night.

As anticipated, Iraqi Special Republican Guards and paramilitaries, backed by fanatical Syrian jihadists, fought fiercely to cut off the Spartans positioned downtown by severing their supply route along Highway 8. In the pitched battles to keep the supply route open at key intersections, the brigade lost three soldiers killed in action and suffered numerous wounded. Resupplied in the middle of the night, however, the Spartans were able to repulse numerous counterattacks on the morning of April 8. With Colonel Perkins and his task force entrenched in downtown Baghdad, the regime essentially evaporated. The next day, on April 9, members of the Fourth Marine Regiment, who had been helping close the cordon of the city from the east, put an exclamation point on regime change. Backed by hundreds of cheering Iraqis, they toppled the giant statue of the dictator in Al-Firdos Square. The bloody reign of Saddam Hussein was over at last.

As the dust of war settled, Baghdad was pure purgatory, the ghosts of the recently departed and the voiceless expectations of an entire nation haunting streets that were otherwise deserted at night, with most Iraqis huddled in their homes and waiting. No one seemed able to answer the deceptively simple question of what was to become of Iraq.

With the unexpectedly sudden collapse of Saddam's regime in Baghdad, U.S. commanders found themselves still in a combat posture and struggling to make the transition to the "Phase 4" tasks of providing security, delivering humanitarian aid, and stabilizing a traumatized society. That difficult transition was complicated by the fact that a chain of command that had remained remarkably disciplined during high-intensity combat operations began to tangle and grate as it collapsed in on Baghdad, with Central Command, Combined Forces Land Component Command, V Corps, Third Infantry Division, and the First Marine Expeditionary Force all descending on the capital and jockeying for their piece of a confused puzzle.

Many of the worst fears of U.S. commanders did not come to pass, in part, at least, because of the unusual speed of the U.S. invasion. Iraqi forces did not have time to torch oil wells in the south and north that had been rigged for demolition in the hopes of causing an environmental calamity on the scale of the first Persian Gulf War in 1991. Saddam did not gas the Kurds in the north or the Shiites in the south as he had in the past, and thus a feared tide of refugees such as the Kurdish exodus in 1991 failed to materialize. Thanks in part to the United Nation's oil-for-food program, which had dispensed between thirty and sixty days of rations to Iraqi families before the war started, there was no widespread famine.

Yet even as the American public were exalting over the toppling of Saddam's regime and the apparent end of the war, so declared on April 14 by the Bush administration, it was obvious on the ground in Baghdad that the critical transition to stability operations would be hampered by the same shortcomings that had bedeviled combat operations, some of them a direct offshoot of Donald Rumsfeld's transformational war-fighting model—namely, stretched-thin forces and long supply lines. There also remained a hard core of enemy fighters who were not so much defeated as run to ground, and who were determined to keep the capital and other parts of the country in a state of violent turmoil.

Even more alarming, with the Iraqi Freedom campaign entering per-haps its most critical phase, the Pentagon seemed to have remarkably few answers to the questions posed by the regime's rapid collapse. For their part, U.S. commanders in the field confessed to me privately that they had mostly limited their planning for post-Saddam Iraq to the positioning of various units throughout the country, awaiting instructions from the Pen-tagon.

Few experts ever doubted that U.S. forces would defeat the Republi-can Guard and Iraq's conventional forces. The key imponderables to the campaign were always the reaction of the Iraqi people to the war and the presence of U.S. troops, the cost in national treasure and the lives of U.S. service members, and America's ability to lay the groundwork for a tran-sition to democracy in Iraq. After all, that was the stated goal of the Bush revolutionaries before launching the war, and in the long run victory de-pended on it. In the critical weeks after Baghdad's fall, however, with U.S. troops still enjoying something of a honeymoon with Iraqis happy to see the last of Saddam, that goal was overshadowed by a growing sense of anarchy and lawlessness.

One morning Col. Steve Hicks explained to me the difficulty U.S. commanders were having in managing that difficult transition. "The col-lapse of the regime in Baghdad happened faster than anyone anticipated, so we're in that inevitable gap between war fighting, when you want all your trigger-pullers and ammunition up front, and stability operations, where the focus is on civil affairs and humanitarian assistance. We're also bound to struggle in a transition period where we're trying to get soldiers to shift from a wartime mind-set of shoot whatever moves, to providing assistance to the civilian population," Hicks told me. "During this phase it will be harder to keep the bad guys at bay, and there's a real potential for unnecessary casualties on the parts of both our soldiers, as well as Iraqi civilians. So we realize this is a critical period, and we need to make this transition fast or we'll alienate the local population and quickly wear out our welcome. If we get this phase of the campaign wrong, we could win the war and lose the peace."

Trying not to alienate the local population, however, was easier said than done. U.S. troops were still unsure, for instance, whether Iraqi irregulars, regime remnants and their foreign allies had quit or simply paused to regroup before launching a campaign of guerrilla warfare and terrorism. Until the situation became clearer, U.S. soldiers had to keep one hand on their weapons at all times, even while dispensing aid and conducting stability patrols. During an interview at his brigade headquarters in Baghdad, with the celebratory sound of AK-47s firing into the sky as backdrop, Col. Will Grimsley of First Brigade confided to me that after so much close-in combat with the Saddam fedayeen, some of his troops got the adrenaline shakes just from seeing a white Toyota truck approach one of their checkpoints.

Inside of V Corps Tactical Headquarters, repositioned at Baghdad International Airport, the transition to Phase 4 was signaled when air-defense, artillery, and close air support officers were sent to the back of the tent, replaced by civil affairs and psychological operations officers at the front. One of these was Col. Tim Regan, a Reservist and commander of the 308th Civil Affairs Brigade that was attached to V Corps. Regan, one of the most senior civil affairs officers in Iraq, was clearly frustrated by the shortcomings inherent in a war plan that from the beginning had relied on speed and agility to rapidly defeat the enemy—necessitating the 'rolling start' to the invasion—but shortchanged the invading force on troops and supplies needed in the war's aftermath.

"In the beginning the plan called for stability operations to begin as soon as maneuver forces had cleared a region, but because we started the attack before all our forces were in theater, the strategy evolved into toppling the Iraqi regime as quickly as possible employing 'economy of force,'" said Regan. "That's a nice way of saying we didn't have enough forces on hand." As a result, he confided, the 308th Civil Affairs Brigade was manned at less than a third of its normal strength in civil affairs officers. "Because the top priority was winning the war and keeping civilians out of the battle space, neither I nor anyone else in the civil affairs community have the resources available in theater to meet the immediate humanitarian needs."

Given ongoing attacks on U.S. forces in Baghdad, and lacking sufficient troops for securing the city, U.S. Central Command's Gen. Tommy Franks judged the capital too dangerous to deploy the Pentagon's hand-picked authority for Iraq, retired Army Lt. Gen. Jay Garner, head of the newly formed Office for Reconstruction and Humanitarian Assistance. While Garner remained in Kuwait and southern Iraq for more than a week after Baghdad fell, V Corps was forced to postpone the assessment of humanitarian needs by many civil affairs teams because of a lack of security personnel. The lack of security also denied U.S. commanders the assistance of numerous nongovernmental relief organizations with expertise in post-conflict operations.

"The expectation of senior leaders was that once the regime fell, civil affairs teams could go through Baghdad very quickly, assessing how to bring power, water, and food distribution back on line," Regan told me in late April. In that sense the fedayeen and terror groups, he said, definitely were interfering with the smooth transition from Phase 3 combat to Phase 4 stability operations. "The situation is still not secure enough for us to go out and make assessments without security forces, and there aren't enough troops to go around," said Regan. "Because of the fear of reprisals from Saddam loyalists, the Iraqi people have also been slower to step forward and help us."

Though it seemed counterintuitive, it became clear in those early days of Baghdad's liberation that the relatively small size of the U.S. invasion force was actually felt more in the stability phase of the Iraqi Freedom campaign than during the war itself. During combat, U.S. forces could concentrate their forces on specific pressure points and centers of gravity associated with the Iraqi military, bypassing many cities in southern Iraq in their steely determination to take the fight rapidly to Baghdad.

After the fall of Saddam and the disappearance not only of Iraqi military forces and police but of virtually all the elements of Iraqi civil society, however, a broad U.S. troop presence was needed to guard administrative buildings, hospitals, and even strategic road intersections in virtually every city in the country. In the part of Baghdad for which it was responsible, V Corps alone had 256 static sites that needed nearly constant guarding. Because those troops were stretched so thin, secondary priorities went unguarded, such as the National Museum of Iraq in Baghdad. As a result, the museum was reportedly looted of centuries' worth of valuable treasures in the weeks after the regime collapsed, adding to a growing sense of anarchy in the capital.

No one felt the pressure of securing Baghdad more than Gen. Buford Blount of Third Infantry. By the time I interviewed him at his headquarters in mid-April, along with P. J. O'Rourke of the *Atlantic Monthly*, news reports of the rampant looting and loss of historical treasures at the museum were dominating the headlines. By that time, virtually all of the reporters who had embedded with Third Infantry Division during the war had dispersed, and it looked like the goodwill between the fourth estate and the U.S. military that was engendered by the unique embed experiment was already fast evaporating.

Just back from the National Museum, General Blount insisted, accurately it would later turn out, that more than 80 percent of the museum's treasures had been safely locked away by its staff in hidden vaults beneath the museum. The top floors had undeniably been trashed, he said, but most of the priceless antiquities associated with the museum had been saved. And then General Blount said something I never expected to hear from a flag-rank officer in the U.S. military.

"You know, I really miss my embedded reporters," Blount told us. "I felt when we had embedded reporters that there was a better flow of information, because they saw the full story and reported the truth. Now the press in Baghdad see 20 percent of the story, and they report that as the whole truth. Thus 'everything' at the museum has been lost to looting. That's why I made sure that Mike Kelly had access to whatever he wanted to see, because I really wanted him to be able to tell the full story of this war, from start to finish. So his death was not only a personal loss. Professionally, Mike Kelly's death was a great loss too."

In the absence of any other authority, the temporary mayor of northern Baghdad by default was a wiry man named Dan Allyn, small of stature with dark eyes and a disarmingly direct manner. Allyn, the commander of the Third Brigade, Third Infantry Division, had an office that consisted of a room without an outside wall in a half-constructed house strewn with rubble. The nearly unobstructed view from his foldout desk was of a nearby mosque with towering spires and palm tree–lined gardens. Virtually every shed and structure between Allyn's office and the mosque contained a hidden arms cache of RPGs and mortar rounds—fallback positions for Iraqi fighters in another "Mother of All Battles" that never materialized. However, seeing such lethal weaponry laying about in piles like so much dirty laundry, and stacked in ammo dumps too numerous for U.S. troops to even guard, much less clear, you couldn't help but worry that if an insurgency did arise in Iraq it would be a very well-armed one.

During a visit by General Wallace and a small entourage, Colonel Allyn explained how he lost a soldier the day before who was shot in the thigh and lost too much blood before he could be medevaced. "If we could have just gotten him out a little sooner we might have saved him," Allyn said matter-of-factly, being shot just another occupational hazard for troops charged with seeing to the immediate needs of Baghdad's more than five million inhabitants.

As part of the campaign to win over residents, Third Brigade's engi-

neers and troops had repaired the local water treatment facility, liberated
the water bottling plant, and reopened a closed school. They were still
working to turn the electricity back on for the northern section of Baghdad, which locals said had been without regular power for more than a
year. In the process, Third Brigade was beginning to learn how to negotiate the labyrinth of local customs and norms of Arab culture with the help
of a Special Forces detachment, a handful of paid interpreters, and a few
soldiers from the Free Iraqi Force, remnants of Ahmed Chalabi's vaunted
Iraqi opposition force that, when finally assembled, numbered less than
one hundred. Chalabi's neocon backers in the Pentagon had seen to it that
the noted Iraqi exile was positioned in southern Iraq, ready to make a
triumphant entrance to the capital when all was ready, but his return had
been delayed by U.S. military commanders who failed to see what base
of support Chalabi could plausibly claim in a country where he was
largely a stranger.

In the meantime, Colonel Allyn said that rather than become em-
broiled in local disputes over the ownership of a cow or goat, his commanders were using emergency funds to encourage local leaders to take
charge in their districts. That honored the semifeudal tradition of the region, where largesse was dispensed through the auspices of local elders
and sheiks. The Americans were also learning the hard way that decades
of brutal dictatorship had wrung the initiative out of Iraqi workers and
contractors. As a result, the Iraqis needed to be told in the most direct and
specific terms exactly what was expected of them. "Basically, we're trying
to do something every day to make the people of Baghdad realize we're
here to try and help them," Colonel Allyn told us.

For all the "can do" spirit and remarkable improvisation on the fly
shown by U.S. commanders and troops in Baghdad, however, the subtext
of our conversations was what the Third Infantry Division did not have
upon entering the city. There was no plan for occupying the city itself and
transitioning to stability operations. There were no predetermined rules
of engagement that would have allowed them to step in for absent police
and put a halt to the rampant looting still under way. There was no guidance on which ethnic and religious leaders to recognize among the mob
that sprang up in a power grab to fill the obvious void of authority. There
were far too few civil affairs officers and translators to help commanders
on the ground negotiate the unfamiliar terrain. Instead, there was a palpable sense of drift in those critical early weeks of liberation, as a vacuum
of power settled over Baghdad like a low pressure zone.

In those early days, with the bloom still on Baghdad's liberation, you
also saw the trust beginning to build between U.S. troops and Iraqis, and
later you wondered about what might have been. "A few days ago, some
of the locals alerted me to an ambush that was being set for my troops,

and we ended up killing twenty-seven bad guys," Allyn told us, conceding that his stability operations were proving more difficult for U.S. troops than the high-intensity combat phase of Iraqi Freedom. "The vast majority of Iraqis are ecstatic that we're here, and the accuracy of the information they've provided us has been nearly 100 percent. We've also seen them beginning to clean up their own streets and the districts, which is a good sign. My primary concern now is to get the locals back to work."

To drive home the point about Iraqi cooperation, Allyn led us to one of Third Brigade's observation posts at a key intersection in northern Baghdad where the giddy possibilities of a free Iraq were on open display. The scene resembled an "open house" day on a U.S. military base, with hundreds of curious and smiling Iraqi civilians milling about the M-1 tanks and Bradleys, and peppering U.S. soldiers with questions in Arabic and broken English. They shouted "Bush!" with the thumbs-up sign, begged to have their photos taken, and tried to sell us warm Pepsi for $1 a bottle. Maj. Jim Barker, General Wallace's gung ho aide, had started classes in Arabic to distract his soldiers from their homesickness, and he returned the favor by trying out his new vocabulary on the Iraqis. Judging from the quizzical looks on the faces of the Iraqi children that surrounded him, Barker still needed to polish his linguistic skills.

The differing reactions of Iraqis to the first appearance of U.S. troops hinted at the deep cultural crosscurrents in Iraq that U.S. commanders only vaguely understood. At another stop on General Wallace's tour that day, Capt. Carter Price remarked on it. "We basically went from having a parade in our honor in Nasiriya, to being engaged in complete battle around Najaf, to a little bit of both in Karbala, back to basically parades again in Baghdad," Price told us. During that journey of discovery, Price and his men learned to look for telltale signs, such as residents having torn down or defaced portraits of Saddam, generally indicating a safe area. "We've also found that if Iraqi civilians are gathered around you in large groups, the situation is probably okay. However, if civilians avoid a particular area, or scatter like a bevy of quail, you had better watch out because a bad guy is probably lurking there."

At another stop at a former Republican Guard compound in Baghdad, the horror of being on the receiving end of U.S. airpower was on vivid display. Some structures on the compound survived virtually untouched, while next to them a pile of misshapen rubble stretched a city block, as if a building's very atoms had been rearranged in a science experiment gone awry. There we met Lt. Col. Jeffrey Sanderson, commander of the 2–69 Armored Battalion. When General Wallace asked what it would take to secure Baghdad, Sanderson gave an "aw, shucks" shrug before nailing it on the head.

"Sir, the only thing I know about civil affairs is what my gut tells me," said Sanderson, his southern drawl as thick as tree sap. "And what my gut tells me, sir, is that we need to turn the lights back on in this city. The problem is, nowhere in my public education in North Carolina or at the University of Kentucky did they teach me how to do that in a city of five million people."

Before taking his leave of the Third Infantry Division that day, Wallace implored the soldiers not to let their guards down or stop watching each other's backs as they negotiated the perilous twilight between war and whatever comes after. "You have traveled farther, and fought more decisively, than any army in history," Wallace told the assembled troops. "I am honored just to be in your presence."

Privately, Wallace asked Colonel Allyn for an opinion from the front line on what it would take to secure Baghdad.

"Sir, there may be a lot of bad guys out there simply trying to wait us out, but so far the locals have been very good at pointing them out to us," said Allyn. "I honestly believe that if we can get the power turned back on, we can keep the people on our side and Baghdad won't be such a tough nut to crack. The one other question I get asked the most by the Iraqis is, what's in store for them?"

Wallace had to think about that one a moment. "You tell them that we'll get out of here just as soon as the Iraqi people are ready to take their future back into their own hands."

Later that night I sat down for an hour with General Wallace for my last interview before leaving Baghdad. Outside the windows of his temporary office in a terminal at Baghdad International the tailfin still loomed over the burned wreckage of an Iraqi Airlines airliner. I reminded Wallace of his comments to the Third Infantry that they had traveled further, faster, and had fought more decisively, than any army in history. Did he really think the bold war plan for Iraqi Freedom, emphasizing speed and agility over mass and sheer numbers, had somehow transformed modern warfare?

Wallace thought it was too soon to draw definitive conclusions. "I have to be careful because wars can be like good wine, they tend to get better with age." However, in monitoring battalions operating independently all over Iraq on a nonlinear battlefield, guided by space- and airborne surveillance systems and successfully substituting precision airpower for massed artillery and formations, Wallace did catch an early glimpse of the "network centric" war fighting that transformation advocates described as almost the holy grail.

"This war was executed almost exclusively at the battalion level and below. The divisions moved guys around the map, but the guys who really did the fighting were the lower echelons at brigade level and below," Wallace said. The ability to successfully distribute brigades on a far-flung battlefield in turn suggested that in the future modular brigades could become more important than venerable divisions as the central organizing principle in the U.S. Army. The model had not worked perfectly by any means. Numerous times Wallace had been frustrated by his inability to transmit information and data to frontline battalions to help them pierce the fog of war. Much of the campaign felt to those at the tip of the spear, such as Lt. Col. Rock Marcone, like a blind "movement to contact" with the enemy, rather than a deliberate attack against known enemy formations. A logistics train still largely mired in the machine age also struggled mightily to keep up with rapid pace of twenty-first-century warfare.

In the end the ability to call in precise U.S. airpower at will, however, masked many deficiencies. "I was continually impressed by the availability of close air support. It was like nothing I ever experienced, even during Vietnam," said Wallace. Indeed, 925 close air support (CAS) sorties had been flown in support of just the Third Infantry Division alone, accounting for 656 enemy combat systems destroyed. Toward the end of the war the average response time to a request for precision air support was down to less than ten minutes. "Most of us old guys refer to Vietnam as the good old days in terms of the availability of close air support, because all we had to do was pop a smoke grenade and tell the pilot over the radio that the target was five hundred meters in front of the smoke. But in this campaign the availability of close air support far exceeded my expectations, as did the ability of my young leaders to employ it to devastating effect."

Finally, I asked Wallace about the decision to jettison the carefully orchestrated Tip Fid, and start the war on a rolling start with lean forces and needed support and reinforcements still pouring into the theater. Wallace's brow furrowed as he thought back on the risks inherent in that plan. One concern Wallace had involved the Fourth Infantry Division. Given the diplomatic debacle that denied it access to Iraq from Turkey, and the rapid fall of Baghdad, Wallace was never able to send the Fourth Infantry Division to tame the Sunni strongholds west of Baghdad such as Fallujah and Ramadi, as originally intended.

"But it's hard to argue with success. All of us would like more predictability in our lives and jobs. But we made this work—that's how I would phrase it. We made it work," Wallace told me of the transformational war-fighting model. "We had some very talented people, and it's a tremendous credit to them that they were agile and flexible enough to adjust to whatever circumstances were dealt us. It was never about success. Success was taken for granted. But success in this war could still have been really ugly."

Later, I talked with one of V Corps' senior staff on background about Wallace's obvious discomfort in discussing Rumsfeld's transformational war-fighting model. "You know, we fought the Iraqi Freedom campaign as a 'just-in-time war,'" he said. "Soldiers at the front would shoot a bullet, and then hope the supply system would deliver another bullet in time, and then they would shoot that one, and so forth. That caused General Wallace and his top commanders to constantly look over their shoulders at their lines of communication, even while managing a complex battlefield at the front. Why would you fight a war like that with so much at stake? We could easily have used overwhelming force, just like the Powell doctrine called for, not only to win the war but secure the peace. So why would you fight a war like that?"

Any hopes that the Pentagon had an executable plan for filling the power vacuum in Baghdad that would quickly get Iraq on the path to reconstruction and democracy were dashed when retired Lt. Gen. Jay Garner rolled into the city on April 21 at the head of a long convoy of SUVs carrying the Office for Reconstruction and Humanitarian Assistance (ORHA). It quickly became clear to U.S. military commanders in Baghdad that Garner and ORHA lacked even the communications equipment, security detail, and manpower to take care of themselves, much less a city of five million inhabitants. Far from filling the power vacuum, Garner and his organization quickly became another drain on already overburdened U.S. military personnel in the capital.

To his credit, Garner, a short, fireplug of a man who had proven his competence by helping manage the Kurdish refugee crisis in northern Iraq in 1991, had only been called out of retirement by Rumsfeld in January. In the scant months he had to plan for the aftermath in Iraq, Garner had initially enlisted the help of officials involved in the State Department's Future of Iraq project, the yearlong planning process that had anticipated many of the difficulties U.S. forces were indeed encountering in Iraq. As a knowledgeable source confirmed to me, Rumsfeld personally ordered Garner to get rid of the State Department's senior representative with experience in the Future of Iraq project. Apparently the State Department official was deemed insufficiently optimistic and gung ho about the Iraq war to suit the neoconservatives around Rumsfeld. A senior State Department official that did make it onto ORHA's staff, who I ran into at the Baghdad airport, confided that relations between State Department officials and the Pentagon appointees in ORHA bordered on dysfunction, once again reflecting the divide at the very top levels of the Bush administration.

The situation that confronted Garner and his staff was certainly worse than anyone had anticipated. Saddam's neglect of Iraqi infrastructure and civil society during a decade of sanctions was stunning in light of his palace-building spree. The country's electrical grid could produce only 50 percent of the electricity the nation needed. The water treatment system only purified 60 percent of the potable water required by the Iraqi people. Agricultural production had dropped by 40 percent during the 1990s. Infant mortality was by far the highest in the Middle East, and most public schools made due with only one book for every six children.

The Pentagon's refusal to deploy enough troops to Baghdad to pacify the capital and halt the looting, however, further crippled Garner's early efforts. ORHA had planned to rapidly rehire Iraqi civil servants and put them to work restoring public services. Fully seventeen of the twenty Iraqi ministerial buildings had been destroyed by looters, however, who picked them clean of desks, chairs, light fixtures, bookcases, and everything else right down to electrical and telephone wires. With no portable generators, Garner's staff couldn't even get the lights turned back on in their own buildings.

As a result of Baghdad Bob's provocations, U.S. forces had also destroyed most of the telecommunications nodes in Baghdad, leaving ORHA with no telephone system or way to communicate effectively with Iraqi civilians. Without an adequate security detail, ORHA staff could only get out of their palace complex into the city and countryside with military escorts, which were unavailable about half the time they were requested. They had only a handful of pre-signed contracts to put Iraqis back to work on reconstruction. To top it off, Garner was forbidden by the Pentagon and White House to talk to the press, meaning there was still no U.S. voice of authority to explain to expectant Iraqis what their future held. The sense of drift worsened.

What Jay Garner did have was a determination to address the dire security situation by rapidly reconstituting the regular Iraqi army which, as opposed to the Republican Guard, was still a respected institution among many Iraqis. Because the Iraqi army had its own command-and-control system and organic mobility, Garner reasoned that it could help in both reestablishing security and in rebuilding roads, bridges, and other infrastructure. Only when newly appointed presidential envoy L. Paul Bremer III arrived in Baghdad in mid-April, he carried a stack of directives that included a decree permanently disbanding the Iraqi army and abolishing the Ministry of Defense. No one seemed to know where the decree had come from, but it was known that Ahmed Chalabi, the darling of the Pentagon neocons, saw the Iraqi army as a direct, home-grown threat to expatriates such as himself who were entering the country with U.S. help.

Garner advised Paul Bremer that abolishing the Iraqi army was a huge mistake, but his warning went unheeded. With Iraq's long, hot summer of liberation just beginning, one of the first edicts of the Pentagon-led occupational authority was to put hundreds of thousands of military-age Iraqi men on the streets without jobs, every last one of them trained to bear arms.

Everyone wondered about the weapons of mass destruction. We all had stories of being snatched out of a welcome dream in the middle of the night by the chilling wail of gas alert, or spending an hour bumping into each other in a crowded tent in gas masks like subterranean moles. We had all spent weeks fermenting in the human musk captured by the charcoal-lined chemical protection suits. One particular gas alert caught me in the middle of a field shower, sending me running into the head-quarters tent half-naked and covered in soapsuds searching frantically for my misplaced gas mask. The bug-eyed staff stared at me like a canary in a coal mine, looking to see if I would begin to dance the "broken chicken." We all knew damn well there had to be freaking weapons of mass destruction.

But where were the stockpiles? In the march through the Iraqi desert we had passed a number of ominous-looking complexes with large earthen bunkers, surely one of them must hold the secret of Saddam's unconventional weapons complex. As April wore on the topic of WMD was thus on everyone's mind, and it was not simply an academic discussion. Over a thousand troops that Central Command could scarcely spare were devoted to the search. More than that, discovery of the weapons would provide tangible justification for the war, and thus help the United States and the Bush administration begin healing the wounds in the international community caused by the conflict.

The topic of the WMD came up one night in the small office at the airport that I had commandeered as sleeping quarters, along with my roommate, V Corps public affairs officer Maj. Dean Thurmond. Thurmond's finely honed sense of sarcasm had been growing on me, even if I couldn't make him understand that it wasn't entirely the media's fault that the U.S. Army was sharing much of the blame for the looting of Baghdad, along with the looters themselves. Then the subject turned to the weapons of mass destruction.

"I can just see the headlines you guys will write if we fail to find the damn things," Thurmond said, tracing the imagined headline in the air with his hand in giant type. "SHOCK AND . . . AWE SHIT!"

On our long journey from Kuwait the soundtrack of Iraqi Freedom had been a mix of radio squawk, the white noise of running generators, and the detonation of various explosives—the distant rumble of artillery, the more immediate thump of mortar fire, the percussive impact of enemy ordnance being detonated nearby, or the whooshing thunder of a Patriot battery intercepting a missile overhead. Yet none of it sounded quite like the sharp crack of a high-explosive round landing inside your own perimeter.

In mid-April the proximity of that retort brought staff pouring out of the V Corps Tactical Headquarters tent on the grounds of Baghdad International Airport. A nearby smoke plume and the unmistakable urgency of soldiers running to the scene confirmed that disaster had struck, although it was still unclear by whose hand. Lying beside a Bradley Fighting Vehicle were the motionless figures of two U.S. soldiers, whose friends and then medics fought desperately to revive. Someone cried out the name of a soldier, but one look at the boy told you that he was mercifully beyond hearing.

In the end it was the hand of fate that had killed another U.S. soldier in Iraq. With no one even in the turret of the Bradley, the electronic surge of an ignition switch had fired what soldiers call a "ghost round," and the 25 mm chain gun proved the bane of its own crew. At dusk the next night, soldiers of C Company, Second Battalion, Sixth Infantry gathered to honor their comrade. They were joined by the members of V Corps TAC that Charlie Company had protected on our long way to Baghdad. On top of a two-step platform, the fallen soldier's rifle was buried bayonet-down, with a helmet resting askew on its butt, the soldier's empty boots on the step below.

The soldier was only twenty years old at the time of his death, not even old enough to buy a drink back in his hometown of Rock Springs, Wyoming. Yet as his tributes made clear, the young man had already found within himself deep wellsprings of the fortitude and selflessness that binds soldiers together in time of war. After the chaplain spoke and the formations bowed their heads in silent prayer, 1st Sgt. Mark Lahan strode before the simple platform of helmet, boots, and rifle for a final roll call.

"Specialist Ulrich!" Lahan barked.

"Yes Sergeant," Ulrich replied, breaking from the formation to go and stand at attention before the platform.

"Private Knobbe!"

"Yes sir, First Sar!" Knobbe made it a formation of two.

"Private Szczublewski!"

"Yes, sir!" And then it was three soldiers standing.

"Private Mayek!" Silence.

"Private First Class Mayek!" Silence of an altogether deeper hue.

"Private First Class Joseph P. Mayek!"

As if in answer, a bugler blew the first piercing notes of "Taps," the infinitely sad refrain of loss set to music, and all the more haunting for being played so far from home. The "missing man" formation of three soldiers wheeled on their heels and marched slowly away without Joseph P. Mayek, twenty years and never a day older. The strains of "Taps" lingered as the day's light began to fail.

The bugler's mournful salute was heard as far away as the 101st Division, which in the same twenty-four hours had lost two soldiers in a grenade accident and another to suicide, a despair that would claim an increasing number of U.S. troops as the occupation wore on. They echoed in the camp of the U.S. Marines in Iraq, where a Marine died that day in another case of suspected blue-on-blue fire. They could be heard as far away as the Fourth Infantry Division then just arriving in Kuwait, where a soldier would be killed in a vehicular accident on his way to Iraq. None present, all accounted for, in a bugler's sorrowful lament to another bad day.

Preparing to hitch a ride out of Iraq on a C-130 in early May 2003, I said my good-byes at the V Corps TAC. Outside I took a walk with Lt. Col. Rob Baker, who had kept a close eye on me ever since Mike Kelly's death. Pretty soon now the Congressmen and their delegations would start arriving—what Rob Baker called the "Hurrumphers!"—and he figured it was a good time to move on. Baker himself was leaving in a few days to have colonel's wings pinned on back in Germany, after which he would take command of a brigade that was slated to deploy to Iraq in just a few months time. Present at the violent creation, Rob Baker would have the rare chance to witness the early struggles of a free Iraq. As we shook hands and said good-bye it occurred to me that amidst all the wanton destruction, friendship remained war's one redemption.

By the time my plane lifted off, the lights at Baghdad International Airport had come back on at night. The temporary deputy mayors of Baghdad reported that it was only a matter of days before power would be restored to parts of the city that hadn't seen electricity for months. Regular aid flights had started to arrive, and the masters of global commerce were already hungrily eyeing the massive reconstruction project that would be required if Iraq was truly to become the center of a new Arabian mosaic. With luck and great good fortune, it was possible that Iraq could grow over time into just another bickering U.S. ally, thankful in its own way but impatient to see an end to the U.S. presence. In the meantime, it already seemed likely that more Americans would perish securing the peace in Iraq than were lost during the war. Years hence, after the last American soldiers had departed, I wondered whether people would even recall what a den of tyranny this place had once been, before the wild boys came and fought, and played "Taps" throughout the land.

CHAPTER 19

Homecoming

AT DUSK on a summer's eve in June 2003, with the marquees and shop signs above nearby 42nd Street flickering alight and throngs of New Yorkers crowding the sidewalks on their evening commute, I emerged from a taxicab outside the neo-Georgian façade of the Harvard Club. Ongoing construction obscured the New York landmark's stately veneer, but inside dark, wood-paneled walls climbed three stories to the ceilings of Harvard Hall, and stern portraiture stared down from the ages, all befitting a temple of power and affluence. In one of the many meeting rooms, the club's Investment Management Group was gathering to talk about gold, while the Bible Study Group was apparently contemplating spiritual enrichment out on the balcony. Elsewhere in the club the architect Daniel Libeskind, whose previous projects included the Jewish Museum in Berlin and the Imperial War Museum in Manchester, England, was explaining his plans to help rebuild a lower Manhattan still visibly scarred by the September 11, 2001, terrorist attacks.

In a third-floor ballroom some of America's leading media magnates, magazine publishers, newspaper editors, and politicians gathered for the presentation of the Eric Brindel Journalism Award of 2003. Named for the late columnist and editorial page editor for the *New York Post*, the Brindel Award was given annually to the "columnist, editorialist or reporter" who best reflected the spirit of its namesake, who according to the award was inspired by "love of country and its democratic institutions, as well as the act of bearing witness to the evils of totalitarianism." That night they were to honor a columnist, editorialist, and reporter all in one. The 2003 Brindel Award was to be given posthumously to Michael Kelly, the author, *Washington Post* columnist, and editor at large of the *Atlantic Monthly*.

At an open bar the actor Ron Silver was holding forth to a pair of attractive women, looking every bit as rapacious as the character he occasionally played on *The West Wing*, only shorter. Recently Silver had taken the conservative counterpoint seat opposite Bianca Jagger in CNN's special coverage of celebrity pundits for and against the Iraq war. Nearby, a *Wall Street Journal* editorial page editor was touting his paper's staunch support of the Bush administration's decision to topple the regime of Saddam Hussein. Media-couple Maurie Povich and Connie Chung worked one side of the room, while on the other New York mayor Michael Bloomberg and his entourage made a late entrance.

"When I saw that Bill Kristol and Rupert Murdoch were both here, I thought to myself, Aha! The 'axis of evil!'" quipped Claudia Winkler, the editor of the *Weekly Standard*, the magazine that editor in chief William Kristol had turned into the broadsheet of the neoconservative movement. Rupert Murdoch, of course, was one of the richest media magnates in the world, who with the help of former Nixon speechwriter Roger Ailes had turned the conservative-leaning Fox News Network into one of the fastest growing news operations in broadcast journalism.

"If you can believe *Vanity Fair*, Bill Kristol here is running the United States government!" Murdoch said, referring to a recent profile of the numerous neoconservatives in Washington who helped shape Bush administration policy.

"When I saw Roger Ailes here, I knew myself that the 'axis of evil' was complete!" said Kristol.

The banter was laced with self-deprecating humor, and the essential melancholy of the evening was lost on no one. Yet there was also a strong undercurrent of triumphalism charging the room, and for that matter the entire nation. President George W. Bush had set the tone on May 1 when he flew out to the aircraft carrier USS *Abraham Lincoln* in a Viking warplane, the President resplendent in a fighter pilot's flight suit. Under a banner proclaiming "Mission Accomplished," Bush declared victory and "the turning of the tide" in America's nineteen-month war against terrorism. "Major combat operations in Iraq have ended. In the Battle of Iraq, the United States and our allies have prevailed—the tyrant has fallen and Iraq is free," Bush said. In his comments to the returning sailors of the *Lincoln*, President Bush also made clear that the revolutionary Bush doctrine was still operative against threats such as Syria, Iran, and North Korea. Regimes with ties to terrorists and who sought or possessed weapons of mass destruction, Bush proclaimed, "will be confronted."

In the opinion of many observers Secretary of Defense Donald Rumsfeld's new doctrine of warfare emphasizing speed and agility and revolutionary technology had also been vindicated by an offensive juggernaut that advanced further in less time than any military campaign in history. Now Rumsfeld had been given nearly total control over the U.S. reconstruction and stability operations in Iraq, and it was time for payback. The Pentagon immediately announced that recalcitrant nations such as France and Germany would be excluded from initial Iraqi reconstruction contracts, signaling that Iraq would be treated as an opportunity to be exploited by the handpicked coalition rather than a burden to be shared among allies.

As for the who's who of neoconservative and conservative opinion makers gathered on June 11, 2003, at the Harvard Club for the presentation of the Eric Brindel Award, many of the attendees were understandably buoyed by the sense that neoconservative philosophy had quite suddenly reached its zenith in early twenty-first-century America. After all, these were influential men and women who were used to thinking about America a certain way against seemingly great odds and, to their minds, much fuzzy thinking. Now they had been drawn together for a melancholy tribute, but at a moment of victory and great import, with the United States embarked upon a generation-shaping struggle and the Bush administration leading a revolution many of them had long advocated.

Certainly the primary question posed by neoconservative commentators in the wake of the Iraq war was alive in the cocktail chatter of the Harvard Club ballroom, just as it infused much national debate in the conflict's immediate aftermath. Armed with such a transformational military, and given the Bush administration's purpose and resolve and revolutionary ideas about American power, what might the nation achieve in this rare historical epoch? What evils might it eradicate for the betterment of the world? What goal could possibly exceed the nation's grasp?

If somewhat less attention was focused on persistent problems in securing both Iraq and Afghanistan, and the question of whether the post-9/11 Bush doctrine was leading to the anticipated reordering of the world to better reflect American interests and spread American ideals, a bound red book handed out to all attendees of the Eric Brindel Award ceremony revealed that the honoree, at least, was grappling with the issue. One of Mike Kelly's last columns for the *Washington Post*, apparently written while we were in Kuwait and reprinted in the handout, summarized his assessment of the stakes involved in the war that was about to begin:

> The U.S. armed forces enjoy a technological superiority like nothing the world has seen before; they are, in a real sense, not even fighting the same war as their opponents or in the same century. No one argues much now about whether these forces are capable of crushing even very serious opposition, and almost no one argues that Iraq offers serious opposition. Rather, the argument concerns whether the employment of this almost unfathomable power will be largely for good, leading to the liberation of tyrannized people and the spread of freedom, or largely for bad; leading to imperialism and colonialism, with consequent corruption of

America's own values and freedoms. This question is real enough and more: probably the next hundred years hinges on the answer.

As the biography reprinted in the Brindel Award handout made clear, Kelly was an unusual candidate for lionization by the Harvard Club crowd. He grew up on Capitol Hill in Washington, D.C., his mother an activist in local Democratic politics and his father a reporter and columnist for the old *Washington Daily News*, a tabloid. In accepting the award on Michael's behalf, Tom Kelly, a diminutive man with an oversize presence and a mischievous grin, described the *Daily News* as the third paper in a three-paper town. It was an old-fashioned kind of place, he said, where middle-aged reporters who had never gone to college strived to deliver all the news that's fit to print.

"Only we viewed what news was fit to print much more liberally than the *New York Times*," Tom Kelly said with a grin. "After all, that's the tabloid creed: most news is worth printing."

Tom Kelly recalled taking his son to work when he was only six years old, and recounted how the boy fell in love with the place and the profession. "Michael paid attention, and he learned valuable lessons at the *Daily News*," Tom Kelly said. "He learned that newspapers should tell the truth, not suppress it out of some high-minded sense of decorum, or out of partisan bent." As a man, Michael Kelly never pretended to believe what he didn't believe, his father continued, nor told a lie in order to get at some greater truth.

"Perhaps Mike's greatest virtue was to take his work seriously, but not himself," said Tom Kelly. "That's another lesson he learned in those early years at the *Daily News*. It's very hard to be pompous on a tabloid."

The mystery was how had the son of a newspaper reporter and a Democratic activist, a man who started his career as an award-winning muckraker for the *Cincinnati Post*, become the sharp-quilled columnist who discerned a moral cause in dethroning Saddam Hussein and a champion of the neoconservatives?

Claudia Winkler, the *Weekly Standard* editor and a childhood friend who worked with Michael Kelly at the *Cincinnati Post*, said she witnessed the transformation firsthand. As a child of the '60s and '70s and a reporter who came of age in the era of Vietnam and Watergate, Winkler conceded that Kelly initially seemed an unlikely candidate for the post of neoconservative polemecist.

"The turning point was the Gulf War, which Michael covered as a stringer for the *New Republic* and the *Boston Globe*," said Winkler. Kelly was in Baghdad when the bombs started falling, she said, and entered Kuwait on the day it was liberated as one of the first reporters to document the pillage of that city by Iraqi forces. He traveled to camps of starving refugees along the Iran–Iraq border after the first Bush administration refused to help the Kurds and Shiites who it incited to rise up against Saddam Hussein, an abandonment that Kelly chronicled in his book on the 1991 Gulf War, *Martyrs' Day*.

One of Michael Kelly's literary heroes was George Orwell, who covered the Soviet Union's role in the Spanish Civil War in 1936 in his book *Homage to Catalonia*. "Every line of serious work that I have written since 1936," Orwell later explained, "has been written, directly or indirectly, against totalitarianism and for democratic socialism as I understand it."

"I think something similar was true of Michael. After 1991 he suddenly saw as precious and fragile things he had taken for granted," Winkler told the assembled crowd at the Brindel Award ceremony. "The liberty that was his birthright as an American he now saw as something to be celebrated and defended. He learned that there is such a thing as political indecency, and he lost all tolerance for those who would apologize for it."

After the Eric Brindel Award ceremony ended, a small group of journalists and editors walked to a nearby restaurant where we ate $40 hamburgers and ordered bottles from boutique vineyards, and swapped Michael Kelly stories until the wine nicely blunted the evening's bitter edge. When the party broke up I slipped into the Algonquin Hotel next door, settled into one of the high-backed, red-velvet chairs in the lobby bar, and ordered a cognac. When the snifter came I inhaled the nutty-sweet aroma, and sat by myself sipping the liquor, something I had done a fair amount of since returning from Iraq weeks earlier.

So Kelly had come by his convictions about a just war to end Saddam's tyranny the honest way, through a sense of personal outrage and betrayal. I was in the middle of reading *Martyrs' Day*, and it was all there in excruciating detail: The surreal neo-Stalinism of Saddam's Baghdad, the orgy of rape and torture in Kuwait so twisted that it shamed even the wretched perpetrators, the cruel fate of orphaned children starving inside pens in Kurdish refugee camps.

That night at the Algonquin was as close as I was likely to get in answering the question that had been bothering me for months: Why had Mike pushed himself and his luck so hard? But in returning to Iraq, Mike was returning to the place of his awakening as a journalist and author with a uniquely informed voice. America was getting a chance to right a historical wrong, in his eyes, and once again Kelly could be at hand to bear witness to the liberation of a tyrannized people. In the lives of nations and men, how many times do you get that kind of second chance?

As I waited for my tab I thought of the award ceremony. Among neoconservatives it had become fashionable to talk about a new and benevolent "American Empire." Thinking of the friends I had made in the war and the one I lost, and of all the U.S. soldiers still fighting in Iraq and Afghanistan, I wondered whether the Harvard Club crowd appreciated just how different that empire looked to those manning its furthest battlements.

Just in the past few weeks I had read how four Marines had, like Mike Kelly, died when their helicopter crashed in a canal in Iraq. A fifth Marine, Sgt. Kirk Straseskie, age twenty-three, of Beaver Dam, Wisconsin, drowned trying to save his buddies. A day earlier, twenty-two-year-old Army Spc. Rasheed Sahib, a local from New York City, was killed in Iraq when a fellow soldier's weapon accidentally fired during cleaning. A first-generation American whose family had emigrated from Guyana, Sahib had dreamed of becoming an FBI agent. He was one of more than forty U.S. soldiers killed just since Saddam's statue was toppled in Iraq in April, while another forty-seven had died in Afghanistan since the Taliban fell the previous December. Somehow I doubted many of them had close relatives in the crowd at the Harvard Club.

When the bill for the cognac came I paid it and pocketed the receipt, determined to file it as a business expense to the company where Michael Kelly worked and my own paychecks were signed. The last time we spoke Mike had promised to buy me a drink, and I meant to hold him to it.

PART IV

Blowback

"A nation grown free in a single day is a child born with the limbs and the vigor of a man, who would take a drawn sword for his rattle, and set the house in a blaze that he might chuckle over the splendor."

SYDNEY SMITH
The Smith of Smiths

CHAPTER 20

Transplanting Democracy

THE C-17 AIRLIFTER banked sharply into a circular dive, descending on Baghdad International Airport in a corkscrew pattern meant to evade surface-to-air missiles. Inside the cavernous belly of the aircraft a small group of Defense Department officials, military aides, and journalists strained at our webbed restraints and prayed that the stomach-churning maneuvers were only a precaution. Riding on twin rails in the center of the aircraft was a chrome-skinned command trailer that housed Deputy Defense Secretary Paul Wolfowitz and his top aides.

In late October of 2003, the Office of the Secretary of Defense had phoned a handful of journalists and asked whether we would care to accompany Wolfowitz on a hastily arranged trip to Iraq. The Bush administration had been taking a drubbing in the press over Iraq, and had publicly complained that the media were accentuating the negative and missing the bigger story of significant progress in Iraq's reconstruction. It was very much with an idea of telling that positive backstory that the trip had been arranged.

There was no question that President Bush and the Pentagon were paying heavily for the administration's triumphalism and runaway optimism following the Iraqi Freedom campaign. In a recent Gallup poll, Bush's approval ratings had dropped to 50 percent, the lowest level of his presidency. The October 6, 2003, cover of *Time* magazine featured a photo of President Bush decked out in his flight suit and smiling on the deck of the USS *Abraham Lincoln*, under the headline "Mission *Not* Accomplished. How Bush Misjudged the Task of Fixing Iraq." The article captured the general tenor of the news coverage of Iraq.

Already by the autumn of 2003 the Bush administration was thus very much on the defensive on the issue of Iraq. Not only had the CIA's Iraq Survey Group failed to find any stockpiled weapons of mass destruction after six months of searching, but head inspector and former CIA analyst David Kay suggested that the weapons might never be found. Interviews with Iraqi scientists indicated that conversations intercepted by U.S. intelligence indicating such weapons existed were really a case of scared scientists telling a murderous dictator whatever he wanted to hear. Saddam may even have been purposefully bluffing about possessing such weapons, some Iraqi officials suggested, the threat of doomsday weapons integral to the intimidating image of a tyrant who ruled by fear. Iraqi officials also explained away well-documented cases of deception of U.N. inspectors as attempts to hide Iraq's conventional weapons programs, some of which violated U.N. restrictions. Whatever the actual case, the failure to find the weapons was a severe blow to U.S. credibility, and was threatening the political survival of British prime minister Tony Blair, America's closest international friend. A poll by the *Times* of London found the British people evenly split over who actually posed a greater threat to world peace, Saddam Hussein or President George W. Bush.

In the intervening months since the war, the American people had also learned that they would overwhelmingly bear the onerous burden of Iraq's reconstruction. While the Bush administration went to great pains to stress that more than a score of nations were part of the Iraq coalition, the international support was a mile wide and an inch deep. Most coalition partners were willing to deploy only symbolic handfuls of troops, and an international donors' conference in Madrid had produced only a small fraction of the anticipated costs of Iraq's reconstruction over the next five years. Meanwhile, U.S. lawmakers were still reeling over the Bush administration's recent request for a whopping $87 billion for reconstruction in Iraq and Afghanistan in fiscal 2004 alone.

So when Paul Wolfowitz disembarked from a C-17 onto the tarmac of the Baghdad International Airport in late October of 2003, and was immediately surrounded by waiting TV cameras and reporters, he was at great pains to cast America's experiment in nation building in a time of violent insurgency as a glass half full.

"I am pleased to be here, again, in free Iraq," Wolfowitz told the press gaggle. "I am in Iraq to thank our brave troops and their international partners who are fighting alongside courageous Iraqis—Iraqis who, in increasing numbers, are putting their lives on the line to defend their country and to build a free, prosperous future of Iraqi self-rule. They are taking the fight to the enemy, whose goal is to destroy the substantial progress being made here, and to take Iraq back to the prison of tyranny from which they've finally been liberated."

From the moment we arrived in Iraq, Paul Wolfowitz was accorded unusual deference. Probably no Western functionary had so captured the imagination of Arabs since British intelligence officer T. E. Lawrence joined the forces under Faisal al Hussein in 1916 and became Lawrence of

Arabia. In the minds of many Iraqi sheiks and governing officials, and of the international press for that matter, Wolfowitz was simply the mastermind of the campaign of regime change and democracy building in Iraq. That Wolfowitz was a Jewish intellectual of Polish descent and the son of an academic and lifelong Zionist seemed largely beside the point.

Certainly the arc of Wolfowitz's advocacy for Saddam's ouster had remained one of the few true constants in U.S. policy-making circles during the tumultuous period between the two Iraq wars of 1991 and 2003. As a senior Pentagon policy official in 1990, he had argued strenuously for using force to oust Iraqi forces from Kuwait, and later had unsuccessfully advocated throwing U.S. military force behind the Shiite and Kurdish revolts that rose up against Saddam in the aftermath of Desert Storm.

A quiet man with the supple mind and ideological purity of a Talmudic scholar, Wolfowitz had become the intellectual godfather of regime change in Iraq back in 1997. At that time he argued in an article in the *Weekly Standard*, which he cowrote with former aide Zalmay Khalilzad, that the United States' only viable option was to use military force to dispose of Saddam. Thus began a campaign of congressional testimony, op-ed pieces, and magazine articles, Wolfowitz's advocacy eventually culminating in regime change being adopted by a Republican Congress and becoming official U.S. policy in the late 1990s. After the September 11, 2001, terrorist attacks, Deputy Secretary of Defense Wolfowitz led the faction that immediately advanced Iraq as a necessary front in the war on terror.

So with the campaign to remake Iraq as the model for a democratic Middle East at roughly the six-month mark, its intellectual architect was ready to take the measure of a grand endeavor that the Bush administration conceded was likely to shape the destiny of an entire generation of Americans. Although the mold of that new American epoch would take years to fully form, the tumultuous forces unleashed in its forging were about to become abundantly clear to all of us who journeyed to Iraq on the eve of the 2003 Ramadan holidays.

For someone driving through Baghdad for the first time since just after the high-intensity phase of the war ended, the signs of positive change were indeed striking. The once-shuttered market stalls and empty sidewalks, the small shops hawking everything from freshly slaughtered poultry to computers, the scores of stores on Karada Out Boulevard selling satellite dishes, all of them bustled with shoppers and rang with the dulcet tones of commerce.

Since I was last in Baghdad, nearly all of the city's hospitals and schools had reopened, and U.S. commanders in Iraq had launched numerous drives to outfit local schools with supplies donated from hometown U.S.A. Through a burgeoning system of neighborhood, district, and city councils supported by U.S. military commanders and the Coalition Provisional Authority (CPA), the Iraqis were also learning the early cadences of democratic discourse. That lesson included regular exercises of a citizen's right to vociferously criticize U.S. and Iraqi authorities through frequent street demonstrations and a raucous free press. "In a recent election for a local council, I personally witnessed the loser coming out and officially congratulating the winner," a member of the Iraqi Reconstruction and Development Council told me in Baghdad, asking that his name not be used. "This has never happened before in Iraq! I thought I was dreaming!"

Yet at every turn in Baghdad, the pathologies, ethnic and tribal divisions, and criminal neglect that were the legacy of Saddam's decades of tyranny were also on open display. Only now the blame for whatever ailed Iraq was predictably being laid at the feet of the CPA and its handpicked allies on the Iraqi Governing Counsel (IGC). Before the war, Secretary of State Colin Powell had warned President Bush that if the United States invaded Iraq it would become the owner of the "hopes, aspirations and problems" of twenty-five million people. Powell and Deputy Secretary Rich Armitage privately called it the Pottery Barn rule: "You break it, you own it." And in their ideological brilliance Paul Wolfowitz and the neoconservatives had been blinded to just how broken Iraq really was.

Under a 1986 decree that made criticism of Saddam's regime a crime punishable by death, for instance, the Baathist regime had killed or imprisoned more than five hundred Iraqi journalists, writers, and intellectuals. Even while persecuting the intelligentsia, however, Saddam's regime had trained thousands of propagandists to run its mammoth Ministry of Information to perpetuate the cult of personality and the culture of the "Big Lie." The result was a society where rumor and conspiracy theories were the coin of the information realm.

Many of the five-thousand-plus professional propagandists who had worked at the Ministry of Disinformation, and who were fired by the U.S. authorities after the war, had peddled their services to the nearly two hundred newspapers and newsletters that quickly sprouted in Iraq after Saddam's fall, more than sixty in Baghdad alone. Not surprisingly, the vast majority were aligned with the various religious, ethnic, and political factions that were vying for power and influence in the country, and most adopted a decidedly anti-American voice and conspiratorial tone. Thus during the summer, *Al Saah*, one of the new Iraqi journals, had published an editorial by a Sunni cleric praising the "martyrs" who were launching attacks on U.S. forces in Iraq. *Al Thaqalain*, a Shiite publication, ran a front-page article claiming that AIDS-bearing prostitutes were pouring into Iraq from Israel. The newspaper *Al Mustaqila* advocated "death to all spies, and those who cooperate with the United States." Meanwhile, papers with a more pro-American perspective were the targets of intimidation and violence.

Eventually, CPA head L. Paul Bremer had been forced to issue strict guidelines forbidding the incitement of violence, the promotion of ethnic and religious hatred, or the circulating of false information designed to promote opposition to the occupation authority. Since then, U.S. forces had closed a number of newspapers and one radio station at CPA's behest. The month before, the IGC had even taken the dramatic step of banning from Iraq for one month reporters from the popular Arab satellite television stations Al Jazeera and Al Arabiya, stations based in Qatar and Dubai, respectively, and both decidedly anti-American. The Governing Council accused the Arab stations, not without justification, of inciting violence and supporting the anti-coalition forces.

Mouafac Harb was director of the U.S.-funded Radio Sawa. "In the Middle East we have lots of satellite TV and radio channels, and a lot of magazines and newspapers, and definitely the Internet. Unfortunately, what is missing among these news organizations is ethics," Harb told me. The Middle East, he said, was "probably the only part of the world where the explosion of satellite channels and media organizations has not improved the education and awareness of the masses. It's the only part of the world where the more the number of channels has increased, the more backward people in the Middle East have become. It goes back to who really funds these channels and news outlets, what their message is, and what they're trying to accomplish."

Though the frustrations of officials were understandable, the CPA's ofttimes heavy-handed approach left a strong impression of a U.S. occupation authority and Iraqi Governing Council antagonistic to a free press, and unwilling to compete in a free marketplace of ideas in post-Saddam Iraq. The larger question was how the U.S. military and CPA were supposed to win hearts and minds and succeed in a historic nation-building exercise amidst such negative stereotyping. On that matter the Bush administration and the U.S. officials in Iraq were strangely quiet, though once again the early polling was not altogether encouraging.

Two-thirds of Iraqis polled in a Gallup survey in the fall of 2003 did believe that within five years their lives would be better than before the U.S. invasion. That hopeful sign came against a backwash of anti-American bile, however, that was sweeping through the region. Extensive polling by the Pew Research Center for the People and the Press, the Gallup organization, and the American-based polling firm Zogby International all showed that despite holding generally favorable views of democracy and globalization, Muslim attitudes in the Middle East, Asia, and Africa were becoming intensely unfavorable toward the United States.

That blowback against perceived American arrogance and a Bush doctrine that had led to two U.S.-led wars of regime change in Islamic countries in as many years, coupled with anger over an Israeli-Palestinian conflict that had devolved into a perpetual cycle of low-intensity warfare and terror, acted as an invisible force working against practically any U.S. initiative in the region. Muslim opinions of the United States had, in the words of John Zogby of Zogby International, "just dropped off a cliff." Disapproval of the United States thus reached 95 percent in Saudi Arabia; 91 percent in Morocco; and 99 percent *in Jordan*, supposedly one of America's closest allies in the Middle East. All of that in the heart of the region where the United States had planted its flag as a beachhead for democratic reform.

As with so many of the United States' immediate initiatives after the fall of Saddam, attempts to reverse that tide of anti-Americanism had suffered from gross miscalculation and plain bad luck. For instance, initial military plans to spare from bombing the Ministry of Information in Baghdad, with its considerable broadcasting assets and equipment, had been scrapped in the face of Baghdad Bob's effrontery. That meant that the CPA's fledgling Iraqi Media Network was short of equipment and handicapped by the decrepit state of the Iraqi infrastructure, as well as by the same general lack of security that had cast a pall over much of postwar Iraq. Polls also showed that most Iraqis viewed the Iraqi Media Network, whose programming was often dictated by military public affairs officers on the CPA staff, as just another propaganda arm of the state. State propaganda was something the Iraqis knew something about.

"I cringe when I hear military officers on the CPA staff dictating content to the Iraqi Media Network, but the real problem is that the Pentagon and the U.S. military are neither trained nor well-suited for such nation-building jobs," Barry Zorthian, a former president of the Public Diplomacy Foundation, told me in an interview. Zorthian had served as the U.S. coordinator for media operations in Vietnam in the 1960s, and just before leaving for Baghdad I had spoken with him on the subject of winning hearts and minds. Given that the U.S. military planned meticulously for war but tended to treat stability operations as almost an afterthought, I asked Zorthian about the Bush administration's unusual decision to put the entire Iraqi occupation and reconstruction under the control of the Pentagon.

"You know, Vietnam was the last major nation-building operation of this scope, where the United States tried to develop the institutions of civil society where they didn't exist," Zorthian said. "I think you can make a pretty good argument that the military won every battle in Vietnam, but we lost the communications war in terms of gaining public support for what we were doing, both among the Vietnamese and at home with the American people. If we don't learn from that experience, something similar could happen in Iraq."

In Baghdad we also witnessed block after block of beat-up cars and taxis wrapped in lines around gas stations, signs of a gas shortage that was confounding the U.S. occupational authorities. A decrepit oil refining infrastructure and intermittent sabotage of oil pipelines had greatly slowed the process of bringing Iraq's oil production back on line, increasing the financial burden on the United States and feeding the inevitable conspiracy theories of Iraqis quick to believe the United States had invaded Iraq for its oil. Why else couldn't Iraqis fill the tanks of their cars in a country sitting atop some of the world's largest oil reserves? On the roadside next to gas stations, peddlers ladled black-market gasoline from open barrels into portable plastic containers, their arms shiny up to their elbows with raw petrol.

During the brutal summer months Iraqis had also learned with some consternation that the same United States that put a man on the moon and toppled Saddam's vaunted armies in less than a month was incapable of instantly transforming an electric grid fallen into decrepitude from decades of mismanagement and from years of international sanctions. Yet even in terms of electricity, signs of improvement were evident, especially now that the heat of Iraq's summer had given way to more bearable temperatures. Electrical power output had returned to roughly prewar levels and was climbing, CPA officials told us, a process facilitated by the decision to turn the project into a high-profile military campaign involving the Army Corps of Engineers.

At a major power plant in Baghdad, we visited what amounted to the boiler room of the Iraqi reconstruction effort, a clanking inferno of pipes and fittings and walkways rising hundreds of feet above the ground, belching steam and black smoke. Practically everything on the grounds was covered in a film of dark soot, including some of the workers. Brig. Gen. Steven Hawkins, commander of Task Force Restore Electricity, explained the challenges of turning the lights back on for twenty-five million people in a country with a patchwork and decrepit electric grid. Two of the plant's four generators were from Germany, he explained, and two from Italy. All but one were down for repair or lack of spare parts. The one operational generator was running at less than optimum power due to its own lack of parts. The story was similar, he said, at Iraq's seventeen other major power plants.

When I asked Hawkins the greatest impediment to producing adequate electricity for Iraq, he didn't hesitate in giving the answer virtually everyone we spoke with identified as the lynchpin in the Iraqi reconstruction effort: security. "Sabotage of the oil and gas lines is really hurting us," said Hawkins. "Many of the power stations run on either crude oil or natural gas. Many of the hundreds of substations are also vulnerable to attack. If we can cut down on the sabotage, I think we'll see steady improvement in Iraq's power generation."

The headquarters of the Coalition Provisional Authority was a sprawling palace complex in central Baghdad crowned with four Rushmore-like busts of Saddam in warlike headgear. Inside the complex, a flag-ranked U.S. military officer briefed us on the one issue on which all others hinged in terms of Iraq's reconstruction and democratic development: Who was the enemy that the United States and its Iraqi allies were fighting, and how could it be defeated?

As U.S. commanders had feared, insurgent forces had only gone to ground in the immediate aftermath of the war in order to regroup, and had grown in coordination and lethality throughout the long, hot summer months. In August alone bomb attacks, many of them bearing the disturbing hallmarks of Al Qaeda suicide operations, had partially destroyed the Jordanian embassy in Baghdad, killing 19 and wounding 50; destroyed the U.N. headquarters and driven the international body out of Iraq, while wounding 100 and killing 23, including the widely respected U.N. chief representative Sergio Vieira de Mello; and wounded 142 and killed 85 near the Imam Ali Shrine in the holy city of Najaf, including the revered Iraqi Shiite leader Ayatollah Mohammed Baqir al-Hakim. That attack was aimed at sparking a civil war between the Shiites and Sunnis that, so far at least, had failed to ignite. Insurgents had also recently stepped up a wave of assassinations of potential leaders of a free Iraq, including Akila al-Hashimi of the U.S.-appointed Iraqi Governing Council.

"Whereas ninety days ago we primarily thought the bad guys were a bunch of disorganized numb-nuts, we're starting to see more signs of centralized command-and-control and some type of organization directing these attacks," a U.S. general explained at CPA headquarters, noting that the average daily number of attacks against U.S. soldiers had doubled since the summer. Increasingly, the enemy was employing "hard-core guerrilla tactics" against U.S. forces, he said, using remotely detonated explosive devices, hit-and-run mortar attacks, and carefully planned ambushes.

Just as frustrating as the hit-and-run guerrilla tactics was the inability of U.S. commanders to draw an accurate composite of the enemy they had faced for going on five months. "We don't have adequate intelligence to diagram out who or which organizations are involved, nor do we have conclusive evidence that Saddam is behind it," said the senior officer. "I will flat out tell you, there is a lot we don't know about who we are fighting, or how percentages break down between Saddam loyalists, foreign fighters, and mercenaries. But we do see enough linkages and threads of communications to suggest a central brain or nervous system behind many of these attacks. We just can't tie it all together to the source yet."

At CPA headquarters Wolfowitz conveyed the message that he had actually flown halfway around the world to deliver, a message that marked a distinct shift in U.S. policy in terms of Iraqi reconstruction. Wolfowitz would repeat it to Americans and Iraqis alike at virtually every stop in his whirlwind tour of the country. Rather than focus any longer on failing efforts to "internationalize" the reconstruction effort and count on further pledges of international troops and donations, Wolfowitz and his top aides stressed to U.S. commanders and Iraqis that they must greatly accelerate the transfer of responsibilities to nascent Iraqi police, security, and governing entities. The Pentagon would help with additional resources where possible, but the subtext was unmistakable: There was a finite window of American forbearance under present circumstances, and with a presidential election season approaching next year that window was closing. Within roughly a month the Bush administration would set a firm deadline for the handoff of sovereignty to a new Iraqi government: June 30, 2004.

"In some ways, the most important subject we want to hear about, principally but not exclusively from the Iraqis, is how we can accelerate Iraqi assumption of responsibility for their own affairs, for their security, for their economy, and for their governance," said a senior Pentagon official on the trip. "That is really the key to success, and we think there has been a lot of progress made already."

In its six thousand years of history, the ancient city of Babylon had seen the passing of many kings and conquerors, from Alexander the Great and King Hammurabi to the Mongol hordes and the armies of Syria, Turkey, Persia, and Germany. The original fortress gate, once the entrance to the Hanging Gardens of Babylon, still bears the visible contours of a "merdog," etched in a sand-colored stone worn smooth by time. A mythical animal from the time of Nebuchadnezzar, the merdog has the forelegs of a lion, the hind legs of an eagle, the skin of a shark, the tail of a snake, and the sting of a scorpion. As modern-day Iraqis awoke in the autumn of 2003, they found outside the fortress gates an army no less the total of seemingly disparate parts, and one unlike any seen even in Babylon's long history.

A riverside palace next to the fortress served as the headquarters for the coalition's multinational division of 9,200 troops from twenty-one different nations, with Poland in the lead. A visit to the palace demonstrated the limitations of an international presence so shallow that a single division had to be cobbled together from Poles, Ukrainians, Latvians, Thais, Danes, Spaniards, Nicaraguans, Dominicans, Bulgarians, and Mongolians. The complexities involved in such an operation rivaled those inherent in the construction of the Tower of Babel, the original site of which lay nearby in the ancient land of Babylonia.

"It's a great challenge, trying to meld the forces of twenty-one countries into one unit," Maj. Gen. Andrzej Tyszkiewicz, the Polish commander of the multinational division, conceded to the Wolfowitz delegation. "We have East Asians, Latin Americans, Europeans. It's difficult just ironing out the language difficulties, not to mention the different cultures and military habits involved."

Although the multinational division was purposely assigned a relatively quiet area of responsibility in the Shiite-dominated region south of Baghdad, this area where U.S. commanders believed liberation would be most welcome had recently become a flashpoint. The tensions in the area were indicative of a growing restlessness throughout much of Iraq over the presence of so many foreign troops on their soil, and a chaffing at occupation by the strongly nationalistic Iraqis that had taken U.S. authorities by surprise. The August 29 bombing in Najaf that killed Ayatollah al-Hakim and scores of his followers had also greatly increased anxiety in the Shiite population, as did the anti-coalition rhetoric of firebrand Shiite cleric Muqtada al-Sadr, whose actions and diatribes against the U.S.-led occupation had become increasingly provocative throughout the summer and fall.

Sadr's militia vaingloriously called themselves the "Mahdi Army," or an army in the service of the messiah. Many of its foot soldiers were recruited from the Shiite slum of Sadr City in Baghdad, named for the cleric's revered father who had been assassinated by Saddam. Recently, members of Sadr's militia had become involved in a gunfight in Najaf that left three U.S. soldiers dead and seven wounded. With Sadr's followers openly confronting U.S. forces and stashing Iranian-supplied weapons inside mosques in the holy city, coalition authorities had decided to act. Only no one believed the Polish-led division was up to the task of confronting the Sadr militia. "One of the dilemmas of the multinational division is that its rules of engagement rule out offensive operations," a senior U.S. officer told me in Iraq. "Given the dynamic situation in Karbala and Najaf, that meant we had to introduce U.S. forces into the mix."

U.S. officials cited their response to the provocations in Karbala as a potential model for future joint U.S.-Iraqi operations. Newly graduated Iraqi Civil Defense Corps (ICDC) forces, backed by U.S. combat troops, raided two mosques associated with Sadr, capturing weapons and arresting more than thirty of his supporters, including two senior Sadr lieutenants. Largely because it was ICDC troops that actually entered the mosques, U.S. officials said the response among Iraqis in Karbala had been relatively muted. No one believed that they had heard the last of Muqtada al-Sadr, however, who was developing a skill for brinksmanship and agitation.

Before we boarded our helicopters, Wolfowitz gave an impromptu press conference. We had just visited a newly opened training center in the nearby town of Al Hillah, where U.S. soldiers had fought vicious battles during the Iraqi Freedom campaign. Now Iraqi women in Al Hillah were learning computer and entrepreneurial skills at the center, and Wolfowitz was clearly energized by the many heartfelt messages of thanks he received there. At one point Wolfowitz had asked how many of those gathered at the center had personally lost a family member or loved one to Saddam's purges, and a majority of the hands in the crowd shot up. But wasn't Wolfowitz daunted, a reporter asked, by the challenges that so obviously lay ahead in Iraq's uncertain march to democracy?

"You know, General Tyszkiewicz just told me something interesting," Wolfowitz replied, referring to the Polish commander. "He told me that fifteen years after the end of the Cold War his country is far better off than they were under Soviet domination or immediately after liberation. Yet Poland still suffers from 18 percent unemployment and many economic challenges. That's a valuable perspective. Instead of comparing Iraq to America, I think you need to compare it to progress made by other countries in the developing world. By that yardstick, I think an awful lot has already been accomplished in just the past six months."

With that we trundled into the helicopters. In the fading light the pilots of our twin-rotor CH-47 Chinook flew a twisting, hard-banking course low over the Tigris River as it wound its way north. Our destination was all the explanation anyone needed for the evasive and stomach-churning flying maneuvers. We were headed straight for the epicenter of the Sunni Triangle, and the dark heart of the Iraqi insurgency.

The headquarters for the U.S. Army's Fourth Infantry Division was a cavernous palace on a bluff overlooking the Tigris River in Saddam's ancestral home of Tikrit. Saddam reportedly never actually occupied the marbled edifice, which had only recently been built in the spree of palace construction that the dictator indulged with lucrative kickbacks skimmed off of the United Nation's oil-for-food program. Yet the continued presence of the Iraqi dictator was as real to the inhabitants of Tikrit as the snake-rattle of automatic weapons fire that echoed in the river valley virtually every night.

"I haven't met anyone in this region who doesn't believe Saddam is alive and out there somewhere, and may be coming back," Maj. Gen. Raymond Odierno, commander of the Fourth Infantry Division, told us that first night in Tikrit. A bear of a man, Odierno and his division had eventually been given the responsibility of securing the Sunni Triangle north and west of Baghdad after entering Iraq through Kuwait last spring. Because the Fourth Infantry Division had not been able to launch a northern front from Turkey during the invasion, it was denied a chance to possibly pacify the Sunni Triangle during major hostilities, and to interdict hardcore Baathists fleeing Baghdad. Now attacks on U.S. soldiers from a regrouped insurgency had increased markedly in the past two months.

Given the former dictator's continuing hold on the Iraqi psyche, senior officers in the Fourth I.D. said that capturing or killing Saddam was still one of their most pressing goals, and they believed their forces had come close to doing just that on a number of raids in the Sunni Triangle. "By the time we got to Tikrit, Saddam had been around for twenty-five years—more than twice as long as Hitler in Germany," a senior officer told us. "And it's going to take some time for us to counter his brainwashing and intimidation, and convince people that he's gone for good."

Although the killing of Saddam's sons Uday and Qusay back in July 2003 was a major victory in the campaign to break the Baathist hold on the Iraqi psyche, there were growing reasons to believe that capturing or killing Saddam himself was critical to pacifying Iraq. For instance, intelligence being assembled by the Iraq Survey Group (ISG), the fifteen hundred-member team created by the director of the CIA to search for weapons of mass destruction, indicated that Saddam may have planned all along to put up only nominal initial resistance to a U.S. invasion before going underground to orchestrate a guerrilla war.

The eventual 2004 ISG report, which was based on numerous interviews with senior Iraqi officials and military leaders, indicated that Saddam told his advisers and military commanders before the invasion to stand their ground for about eight days, after which Hussein would "take over." The report also revealed that from August 2002 to January 2003, Iraqi commanders across the country had been ordered to hide weapons in the countryside. An index to the report would reveal that a branch of

Iraqi intelligence trained fighters from Syria, Yemen, Egypt, Lebanon, and Sudan in explosives and marksmanship in anticipation of a guerrilla war.

"Saddam believed that the Iraqi people would not stand to be occupied or conquered by the United States and would resist—leading to an insurgency," the thousand-page report, signed by chief weapons inspector Charles A. Duelfer, would later reveal. "Saddam said he expected the war to evolve from traditional warfare to insurgency."

The leaders of the Fourth Infantry Division were confronted every day with signs of that growing insurgency, including increasing acts of intimidation and reprisal against U.S. collaborators. "Iraqis coming forward with information are the most important intelligence sources we have, but retaliation and threats against them is a huge problem," Odierno told Wolfowitz and his staff. Stories abounded in Fourth I.D. headquarters of such reprisals, such as that of a young woman who objected when the fedayeen tried to bury weapons in her front yard, and then was forced to watch her husband and son being shot to death in reprisal. "Those kinds of stories play on the psyche of the Iraqis," Odierno said.

Despite the sharp increase in attacks on U.S. troops in the Sunni Triangle, Fourth I.D. officers still surmised that Baath Party loyalists were fighting a desperate rearguard action in Saddam's last stronghold. At least from Fourth Infantry Division headquarters, the light was clearly visible at the end of the tunnel.

"They've largely surrendered the north and south, and are funneling in fedayeen and foreign fighters from outside in an attempt to defend the heartland," General Odierno told us. "While they've had some success in scaring the public and monopolizing press coverage, they also know that as long as U.S. troops stay, they cannot win. Each day we get stronger, our actionable intelligence gets better, and we continue to improve infrastructure and win more Iraqis to our cause. Their only hope is to sway U.S. public and congressional opinion to force us to pull out."

Out of deference none of the Washington delegation mentioned the state of considerable flux in U.S. public and congressional opinion in terms of Iraq. Even after a recent prime-time speech by President Bush that argued in lofty tones that the sacrifices in Iraq were a necessary part of the administration's response to the 9/11 terrorist attacks, most Americans (51 percent to 41 percent) opposed Bush's request for $87 billion, much of it for reconstruction and military operations in Iraq, according to an NBC/*Wall Street Journal* poll.

Like most other U.S. units in Iraq, Fourth Infantry Division commanders had steadily adjusted their tactics to focus more on targeted raids based on specific intelligence, rather than random searches that inevitably alienated local Iraqis. Since September, such raids had led to the successful interdiction of 175 "targets," they said, leading to the arrest of 1,315 enemy detainees, including 46 suspected bomb makers and 6 senior Baathist financiers. The statistics and charts all seemed encouraging, even if they did relatively little to illuminate the true nature and size of the enemy forces, or the overall success of their campaign of intimidation and sabotage.

What Wolfowitz was determined to stress in his discussions with the Fourth Infantry Division leaders, however, was the new U.S. strategy of dramatically shifting responsibility to Iraqi forces. He pressed the commanders to accelerate training and deployment of the ICDC, border guards, and police in the Sunni Triangle. To date, the Fourth I.D. had already recruited more than 12,650 such forces in an attempt to put an Iraqi face on security operations. Nationwide, coalition authorities said that they had deployed a total of 86,000 Iraqi security troops and police, though they were certainly not visible on the streets and the actual numbers were very difficult to substantiate.

The man most responsible for training ICDC forces in the Fourth I.D.'s area of operations was Lt. Col. Steve Russell. The division had been able to largely weed out bad apples and potential spies, he told us, by vetting recruits with local sheiks. Meanwhile, at checkpoints, ICDC troops proved their worth and the soundness of the new U.S. strategy of rapid transfer, he said, by pointing out cars or drivers that represented potential trouble long before they could pose a danger to U.S. forces.

"Because they've lived here all their lives, they notice when things aren't right long before we can," said Russell, whose Fourth I.D. comrades had conducted more than three thousand joint patrols with Iraqi forces just since September. "They gather intelligence from friends and families in the region, and receive intelligence tips, that we simply aren't privy to. They can go into Iraqi homes and mosques without causing a furor or resentment. We can't."

Even in the Sunni Triangle, Fourth I.D. trainers said they had exceeded their recruiting of Iraqi forces, and interviews with several of those volunteers suggested that while Saddam was certainly feared in his hometown, he was not exactly widely loved by the man in the street. "He stole all of our oil, and hurt a lot of people around here," said one Iraqi trainee, who out of fear of reprisal identified himself only as "Joseph." "These fedayeen, all they are doing is fighting for money. That's not being a good Muslim. We are not fighting for money. We're fighting for our country. And one day, after the Americans help us get rid of the rest of Saddam's forces, we'll have our country back."

Colonel Russell gave a demonstration of a training session for ICDC troops. With a U.S. sergeant barking orders, a three-man Iraqi rifle team practiced the synchronized "cover and advance" tactic of a squad under fire. Only the Iraqis clearly hadn't gotten the hang of it, advancing together uncertainly and stopping in unison in a fashion that would prove suicidal in an actual firefight. The louder the U.S. sergeant barked at them in English, the more flustered the Iraqis became, until an Iraqi interpreter stepped in and shouted at the sheepish-looking ICDC troops.

Observing the hapless display, I was reminded of experts who insisted that it would take at least three years to build a competent paramilitary force out of such raw material. Judging by the message that Wolfowitz was bringing to U.S. and Iraqi commanders, it was clear that those Iraqi men didn't have a year, much less three, before they could expect to man the front lines in the fight against the Iraqi insurgency. As we walked away an obviously frustrated U.S. sergeant was relaying a message to the men through the Iraqi interpreter. "Tell them that they would be dead," he said, and pointed at each in turn. "Go ahead, tell them. If they tried that under fire, they would be dead men."

Before escorting Wolfowitz and our entourage to the helicopters, Odierno drove us out to a lonely road crossing near a canal bordered by tall grass. Under different circumstances the spot would be scenic, but as with hundreds like it throughout Iraq the canal side was mostly notable as an ambush site. A week earlier, on October 18, 2003, 1st Lt. David Bernstein of Phoenixville, Pennsylvania, and Pfc. John Hart of Bedford, Massachusetts, were both killed on that spot in a coordinated ambush employing a machine gun, RPGs, and small arms. They were among the more than 170 U.S. soldiers who had died in Iraq since President Bush declared major hostilities over on May 1.

"When we first got here the attacks tended to be by small, undisciplined groups who would give up and run at the first indication of a fight," explained Odierno. "More recently, the ambushes directed at us tend to be a little more organized. We can't prove it, but we think that indicates the increased presence of foreign fighters in this region."

As the Wolfowitz delegation lifted off from Tikrit, many of us breathed a sigh of relief at leaving the Sunni Triangle behind. Every Fourth I.D. soldier seemed to have a story about a harrowing firefight, a close call with a roadside bomb, of buddies who had lost limbs and lives. Time in the Triangle rarely passed uneventfully. Thankfully, the next stop for the delegation was Kirkuk, by all accounts a multiethnic success story in the relatively calm Kurdish region of northern Iraq. By the time we arrived, word reached us that just after our departure from Tikrit a U.S. Army Blackhawk helicopter there was hit by RPGs and forced to crash-land in flames.

"When you first arrived in Iraq, we thought you wore the ring of Solomon!" laughed Sheik Ali Khalid Al Iman, welcoming Paul Wolfowitz to a roundtable discussion with local Kurdish, Arab, and Turkmen religious leaders in Kirkuk, held in the shade of a long pavilion. "Now we see from your behavior that you may even be one of us, because you come hoping to try and help us solve our problems. And as you can see at this table, we are of three ethnic groups, and two strands of Islam, Sunni and Shiite, and there are no problems among us."

The stop in Kirkuk had clearly acted as a balm to Wolfowitz's spirits. We had walked with him to the pavilion through the city's main market street, which wound toward an old fortress sitting atop a nearby hill. Wolfowitz was greeted by the Kurds on the street almost as a returning hero. Although U.S. officials still feared the Kurdish region could turn into another flashpoint over the issue of resettlement of Kurds and Arabs displaced during Saddam's rule, on this day the talk among the imams was of blessedly mundane matters. The assembled religious leaders wanted all liquor stores closed for the upcoming religious holiday period of Ramadan. They also wanted to know if Wolfowitz could reconvene the old Council of Elders in Baghdad, which traditionally would decide when the moon was ripe enough to declare the start of Ramadan.

"I am very impressed by your spirit of cooperation," Wolfowitz told the religious leaders. "That makes us allies in the most basic sense, because we share the same goals. I promise you that I won't consider my work here finished until people are doing well again, and a new, elected government is established in Iraq."

After the United States had initially abandoned the Kurds to slaughter and exodus at the hands of Saddam's Baathist forces in 1991, Paul Wolfowitz was promising that the United States would see it through this time. Looking into the faces of those Iraqis whose lives now depended upon it, you hoped that he was right. Before leaving Kirkuk, the Wolfowitz delegation visited a police station where U.S. military police were training local Iraqi police. Lt. Col. Dominic Caraccilo of the Fourth Infantry Division explained how they were trying to acquire cars and radios and other fundamentals for their Iraqi counterparts, but that it was slow going squeezing the equipment out of the coalition supply chain. Outside, the Iraqi police stood in formation and Wolfowitz went down the line shaking each of their hands in turn, the architect of Iraqi liberation thanking these unlikely foot soldiers for assuming one of the most dangerous jobs in all Iraq.

Walking away from the police station I struck up a conversation with *Washington Post* columnist David Ignatius, who had recently been in Fallujah, a stronghold of the former Baathists in the Sunni Triangle. In a tragic case of misidentification, U.S. troops in Fallujah had recently opened fire on Iraqi police who were involved in a car chase, killing eight of them. "I can tell you, in Fallujah you certainly no longer get the sense that the cops and the occupation forces are all in this together," Ignatius said.

CHAPTER 21

The Ramadan Offensive

ON THE NIGHT BEFORE Ramadan, members of the Iraqi Governing Council held a cocktail party for Paul Wolfowitz and his delegation at the Al Rashid Hotel in Baghdad. Over drinks I sidled up to Ahmed Chalabi and Bill Luti, respectively the Iraqi exile and the man who helped run Iraq policy from the Pentagon's Special Plans Office. Both men were understandably commiserating over their recent news notices.

Despite the fact that much of the discredited intelligence on Saddam's supposed weapons of mass destruction was traceable to the Iraqi defectors Chalabi had personally made available to U.S. journalists and Pentagon officials, the wily exile was still receiving hundreds of thousands of dollars from the Pentagon each month for his intelligence contributions. Chalabi was also associated with two of the most controversial—some would say ruinous—decisions of the Iraqi reconstruction effort to date: the complete dissolution of the Iraqi army, and a tough "de-Baathification" effort that Chalabi was zealously managing from Baghdad, purging the ranks of the new government of even low-level bureaucrats with Baath Party connections. Taken together, those decisions not only shut down the only two functioning institutions still operating in Iraq at the start of the war, they also guaranteed that much of the Sunni population and hundreds of thousands of former Iraqi soldiers would feel disenfranchised, with little stake in their country's future. Together the two initiatives helped ensure, however, that Chalabi and the other exiles favored by the Pentagon faced no direct threat or political competition from former regime officials.

For his part, Luti's Special Plans Office was the subject of various investigations into the failure to find weapons of mass destruction. Of special interest was the intelligence shop's close ties both to Chalabi and Vice President Cheney's office. Many intelligence analysts believed that the Special Plans Office that Luti ran on a day-to-day basis had essentially acted as a backdoor conduit to the highest levels of the U.S. government for intelligence that could not withstand the close scrutiny of regular intelligence channels. Luti and his boss, Undersecretary of Defense for Policy Doug Feith, had also come in for heavy criticism for their failure to anticipate many of the worst-case scenarios that were unhappily unfolding in Iraq. As if that wasn't enough, the FBI was also investigating Luti and other officials in the Office of Special Plans for possibly passing classified information to the Israelis.

"According to the press, I'm supposed to be 'smug' and 'parochial,'" Chalabi said with a shake of his head.

"And I'm supposed to be Satan himself!" rejoined Luti, a former Navy captain.

"This is a hard business," Chalabi agreed, shaking his head again.

The problem in Luti's view was not a lack of planning for post-Saddam Iraq by the Pentagon, but rather the CIA's prediction that the Iraqi army would turn against Saddam Hussein, instead of collapsing like a house of cards. As for the ongoing "troubles," Luti mostly blamed the tactics of the Army's heavy armored forces who had assumed responsibility for Baghdad and most of the Sunni Triangle in the spring. The light infantry of the 101st Air Mobile Division in the Kurdish north, and the Marines in the Shiite south, had fared much better in his view. I didn't bother to point out at the time that it was Baghdad and the Sunni Triangle, and not the north or south, that were the epicenter of the growing insurgency.

As for Ahmed Chalabi, he was already beginning to irritate his American benefactors in Baghdad by publicly lobbying for a faster transfer of sovereignty to the unelected Iraqi Governing Council, where he had recently served a one-month tour as president.

How long, I wondered, did Chalabi think U.S. military forces would need to stay in Iraq?

"Iraq is a country surrounded by six countries which between them have more than two million men under arms," he told me. "We have no army, nor are we likely to get one. So I think the longer America stays in Iraq, the better."

One or two years?

"Longer," said Chalabi. "Surely longer."

Later at the Al Rashid reception I asked another member of the Iraqi Governing Council whether he thought the security situation was improving in Baghdad. He advised caution, warning that it was wiser not to travel in the large Chevrolet Suburban SUVs favored by coalition and IGC officials. "Better to travel by taxi so as not to present such an obvious target," the Iraqi told me. "Because the Baathists are once again getting more organized in Baghdad. I can feel it."

Everyone seemed drawn to their windows the next morning. Dawn had just broken over Baghdad on October 26, the soft light muting the city's infinite palette of brown into a single muddy hue. Against that backdrop a car caught the eye of U.S. observers stationed on a nearby rooftop: It was pulling what looked like a portable generator down a largely deserted street outside the barricaded Green Zone that housed the Coalition Provisional Authority. As a precaution, an Iraqi paramilitary patrol was dispatched. For some reason, the trailer was painted a bright, incongruous blue.

On the upper floor of the Al Rashid Hotel, some nine hundred yards away, the entourage accompanying Wolfowitz were crawling out of our beds to the accompaniment of 6:00 A.M. wake-up calls. The night before, I had sat in the bar of the Al Rashid with a motley assortment of soldiers, contractors, ex-military types, nurses, mercenaries and reporters—adventurous men and women a long way from home, with stories to tell and no one to tell them to but each other. I wasn't particularly happy, then, to see the crack of dawn.

I was in the shower when my roommate, Steven Hayes of the *Weekly Standard*, heard a sizzle-whoosh as if from a giant Roman candle somewhere outside. Like nearly everyone else who heard the sound, including Paul Wolfowitz himself, Hayes was drawn to our window. In that instant before the thunderclap, those who saw the mesmerizing contrails of the approaching rockets knew they were in exactly the wrong place at the wrong time, and that their lives were about to change.

The fusillade of 68 mm and 85 mm Katyusha rockets caught the Al Rashid broadside in a rapid succession of sledgehammer blows that sheared off chunks of concrete and vaporized bulletproof windows into mists of jagged glass. The rockets burst into hotel rooms and blew locked doors into hallways. For a few endless moments after the attack, the entire hotel was quiet, as if holding its collective breath. Then the Al Rashid exhaled pure pandemonium.

When I ran out into the hall in my towel, the eleventh floor was already nearly ankle-deep in water and filled with acrid smoke and clumps of debris. Half-dressed men carrying guns spilled into the hallway, screams and shouts of "Fire!" echoed off the walls on various floors, and the order was given to evacuate. A few doors down Stephen Hayes peered into a room that had sustained heavy damage, and then disappeared inside. A few moments later Hayes emerged shouting for a medic, his face registering a grim prognosis.

The emergency-exit stairway was covered in glass from shattered partitions, and the wounded were being carried down in sheets that doubled as makeshift stretchers. An alarm whooped and reverberated as the stairwell filled with thick smoke, the way down clearly marked on each step and landing by boot prints outlined in thickly pooled blood.

"They do this every time. Every time we do something positive, the bad guys try and reverse the psychology with their own negative act," Brig. Gen. Martin Dempsey, commander of the Army's First Armored Division in Baghdad, explained as he briefed Wolfowitz and the rest of our delegation on the afternoon of the rocket attack. The positive gestures in this case were the relaxation of curfews in advance of the start of the Ramadan holy month, and the reopening of the 14th of July Bridge to ease traffic congestion in downtown Baghdad. The bridge's reopening created a traffic thoroughfare right down the middle of the Green Zone complex. The makeshift rocket launcher in the blue trailer had been parked on a side street just off 14th of July Street.

"I don't think this fight will be won when the enemy raises a white flag," Dempsey said, briefing us in a sweltering tent on the compound housing the headquarters of his Second Brigade, which had responsibility for securing the Green Zone. "It'll be won when we can do more positive things than he can do negative."

That seemed a tall order given the seemingly infinite opportunities for mayhem in Iraq. First Armored Division commanders remained optimistic, however, and they mostly discounted the likelihood that the rocket attack was targeted at Wolfowitz specifically. They described the improvised nature of the rocket launcher—what Dempsey called a "Rube Goldberg" device—as a likely sign of the enemy's weakness and lack of sophistication. They saw the attack itself as a sign of desperation from an enemy that realized each day that U.S. authorities were making progress improving security in Baghdad. The enemy's increased difficulty in finding recruits, the commanders said, was reflected in the rising price for a contract hit on American forces, which had spiraled from $300 shortly after Baghdad fell to roughly $5,000 by October of 2003. Though the Al Rashid attack was certainly sensational and would no doubt create an uproar in the press, First A.D. commanders said that tactically the damage it inflicted was insignificant. The numbers were all on our side.

Among the assembled commanders a familiar voice cut in. "Oh, you don't have to worry about Kitfield there getting too excited by a rocket attack. This stuff is all old hat to him!"

Turning, I saw the commander of Second Brigade, First Armored Division, his face framed by a low-swept helmet bearing the full-bird insignia of a colonel in the U.S. Army. The familiar jutting jaw gave way to a wide grin that was the most welcome thing I had seen in this country.

"Welcome back to Baghdad, James," said Col. Rob Baker.

The First Armored Division had prepared to fight a high-intensity war in Iraq, and instead found itself responsible for a city of more than five million inhabitants that was caught somewhere between post-regime anarchy and insurgency. Though we could only begin to sense it as Rob Baker and I drove around Baghdad in his armored Humvee that afternoon, the events of that morning and the coming days were about to tip the balance in that equation toward all-out guerrilla war, and Baker would play a central role in the drama.

Two weeks after the attack on the Al Rashid, Baker would launch Operation Striker Elton, named in honor of singer Elton John's hit "Rocket Man." On November 8, 2003, Striker Elton targeted eighteen houses in a simultaneous strike that netted thirty-six suspected insurgents, twenty-nine of whom were later imprisoned for their complicity in the rocket attack on the Al Rashid. One of the most successful operations in Iraq to that date, Striker Elton heralded a new and more intense phase in the U.S. Army's counterinsurgency campaign in Iraq, one focused on human intelligence, rapid counterstrikes, arrests, and aggressive interrogations of suspected insurgents.

That new phase would lead U.S. forces in Iraq to score many victories against the insurgency in an increasingly intelligence-driven guerrilla war, including the December 2003 capture of Saddam Hussein himself. As part of that operation, U.S. commanders would discover intelligence indicating that the former dictator and his inner circle were indeed responsible for financing and coordinating many of the attacks on coalition forces, accounting for at least one of the "unseen hands" U.S. officials had felt directing attacks.

That heightened phase of counterinsurgency would also steer the U.S. military, however, into waters uncharted by its own doctrinal manuals and outside the bounds of much of its traditional training. If Pentagon civilians such as Paul Wolfowitz and Donald Rumsfeld grasped the irony of what they had done, however, they didn't let on to reporters. In insisting on a transformational model of warfare and later denying calls on Capitol Hill for an increase in U.S. troop strength, Defense Department officials had essentially taken a capital-intensive, high-tech U.S. military, stripped it lean for a sprintlike invasion of Iraq, and then had left it mired, undermanned, in a manpower-intensive marathon of occupation and counterinsurgency. Certainly it seemed likely that my friend Col. Rob Baker and other U.S. commanders and troops would continue to struggle mightily to stabilize Iraq under such conditions. After all, the U.S. military very purposely got out of the counterinsurgency business after Vietnam.

The strategic nature of the Ramadan Offensive became clear the morning after the Al Rashid rocket attack. Between 8:30 and 10:15 A.M. on October

27, 2003, a coordinated wave of four suicide bombings killed 40 people, wounded 224, and plunged Baghdad into chaos. The chosen targets— four Iraqi police stations and the offices of the International Red Cross— were picked to counter the new U.S. strategy of greatly accelerating the handoff of security responsibilities to Iraqi authorities, and of eliciting greater international assistance in Iraq's rebuilding. The message from the guerrillas was clear—side with the United States in this struggle under fear of death. Anyone who failed to receive that message was left with the example of Faris Abdul Razzaq Assam, one of Baghdad's three deputy mayors, who was assassinated on the same day as the Al Rashid attack by two executioners who shot him at point-blank range at an outdoor café. His slaying was just the latest in a long string of assassinations of Iraqi officials who dared cooperate with U.S. authorities. The string of executions would grow.

Iraq was not Vietnam, of course, and the differences in the two wars were probably as instructive as their similarities. When Vietnam analogies began appearing in much of the press coverage around the time of the Ramadan Offensive, it wasn't because defeat in Iraq was imminent or inevitable. Rather, for those of us who witnessed the events firsthand, the *potential* for defeat in this grand endeavor on which the United States had sacrificed and gambled so much suddenly became quite clear, and the likely contours of that failure seemed hauntingly familiar.

Certainly, the United States had not faced a moment so fraught with risk since January 31, 1968, when North Vietnamese and the Viet Cong launched an early morning offensive in South Vietnam to coincide with the Tet Lunar New Year holidays. Just as in October of 2003, the U.S. military plausibly argued at that time that the offensive was a last, desperate act of a foe that was losing virtually every battle on the ground. Then as in 2003, the Pentagon was likewise developing a strategy for rapidly handing over security responsibilities to local authorities, in that case through Vietnamization.

In 1968 President Lyndon Johnson had likewise refused to suspend his cherished Great Society programs or call up the Reserves in order to focus the energies of the country fully on the war, just as George W. Bush refused to scale back historic tax cuts or increase U.S. troop levels to win decisively in Iraq. Perhaps most importantly, with both the Tet and Ramadan Offensives, an enemy that was hopelessly outgunned in every conventional sense tried to change the terms of the debate with an unconventional war of terror and attrition aimed directly at the will of the American people.

The U.S. military never forgave the press for what it perceived as the media's unwitting complicity in that strategy, or for missing the backstory of how the Tet Offensive was a military setback from which the Viet

Cong never really recovered. For its part, the media criticized the Pentagon for never fully leveling with the public about the extent of the enemy and the likely sacrifices in national treasure and blood defeating him would require, and U.S. political leaders for never adequately fortifying the will of the American people against the challenges of Vietnam.

In some ways, the Wolfowitz trip had been an attempt by both sides—the Pentagon and the media—to avoid a repeat of 1968. To get it right this time. Only that would have required agreeing on a common narrative to describe what happened on a journey to Iraq on the eve of Ramadan 2003. And that, as it turned out, was harder than either side anticipated.

The Wolfowitz delegation left the coalition's headquarters by helicopter on the night of October 26, no one wanting to chance driving a convoy through "Ambush Alley" that the main road leading to Baghdad International Airport had become. Looking out the open rear door of the giant CH-47 chopper, I could see the rear gunner silhouetted against the bright lights that shimmered over the city and reflected off the dark ribbon of the Tigris. The backwash from the Chinook's turbines wafted through the darkened fuselage like one last, hot breath from Iraq.

Before boarding the helicopters Paul Wolfowitz had a long dinner with Abdel-Aziz al-Hakim, a member of the Iraqi Governing Council and the head of the Supreme Council of the Islamic Revolution, an organization with close ties to the Grand Ayatollah Ali al-Husseini al-Sistani, the top Shiite cleric in Iraq. The two men discussed one of the most important outstanding questions posed by a free Iraq: Could the nation's Shiite religious majority embrace democracy and pluralism? Despite having close ties to Iran, where he spent time in exile from Saddam, al-Hakim assured Wolfowitz that the Shiites didn't seek an Iranian-style theocracy of the mullahs for Iraq, which would almost certainly provoke a civil war. Al-Hakim, whose brother the Ayatollah Mohammed Baqir al-Hakim had been assassinated in Najaf two months earlier, insisted that Iraqis had suffered and sacrificed too much already in war and civil strife.

"Sixty-three members of my family have been murdered already," al-Hakim told Wolfowitz. "I don't want to be number sixty-four."

Our last stop before loading up the helicopters had been at the U.S. hospital in the Green Zone, where Wolfowitz visited those seriously injured in the morning's rocket attack. The wounded offered a revealing cross-section of the civilians and soldiers who were risking their lives to help in Iraq's transition. There was a secretary from the State Department who had volunteered for duty in Iraq; a British national working to remove Saddam's face from the Iraqi currency; an official from the U.S. Department of Labor who was helping establish Iraq's Labor Ministry; and a civilian from the U.S. National Imaging and Mapping Agency involved in intelligence collection. The last person Wolfowitz visited was an Army colonel who was so badly wounded that he remained behind an oxygen mask. When Wolfowitz detected an accent, he asked where the man was from?

"I live in Arlington, Virginia, sir, but I grew up in Beirut, Lebanon."

"What do you think about this idea of building a new Middle East," Wolfowitz asked the officer.

The man raised his hand in a thumbs-up gesture.

The officer that Steven Hayes had tried to assist a few doors down from our room at the Al Rashid was Lt. Col. Charles Buehring, a military intelligence briefer for the CPA. Chad Buehring was a graduate of The Citadel and, along with his wife, Alicia, the proud parent of sons Nick, twelve, and Drew, nine. All were on hand a few weeks later, along with Paul Wolfowitz, when they gathered at Arlington National Cemetery to bury Lt. Col. Buehring, the highest-ranking officer killed in Iraq to date. Before the Buehring family was left to endure the silence of his passing alone, a bagpiper in a gray kilt played a mournful "Amazing Grace."

After visiting the critically wounded in Baghdad that day, Wolfowitz had spoken with reporters briefly before we all embarked on the long journey home. "The victims of this attack, including our colonel who tragically died, are real heroes," Wolfowitz said. "The criminals who are responsible for their deaths and injuries are the same people who have abused and tormented Iraqis for thirty-five years. There are a small number of dead-enders who think they can take this country back by destabilizing it and scaring us away. They are not going to scare us away. We're going to finish this job despite the last, desperate acts of a dying regime of criminals."

It was exactly the right tone to honor the fallen, of course, and from the air that night, looking down over the city, I could almost imagine Baghdad as just another capital with a river running through it. I didn't want to think about the ethnic and religious patchwork that the view obscured, or the demons spawned by decades of tyranny that had been let loose on the land. I didn't want to think about all the heroes, American, Iraqi, and coalition alike, who were yet to be sacrificed to the cause. I didn't want to think that the Ramadan Offensive had only just begun. Just for a moment, I wanted to see the landscape below the way Paul Wolfowitz saw it—without doubts or fears of ignoble failure. I wanted to believe.

CHAPTER 22

Transformation and Revolt

FOR A MOMENT we were back in Iraq, the Third Infantry Division spearheading an assault on another dusty cinder block of a town hard by the desert, a place not unlike Al Kifl, and the bad memories came flooding back. A company of the Third Brigade, Third Infantry Division, had been ordered to secure the town and detain a scientist suspected of helping develop weapons of mass destruction. Only the villagers had caught rumor that U.S. soldiers had fired into a crowd in another nearby town the day before. No way were the locals cooperating. Irate civilians were yelling in the faces of U.S. soldiers, local police officers didn't understand or were refusing to obey orders to drop their weapons, and word was coming over the tactical radio that insurgents had seized the road behind Charlie Company and cut them off from reinforcements. About that time the company began taking sniper fire and RPGs, and before you knew it U.S. soldiers were down.

That's when the memories came unbidden to Capt. Vern Tubbs, Charlie Company commander, who less than a year before had helped spearhead the Third Infantry Division's march to Baghdad.

"With all the confusion, I started to get some flashbacks, you know, like I'd seen this before," Tubbs told me after the excitement ebbed. "Only in Iraq, I was a lot more scared."

We were standing in a wide-open pan in the middle of the Mojave Desert in early January 2004, the horizon ringed by low hills that shimmered blue in the near distance. Seen from above in a helicopter, this largely deserted region inhabited by wild burrows and goats looked like a wasteland, God's own gunnery range. In actual fact, Charlie Company commander Capt. Vernon Tubbs and his troops were all wired into a sophisticated, computerized range system that used lasers to correspond exactly with the ranges and accuracy of their weapons. In a windowless building back at base camp controllers played Wizard of Oz, conjuring up virtual armies on their computers and sending them out into the ether to give the exercise the depth and feel of an actual war zone. Those armies appeared on Third Brigades' command-and-control monitors and electronic sensor systems, just as they had during Iraqi Freedom, only this time the enemies laying in wait were only ghosts in the machine.

Meanwhile, the village where Charlie Company had "fought" was actually a mock-up called a MOUT, short for Military Operations in Urban Terrain. The "Iraqi villagers" were carefully coached stand-ins. Though it stretched to the edge of sight, the valley we were in was just a sliver of the Army's vast National Training Center (NTC), its premier training ground for maneuver warfare.

A group of Army visionaries were responsible for carving this large swath out of California's Mojave Desert in the 1970s. As young officers they had taken a poorly trained and ill-prepared draft Army into Vietnam, and in places like the Ia Drang Valley they watched it get mauled in early confrontations with a seasoned foe. Just as U.S. troops had been badly bloodied in early battles of previous wars, whether at "Frozen Chosin" Reservoir in the Korean War or at Kasserine Pass in North Africa during World War II. Each time commanders relearned the hardest lesson of them all, namely that a U.S. soldier's chances of survival and success grew exponentially with his combat experience. After Vietnam a group of officers had promised themselves never again would green and unprepared American soldiers be led to slaughter. So they adopted the ethos of the Roman legions: Their drills would be bloodless battles, and their battles bloody drills.

The result of that pledge was the National Training Center, a place where Army units could be exposed to the rigors and hard lessons of combat in bloodless battles with the NTC's notoriously disciplined Opposing Force, or OPFOR. It was here in the 1980s that the Army had honed the concepts and skills behind AirLand Battle doctrine—combined and coordinated assault, maneuver, deception, deep strike—that were designed to counter the Soviet army, but proved doubly devastating against the hapless Iraqis during Operations Desert Storm in 1991 and Iraqi Freedom in 2003. The NTC was where the U.S. Army went to get better after defeat and learn from its mistakes even in victory.

When a top-level Pentagon delegation flew out to a remote corner of the NTC in early January of 2004 to witness the Third Infantry Division's first rotation through the center since it fought in the Iraq war, however, it was with an even grander purpose in mind. They were there as part of an audacious campaign by Defense Secretary Donald Rumsfeld and his Pentagon team of civilians to use the momentum and stresses created by the Iraq and Afghanistan wars to succeed where they had notably failed before the 9/11 terrorist attacks—to fundamentally and irreversibly transform the U.S. military. Just as their fellow Bush revolutionaries had used the 9/11 attacks as a catalyst for a hoped-for reordering of U.S. foreign policy and international relations, unshackling U.S. power from traditional constraints and alliances with preemption and unilateralism, so too was the Rumsfeld team using the resultant wars to realign the primary instrument of U.S. power to the demands of the assertive Bush doctrine.

The mere presence of the Third Infantry Division underscored the urgency the Pentagon placed on that effort. Only back in the United States for a matter of months since its occupation of Baghdad, the division had become the prototype of a "modular" redesign of the entire U.S. Army. General Wallace's epiphany during the war—on seeing brigade combat teams roam virtually autonomously over hundreds of square miles of nonlinear battlefield in Iraq, networked by satellite communications and surveillance and able to call in lethal, precision fires at will—had emboldened Pentagon leaders.

In the future, Brigade Combat Teams—and not venerable Army divisions—were thus to become the central organizing construct for a modular, more interchangeable U.S. Army that could be rapidly assembled in Lego-block fashion and tailored to particular contingencies. That reflected an effort under way by all the services to become more expeditionary and flexible in their ability to rapidly reconfigure themselves for real-world missions.

On that day at the NTC, Army Chief of Staff Gen. Peter Schoomaker was present as an observer, and he assured me that by the time the last Third Infantry Division brigade rotated through the NTC later in 2004, the division that had spearheaded the Iraq invasion would be all but unrecognizable, broken down into lighter, more independent and deployable Brigade Combat Teams. And that was just the beginning of the transformation he anticipated for the U.S. Army.

"Because of what we've learned in recent combat operations in Iraq and Afghanistan, we're now putting people through training scenarios where there are no solutions," General Schoomaker told me. In the past, he said, Army commanders were judged on how well they complied with established doctrine and used it to organize their forces and accomplish the mission. "Today we're designing training scenarios that put people in a continual zone of discomfort. If they start getting comfortable because they may have mastered certain tasks, we ratchet up the pressure so that they're back in the zone of discomfort. That's how you stretch yourself, and it's the kind of organization we want the Army to be. We want an adaptive organization, full of thinking, adaptive problem solvers."

According to General Schoomaker, the most important thing to understand about transformation was that it was more about people and culture than equipment or organizations. "It's about intellect, judgment, and the development of leaders and soldiers," Schoomaker said. "You've got to make that intellectual transformation before you can make the visible transformation. And you've got to get through some emotional blockades to make the intellectual transformation."

Just the presence of General Schoomaker at the NTC was vivid proof of the emotional blockades Secretary Rumsfeld was willing to bust through in order to realize his vision of transformation. A strapping man who would have looked more natural atop a rodeo bull than sitting behind a desk, Schoomaker had spent most of his career in Special Forces, and he was one of the original members of the elite Delta Force counterterrorism unit that had very nearly been stranded in the Iranian desert in the aborted 1980 attempt to rescue U.S. hostages in Tehran. He had been retired from the active force for years, however, and Schoomaker's selection to come back and lead the active Army to the promised land of transformation was just one indication of the extraordinary tensions that had flared between Rumsfeld's OSD and the Army's top leadership.

Many experts considered the period of discord between Rumsfeld and the Army preceding the Iraq war as the most serious civil-military breach since the post–World War II "Revolt of the Admirals"—when the Navy publicly opposed Pentagon plans to put all its nuclear eggs in the Air Force's basket—or later disagreements between former Defense Secretary Robert McNamara and the Joint Chiefs over Vietnam.

Fallout from those battles between Rumsfeld's OSD and the Army included the firing of Army Secretary Thomas White in 2003, and an almost-unprecedented feud between senior civilians and former Army Chief of Staff Gen. Eric Shinseki. Rumsfeld and Shinseki had disagreed over the pace of Army transformation, over OSD's cancellation of the Army's proposed Crusader artillery system, and over the number of Army troops that would be needed during and after the war in Iraq. Rumsfeld and Wolfowitz had publicly scoffed at Shinseki's prescient prediction that it would take as many as two hundred thousand troops to subdue a fractious postwar Iraq. All of which convinced Rumsfeld and his civilian team that a reluctant and hidebound Army had failed to get appropriately in line on transformation, and needed a lesson. As a result, Rumsfeld's office had leaked the name of Shinseki's designated successor more than a year before the scheduled end of his tenure, making the Army Chief of Staff a lame duck on a very long and awkward flight.

"That put Shinseki in a horrible position, even though he had fought hard to begin transforming the Army into a lighter, more mobile force long before Rumsfeld became Defense Secretary," a senior Army civilian told me on background. "The truth is that Rumsfeld and his small coterie of advisers want to run everything from the top, and they don't want service secretaries or service chiefs who will question their decisions or visions."

When Shinseki's designated successor, Vice Chief of Staff of the Army Gen. Jack Keane, decided he didn't want to take the Army's top job after all, Shinseki was succeeded not by an active-duty general from the conventional Army—three of whom declined the job—but by retired General Schoomaker. The request to come back to the Pentagon and out of retirement was so unprecedented that when Schoomaker took the call, driving in his pickup truck near a friend's ranch in Waco, Texas, he originally thought the caller was joking. It was no joke for the two- and three-star generals who Shinseki had groomed before his departure, however, many of whom were shown the door in an OSD-dictated housecleaning. In a thinly veiled swipe at senior Pentagon civilians, none of whom bothered to even show up at his retirement ceremony, Shinseki cautioned in his speech to "Beware the twelve-division strategy for a ten-division Army."

Though OSD considered the Army the lynchpin of its transformation efforts, the transformation campaign was certainly not limited to green-suiters. The Third Infantry's exercise at the NTC represented just a single skirmish in a larger, groundbreaking war game, for instance, that linked the Western training ranges of all the individual armed services: the Army's NTC, the Marine Corps' Twenty-nine Palms training ground in California, the Air Force's Nellis base and training range in Nevada, and the Navy's training center in San Diego. That joint war game, itself a prototype for future joint training exercises, was designed to capitalize on the unprecedented levels of service coordination and synergy displayed during Iraqi Freedom.

Wars change military organizations as surely as they chart the course of nations, and at the NTC you could begin to see how the Iraqi Freedom campaign was already transforming the U.S. military. The theme of the first-of-its-kind war game, for instance, was close integration of U.S. airpower and fast-moving ground maneuver forces. Joint Forces Command, which Rumsfeld had empowered to act as the center for military transformation and for "lessons learned" from the Iraq war, had singled out that capability as perhaps the single greatest achievement of Iraqi Freedom. Rumsfeld had handpicked his former military aide, Adm. Edmund Giambastiani Jr., to command Joint Forces Command, and had given him $207 million in fiscal 2004 for research and experimentation—more than three times what Joint Forces Command had received in 2000—to rapidly institutionalize the lessons of Operations Iraqi Freedom and Enduring Freedom in Afghanistan.

Certainly when Air Force, Marine Corps, and Navy pilots returned from Iraq and Afghanistan, the aviators were rightly demanding training that better reflected the way they actually fought in wartime—working together in tandem in support of ground troops. Fully 79 percent of the ordnance delivered from the air over Iraq during the invasion had been dropped in support of ground operations, for instance, and no one on the ground knew or cared which service insignia the pilots wore. One of the innovations being tested by the Third Brigade's exercise was thus to assign Air Force "joint tactical controllers" down into smaller-sized Army units at the very tip of the tactical combat spear, empowering even company-sized units with the ability to directly call in lethal firepower from the air.

As a military reformer and former nuclear submariner, Joint Forces Commander Admiral Giambastiani followed in a long line of Navy iconoclasts noted for their willingness to challenge conventional wisdom. "We've progressed from joint operations that focused on de-conflicting the individual armed services, to coordinating their operations by stitching together the seams that separate them, to focusing today on joint interdependence in operations that are collaborative, network centric, and capabilities-based," Admiral Giambastiani told me in an interview. The goal was no longer just to have two or more service departments working cooperatively together, he said, but rather to recognize that any major crisis the U.S. military responded to would require a truly "Joint Force." "By Joint Force I mean one that is oriented toward producing desired outcomes, rather than one that is worried about who achieved what particular effect," said Giambastiani. "It's based on a recognition that the joint whole is greater than the sum of its service or interagency parts, and that those parts include not only the individual services but also Special Operations Forces, coalition partners, and nongovernmental organizations. All of the players involved."

When I asked him about the apparent turnaround in the attitude of the uniformed leadership toward Rumsfeld's transformation agenda, Giambastiani pointed out that two of the seminal military reforms during his career—the 1973 move to an all-volunteer force and the 1986 Goldwater-Nichols reforms dictating more joint interoperability—had been imposed on a reluctant military from the outside, either by the executive branch or Congress or both.

"In neither of those cases did the military willingly embrace the reforms. In fact, to the best of my knowledge senior flag and general officers at the time fought them hammer and tongs. Yet today I don't think you could find a senior officer who would like to return to the draft or the pre–Goldwater-Nichols days," said Giambastiani. With pressure to transform coming both from Secretary Rumsfeld's office and from the demands of ongoing combat operations that were badly straining U.S. forces, "we've accelerated the process of change significantly, to the point that the breadth and depth of the changes that are transforming the U.S. military are really unbelievable. Part of that is due to how busy the U.S. military is today. There's no better time to transform than when people are engaged across the entire spectrum of operations, from fighting wars and conducting combat operations to engaging in peacekeeping and stability operations."

That theme—that wars provided helpful impetus for transformative change—was repeated continually during my visit to the National Training Center. One notable observer that day at the NTC was retired Navy Vice Adm. Arthur Cebrowski, director of the Pentagon's influential Office of Force Transformation, and another of Rumsfeld's handpicked reformers. Cebrowski was also a brilliant Navy theorist, and his pithy and often insightful metaphors for the process of information-age transformation made him a popular speaker, almost a three-star Alvin Toffler. At other times his meanderings on the subject could devolve into futuristic mumbo jumbo that had the boots-on-the-ground operators in uniform rolling their eyes. Cebrowski conceded to me that the ability of transformation advocates like himself to overcome venerable resistance to such radical change was due in large part to many of the guardians of service traditions being preoccupied by wars around the world.

"You never want a war, but if you're an advocate for military transformation and a war occurs, it can prove a powerful catalyst and opportunity for transformation," Cebrowski told me. "You can call it necessity being the mother of invention. But under the kinds of stress that wars create in military organizations, a certain open-mindedness appears. Essentially, no one thinks of new ideas quicker, or learns faster, than someone being shot at."

At Rumsfeld's direction, the Joint Staff had thus used the Iraqi Freedom campaign to rewrite strategic war plans to reflect the ability to rapidly defeat sizable foes such as North Korea and Iran with fewer forces, thus enabling the Pentagon to resist calls in Congress to increase the size of the U.S. military to relieve increasingly evident strains. Equally important, the Rumsfeld team was conducting a Global Posture Realignment to reconfigure the global footprint of military bases, and planning to bring tens of thousands of forward-deployed forces home from Europe and Asia in favor of a more expeditionary force based largely in the United States.

"To a large extent, we're moving away from the concept of large, forward-operating bases with lots of infrastructure around the world to a lighter footprint that focuses on lightly manned sites and cooperative security locations that give us more flexibility," Douglas Feith, the Undersecretary of Defense for Policy who was responsible for the Global Posture Realignment, told me in his Pentagon office. In person, Feith had the fresh-scrubbed appearance of a choirboy, but like all of the neocon-servative true-believers he had an unshakable faith in his own theories that allowed him to think in grand, sweeping terms. Feith billed the Global Posture Realignment as the most profound reconfiguring of U.S. forces abroad since America became a dominant world power after World War II.

"In a world full of strategic surprises, it doesn't make sense to try and predict where you will fight and against whom. So in freeing ourselves from that orthodoxy of the Cold War, the focus becomes developing more agile forces that can move quickly to wherever they are needed," said Feith, who also pitched the salutary effects of global war on the transfor-mation effort. "At Secretary Rumsfeld's direction, we are taking advan-tage of a historic opportunity to implement a degree of change that might not otherwise be possible in normal times, because as a practical matter when you move so many forces around the globe, the resetting process gives you an opportunity to do things differently."

At Rumsfeld's behest the services were also recalibrating the mix and makeup of active-duty and reserve forces, and of soldiers and civilians on the Pentagon payroll, in ways that were redefining what it meant to be a soldier and a citizen soldier in the service of the Republic. In the future Rumsfeld's team wanted to deploy active forces more rapidly, without so many time-consuming and politically unpopular call-ups and mobiliza-tions of reserve forces. For their part, citizen soldiers would no longer be thought of as a strategic reserve for times of dire crises, but rather as active-duty fill-ins who could expect to come off the bench every so often and deploy overseas for as long as a year. OSD officials were also funda-mentally changing the rotation and deployment models that lay at the heart of military life, sacrificing forward deployments and regular re-gional tours for the ability to surge more U.S.-based forces quicker to ac-tual crises. They were also further honing that force to become even more dominant on the conventional battlefields of the future by investing addi-tional billions of dollars in cutting-edge technologies.

Taken together, those ambitious Rumsfeld reforms surely did repre-sent a fundamental makeover of a U.S. military that was already not only the world's best, but also the busiest. The dim contours of the trans-formed military that Rumsfeld and his team had envisioned early on was thus beginning to take recognizable shape by early 2004.

Instead of living on permanent overseas bases that anchored Ameri-can alliances around the world, the bulk of the transformed force would be based in the United States and deployed frequently to austere staging areas and global hot spots. Those far-flung forces would also rely more on space-based communications and surveillance, long-range precision bombs and missiles, and just-in-time logistics capabilities modeled after

Federal Express to provide the support and lethality traditionally associated with forward-operating bases and heavily massed forces. Assurances to the contrary notwithstanding, such a globe-spanning, space-dependent force on the cutting edge of the revolution in military technology would find it increasingly difficult to act in tandem with allied militaries that could never hope to match such capabilities.

I had no doubt that the pressures of a global war on terror, coupled with the innovations and improvisations that naturally bubbled up from the front during two, nontraditional wars, combined with the Pentagon's relentless pressure on the services to transform themselves, all had made the services vastly more malleable and accepting of change. The scene at the western training ranges made clear that a new, more joint and agile military mold different in significant ways from the Cold War and post–Cold War models of the past half century was undoubtedly taking shape. Much of that was undeniably to the good.

Yet as I boarded the small Air Force jet with Paul Wolfowitz at Palm Springs, California, for the trip home, I couldn't shake a deep sense of unease brought on by what I had witnessed and heard at the NTC in January of 2004. As we settled in for the flight, Wolfowitz reiterated his and Rumsfeld's belief that the stars were finally in alignment and the key players in position to implement truly radical and lasting military reforms. "One might have expected the wars to put transformation on hold, but in fact they allowed us to accelerate it, because the battlefields of Afghanistan and Iraq provided real-world demonstrations of the value of some of these transformational concepts," Wolfowitz told me in an extensive interview. "For instance, we absolutely broke the Desert Storm paradigm which held that the larger your force, the less risk you assume. Iraqi Freedom suggests a new paradigm for the future where speed and surprise become more important than military mass."

The enormous stress that the Iraq and Afghanistan wars and their difficult aftermath placed on personnel and military organizations, Wolfowitz continued, also created helpful incentives for the Pentagon to use its people more efficiently. "As we've just seen with the Army's reorganization of the Third Infantry Division, the dislocations of war also give us a real opportunity to reshuffle the deck and overcome fears of innovation."

Each time I listened to Rumsfeld's handpicked revolutionaries, however, I kept thinking that the "creative tension" of war they were all so enamored with was tearing at the lives of people whose names and faces were real to me. In their determination to exploit those pressures in the name of transformation, I also knew there was every possibility that Rumsfeld and his senior aides could damage the U.S. Army, and in ways that would be difficult to reverse.

Anyone looking for signs that the world's most powerful military was being fundamentally reshaped in early 2004 could also be excused for wondering where the official notice was posted. Wars and occupation in Iraq and Afghanistan were preoccupying Capitol Hill and Washington's media establishment, and sucking the analytical oxygen out of Washington's Beltway bubble. Thus some of the traditional checks and balances that kept radical reforms from going awry were noticeably absent.

After being in the bowels of the beast during Iraqi Freedom, and having recently witnessed how the U.S. military was struggling mightily in post-Saddam Iraq, I had also acquired a marked skepticism toward grand pronouncements from this Pentagon. The same group that was now pushing for such a profound and fundamental change in the U.S. military had repeatedly shown themselves capable of gross strategic miscalculation, whether in the diplomatic debacle they helped engineer before the Iraq war or in the inadequate planning for operations in post-Saddam Iraq and post-Taliban Afghanistan. Nor did anyone at the NTC seem interested in talking about the great risks inherent in Rumsfeld's transformational war plan for Iraqi Freedom.

In talking to Pentagon civilians and uniformed leaders at the NTC, I was also reminded of the brutish way Rumsfeld and his inner circle dealt with dissent. Time and again those who disagreed with their vision were cut off at the knees, General Shinseki being the most prominent but hardly the lone example. By early 2004 it was clear that such intolerance for dissenting views was a marked characteristic of the Bush revolutionaries, especially the Pentagon clique, who seemed to prefer debating the radical restructuring of the U.S. military in an echo chamber.

All of those concerns and more were crystallizing in my mind at the NTC when I had felt a tap on my shoulder, and turned to see Maj. Jim Barker. I had last seen Barker mumbling unintelligible Arabic at a crowded street fair in Baghdad on a long-ago day of liberation. That had been one of the best days of my life just after one of the worst, and Barker and I clapped shoulders and smiled. Then he pointed to a lone figure standing away from the crowd of VIPs and generals observing the Third Brigade's maneuvers.

Approaching the figure, I noted the three stars on the helmet and extended my hand before I was clasped in a bear hug. Lt. Gen. Scott Wallace had flown in from Ft. Leavenworth, Kansas, where he headed the Army's Combined Arms Center, to see the transformed Third Brigade Combat Team put through its paces. Given the general tenor of the times and his run-in with Rumsfeld during the war, I could well imagine why he might be standing aside from the other group of senior Pentagon and uniformed leaders.

Knowledgeable friends told me that Lt. Gen. David McKiernan, the former senior commander in Iraq and Wallace's direct superior during the war, had been all but banished to the hinterlands after some of Rumsfeld's inner circle judged him insufficiently enthusiastic in front of the television cameras when asked about the situation in post-Saddam Iraq. After complaints about his handling of a confused situation in Iraq made infinitely worse by the lack of adequate OSD planning, former Third Infantry Division commander Gen. Buford Blount would also fail to make his next promotion, retiring before the end of 2004. The senior officers most directly responsible for achieving a great wartime victory for the United States had seemingly been ushered quietly out to pasture, while Pentagon revolutionaries who themselves had never seen combat continued to fundamentally transform U.S. combat power.

As we got to talking about the transformation of the Third Infantry Division, Wallace said that he indeed had caught a glimpse of a new, faster, and more fluid style of warfare during Iraqi Freedom. "That war certainly changed my way of thinking, and I'm pretty sure that's universal throughout the military," Wallace told me. "Being able to successfully distribute forces so widely on that battlefield, while leaving a lot of white space between brigades, convinced me that brigades probably will be more important in the future and that we should reorganize to become more modular. The effectiveness of that joint Air Force/Army team also convinced me we can afford to break the Army down into smaller, brigade-sized units and still retain that lethality."

I pointed out that Wallace knew better than most the risks and gambles inherent in the transformational war plan for Iraqi Freedom, vulnerabilities that a more competent and determined enemy might have exploited. He didn't disagree. Nor was the war truly over, I pointed out, recounting my trip to Iraq in October. That set us to talking about the struggles the Army and some of our mutual acquaintances were coping with in countering a violent insurgency in Iraq. Scott Wallace eventually gave voice to the thought that had troubled me ever since the trip to Iraq during the Ramadan Offensive, and which lay at the crux of a revolutionary Bush doctrine premised on confronting rogue nations militarily as a way to spread democracy.

"I'm beginning to think that in wars of regime change, which may well be the wars we're most likely to fight in the twenty-first century, the military campaign is not the decisive phase of the conflict," Wallace told me. "In the military we're taught that the high-intensity phase is decisive, when in actual fact it may only set the necessary conditions for success. The fight we're engaged in right now in Iraq may actually prove the decisive phase."

The silence surrounding Rumsfeld's fundamental restructuring of the U.S. military was practically deafening in Washington, D.C. On returning to the capital after visiting the western training ranges, I had decided to put some of my concerns about the Rumsfeld transformation to the test. Certainly the almost eerie silence on the subject that seemed to permeate Washington seemed cause enough for concern. That the Bush administration could perform such radical surgery on the very sinews of American power and have it go largely unnoticed seemed to me proof of the extraordinary period of upheaval that was roiling the nation, and the uncommon dangers it presented.

The Washington media and think tank establishments were largely consumed in covering and analyzing the complex aftermath in Iraq and Afghanistan. There was also a pronounced bias in the media to think of defense transformation only when major weapons programs were cut to fund new, more cutting-edge systems. Since the September 11 terrorist attacks, however, Congress had appropriated $289 billion more for defense than would have been spent had the defense budget been held to the inflation rate, at least temporarily allowing Rumsfeld and OSD to avoid pitting the services' prized weapons programs against one another. Thus the services no longer viewed transformation as a stalking horse for cuts to their budgets or end strength.

After swallowing the largest bureaucratic reorganization of the federal government since just after World War II, Washington was also still trying to digest the Department of Homeland Security. Major intelligence reform of a like not seen since creation of the Central Intelligence Agency more than fifty years ago was likewise looming on the horizon.

Given the controversial aftermath of the war in Iraq, certainly the Republican-controlled Congress showed little interest in probing deep into the lessons learned from the Iraq war on the eve of a presidential election season, an unfortunate abrogation of its duty to oversee the raising and maintaining of the nation's armed forces. That was in stark contrast to the last major reform of the U.S. military, the 1986 Goldwater-Nichols Act that forced a heretofore unprecedented degree of joint cooperation on the services and greatly empowered the Chairman of the Joint Chiefs of Staff at the expense of the individual service chiefs. Widely considered one of the most successful reforms in U.S. military history, the bipartisan Goldwater-Nichols Act was the culmination of years of congressional hearings, exhaustive studies by think tanks and the war colleges, and in-depth media analyses. The same was true about the decision in 1973 to transition from a conscription army to an all-volunteer force, though it was motivated less by military need than the desire on the part of the Nixon administration to undercut the antiwar movement.

Part of the silence on defense transformation, I suspected, was welcome at the Pentagon. Joint Forces Command, for instance, the official keeper of the lessons learned from Iraq, had testified at a single congressional hearing, given one early press conference on the subject, and produced a mostly classified report. Shortly after the war, Rumsfeld and Marine Gen. Peter Pace, his handpicked vice chairman of the Joint Chiefs of Staff, had privately briefed a number of independent defense experts on the lessons learned after the Iraq campaign. Not surprisingly, the briefing amounted to a ringing endorsement of transformational warfare by high-tech and lean forces that Rumsfeld and his team had pushed since entering the Pentagon. According to sources that had seen the brief, virtually nothing was said of the risks-versus-rewards tradeoffs of transformational warfare as conducted in Iraq, or whether victory against such a hapless foe actually justified the profound changes that were following in its wake. "Basically, the Pentagon and the U.S. military are grading their own homework," a noted defense expert who had seen the classified brief told me. "Without more independent analysis, we may never know the true lessons of the Iraq war."

Dan Gouré is a longtime defense analyst with the Lexington Institute, a defense consulting firm, and one of the leading experts in Washington on the U.S. Army and defense transformation. He too was struck by how nearly all the lessons learned coming out of Iraq seemed to reinforce Rumsfeld's arguments for transformation. "That raises the question of whether some of the good news on that war is in fact too good to be true," Gouré told me, noting that Rumsfeld's deft bureaucratic maneuvering had left few senior leaders in uniform willing to challenge the transformation juggernaut. "Rumsfeld and his team have methodically put in place military leaders who share their vision, and they brilliantly seized the bureaucratic and organizational high ground in the Pentagon by taking control of the strategic war plans, thus allowing them to control the risk calculations that the military used to sidetrack past reforms. As a result, I do think they have the potential to institutionalize the most radical restructuring of the military really since the 1940s."

Andrew Krepinevich, head of the Center of Strategic and Budgetary Assessments in Washington, D.C., is one of the nation's preeminent military analysts and advocates for transformation. Like a number of experts I spoke with, Krepinevich noted that Rumsfeld's transformation effort was overwhelmingly focused on the high-intensity combat phase of military operations. In other words, shaping a military that could do even better what Central Command accomplished so expertly in the roughly three weeks of the Iraqi Freedom campaign.

"I think in Iraqi Freedom we did get an early glimpse of a type of network-centric, nonlinear warfare that is transformational, in the sense that it is likely to eclipse the combined-arms, mechanized, heavy forces model that has dominated land warfare since the advent of blitzkrieg," Krepinevich told me. The Pentagon's emphasis on further perfecting the ability of U.S. forces to dominate the conventional battlefield of major force-on-force engagements, he said, would certainly be useful in dissuading potential adversaries from challenging the United States with conventional forces.

"The problem is we're already so good no one wants to fight us that way anymore, and it's difficult to imagine many potential enemies deciding to engage in a combined-arms fight out in the open with U.S. forces," said Krepinevich. Instead, growing U.S. predominance in conventional warfare was likely to push potential adversaries to confront the United States at the high and low spectrums of conflict, through unconventional or "asymmetrical" warfare. At the high end, that could mean acquiring weapons of mass destruction as a deterrent against overwhelming U.S. conventional power. At the low end, it might translate into guerrilla operations and terrorism, the traditional forms of warfare of the weak against the strong. That, in fact, was exactly the direction North Korea and Iran had taken in accelerating their nuclear programs in response to the U.S.-led war on global terrorism and their inclusion in the "axis of evil." It was what the Taliban were doing in Afghanistan, what Baathist remnants and insurgents were doing in Iraq, and what Al Qaeda had done all along.

Pentagon civilians also seemed little inclined to discuss how the same Rumsfeld-tailored force that was so successful in rapid regime change in Iraq was proving utterly inadequate to the job of stabilizing the country in the war's aftermath. A transformed military that was configured primarily to fight high-intensity, network-centric warfare might in the future lack the manpower, heft, and sustainability to clean up and police the messes it created in places such as Iraq and Afghanistan.

A recent study by the National Defense University (NDU), for instance, strongly suggested that the Pentagon's new war-fighting model failed to adequately take into account the manpower-intensive work of counterinsurgency and stability operations inherent in wars of regime change. "Success in Afghanistan and Iraq demonstrated that the new war-fighting model is very successful in the first, high-intensity phase of conflict, but there are unintended consequences," Hans Binnendijk, director of NDU's Center for Technology and National Security Policy, which helped produce the report, told me in an interview. "In both instances, the United States deployed relatively small forces very rapidly, and they won quickly and in very dominant fashion with minimal collateral damage. The net result is you end up in theater with far fewer troops than in traditional wars, and with an enemy that is defeated but not exhausted. And quite suddenly you are in a postwar period without adequate forces or planning for the next phase of nation building."

Time and again, analysts I spoke with mirrored the concern that the Pentagon under Rumsfeld had yet to fully come to terms with the implications of their own transformative war-fighting models and doctrine of preemption, or to match their rhetoric over the importance of establishing a viable democracy in Iraq with the means to accomplish that mission. Rumsfeld and company always fell back on the argument that U.S. military commanders in Iraq had never asked for more troops, for instance, knowing that the U.S. military is by nature a fundamentally "can do" organization whose senior leaders are little inclined to buck their civilian masters in wartime with unwanted requests. Any question about how Rumsfeld felt about requests for more troops for Iraq, and how he was inclined to deal with such insubordination, had been answered conclusively by the Shinseki affair. There were even reports that some base commanders in Iraq had requested more troops, but had been turned down by their immediate superiors. More than anyone else, senior U.S. military leaders understood that there were simply no excess troops to commit to Iraq without further stressing an already overstretched force structure.

"Rumsfeld doesn't really buy into all this nation-building and stability-operations business, so he's basically ignored what's happened in the aftermath of Iraqi Freedom, because it forces a different answer than he wants to hear in terms of Army troop strength. When he doesn't like the answer, Rumsfeld typically changes the question," said Thomas Donnelly, the longtime national security analyst with the American Enterprise Institute, the epicenter of much of the neoconservative argument for deposing Saddam Hussein in the first place. Donnelly catalogued that strategy-and-means mismatch in the 2004 report *Operation Iraqi Freedom: A Strategic Assessment*. "If you seriously try to imagine what President Bush's commitment to transform the Middle East with democracy means for the military, it's going to be an incredible strain, as we police a very screwed-up Iraq and this region for longer than most of us will be alive," Donnelly told me. "The armed services are in denial about the implications of that."

Ivo Daalder is a senior national security analyst at the Brookings Institution and former National Security Council official in the Clinton administration. "Rumsfeld's transformation strategy, with its focus on over-the-horizon warfare and lean ground forces, ignores the fact that modern wars of regime change involve two phases," Daalder told me in an interview. "The type of warfare they contemplate is good for the first phase of killing bad people and toppling regimes, but we're finding out in Iraq and Afghanistan that it's horrendous in the second phase of trying to stabilize a nation and assist good people in rebuilding it. And without that second phase, the first phase is worse than useless. If we don't solve the problems created in the aftermath of Saddam Hussein's ouster, for instance, Iraq and the region will be worse off than before."

At the center of the Bush doctrine and Pentagon transformation I also sensed the same troubling ideological bent, which led the Bush revolutionaries time and again to focus on the hard-power/military force side of every equation, almost to the point of blinding them to other possible solutions and the need for follow-on approaches. Transform yourself into a hammer, as the saying goes, and suddenly every problem looks like a nail.

One obvious example of that mind-set was the national missile defense system that was scheduled to be operational by the end of 2004. Because the Pentagon had successfully circumvented traditional testing milestones in deploying the system, there was no way to independently assess whether it actually worked. But the Bush administration and Pentagon had lavished scores of billions of dollars on the program, with more surely to come.

When it came to adequately securing Russia's vast stockpiles of nuclear fissile material, warheads, and chemical and biological weapons, on the other hand, the Bush administration was far more miserly. Collectively called the Nunn-Lugar "cooperative threat reduction programs," those efforts had been consistently cut or underfunded by the Bush administration. For the fiscal year starting in October of 2004, for instance, Bush would cut Defense Department efforts to secure such foreign stockpiles by $41 million, which amounted to 9 percent of the total budget for such programs. Yet many experts, including Bush's own CIA Director George Tenet, believed that the possibility of such weapons or materials falling into the hands of terrorist organizations that sought them, such as Al Qaeda, was the single greatest threat facing America.

After watching the Third Brigade's maneuvers at the NTC in January 2004, and talking to Pentagon civilians who viewed wartime stress as a helpful antidote to "hidebound" service bureaucracies, my concern was also growing that in their zeal to transform the U.S. Army the Rumsfeld team could actually do it serious and lasting damage. I had written extensively on how a similar dynamic of overstressed troops, rapid change, and inadequate funds had turned the U.S. Army of the 1970s into a "hollow force." At the NTC, some of those same stresses were right in front of my eyes.

At the end of the year, for instance, the Third Infantry Division was already slated to return to Iraq after only roughly a year at home. During Vietnam the services had all discovered that the accrued stresses of such back-to-back combat tours prompted professionals to opt out of the military by voting with their feet, presaging a retention crisis. That's why both the Navy and Marines began limiting deployments to six months in the early 1980s. Families of Third I.D. soldiers who had only recently readjusted to the normal pace of military life would soon be torn asunder again by the strains of a yearlong combat deployment.

Other signs of strain were evident at the National Training Center. The Army was stretched so thin that it would soon announce that for the first time ever, it was deploying the permanently stationed Opposing Force (OPFOR) at the NTC, as well as the OPFOR at the Joint Readiness Training Center (JRTC) in Louisiana, to operations in Iraq. Within the past two years, virtually every other combat-capable unit in the active force had already been deployed to either Iraq or Afghanistan.

In order to keep units preparing for deployments to Iraq and Afghanistan fully manned, the Pentagon had also instituted a series of "stop loss" decrees barring more than 7,800 soldiers from leaving the Army even if their original enlistment periods were up. Increasing numbers of those soldiers were challenging the stop loss measures in courts as essentially a backdoor draft.

Meanwhile, because of the stresses on Army forces and the failure to receive the help of an anticipated multinational division in Iraq, the next rotation for Iraq slated for spring 2004 would consist of 40 percent Guard and Reserve forces, some of them on their second deployments in recent years and unaccustomed and unprepared for yearlong combat tours. That deployment would include some of the roughly 5,700 Individual Ready Reservists the Pentagon has activated involuntarily, many of them former active-duty soldiers who had fulfilled their initial tours of duty. As many as one-third of the soldiers tapped from the Individual Ready Reserve had reportedly failed to report to duty. In a number of cases the Army was also forced to remobilize the same Reserve unit twice within the same twenty-four-month activation period, a line that force planners conceded they crossed only with reluctance. Later in the year those stresses would come to a head, and a poorly trained and equipped Reserve transport unit would essentially mutiny in Iraq, refusing to deliver critical fuel supplies from Tallil Air Base further north because of a lack of armored trucks and adequate security.

Such extraordinary measures and events came against a backdrop of recent figures that showed that National Guard recruiting nosedived 12 percent below goal in the first three quarters of 2004. The Army was likewise well below its desired level of recruits in its delayed-entry program, a potential early indicator of recruiting problems to come. By the time recruitment or retention problems become evident, the U.S. military could be in a downward spiral from which it could take many years to recover. That's because in a hierarchal structure such as the U.S. military, you can recruit bodies but you cannot recruit experience. It takes the Army eight years to replace an experienced E-6 staff sergeant, for instance, who declines reenlistment. Molding a midcareer major takes ten years.

Charles Moskos is the nation's preeminent military manpower expert, and a sociology professor at Northwestern University. "I think the drop in the delayed-entry program and Guard recruitment are warning signs of serious recruitment and reenlistment problems coming next year," Moskos told me in 2004. "I know the Pentagon's line is that they can manage this, but the fact is they just don't have enough boots on the ground. I think they're standing on a precipice."

A visit with Army force planners who shuffle all the numbers on unit rotations in windowless offices in the bowels of the Pentagon was instructive on that point. Talking to the number crunchers, it was easy to see why Rumsfeld and his team found the stresses on the Army a helpful lubricant to transformative change. In looking at the long-term trends, however, you could also imagine how the pressures OSD was piling on the Army could eventually cause the wheels to come off.

The redesign of the Army into Brigade Combat Teams was as much about creating a sustainable rotation base, for instance, as it was about capitalizing on the lessons of Iraqi Freedom. In wringing ten new Combat Brigade Teams out of its present force structure by 2006 (increasing the active-duty Army to forty-three Brigade Combat Teams from its present level of thirty-three active brigades), Army force planners figured they could create a rotational base capable of sustaining deployment of eight to twelve brigades on six month tours, with roughly eighteen months in between deployments.

The subtext of those numbers, however, was an Army that simply could not maintain its present level of effort without potentially catastrophic results. Like the Third Infantry Division, major units returning from a one-year deployment to Afghanistan and Iraq, for instance, could count on only one year of "dwell time" before they deployed again to combat operations for a full year. As the Pentagon learned in the 1970s, such a 1-to-1 ratio of deployments to down time, with yearlong combat tours, eventually broke the force. Notably, in three recent instances, the Army had not been able to give units even one full year of downtime and reconstitution between combat deployments (according to Army force planners the Second Brigade of the Tenth Mountain Division got 208 days; the Third Brigade of the First Armored Division 283 days; and the Third Armored Cavalry Regiment 340 days).

Even with ten extra Brigade Combat Teams in 2006, Army force planners conceded that they would not be able to reduce the length of tours to six months unless the requirement for U.S. troops in Iraq dropped dramatically. At its anticipated 2006 end state, for instance, the Army would be able to deploy a maximum of twelve brigades on six-month rotations. Operations in Iraq and Afghanistan, however, were at the beginning of 2004 requiring eighteen brigades and forty thousand additional support troops.

In a bid to get more boots on the ground quickly, the Army was quietly exceeding by thirty thousand troops its authorized end strength, using emergency authority and supplemental funding granted by Congress for the global war on terrorism. Pentagon officials had resisted calls from Congress and many retired flag-rank officers, however, to make that increase permanent in order to relieve stains on the force. OSD officials feared that expensive increases in manpower would drain funds from their prized efforts to transform the military into a leaner, more high-tech organization.

"If we have to sustain the present level of effort with our current force structure, then we can't get to the six-month tours we know our units need to adequately service equipment, send troops to professional development schools, and prepare in our training centers," a senior Army force planner conceded to me. "You have to remember that all the modeling and war-gaming we did in shaping the present force was based on an entirely different world. We never envisioned having to maintain our force on this extended plateau of combat operations that we find ourselves on."

As I studied the aggregate numbers of the force planners, I saw the faces of the friends I had made in the Army during Iraqi Freedom, and worried about the force that had so expertly and unquestionably done America's bidding. I thought of my friend Lt. Col. Rob Baker, who at the end of his scheduled tour in Iraq would be deployed to a combat zone for fourteen of the preceding sixteen months. The Army recently conceded that, for the first time since the all-volunteer force was established in 1973, as many as forty-five thousand soldiers were likewise serving such tours after rotating out of units coming back from war and into units just deploying. I talked to Lt. Col. Rock Marcone, perhaps the most promising battalion commander to fight in Iraqi Freedom. Marcone wasn't altogether sure, but after finishing his present assignment as a trainer at the NTC, he was thinking about leaving the Army.

I also called my friend Lt. Col. Eric Wagenaar, the deputy operations officer for V Corps TAC during the war. Wagenaar had recently returned to Germany from Iraq, his third extended deployment to the Middle East in the past decade. "I understand when Secretary Rumsfeld says we have enough people in the Army, and that they're just in the wrong places and positions. Okay, Roger that," said Wagenaar, whose mother had died during the Iraqi Freedom campaign, leaving him unable to even attend her funeral. "When I look at my own ten-year-old daughter these days, and start adding up the time I've spent in the desert and away on deployments, I realize that I've missed 30 to 40 percent of *her* life. It kind of gets you to thinking, you know? That's just the reality of being a soldier in today's Army."

The Pentagon's Global Posture Realignment raised similar fundamental issues. By withdrawing seventy thousand forward-deployed troops from overseas bases in Europe and Asia back to the United States, OSD officials insisted that they were freeing the nation from the "orthodoxy of the Cold War." It was certainly true that the current U.S. footprint of overseas bases was largely a legacy of the Cold War. The Soviet threat that had originally justified the deployment of such substantial U.S. forces to Germany had disappeared. There was little reason to keep U.S. forces deployed along the South Korean demilitarized zone, where they were essentially hostages to a North Korean first strike. There was also some truth to the argument that a largely U.S.-based, expeditionary force offered added stability for families who could remain at stateside bases while service members were regularly deployed to hot spots around the globe, allowing children to settle into schools and military families to purchase semipermanent homes.

Due in large part to the Bush administration's hard-line stance on Iraq and North Korea, however, the United States' strategic alliances with NATO and South Korea were at their lowest ebb in decades. Just at the time when the United States was pleading for European help in dealing with a fractious Iraq, and trying to present a united front with South Korea against the accelerated nuclear weapons program of Pyongyang, the Rumsfeld Pentagon was sending signals that it wanted to withdraw tens of thousands of troops from those alliances. Once again, the Rumsfeld revolutionaries seemed willing to gamble venerable alliances that took generations to construct based on the premise that our allies would surely see the innate wisdom and logic of their proposals.

"From a purely strategic and military standpoint some of the proposed changes in our force posture in Europe and Asia make sense, but the timing couldn't be worse," said Michelle Flourney, a defense expert and senior adviser at the Center for Strategic and International Studies in Washington. "Rightly or wrongly, U.S. troop levels abroad have always been viewed as a symbol of our commitment, and given the strains the Iraq war and North Korean crisis have created in our alliance relations, our allies will likely make the wrong assumption about what signal we're really sending."

For a global superpower, there were also many intangibles that accrued from the sizable, forward presence of U.S. troops that were in danger of being sacrificed on the altar of efficiency and a more expeditionary military model. Congressional delegations of lawmakers and staff from the Foreign Relations and Armed Services Committees routinely visited far-flung commands and U.S. troops stationed overseas, for instance, where they became versed in arcane matters of regional politics, local public attitudes in alliance countries, and the basics of alliance mainte-nance. Pulling many of those troops back to bases in the United States would throw them into the sphere of domestic pork-barrel politics, in es-sence reducing a key political constituency for international engagement.

From a purely military standpoint, a number of experts I spoke with also cautioned that the U.S. military could forfeit many important intangi-bles in a wholesale move of troops back to the United States. One of those was retired Maj. Gen. Bill Nash, an analyst at the Council for Foreign Re-lations who led NATO troops into the former Yugoslavia in the mid-1990s to quell the Balkan wars. "Superficially the Pentagon can argue that we are not lessening our commitment to NATO or South Korea, but the prac-tical, day-to-day reality will be that we will have less capacity to partici-pate in the full range of activities that undergird those alliances," Nash told me. "Under this new construct the Pentagon is proposing, we will try and substitute periodic exercises for forward presence, and as a net result we'll lose much of the familiarity with other militaries and other peoples that we gained from sizable forward presence in Europe and Asia. I personally think America is well served by a military that is very comfortable operating in foreign lands."

Retired Gen. Barry McCaffrey was a division commander in the 1991 Persian Gulf War, a four-star commander in chief of Southern Command in Panama, a senior planner on the Joint Staff, and someone who spent much of his Army career in Europe. He also believed the Pentagon's pro-posed realignment carried potentially serious drawbacks. "Someone has to explain to me how it makes strategic or fiscal sense to pull sixty thou-sand troops out of Europe from bases that are largely paid for by Ger-many and NATO, forcing us to buy more expensive airlift and sealift in order to send them back to hot spots that are closer to Europe in the first place," McCaffrey told me in typically outspoken style. "I also believe that NATO is in serious trouble, and the Europeans are not going to see this as a move to enhance international cooperation. The message they are likely to get instead is that the U.S. military is pulling back into for-tress America, we will enhance this unilateral capability to rapidly deploy anywhere in the world, and the next time you see us we'll be shooting. We did that in the last century and each time we returned to Europe it was to fight a war."

McCaffrey, who retired in the 1990s as the most highly decorated of-ficer in uniform to take the job of "Drug Czar," or director of the Office of National Drug Control Policy, also had serious concerns about the effect of the Pentagon's transformation on an overstressed Army. "The Army is accelerating toward a cliff right now, and if the course isn't changed, we could break it over the next five years," he said. "We as a nation have done it before at the peak of our power. We broke the Army after World War II, and paid for it in Korea. We broke the Army after Vietnam, and paid for it with the 'hollow force' of the 1970s. We are doing it again with an Army that is overcommitted and underfunded. If we end up in an unanticipated war with North Korea or Iran, we could pay a very heavy price as a result."

Those comments underscored another primary tenet of the Rumsfeld transformation that had been bothering me. Collectively, the initiatives made it easier to wield dominant U.S. military power, but in service to a doctrine of preemption and ad hoc coalitions of the moment that was demonstratively isolating and weakening the United States at a critical period in its history. For instance, not only did the Rumsfeld transformation put a high premium on unilateral capability, but it also made it easier to wield military power without even rallying the will of the American people.

As just one example, the Pentagon was billing as transformational a wholesale movement of jobs and missions from the Reserve forces into the active duty military in order to make it possible to deploy the active force with fewer time-consuming, lengthy, and disruptive Reserve call-ups. Yet visionary Army Chief of Staff Gen. Creighton Abrams had made the new all-volunteer Army so dependent on the Reserves after the American troop pullout from Vietnam in 1973 precisely because Lyndon Johnson had refused to call up the Reserves during the 1960s, thus failing to mobilize the nation behind the Vietnam War effort and leaving the military to fight a war alone halfway around the world without strong public backing. The subsequent tearing of America's social fabric literally took decades to mend. To anyone who would listen, Creighton Abrams made his feelings on the matter clear. "They're never going to take us to war again without calling up the Reserves."

The Bush revolutionaries were arguing instead that the new threats revealed by the September 11 terrorist attacks and their aftermath necessitated the wholesale abandonment of such "Cold War orthodoxy," including quaint ideas about the need to mobilize the nation for war and outdated vestiges of the Cold War containment strategy. In place of that forward-deployed, alliance-dependent deterrent force optimized to contain the forces of tyranny, Rumsfeld and team were proposing a largely

U.S.-based expeditionary force poised for rapid and more unilateral action in the service of a new strategy of preemption and confrontation.

Historically important armed forces have always been a reflection of the societies they serve, mirroring strengths and often exaggerating societal weaknesses. The massive, overcentralized, and brutish Soviet army was a blunt force extension of Soviet society itself, for instance, just as military historians have noted that the Roman legions and their offensive style of warfare fit well the ambitions of the Roman Senate and the emperors of Rome. What had nagged me all along about the Bush revolutionaries and their vision for transforming the U.S. military—the fortress of missile defense, new nuclear bunker buster bombs that lowered the threshold of the "unthinkable," domineering lethality, and professional legionnaires postured not for engagement or deterrence or nation building, but maximized for something akin to perpetual war—was what such a force said about America itself.

CHAPTER 23

Nation Building in a Time of Terror

DRIVING THROUGH the dark on St. Patrick's eve of 2004, the largely deserted streets of Baghdad seemed lonely and wild. As our convoy of Humvees passed beneath each bridge, a gunner standing through the roof of the lead vehicle swiveled and shined a searchlight on the overpass above. Gunners in the trailing vehicles turned and swept their automatic weapons in the light's arc looking for telltale movement. Another tic of urban survival learned the hard way.

Just past midnight the convoy turned off the road into a darkened dirt lot. Beneath a hazy blue halo cast by the lights and billowing smoke of a nearby power plant, Col. Rob Baker, commander of the Second Brigade, First Armored Division, set up a mobile tactical operations post for a mission months in the making. From the rear seat of Baker's command vehicle, I could see a computer screen displaying a detailed map of the city and the positions, tracked by satellite and updated every few seconds, of Second Brigade's various strike forces.

Shortly after 1:00 A.M. Baker gave the signal, and his strike teams descended on their targets, breaking the night quiet with shouts in Arabic and the hammering of doors. Soon calls started flooding in over the tactical radio. In rapid succession, "Zulu Zero Five," "Seven," "Eight," and "Nine" were positively identified and captured, landing into U.S. custody suspected insurgents responsible for attacks on U.S. and coalition forces using rockets and improvised explosive devices, or IEDs, the bane of existence for many U.S. forces in Iraq. Soon Baker's troops also snagged "Yankee Zero One," the suspected ringleader of the Sokum Al-Mujaheddin, or "Eagle Militants," a terrorist cell strongly suspected in the December 31 car bombing of the Nabil Restaurant in Baghdad. That attack killed eight and wounded, among others, three *Los Angeles Times* reporters.

Operation Iron Promise was in full swing, representing the type of precise, intelligence-driven counterterrorism operation that the First Armored Division could only have dreamed of mounting a year ago, when it took up residence in Baghdad unsure of who or even what it was up against. By the spring of 2004, at the one-year mark in the U.S. liberation and occupation of Iraq, such operations represented the most potent weapon in the U.S. arsenal against an ever-shifting and increasingly lethal Iraqi insurgency. In operations such as Iron Promise, it was U.S. troops who swept out of the night to seize the initiative from an enemy who in the daytime was able to hide in plain sight on the busy streets of Baghdad.

Before long the two most coveted targets of the evening—Zulu Zero One and Zulu Zero Two—also fell into Second Brigade's hands. Zero Two, dubbed "King of the Wahabis," was an influential imam who regularly preached jihad against the U.S. occupation at his Baghdad mosque, and whose followers were suspected in numerous attacks. Zulu Zero One, owner of a local computer store, had ties to the true prize, the most wanted terrorist in all Iraq—Abu Musab Al-Zarqawi.

In defending their decision to invade Iraq as a centerpiece in the war on international terrorism, Bush administration officials had argued that they would rather the United States fight the terrorists in Iraq than on the streets of America. Saddam Hussein's ties to Al Qaeda before the Iraqi Freedom campaign were largely anecdotal and tenuous at best, as noted by the bipartisan *9/11 Commission Report* on the terrorist attacks, which found no operational linkage between Saddam's regime and the Al Qaeda operatives who organized the 9/11 attacks. After the U.S. occupation of Iraq, however, the networks of Islamic terror had shown every sign of obliging the Bush administration in making Iraq a key battlefield, infiltrating across Iraq's porous borders in growing though still relatively small numbers, and finding ready recruits among Iraq's Sunni fundamentalists, and the militant remnants of Saddam Hussein's Baathist Party.

With most of the top leadership of the Baathist resistance in Baghdad captured and its remnants retreating to Sunni strongholds such as Fallujah, its cell structure had been largely dismantled in the capital. Yet Second Brigade commanders had tracked a steadily growing presence and increase in activity by Islamic terrorists associated with Zarqawi. A Jordanian high-school dropout and ex-convict with a taste for personally decapitating prisoners, and a knack for building clandestine networks, Zarqawi had a history of brazen attacks and clear ties to Osama Bin Laden and Al Qaeda.

With a rotation of new units under way in the early spring of 2004, and more than two hundred thousand U.S. troops in the midst of the largest relief-in-place of U.S. forces in a combat zone since World War II, U.S. commanders in Baghdad hoped with Iron Promise to buy their replacements a little breathing room. As new units settled in, the outgoing

First Armored Division hoped to give them a brief respite from the relentless probing of terrorists and insurgents that surely awaited them.

Almost daily rocket and mortar attacks, for instance, had become part of Baghdad's background noise by the spring of 2004. At night I would gather with senior Second Brigade commanders on the third-floor balcony of the Al-Sijood palace in Baghdad that served as their headquarters, where we smoked cigars and frequently watched the glittering contrails of rockets launched into the Green Zone from across the adjacent Tigris River. Within the Second Brigade's area of operations, which included the Green Zone, the most heavily guarded real estate in all of Iraq, the past week alone had brought thirteen separate attacks—four by rocket, three by improvised explosive devices, two by grenades, two by small arms, one by mortar, and one by car bomb.

"We think Zarqawi has outsourced terror operations in Baghdad to local Iraqi Mujaheddin terror cells, which we now see as the greatest present threat in our area of operations," Baker told me on the night of March 17, 2004, during Operation Iron Promise. "My intent is to take a big chunk out of their operations tonight as a way to buy some operational space for the unit replacing my brigade, and hopefully make the handoff without a major attack or disruption by the enemy."

Down a muddy alley cordoned off by U.S. troops and up a cement staircase, Rob Baker led the way into a two-room flat where a suspected insurgent with a long black beard and dark robe lay on the floor, his hands secured behind his back with plastic handcuffs. A half-eaten meal sat on a tray, and an Arabic interpreter in a U.S. Army uniform was sifting through papers looking for evidence, pointing out news reports in Arabic praising Osama Bin Laden's war with the United States. Nearby a soldier stood guard over the man's wife.

After surveying the scene, Colonel Baker drove to the computer store owned by Zulu Zero One. On a deserted street under a brightly lit sign advertising the "Aldijar Internet Café," U.S. soldiers were blowtorching the iron gate of a small computer store, their protective masks illuminated in a fiery shower of blue sparks. Once inside, they confiscated the shop's computers for intelligence exploitation. An Iraqi interpreter pointed out two entries in a ledger found inside the store. Next to entries reading "enriched uranium," and "anthrax," was the figure $3 million.

What fevered dreams of holy war possessed the owner of the sad little computer store, and how he ever intended to raise $3 million, I couldn't begin to imagine. With the capture of the owner and confiscation of relevant intelligence to be exploited, however, the First Armored Division's Operation Iron Promise had borne the kind of fruit that would almost certainly sustain future operations against terror cells operating in Baghdad. U.S. commanders referred to such raids, which required months of painstaking intelligence and detective work, as "the gift that keeps on giving." Of the twenty-two suspected terrorists and insurgents on Second Brigade's target list, sixteen were taken into custody in just a few hours without firing a shot. Nearly all had ties to attacks targeting U.S., coalition, and Iraqi security forces or civilians. As was so often the case in Iraq, however, a night full of promise soon revealed an equal share of unforeseen menace.

Before returning to base for some much-needed rest, Col. Rob Baker made a final stop in the early morning hours of March 18. In the harsh arc lights of television cameras and rescue crews, the scene outside the former Lebanon Hotel in Baghdad looked like the set of a Hollywood disaster movie. The crater where the suicide car bomber ignited an estimated 1,000 lbs. of explosives hours earlier was the size of a small swimming pool and filled with brackish water from a broken water main. The inability of stretched-thin U.S. forces to even post guards at Iraq's ubiquitous ammo dumps following major hostilities was now coming back to haunt occupation authorities, who were facing insurgents with a seemingly inexhaustible supply of explosives. Many of the car bombs were rigged from standard-issue artillery shells.

On one side of the street in front of the Lebanon Hotel, the burnt and crumpled husks of cars lay in a pile where they were haphazardly swiped by the force of the blast. The façade of the hotel itself had been stripped away to its charred support structures. Across the street a fire from a broken gas main burned uncontrollably in an exposed room without walls on what had been the second floor of a house. Beneath it a backhoe pawed at the rubble where families had gathered earlier in the evening. A small crowd waited along the street for the pile of rubble to surrender its dead.

With the backhoe's grim probing as backdrop, Baker was interviewed by a CNN television crew. He pointed out that the offensive raids of that evening were the only viable defense against such future horrors, but the mention of Iron Promise would predictably be buried beneath an avalanche of car-bomb coverage. Once again the terrorists had successfully seized the news cycle with wanton destruction, drowning out the more muted message of steady progress. Baker, who by then had spent the better part of sixteen months in Iraq, knew the drill by heart. He had walked through the detritus of five car bombs in just one year in Baghdad, at times having to pause and literally scrape off the flesh and human viscera that clung to his boots like slop. No one had to explain the terrorists' macabre public relations campaign to Baker.

Just before we turned in early that morning back at the palace complex, I asked Baker who he really thought had won the night, the U.S.-led coalition or the terrorists? The question was simple enough, but as I was discovering once again, in Iraq the truth always looked different depending on the angle of approach. How do you weigh a quiet operation that likely thwarted numerous future car bombings, Baker asked me, against one terrorist spectacular? What value do you place on visible but halting steps toward Iraqi reconstruction and self-governance that were sometimes purchased with the lives of American and coalition soldiers, not to mention with the blood of numerous innocent Iraqis? What was the window of forbearance for an Iraqi people already chaffing at the yoke of occupation and the mayhem wrought by terrorists, and an American public clearly wearying of the onerous burden of Iraq in terms of lives and national treasure lost?

With the Bush administration's epic campaign of nation building in a time of terror and insurgency at the one-year mark, the question of who was winning and who was losing in Iraq was very much on the minds of the American people. I had figured that there was no better place to look for answers than in the company of U.S. soldiers who had spent the last year on the ground in Iraq. As Rob Baker and other men and women of the First Armored Division knew all too well, however, the very concepts of "victory" and "defeat" in Iraq depended on your answers to a host of existential questions.

The Army clearly had no doctrine for this. With the strong encouragement of the American people and the body politic, the U.S. military had gotten out of the counterinsurgency business after the Vietnam War. Culturally, materially, doctrinally, philosophically—the U.S. Army had moved on. Been there, done that, had the scars to prove it. So having prepared to fight rapid, offensive war in Iraq based on Secretary Rumsfeld's transformational war-fighting concepts, the First Armored Division had instead found itself negotiating a minefield of cultural sensitivities in a very alien landscape, all the while trying to stabilize a city of more than five million citizens caught in the cross fire of an all-out insurgency and terrorist campaign. It was exactly the kind of nation building that Rumsfeld and President Bush had disparaged on first entering office nearly four long years ago.

With the benefit of hindsight and ground truth in Iraq, it was clear to me just how vaguely the Bush administration and the Pentagon understood the challenges inherent in planting the American flag so firmly in Iraqi soil, and in staking U.S. credibility on building democracy in a country traumatized by decades of tyranny, in a region seething with nationalism and anti-American fervor. Many of the missteps of the Pentagon and the Coalition Provisional Authority over the past year could be traced back to that fundamental miscalculation.

As a direct result, the burden of keeping the situation in Iraq from spinning out of control while the United States tried to adjust a deeply flawed reconstruction and nation-building plan on the fly had fallen to military units such as the First Armored Division. Essentially, their year in Iraq had amounted to a crash course in the hard lessons of counterinsurgency warfare. And as was the case during the Iraqi Freedom campaign, the U.S. military was proving once again that perhaps its most transformational attribute was the tactical adaptability and innovation of its officer corps and soldiers.

Col. Rob Baker had to wrestle with the same conundrum confronting every U.S. military commander in Iraq, regardless of their unique circumstances: How to win if not the hearts and minds, at least the grudging respect and tacit cooperation of the Iraqis they are trying to help, while at the same time aggressively pursuing a deadly insurgency. In the case of Second Brigade, the question was infused with special urgency, given that their area of operations included the most tempting targets for terrorists in the entire country. Not only was Second Brigade responsible for securing the Green Zone that was home to the CPA and the Iraqi Governing Council, but 70 percent of the embassies of coalition partners resided in its area of operations.

Intuitively, Rob Baker and his officers grasped that they had to adjust U.S. Army tactics and procedures to Iraqi cultural sensitivities. With little detailed intelligence of the enemy, for instance, First Armored units had initially responded to attacks with broad security sweeps that paralyzed entire sections of the city. In one such early "cordon search," Second Brigade had entered roughly fifteen hundred Iraqi homes on Haifa Street. If U.S. soldiers felt a home represented a threat, soldiers followed Army doctrine and training that emphasized blowing down doors with explosives, putting boots in the backs and bags over the heads of detainees to discourage resistance, and separating individuals into separate rooms so they couldn't check stories with one another.

"Whenever I talked with Iraqi tribal leaders afterward, they would ask why we had to be so insulting in our searches?" Baker told me, noting that given decades of subjugation, the Iraqis he had come to know were hypersensitive to humiliation and feelings of inferiority. "So that boot in the back was an enormous insult. Separating women into different rooms suggested to the men that we were harming them."

As a result, Second Brigade changed its tactics. Strike teams always included female searchers and Iraqi interpreters, and they generally kept men and women in the same room during questioning. Blowing down doors was discouraged in most cases, and whenever possible raids were conducted in conjunction with members of Iraqi Civil Defense Forces to put an Iraqi face on operations and mitigate cultural misunderstandings. When Second Brigade troops raided a mosque, they first put plastic slippers over their boots to avoid defiling prayer rugs, and handed out flyers in Arabic to explain exactly why the imam was arrested. Imams from a Religious Advisory Board that Baker had established were invited to go along on mosque raids to ensure against unintended blasphemy. Baker had established the religious advisory boards to explain Second Brigade actions to leaders in the Sunni, Shiite, and Christian communities in a give-and-take that would have been unthinkable during the reign of Saddam, when religious divisions were purposely exploited.

Raiding teams knew that they were sometimes assuming extra risk in taking a less threatening posture during their operations. "But I know in my gut that this way works better," Baker told me. "From the beginning I instinctively knew that if we didn't respect their cultural sensitivities, for every miscreant we caught we'd inspire five more. That would create a cycle of endless violence."

Convinced that attempts to protect such large and inviting targets with static defenses alone would fail, Colonel Baker and Second Brigade also initiated an aggressive outreach to win the support of the local Iraqi community. Despite the Coalition Provisional Authority's prohibition against brigade commanders holding their own press conferences, another failed attempt to try and micromanage the news in Iraq, Baker began holding bimonthly "press huddles" to which he invited and answered the questions of Arab media outlets, including the influential and frequently adversarial Al Jazeera and Al Arabiya television networks. By contrast, CPA head L. Paul Bremer and the Iraqi Governing Council had taken to responding to the undeniable provocations of Al Jazeera and Al Arabiya by periodically banning their reporters from Iraq.

At the start of one such press conference I attended, Baker began with a prepared statement summarizing the Second Brigade's capture of sixteen suspected insurgents during Iron Promise, stressing that the operation represented the first time that the nascent Iraqi army had participated in offensive operations with their American counterparts. Baker noted the death toll in the bombing of the Lebanon Hotel, which killed seventeen Iraqis and wounded many others. He outlined nearly a thousand small reconstruction projects Second Brigade was funding with $13.5 million in Commanders Emergency Response Funds (CERP), making Second Brigade by far the most aggressive unit in Baghdad in terms of utilizing the CERP funds to employ local Iraqis and improve their neighborhoods. He talked about the nearly six hundred new recruits who had volunteered and been signed up for the Iraqi Police Academy.

When he was finished, Baker opened the floor to questions. The first was from an Arab reporter asking about a U.S. investigation into the killing of two reporters from Al Arabiya on a recent night at a U.S. checkpoint.

Baker told the Arab reporters that the investigation into the incident was not completed, but shared what he knew about the incident. When the investigation did indeed point to a tragic case of misidentification and misunderstanding on the part of U.S. soldiers as well as Arab reporters, Baker owned up to the mistake and then called in all his battalion commanders and for hours meticulously poured over Second Brigade's "rules of engagement" (ROE) for spot checkpoints. The ROE was adjusted in ways that might lead to a miscreant getting away in certain circumstances, but was more likely to avoid Iraqis or Arabs being shot to death because they didn't understand the correct procedure to follow at checkpoints. Baker not only talked the talk to the Iraqis, he walked the walk.

Nowhere was that more clear than at one of the Neighborhood Advisory Councils that I attended in Second Brigade's area of operations in Baghdad. Because Baker had given the councils authority to prioritize and pick reconstruction projects for funding from his CERP account, positions on the councils were highly coveted within local communities. At the long council table I saw sheiks, imams, female civil engineers, bureaucrats, all engage in a lively but polite exchange about how $2.2 million from Second Brigade's cleanup fund could be spent in their neighborhood.

Maj. Doug Whitehead, a Reserve civil affairs officer who was Baker's liaison to the council, nodded his head at the unmistakable sound of grassroots democracy in action. "These meetings are almost exactly the same as the city and county contract meetings I regularly attend in Miami, where we talk about beautification projects, sewer issues, and road repair," said Whitehead, an environmental engineer who in his civilian life ran the largest landfill in south Florida.

In explaining the importance of the Neighborhood and District Advisory Councils to the Iraq reconstruction effort, Whitehead pointed to the mundane example of trash pickup. When Second Brigade first arrived they had bought garbage dumpsters for all the major neighborhoods in an effort to clean up Baghdad's trash-strewn streets. Within weeks the dumpsters, made of high-quality, galvanized metal, had been cut up for scrap by scavengers. "After we set up the Neighborhood Councils, however, they took ownership of those dumpsters, and we haven't had a problem since," said Whitehead. "Essentially, we're spending as much of the CERP funds as we can justify on all these little projects as a way to buy Iraqi patience for the big projects to come. In the future, hopefully those big projects will markedly improve their lives."

When I asked how Second Brigade officers kept their spirits up given the size of the challenge in rebuilding Iraq, Whitehead said it was a subject the soldiers often discussed among themselves. "It's kind of like listening to my uncle talk about World War II," said Doug Whitehead.

"Basically, I think this may be the most important thing we as Americans ever do."

The problem was that the big projects promised by the CPA were languishing badly, victims of the uncertain security environment, frequent sabotage, and poor management that characterized the macro-reconstruction effort. After a year the patience of Iraqis looking to see if the occupational authorities could live up to their promises was clearly wearing thin. As the CPA's own figures would later show, for instance, of the $18 billion in emergency reconstruction funds that Congress had appropriated the previous year, virtually with no strings attached, less than $1 billion had been spent. Meanwhile, of that $1 billion the overwhelming majority had been allocated to U.S. and coalition firms such as Halliburton for long-term construction projects, with minimal money directed at improving security and virtually none focused on creating local jobs for Iraqis.

Before the council meeting, I shared hot Iraqi tea with Yahia Mohamed Ali, chairman of the Kharkh District Advisory Council, and talked to him about the impact of the constant attacks and the general lack of security in Baghdad. Many of the council members, I had noticed, had arrived at the council meeting with armed personal guards and looking over their shoulders. "I myself have received personal threats, but there must be people willing to help build a better Iraq," said Yahia, speaking through an interpreter. "If people refuse to take part or hold back, who will take responsibility for rebuilding schools, for facility restoration, for sewage treatment, for helping to recruit Iraqi security forces?"

While Yahia personally believed Syria was letting terrorists freely cross its borders in order to inspire local Islamic fundamentalists and sow instability in Iraq, he said most Iraqis placed the blame for the lack of security squarely on the shoulders of the Americans. "The Arabic media is constantly playing up this idea that the Americans are to blame for the attacks, even if the blood of the victims is most directly on the hands of the Wahabis," Yahia Mohamed Ali told me, referring to Islamic fundamentalists. "Really, most Iraqis think the Americans are somehow behind or to blame for the attacks."

The absolute necessity of establishing a baseline of security was the first lesson of counterinsurgency warfare, and the reason why most successful campaigns against determined insurgencies took a decade or more. That was why the Pentagon's decision in 2003 to accelerate the handover of security responsibilities to new homegrown Iraqi security forces was so critical. Only competent and well-equipped Iraqi security forces would eventually have more at stake and greater staying power than the insurgents themselves.

In the meantime, however, U.S. forces knew they had to at least keep insurgents from gaining a stranglehold on Iraqi society. As the noted Communist insurgent Mao Tse-tung famously proclaimed, "The people are like water and the army is like a fish." A population cowed by intimidation and angered by foreign occupation offered a deep reservoir indeed for insurgents, who only had to patiently keep the tributaries of nationalism flowing until the U.S. occupation was swamped. Though you wouldn't guess it from the Bush administration's reassuring comments about progress in Iraq, U.S. forces were thus in a desperate race against time. Success in the interim meant keeping the pools of insurgent support sufficiently drained to target the rebels.

Certainly that reality was not lost on Second Brigade commanders, and indeed helped explain their aggressive outreach to the local community. "From the outset we were determined to make a little progress every day in winning the support of what we call the 'silent majority,'" said Lt. Col. Jim Danna, a wise-cracking and profane New Jersey native and the Second Brigade executive officer. Between the relatively small percentage of Iraqis who violently opposed the U.S. occupation, and an equally small percentage who supported the coalition unquestioningly out of hatred for the former regime, Danna and his colleagues believed there was a sizable majority who were essentially sitting on the sidelines trying to determine whether the U.S.-led coalition or its enemies were going to win the struggle for Iraq's future. "In that fight we've discovered that money is a very powerful tool," he said. "We've seen a direct correlation between our support of local reconstruction projects, for instance, and the willingness of local Iraqis to come forward with useful intelligence on the enemy."

Of all the surprises and revelations in a year full of them, that epiphany on the critical importance of human intelligence in fighting a counterinsurgency war stood out for Second Brigade commanders. As Operation Iraqi Freedom had demonstrated the previous year, a heavy U.S. armored division maneuvering on the battlefield and probing enemy formations with state-of-the-art satellite and robotic surveillance systems, represents the world's most fearsome fighting machine. As U.S. commanders soon learned in patrolling the urban labyrinth of Baghdad, however, without the eyes and ears of the local Iraqis they were fighting blind against an enemy hiding in plain sight.

The realization of the critical role human intelligence played in counterinsurgency warfare explained why Col. Baker relieved his first chief intelligence officer, or "S-2," early in the deployment. Baker turned for help instead to a bulldog of a major with a Kojak haircut and an attitude to match. Maj. Larry Wilson, an Indiana native by way of Northwestern Missouri State and the Command and General Staff College, had already served as a Brigade S-2 and didn't need a lateral assignment, thank you very much. Convinced that he would be given the latitude to make a difference for a combat brigade badly in need of help, however, Wilson set out to develop a brigade intelligence shop unlike any in the conventional U.S. Army.

Stretching Army regulations beyond recognition, Wilson established the "Striker Service Agency" to put Iraqi informants and surveillance teams throughout their area of operations on Second Brigade's payroll. Though resistant at first, battalion commanders were graded on their ability to recruit and run informants in an ever-widening intelligence gathering network that included former Iraqi intelligence agents, military officers, police, university professors, local politicians, imams, taxi drivers, and even prostitutes.

Rather than send prisoners and captured documents and computer hard drives up to division headquarters as was customary, Second Brigade's intelligence shop built its own jail and began conducting its own interrogations and document exploitation. The rapid turnaround of "actionable intelligence" in turn quickly led to yet more arrests, and more focused and probing interrogations. The result was steadily increasing visibility into the complex and interwoven networks of terror and insurgency in and around Baghdad, and the leadership hierarchies that guided them.

As an increasingly important player in the intelligence-gathering community in Iraq, with its own homegrown product, Second Brigade also became more adept at bartering and sharing intelligence data with other agencies operating in and around Baghdad, which included the FBI, Britain's M16 intelligence service, and Task Force 121, an elite counterterrorism unit of Special Forces commandos and CIA agents that was responsible for capturing Saddam Hussein and targeting Zarqawi and other high-value targets. At the tip of America's spear, Second Brigade was exhibiting the same "jointness" in intelligence and counterterrorism operations that U.S. forces had shown in conventional operations during the Iraqi Freedom campaign.

Daily "targeting briefs" in Second Brigade's tactical operations center thus came to resemble nothing so much as an Arabic genealogy course, with the tribal and familial ties connecting various insurgents and their operating cells laid out in family tree schematics, each branch of the tree capped with the picture, name, aliases, and preferred mosque of a suspected terrorist or insurgent. Nearly all of the brigade's operations were driven by such focused human intelligence targeted at specific suspects.

During one intelligence brief on Second Brigade operations that I witnessed, Brig. Gen. Mark Hertling, deputy commanding general of First Armored Division, indicated with a laser pointer the leader of a local cell of Baathist insurgents.

"Do we know where this guy is," Hertling asked.

"Yes sir, he's in Jordan getting medical treatment," said Wilson.

"Are you sure?"

"Yes sir," Wilson replied with a wolfish grin. "We happen to have a good ultrasound on his prostate, which is about to fall out. You could say we're hot on his tail!"

Operation Striker Elton, which Second Brigade had launched in response to the rocket attack I had survived the previous October on the Al Rashid Hotel, had represented the first major test of the new model of intelligence-driven operations. Launched on November 8, 2003, Striker Elton had netted thirty-six suspected insurgents, twenty-nine of whom were later imprisoned for their complicity in the Al Rashid rocket attack and other insurgent operations.

In the intelligence bonanza that followed the capture of Saddam Hussein on December 14, Second Brigade commanders also came to realize that Striker Elton had actually taken down one of Saddam's three insurgent cells in their area of Baghdad, dealing a crippling blow to the former regime's operations in their region. The operation also netted Shawki Al-Kubesyi, thought to be the top financier of foreign fighters entering into Iraq to fight the coalition. The Brigade's first precision, human intelligence–driven operation had thus been a resounding success.

By the spring of 2004, the general outline of the terrorist pipeline that fed into Baghdad was relatively well understood. Front companies, many of them based in the United Arab Emirates and the other Gulf states, funded a sort of terrorist pilgrimage of jihadists primarily through Syria and Jordan and across the Iraqi border. The path typically led through radicalized mosques, on to local terrorist training centers in Iraq, and then to safe houses scattered throughout the country. While the number of foreign terrorists in Iraq was still considered relatively small, many acted as facilitators in forming cells and recruiting local Sunni Islamic fundamentalists and militant Baathists.

After the Ramadan bombings and the ambush and murder of seven Spanish soldiers on November 29, 2003, the insurgents' strategy of isolating the United States by targeting its international and local partners in Iraq's reconstruction became clear. Sensing that shift, Colonel Baker refocused Second Brigade's informants and intelligence gathering network on the operations of the Zarqawi and Ansar al Islam networks, the most active terrorist groups in Iraq. A break they were hoping for came on January 13, 2004, when a red Opel station wagon carrying three Iraqis over the 14th of July Bridge in Baghdad tested positive at a U.S. checkpoint for bomb residue.

Interrogations of the three men, and rapid intelligence exploitation, eventually led Second Brigade and Special Forces units to a farming complex outside of Baghdad that was used by the Zarqawi network as a training camp for foreign fighters and Iraqi mujaheddin. The "Zarqawi Farms," as they were dubbed, contained one of the largest weapons caches ever captured in the possession of insurgents. The raid and multiple arrests on the Zarqawi farm complex and subsequent interrogations, in turn, were pivotal in developing the target list for the Iron Promise raids of March 17.

"You can trace the Iron Promise raids in March, and the raid on the Zarqawi farms in February, all back to those three guys crossing the 14th of July Bridge in an Opel station wagon in January, but that's the nature of counterinsurgency warfare," said Larry Wilson, whose expertise in counterinsurgency intelligence gathering would lead to his transfer later that year to an elite Special Forces unit operating in Iraq. "You get a break or a lead, and through rapid and persistent intelligence exploitation you keep pulling that thread until you see where it leads. That's the only way we'll seize the initiative in this fight, by keeping the bad guys running for their lives rather than planning future attacks."

At one point, Wilson invited me to sit in on an interrogation in "The Cage," a holding facility of chain-link cells where Second Brigade kept prisoners swept up in its operations until they were sent up to a division-level prison for longer incarceration. Those prisoners who were released directly from The Cage were offered a free taxi ride home. Unbeknownst to them, however, the Iraqi taxi driver was one of the many informants on Second Brigade's payroll. More than a few had so incriminated themselves on the ride home that they never actually got to spend time there.

Sitting in on the interrogation of an Iraqi prisoner captured during Operation Iron Promise, I realized to my surprise that it was the same long-bearded man I had seen laying down handcuffed on the floor of his apartment on the night of the raid. Listening as the Iraqi was interrogated by a young Army specialist practically just out of boot camp, I was struck once again at how the focus on intelligence gathering and interrogation really stretched standard Army doctrine and training.

After the interrogation I talked with the young Army interrogator, who conceded that he had no real expertise in Iraqi culture and relatively little training as an interrogator. Like so many other soldiers in Iraq, he had been pressed into unfamiliar duty based on unanticipated demands being placed on an overstretched force. The young soldier had, however, conducted nearly three hundred interrogations in what amounted to a crash, on-the-job training course. "This guy was pretty typical, in that rarely will a prisoner admit to doing anything wrong," said the specialist, who asked that I not use his name. "More often they'll admit to associations with people in a way that they don't think will be incriminating, like they know so-and-so to say hi to on the street. It's easy to tell when they're lying, however, because they become evasive under pressure."

When I asked what would happen to the man, whose wife I remembered sitting on their bed under guard and looking forlorn in their tattered little apartment, the Army specialist said the Iraqi was being sent up to the division-level prison, a place on the northwestern outskirts of Baghdad called Abu Ghraib.

On March 18, 2004, the Iraqi Civil Defense Corps had celebrated the opening of its first of eight planned battalion headquarters in Baghdad, and I was eager to visit the unit and gauge progress in what had become the lynchpin in the entire democracy-building experiment in Iraq. Ever since Paul Wolfowitz and the Pentagon had announced the new strategy of rapidly handing over security responsibilities to Iraqi forces in October of 2003, everyone who worked for the U.S.-led coalition in Iraq understood that they were operating against a stopwatch. Time and history were definitely not on the United States' side in terms of preparing Iraq for the leap from tyranny and dependency to some form of functioning democracy in a matter of months rather than years.

In contrast to nation building in postwar Germany and Japan, where power and responsibility was transferred gradually over a period of many years, in Iraq the U.S.-led coalition was essentially imposing a crash course in democratic self-governance. On June 30, 2004, the U.S.-led Coalition Provisional Authority planned to transfer Iraqi sovereignty to a Baghdad government of still indeterminate nature. By the end of 2005, less than two years after Saddam's fall, a freely elected Iraqi national assembly was slated to have voted on a permanent constitution. By any historical standard, that schedule amounted to the nation-building equivalent of shock therapy.

Defense Secretary Rumsfeld had promised that U.S. forces would remain in Iraq as long as necessary, and not a day longer, whatever that meant. The body language of the U.S.-led occupation in Iraq, however, spoke louder than platitudes and sent a very pointed message: The burden of Iraq's internal security had to shift rapidly onto the largely untested shoulders of Iraqi security forces.

Brig. Gen. Curtis "Mike" Scaparrotti, an assistant division commander for the First Armored Division who was responsible for helping Iraqis stand-up security forces in Baghdad, tried to explain the rush. "One of the major differences between this operation and Germany and Japan after World War II is one of culture," he told me at First A.D.'s headquarters at the Baghdad International Airport. "I just don't believe the

Iraqi culture will indefinitely support U.S. forces in the numbers and day-to-day proximity that we are today."

That assessment was backed by numerous polls showing that while a majority of Iraqis were optimistic that their lives would eventually improve, many were already tired of the presence of foreign troops on their soil. A *USA Today*/CNN/Gallup poll published in April 2004, for instance, found that 57 percent of Iraqis thought that foreign troops should leave their country immediately even if security suffered, and 71 percent identified coalition troops as "occupiers." A May 2004 poll by ABC News, BBC, and the German network ARD revealed that more than half of the Iraqi respondents said that life was better *under Saddam*, and only 25 percent expressed confidence in coalition forces.

"If we stay here indefinitely and continue to change all the lightbulbs in this country, the Iraqis will allow us to do so and increasingly resent us for it at the same time," an Army general told me in Iraq. "That's the nature of the schizophrenic relationship between the West and the Arabian peninsula. Sometimes, I swear to you, I feel like letting Saddam out of prison and saying, okay, you want him back, you got him."

Gen. John Abazaid, commander of U.S. Central Command with responsibility for U.S. military operations in the Middle East, referred to it as a process of "descending consent." Abazaid had postulated that the U.S.-led coalition was somewhere around the halfway point in a roughly two-year grace period for helping Iraq make the leap to greater self-sufficiency and independence. After that point a massive U.S. presence of more than one hundred thousand troops risked provoking a general backlash. As events would soon reveal, Abazaid was off in his calculation by about half.

As a result of that timetable and assessment, however, by late March 2004 First Armored Division had already pulled two-thirds of its forces back to operating bases on the outskirts of the capital where they could conduct targeted operations and otherwise act primarily in support of Iraqi police and security forces. While commanders knew they paid a price in terms of keeping their fingers on the pulse of the city and gathering intelligence, the new "standoff" configuration offered the potential advantage of making U.S. forces less visible and intrusive in the everyday lives of Iraqis.

The security organizations left shouldering the added burden of Iraqi security as U.S. forces pulled back certainly looked impressive on paper. According to the Coalition Provisional Authority and Pentagon they numbered over two hundred thousand strong, including seventy-four thousand police, ninety-two thousand facilities protection and border-control forces, and three thousand of a planned forty thousand Iraqi army troops. Because they were mentored by U.S. military trainers and conducted operations in close coordination with U.S. units, however, the cream of the crop in terms of Iraqi security forces were the thirty-four thousand troops of the Iraqi Civil Defense Corps (ICDC). Though originally envisioned as a sort of Iraqi National Guard, the ICDC was actually being groomed to take over counterinsurgency and counterterrorism operations as U.S. forces receded into the background. "I keep briefing the importance of the ICDC to our plans to anyone who will listen," a senior U.S. commander in Baghdad told me. "Because, ultimately, these guys are our ticket out of here."

Sometimes in journalism you have to understand the macro, bird's-eye view of events to make sense of what you see up close on the ground. There are other times when the wider truth is only revealed through the smallest detail. In the case of the Bush administration's "Iraqification" effort, the centerpiece of its campaign to transform the Middle East with democracy, the truth was shown to me by a young Iraqi man I would never even meet. At its essence the story of Mahmood Kameel was ultimately about the betrayal of someone who risked his life believing everything the Americans had to say about his country.

The walled compound that houses the headquarters for the 302nd Battalion, the first ICDC unit established in Baghdad, lies in the middle of the neighborhood of Sadahmiya, childhood home of Saddam Hussein. Outside the compound's gates, slablike archways rise in solitude hundreds of feet above the desert floor, portals into Saddam's boundless megalomania. Before war interrupted construction, the Iraqi despot and unlikely religious patron was erecting the world's largest mosque on the site to curry favor with Islamists. By March 2004 Sadahmiya had become the most dangerous neighborhood in Baghdad for U.S. troops of the Second Brigade. Nearly 70 percent of the casualties suffered by the brigade over the past year had occurred in this troubled area.

When the 302nd ICDC Battalion commemorated the opening of its headquarters on March 14, it was thus a cause for celebration for both U.S. and Iraqi officials. After the obligatory staff photograph outside the headquarters building, the battalion's chief intelligence officer pulled aside Capt. Justin Tancrel, Second Brigade's chief liaison with the new Iraqi security force. A clearly agitated Capt. Mahmood Kameel pleaded to be issued a pistol, insisting that his life was in danger. Justin Tancrel had no reason to doubt it.

For weeks Tancrel, a lanky British paratrooper attached to Second Brigade, had tried in vain to procure sidearms for senior officers in the battalion headquarters to protect themselves traveling to and from work. Days earlier he had even gone to shake the hand of the battalion's chief supply officer, only to find it bandaged from a gunshot wound from an attacker. The U.S. chain of command in Iraq had tried to equip frontline ICDC soldiers with AK-47 automatic rifles, many of them hand-me-downs seized in raids, but new equipment for the Iraqi forces trickled in at a miniscule pace from an overstressed supply line. Iraqi enlisted personnel were not even allowed to take their rifles home, and officers refused to carry them off duty for fear of being recognized as someone who was cooperating with the U.S.-led coalition. In Baghdad in the spring of 2004, a public label of American collaborator often amounted to a death sentence.

After talking with Captain Mahmood, Tancrel once again pleaded in vain for sidearms from a U.S. supply chain in Iraq that was overburdened by the requirement to rapidly equip its own forces with flak vests and armored Humvees for counterinsurgency war, let alone outfitting roughly two hundred thousand new Iraqi security forces hired in just the past year. Almost none of the $18 billion Congress had appropriated for Iraq had been spent arming, equipping, and training Iraqi forces that were badly in need of all three measures. Defense Secretary Rumsfeld and his civilian team in the Pentagon had just left it to already stretched-thin U.S. forces in Iraq to stand-up their Iraqi counterparts and equip them out of the Army's already threadbare hide. For its part, Central Command and the U.S. command chain in Iraq were displaying a marked propensity for underestimating the strength of a still growing insurgency, and overestimating the capabilities of nascent Iraqi security forces.

The day after Tancrel made his unsuccessful request for pistols, he entered the converted airport tower that served as the new home of the 302nd ICDC Battalion staff. Immediately Tancrel sensed something amiss. A funereal quiet hung over the entire headquarters. That morning, he was told, Captain Mahmood and five other ICDC soldiers had been attacked by insurgents on the way to work. According to eyewitness accounts and an investigation report I read, a blue Opel station wagon with tinted windows had pulled unnoticed alongside the off-duty ICDC soldiers' car. After raking it with automatic weapons fire until it swerved and stopped, the rebels did a strange thing. The driver of the Opel strolled over and pulled Mahmood and three other wounded ICDC troops out into the street, almost as if he knew they would be unarmed. As his two compatriots called the ICDC troops "American spies" and shouted "Allah Akhbar!" the driver put a gun into Mahmood's mouth and blew out the back of his head. Three other ICDC soldiers were executed in turn before the attackers sped away.

The grisly fate of Mahmood Kameel and his compatriots was tragically commonplace in Iraq. Between the end of major hostilities and September of 2004, Pentagon figures would reveal that more than 720 Iraqi security forces would be killed by insurgents and terrorists who had clearly taken note of the U.S. strategy of turning over security responsibilities to homegrown forces. Just in the week after Mahmood's death, insurgents would murder two twin brothers in police uniform; kill a provincial police chief and nine police recruits in an ambush of their vehicle; and target a police chief's home in a suicide car bomb attack. Mahmood's was just a single face among many in a morgue full of grim statistics, but a face that spoke to a larger truth.

Soon after the March 15 murder of Capt. Mahmood Kameel and the three soldiers, other members of the 302nd ICDC Battalion began receiving letters from a group calling itself the "Mujaheddin of the Allah Akbar Forces." "Consider this warning as the last warning to you and your friends in the ICDC. Anyone betraying our country and our people is dead," read the message, a copy of which lay in the investigation file. A 302nd Battalion officer found a similar warning spray painted on the wall in front of his car in a parking lot. "We are watching you, spy!"

Almost no one doubted that the Mahmood murders were an inside job, or that the ranks of the nascent Iraqi security forces were riddled by infiltrators and spies. That was an almost inevitable result of the CPA's decisions to disband the Iraqi army and create an entirely new Iraqi security structure from scratch on an aggressive time line with insufficient resources and oversight.

"Almost any man who goes to the U.S. Army with rudimentary papers can get hired for the ICDC," Col. Hayder Abdul Rahsul, commander of the 302nd ICDC Battalion, told me in an interview. "We need tighter checks because not enough is known about these peoples' families. I think more insurgents probably are infiltrating our ranks."

Indeed, infiltration was an occupational hazard of a project that called for rapidly hiring tens of thousands of military-age men in a country where no one seemed to have a history predating the fall of the Saddam Hussein regime. "There's a strange void in the lives of most of these Iraqis in terms of documentation and paperwork, and most of them are terrified to admit what they did during Saddam's reign," Captain Tancrel told me. Coalition regulations barred senior officers from Saddam's former security forces from positions in the new Iraqi security forces, and U.S. officials had attempted to vet recruits through neighborhood and regional advisory councils. "But with so many men recruited so fast you can't investigate everyone, and we definitely believe their ranks are infiltrated by former regime loyalists and spies. I know for a fact that former members of the Republican Guard have slipped through."

After the horror of the murders, Second Brigade commanders scrounged a number of hand-me-down pistols seized in raids and gave them to the 302nd Battalion officers. That was par for the course. Frequently, the ICDC had to rely on sympathetic U.S. soldiers to donate critical equipment such as computers and flak vests out of their own stocks and pockets. In a wartime bureaucracy catch-22, however, CPA regulations barred U.S. commanders from transferring ammunition to the ICDC except for training purposes. As a result, even after Mahmood's murder, 302nd Battalion officers were carrying around sidearms without bullets.

"We're in a kind of ridiculous situation at the moment, and it's intensely frustrating," Tancrel told me, obviously still agonizing over the foreshadowing of Mahmood Kameel's death and his inability to do anything about it. In the spring of 2004 critical equipment needed for the ICDC to conduct even rudimentary missions was only starting to trickle in. A contract dispute had been allowed to hold up for months the procurement of tactical radios for the 302nd, for instance, as if the urgency of the situation in Iraq allowed for normal accounting procedures. The first trucks for the unit had only begun to arrive at that point. Most ICDC soldiers still got by with a single well-worn uniform. "We're telling the ICDC they are absolutely the main effort in terms of the coalition transferring security duties back to the Iraqis, but because no one anticipated all of these details and demands in advance we can't even arm or equip them properly yet," said Tancrel. "Meanwhile, we're all constantly looking at the sand clock running out and rushing the ICDC to meet unrealistic goals. Sometimes it makes me nuts."

Almost no one I spoke with in Iraq doubted the wisdom of the strategy of turning security duties back to the Iraqis. Against an increasingly lethal insurgency, U.S. commanders needed the homegrown intelligence network and the home-turf expertise of viable Iraqi security forces. First Armored Division had even created an Iraqi intelligence agency modeled on U.S. collection efforts called the "Collection, Management and Analysis Directorate," and a Joint Coordination Center for managing joint U.S.-Iraqi operations.

Maj. Gen. Martin Dempsey, commander of First Armored Division, put it this way: "Intuitively I think relying more on Iraqi security forces is absolutely the right way to go," he told me. "The threat is evolving from the 'C' students of insurgency in terms of the Saddam fedayeen and former regime types, to the 'A' and 'B' students with the Islamic terrorists, and we're going to need the help of indigenous Iraqi intelligence and security forces fighting on their home court."

After announcing the shift in strategy toward rapidly handing over security responsibility to the Iraqis—essentially painting a target onto the backs of the Iraqi forces—Pentagon civilians had done little to follow through on their own initiative. Precious months had expired, and in what amounted to a clear dereliction of duty the Rumsfeld team had failed to give the mission the priority, funds, and oversight it clearly warranted. For its part, the CPA did not even amend or streamline peacetime contracting procedures that were bottlenecking critical equipment for Iraqi security forces. Stretched thin by ongoing operations in Iraq, an un-dermanned U.S. military had only limited personnel to devote to the task of training and overseeing Iraqi forces, and U.S. military leaders vastly overestimated the success of those limited efforts.

Tragically, the only group that seemed to have taken Rumsfeld and Wolfowitz's rhetoric on the matter seriously were the insurgents them-selves. With equipment to new Iraqi forces still trickling in, mass recruit-ment drives under way that were easy to infiltrate and target, and with Iraqi security forces struggling to master even the rudiments of their jobs, Iraq's terrorists and guerrilla insurgents identified them as the weak link in the U.S. strategy for Iraq. The inevitable result were a string of inci-dents culminating in the deadliest such attack of 2004, when in October insurgents dressed as policemen would stop three minibuses of unarmed Iraqi soldiers at a false checkpoint and methodically kill forty-nine of them, most with a single bullet to the head. Just like Mahmood Kameel.

"Everyone understands that the shelf life of the U.S. presence, and our chance to make a positive impact, is slipping away," one U.S. com-mander in Baghdad told me in March 2004. "I still worry, however, that people in Washington assume that the day when Iraqi security forces will be ready to stand on their own is actually closer than is actually the case. Pitting Iraqi security forces against the Zarqawi network and the insur-gency at this point would be like putting minor league batters up against a big league pitcher like Roger Clemens."

We pulled up in front of the low-slung office building near a major Bagh-dad intersection, two Humvees in tandem, the trailing vehicle containing Col. Rob Baker's security detachment and special electronic equipment capable of jamming roadside bombs, assuming that their intelligence shop had correctly identified the detonation frequencies. Another day on Baghdad patrol, another crap shoot.

As we drove slowly by the building, Rob Baker peered into the shut-tered offices of a newspaper. Just days before the Coalition Provisional Authority had ordered Second Brigade to shut down the publication, the mouthpiece of renegade cleric Muqtada al-Sadr, and to arrest one of his chief lieutenants. The order had prompted a lot of grumbling in Second Brigade headquarters. Rob Baker, who had led the raids to quell an al-Sadr uprising in Karbala the previous fall, couldn't understand why Am-bassador Bremer and the CPA would choose this of all times to rile the firebrand cleric. They were in the midst of one of the largest reliefs-in-place in U.S. military history, after all, and his experienced troops were set to leave Iraq during the next few weeks as green replacements took their place and tried to get their bearings. Luckily, the streets outside the newspaper offices that had been filled by protestors the day before now bore only normal midday traffic, and Baghdad seemed relatively quiet.

When we drove through the campus of Baghdad University, where Second Brigade had donated hundreds of thousands of dollars in reconstruction aide, young students dressed in modern garb and traditional robes alike gave us only perfunctory looks. Passing the Baghdad Zoo, Baker recalled how the CPA and military commanders had lavished reconstruction funds on the facility in order to get it quickly reopened after the war, not wanting to repeat the public relations disaster of the Kabul Zoo, where a mangy and neglected lion became an international symbol of the lagging reconstruction effort in Afghanistan. Only later did the Americans discover that Saddam Hussein had reserved the Baghdad Zoo as a private perk for senior Baath Party officials, and it was a hated symbol among many Iraqis. Now that you've taken good care of the beasts, the local sheikhs told Rob Baker, maybe you could help us. "After that I pledged that before I put any more of our great ideas into practice, I'd run them by the local Iraqis first," Rob Baker told me, laughing.

It was late March of 2004, and we were on a farewell tour of sorts as the First Armored Division—"Old Ironsides"—packed up to leave Iraq. As such farewell tours must, ours ended at a memorial service for the First Armored Division soldiers who would never make it home. At the memorial ceremony, held at a facility called Freedom Rest near the 14th of July Bridge in Baghdad, First A.D. commander Maj. Gen. Martin Dempsey spoke of the dead.

"The enemy didn't take the lives of these soldiers," he said. "They gave them in the cause of freedom."

After the ceremony I was looking at the eighty-two names on the First A.D. memorial plaque with Brig. Gen. Mark Hertling, deputy commanding general of First Armored Division, who pointed to some of the etched names and recalled the lives reflected there. There was Pfc. Rachel Bosveld from Oshkosh, Wisconsin, a military policewoman who died nine days shy of her twentieth birthday. A surrogate sister to her whole squad, Bosveld had already received a Purple Heart for wounds she sustained in an earlier ambush. The Sunday evening before she was to receive the medal, Bosveld was killed by mortar fire in the badlands surrounding Abu Ghraib prison.

And so it went on down the line. Pvt. Jonathan Falaniko was in an engineering brigade commanded by his father. After the boy was killed, Command Master Sgt. Ioakino Falaniko accompanied the body back home and buried his son, before returning to Iraq to finish the job they both had started. While most of America was celebrating New Year's Eve of 2003, Command Sgt. Maj. Eric Cook was dying from wounds sustained in Iraq. Spec. Chris Holland was a medic badly shaken up by the trauma of treating wounded under fire, but he overcame the fear because troops needed him, and they continued to need him right up until Holland himself was killed in a subsequent action. Sgt. 1st Class Clint Ferrin was a popular noncom and gung ho paratrooper killed just the week before by a roadside bomb. Staff Sgt. Chris Swisher and Pfc. Sean Silva were lured into an alley in Sadr City by a woman who claimed she needed help and then led them into an ambush. As soldiers came to their aid, Swisher and Silva were said to be holding onto one another as the life seeped out of them both.

"Leaving so many troops behind reinforces how important it is that the United States sees this mission through to the end. That's why our motto at these memorials is 'Make It Matter,'" Gen. Hertling said. "I only hope First Armored can make it out of here without putting any more names on that plaque."

After Hertling left I was writing down some of the names, thinking about a lost world of courage and companionship and the fragile fingerprint left behind on a wall at Freedom Rest, when I was struck by the very first name on the plaque. The first among so many First Armored Division soldiers sacrificed to this cause was a young man from Rock Springs, Wyoming, who had helped protect the V Corps TAC on our long road to Baghdad, felled by a "ghost round" on a day of liberation already so many lifetimes ago: Pfc. Joseph P. Mayek, twenty years and never a day older.

CHAPTER 24

Razor's Edge

AT FIRST GLANCE the carcasses looked like something in a slaughterhouse, strung up and dripping. Only when you realized that pieces were missing did it register that they were human, and by then it was too late. No matter how fast you averted your eyes, the picture stayed with you forever.

"You're American, you should see this," the Kuwaiti newsstand clerk said before putting the Arabic newspaper on top of my *International Herald Tribune*. "You should be *very* careful."

I had just arrived in Kuwait unshaven and exhausted, having spent the previous twenty-four hours hitching a ride on a C-130 cargo plane out of Baghdad, after an always tense drive to the airport along "Ambush Alley." The four American security contractors in the photographs hadn't been so lucky. After insurgents, possibly aided by Iraqi police, had ambushed their vehicle in the Sunni stronghold of Fallujah, an Iraqi crowd that included young boys who looked no more than ten or twelve had literally ripped them apart before stringing some of the bodies up on a bridge span. You could only pray that the men were killed in the initial attack.

CPA officials talked tough about bringing the perpetrators to justice, and the U.S. Marines mounted an assault on the city, but at the same time residents of Fallujah were rising up in revolt west of Baghdad, armed followers of Muqtada al-Sadr launched uprisings in Baghdad's Sadr City and in the southern region around Najaf. In rapid succession the southern cities of Najaf, Karbala, Diwaniyah, and Al Kut fell to Sadr's rebels, underscoring the United States' shaky grip on Iraq. Fears that the mounting violence might ignite a general uprising and spread throughout the country forced U.S. commanders to back off initial vows to retake Fallujah and capture or kill al-Sadr, raising serious questions about U.S. resolve.

Given the CPA's provocations, the uprising by al-Sadr's forces was utterly predictable, and just as predictably, more than 50 percent of an underequipped and poorly trained Iraqi National Guard and police force refused to fight. Some units declined to board aircraft transporting them to the fray, others joined the rebels, but most just stayed home.

Of course, the First Armored Division wasn't going anywhere. The insurrection in the south had totally severed vital supply lines connecting U.S. forces in and around Baghdad to their logistics base in Kuwait. Col. Rob Baker and Second Brigade were tasked with relieving a besieged Spanish unit in Najaf and wresting control of Al Kut back from the rebels as a first step in reestablishing secure supply lines. In the midst of the fighting, the soldiers of First Armored Division were informed that they would have to stay in Iraq for at least an additional three months, and before long the memorial plaque in Freedom Rest would be taken down for fresh etchings. In the end, April 2004 would prove the cruelest month of all for U.S. troops in Iraq, with 137 troops killed and another roughly 1,000 wounded. According to an Associated Press tally, an estimated 1,360 Iraqis were killed in the same month. And still there were deadlier months yet to come in Iraq before the year was out.

In the midst of that desperate struggle, photos were published worldwide depicting abuse, sexual humiliation, and torture of Iraqi prisoners by U.S. soldiers at Abu Ghraib prison. The abuse story could not have come at a worse time. U.S. officials who had hoped to mark the one-year anniversary of operations in Iraq with sober but upbeat reflections on the numerous and significant accomplishments in reconstructing Iraq were thus consumed instead with trying to explain the unfathomable, even while much of the country burned.

Meanwhile, terrorist train bombings in Madrid linked to a still active and lethal Al Qaeda killed 202 Spaniards in March 2004 and prompted a new government in Madrid to withdraw its troops from Iraq in May. Honduras and the Dominican Republic would soon follow suit and pull their own troops. They would not be the last coalition partners to abandon the effort over the course of the year. The United States' grand endeavor of nation building in a time of terror and insurgency teetered on the sharp edge of a razor.

The mission to bring democracy to Iraq at the point of a gun had probably never had high tolerances for error, and by the awful spring of 2004 the Bush administration's myriad errors and miscalculations in the invasion's aftermath were compounding dangerously. Reporting on the crisis from Kuwait, I remember waking up one night from a nightmare and hearing the incantation of morning prayers drifting through my window from a white-spired mosque across the street from the hotel. In my dream I had been laying in wait outside a darkened house, and when a large Arab armed with a scimitar crept up I shot and killed him. Then his brother came and I shot him too, but he was only wounded and we talked. The Arab kept telling me, over and over, that his brother meant no harm. I tried to give him gifts as recompense for his brother's life, but the Arab took a baseball bat and knife from my mantle and said that, sorry, he would use them to kill another American as revenge. Right before waking I had been following the Arab out the door, begging him to take a game of Monopoly instead. For some reason it was important that the Arab accept the Monopoly game.

Sitting awake with the night sweats, it occurred to me that after everything that had happened, I still couldn't answer the question Shafeeq Ghabra had put to me in that same city almost exactly a year ago. Did this thing America was doing represent a promising new beginning, or the beginning of the end?

The clock on my bedside read 4:12 A.M.

When Deputy Secretaries of Defense and State Paul Wolfowitz and Richard Armitage, respectively, appeared together before the Senate Foreign Relations Committee on May 18, 2004, the hearing room was packed and buzzing with expectation. Inside the Bush administration's top echelons, it had long been an article of faith that muscular leadership in the post-9/11 world meant never having to say you're sorry. Admitting mistakes and signaling course corrections were considered signs of weakness. As a result, President Bush and his senior lieutenants almost never did the former, and only reluctantly acknowledged the latter. By the spring of 2004, however, serious mistakes were the one thing senior Bush administration officials could no longer plausibly deny.

Inside cavernous Room 106 of the Dirksen Senate Office Building, with its large American eagle emblem offering official imprimatur and towering walls of polished wood lending the drama a stately air, television cameramen, photographers, and reporters jockeyed for position. The atmosphere was a cross between a high-profile courtroom showdown and a heavyweight title fight. Though stylized and scripted, such hearings were a time-honored Washington ritual, and in times of crisis they could prove cathartic. Politicians would inevitably grandstand before the cameras. Administration officials would offer excuses and pronounce their mea culpas. The pundits would pontificate. The question that hung over the noisy proceedings was whether all of this attention might nudge the superpower ship of state toward a course correction that avoided calamity.

"Listening to your opening statements you would never know how distraught many Americans are," said Sen. Barbara Boxer, the liberal California Democrat. Boxer recounted the comment of a businessman and constituent who said the "American brand" was being pummeled by the barrage of photographs depicting sexual humiliation and torture of Iraqi prisoners at the hands of U.S. soldiers. As was the case in previous conflicts, the photos had galvanized public opinion in a way that a whole forest worth of newsprint could never match, recalling the famous image of a naked Vietnamese girl being scorched by napalm; of blindfolded Americans being held hostage in Iran; of the bodies of U.S. soldiers being dragged through the streets of Mogadishu. In this case the images had tapped into a deep unease among the American public about the course of events in Iraq.

"I didn't hear where we are changing our course, and this is the moment for a course change if ever there was one," Boxer continued. "The essence of our country has taken an enormous hit around the world because of this prison scandal. That's really seared the soul of America. I know the terrorists are worse, but our strength is that we're better than they are."

Sen. Chuck Hagel, the maverick Republican from Nebraska, had served in Vietnam and knew something about the risks entailed in fighting a war that was losing public support. "I don't completely subscribe to polls, but last week it was reported that a poll conducted by our own Coalition Provisional Authority found that 82 percent of the Iraqi people disapprove of the U.S. presence in their country, and a large proportion backed Muqtada al-Sadr," said Hagel. "I want to stress that politics is the essence of this effort, and if we lose the Iraqi people, we've lost. And that poll was taken *before* the prison abuse scandal broke."

Part of the frustration evident in the hearing room could be explained by the failure to find the weapons of mass destruction that were the chief reason for invading Iraq. Without weapons stockpiles, the Bush administration had focused on the liberation of tyrannized Iraqis as its key justification for the war. Fairly or not, the graphic pictures of U.S. Reservists sexually humiliating Iraqi prisoners had undermined even that rationale for the war. In a May 2004 CNN/*USA Today*/Gallup poll, a majority of Iraqis had reiterated their desire for the United States to leave Iraq immediately. For the first time, a majority of Americans also disapproved of President Bush's handling of Iraq.

In the Abu Ghraib scandal there were also disturbing yet familiar hallmarks of Secretary Donald Rumsfeld's leadership, including a constant prodding of the uniformed military to stretch the rules and bend the regulations, in this case the Geneva Convention on the treatment of prisoners of war that were also designed to protect captured U.S. soldiers. An independent panel headed by former Defense Secretary James Schlesinger would eventually blame senior Pentagon leadership for allowing interrogation methods used on suspected terrorists and unlawful combatants at Guantánamo Bay in Cuba, where the Bush administration insisted the Geneva Convention did not apply, to "migrate" to Iraq where the

Pentagon said prisoners were protected by the convention. Later in the year, the International Red Cross would charge that those psychological and physical interrogation techniques honed at Guantánamo were tantamount to torture.

How did drastic interrogation techniques designed to illicit perhaps lifesaving information from suspected Al Qaeda terrorists at Guantánamo, or "Gitmo," migrate to Abu Ghraib, where Iraqis of every conceivable stripe who were swept up in U.S. operations were routinely sent? One obvious path occurred in August 2003, when Rumsfeld's right-hand man and Undersecretary of Defense for Intelligence Steve Cambone sent the commander of Guantánamo, Maj. Gen. Geoffrey Miller, to Abu Ghraib to improve the actionable intelligence gained from interrogations. Senior military officials told investigators that General Miller handed out the Guantánamo interrogation procedures to battalion commanders at Abu Ghraib.

Obviously the abuse depicted in the photographs went far beyond even those strident techniques. The backstory of Abu Ghraib was once again of a stretched-thin U.S. Army operating in a combat zone and struggling to comply with pressure from on high for better results, ratcheting up the interrogations on some of the forty-five thousand Iraqi detainees who passed through a prison manned by a poorly trained and undermanned Reserve military police unit. Investigations would show that overwhelmed soldiers in a dangerous prison were unclear as to who was even in charge, and how far they should go to help get information. In such a cesspool turds will float to the top.

The sexual humiliation and abuse that resulted from that dynamic had virtually no antecedent in U.S. military history, and was another sign for many senior military officers that the incredible strains the Pentagon civilians were putting on the Army, and their bend-the-rules mentality, were corrupting the Army's very culture, possibly introducing a rot at the core. As one retired four-star Army general put it to me, "When I saw pictures of uniformed soldiers terrorizing *naked* prisoners with dogs, I couldn't believe that was the U.S. Army. Where did that come from?"

When asked at the Senate hearings what miscalculations led the United States to such a desperate position in Iraq, devolving from "liberator" to a hated "occupier" known for abusing prisoners in just the space of a year, Wolfowitz was both defensive and contrite.

"Senator, when people start listing the miscalculations in Iraq they rarely list the bad things we counted on happening that didn't happen because our military campaign emphasized speed over mass. Because of the enormous speed of our advance we didn't face major destruction of the oil fields or extensive urban fighting," Wolfowitz testified. "However, we clearly thought we could proceed with occupation much longer than the Iraqis had patience for. In response we have considerably speeded up the transfer of sovereignty and movement toward elections. This label of occupying power is onerous, and I'll be glad to be rid of it after June 30th."

Pressed by numerous senators, Wolfowitz also conceded that the Pentagon had badly misjudged the nature of the enemy in Iraq. Of all the things the administration underestimated, he said, chief among them was the resilience of an insurgency sustained in large part by former regime elements.

"No one predicted that Saddam would be funding attacks against Americans with many hundreds of millions of dollars for months after his regime fell, or that after his capture the killers in his intelligence services who number in the thousands would continue to prove so much tougher than anyone imagined," said Wolfowitz. "Or that they would bring in foreign fighters and work with the likes of Mr. Zarqawi to conduct urban guerrilla fighting. I would also say that we were probably too severe in the de-Baathification process, which is why Ambassador Bremer is now modifying that program, though such moves have prompted hard comments by the Shiites that we may be opening the door back to power for the Baathists."

The remaining hope, Wolfowitz said, lay in the many Iraqis who were risking their lives to stand up for a new, elected government. "I think we were probably slow in empowering those Iraqis," Wolfowitz admitted to the senators. "Perhaps because we anticipated something closer to peacekeeping operations in Iraq, rather than the war we're still fighting."

For his part, Armitage most regretted not immediately conducting on a national level the kind of outreach to tribal elders and sheiks that some commanders at the local level like Col. Rob Baker had begun instinctively. "The single thing I would have done differently would be to more rapidly bring the sheiks into our consultations," Armitage told the lawmakers. "We thought we could deal directly with the Sunni, Shiite, and Kurdish communities on our own, which was wrong. We just didn't fully anticipate the degree to which this is a tribal society, and if we had gotten the tribal sheiks involved earlier I think we'd be much further along right now."

In actual fact, many of those pitfalls the Pentagon had stumbled into in Iraq had been predicted by the National Intelligence Council (NIC), an independent group of senior analysts who advise the director of central intelligence. In two classified reports prepared for President Bush in January of 2003, months before the war, the NIC had warned of a possible insurgency against the new Iraqi government and American forces, and suggested that rogue elements from Saddam's security and intelligence forces could work with terrorist groups to wage guerrilla warfare. The

Bush revolutionaries in the Pentagon and Vice President's office, however, had judged the NIC's warnings as overly pessimistic, and the status
quo in Iraq as unsustainable. That was certainly an arguable case. Now
they had to contend with the disquieting fact that the NIC's warnings and
gloomy scenarios had largely come to pass.

Some of the lawmakers on the Senate Foreign Relations Committee
that I spoke with took the out-of-character apologies and policy reversals
emanating from senior Bush officials in the wake of the prison scandal as
a welcome, albeit belated indication that the Bush administration finally
grasped just how serious the situation had become in Iraq.

"The follow through in Iraq has been profoundly disappointing, to
say the least," Sen. Richard Lugar (R-IN), chairman of the Senate Foreign
Relations Committee, told me in an interview. "When we pointed out in
hearings before the war that there had to be an interim strategy for what
our armed forces were to do after major hostilities were over, senior Bush
administration officials—some of who I call the 'dancing in the streets'
crowd—essentially told us not to worry. The Iraqis would be very appre-
ciative of our getting rid of Saddam, they were educated people, they had
lots of oil reserves, etc. The Pentagon insisted this country would not be
a basket case, and that our armed forces would not have to stay around
long."

Even when Lugar called hearings before the war, and asked the Pentagon to send officials to Capitol Hill who could explain the plan for
Iraq's stability and reconstruction phase, it was to no avail. "The Pentagon stiffed me," Lugar told me. "[ORHA commander Gen. Jay] Garner
couldn't find the time to testify. Meanwhile, Secretary Rumsfeld just kept
repeating at his press conferences that Iraqi oil would pay for everything,
but that was no substitute for having a plan that could have kept the Iraqi
government from disintegrating."

In the same series of hearings on Iraq in late May of 2004, the Senate
Foreign Relations Committee heard from Anthony Cordesman of the
Center for Strategic and International Studies. He was not quick to forgive
the architects of the Iraq quandary. "First, it is simply too late to deal with
the most serious problem we face: the fact that a small group of neoconservative ideologues were able to substitute their illusions for an effective
planning effort by professionals using the interagency process," Cordesman testified, noting that forty years earlier he had himself gone to work
for the Office of the Secretary of Defense in similar circumstances. "At
that time an equally small group of neoliberals were able to do the same
thing. These 'Best and Brightest' trapped us into a losing war, and their
names are written invisibly on the body bags of every American who died
in that conflict. This time, it is neoconservatives, not neoliberals, who
trapped us into war without setting realistic and obtainable goals, and

without a realistic and workable approach to creating stability and security, and dealing with nation building. Once again, we find that incompetence kills just as effectively as malice."

———

After just returning from Iraq and attending the Senate hearings, the question that had been growing in my mind was what could still be realistically salvaged in Iraq? How could America as a nation still, in the motto of the First Armored Division, "Make It Matter"? In terms of President Bush's grand vision of a democratic Iraq serving as a catalyst for reform throughout the Middle East, that foundation of the post-9/11 Bush doctrine was looking shaky. Even some of the conservatives who had originally championed the Bush policy on Iraq were warning that rather than visions of a transformed and democratic Middle East, the Bush administration should articulate to the American people how defeat in Iraq was just not an option.

At a talk at the Council on Foreign Relations that I attended in May 2004, for instance, Sen. John McCain (R-AZ), another Republican maverick who had strongly supported the Bush administration on Iraq, aptly framed the stakes involved in Iraq. After spending five years in a North Vietnamese prisoner of war camp before being released on the eve of South Vietnam's collapse and Saigon's fall, McCain also knew something about consequential moments in history and repercussions that could ripple down through the decades.

"In terms of America's security, I think this is the most critical moment in a generation," McCain told the audience. "If we fail in Iraq, we will have taught our enemies the lesson of Mogadishu, only one hundredfold: If you inflict enough pain, America will leave. Iraq will then descend into chaos and civil war. Warlords will reign. There will be bloodletting. We will have energized the extremists and created a breeding ground for terrorists, dooming the Arab world. Unfortunately, as we continue to see large numbers of American casualties a year after Americans were told that major combat was over, I fear U.S. public support is eroding. So I think we need to admit that serious errors have been made, increase our troop strength in Iraq, and do what's necessary to turn this thing around."

Serious errors have been made. Corrections are under way even as we stay the course. The strategy is sound though the tactics are shifting. Even as President Bush continued offering lofty rhetoric about the transformational promise of a democratic Iraq in the late spring and early summer of 2004, his still deeply divided foreign and military affairs teams faced their most difficult wartime test. The window for salvaging an acceptable outcome in Iraq was fast closing. Their ability to stave off a catastrophic defeat and reverse the precipitous slide in U.S. standing around the world would largely determine whether the Bush revolution in foreign and military affairs ultimately made America stronger or weaker.

Taken together, the series of Bush administration policy changes and reversals on Iraq undoubtedly amounted to a major course correction. The chief question was whether those changes represented a fundamental change in the Bush administration's worldview given the hard lessons of Iraq, or just tactical adjustments as the Bush revolutionaries attempted to ride out a difficult situation in Iraq through the November elections.

A senior White House official I spoke with at the time made no apologies for the fateful decision to put the Pentagon in almost complete charge of a nation-building exercise for which it had little experience, suggesting no change in the Bush administration's proclivity for focusing more on U.S. military power than diplomatic tools. "Look, we as a nation haven't done that much nation building period, and we didn't think that Bosnia and Kosovo [where United Nations and State Department entities were ultimately in charge] represented a very successful model," the official said. "Because there were still military operations ongoing, and we wanted to retain unity of command, we put the Pentagon in charge of the whole operation and let them run with it."

After opposing calls to give the United Nations a more central role in Iraq for more than a year, however, the Bush administration did an about-face in the spring of 2004, asking U.N. envoy Lakhdar Brahimi to identify a caretaker government and oversee the transfer of power to it on June 30. That change in policy predictably infuriated Iraqi exile Ahmed Chalabi, no favorite of Brahimi's, and a member of the Iraqi Governing Council that would soon be disbanded. Ever the survivor, Chalabi responded by trying to reinvent himself as a populist and reaching out to form an alliance with Muqtada al-Sadr. In May, U.S. and Iraqi forces even raided his house looking for evidence that Chalabi leaked classified documents to Iran. The alliance between Ahmed Chalabi and Pentagon neoconservatives that had proved so fateful in steering America toward war with Iraq was permanently shattered.

In another shift, the Bush administration was actively lobbying the NATO alliance to assume a greater role in Iraq, though predictably under the circumstances, their pleas had gone unanswered. Instead, thirteen members of the Iraq coalition, many of them NATO members, would soon announce plans to withdraw their troops by early in 2005, amounting to a drop in coalition troops—other than U.S. and British—of about one-third. Largely as a result, the Pentagon announced that it would not cut back troop levels in Iraq in the summer of 2004 as planned, but rather would keep roughly 138,000 troops there through 2005. That announcement reignited the debate about Rumsfeld's continued refusal to increase the permanent end strength of the U.S. Army. The Bush administration also abandoned its plan to delay asking Congress for an additional $25 billion for Iraq until after the November presidential election, instead making the unpopular request in the spring.

Inside Iraq there were also signals of a major course correction. As Paul Wolfowitz testified to the Senate, Ambassador Bremer finally relaxed restrictions barring former Baath Party officials from holding many government jobs, and U.S. commanders desperately trying to reconstitute Iraqi security forces began reaching out to militias and to former Iraqi army officers. Both moves were an attempt to mitigate the most misguided decisions of the U.S. occupation, the sweeping "de-Baathification" drive led by Chalabi that radicalized much of the Sunni community, and the wholesale disbanding of the Iraqi army and security forces.

The April insurrection, and generally dismal performance of Iraqi security forces, also revealed that the Pentagon's often touted number of two hundred thousand Iraqi security forces in the field was about as reliable as Vietnam-era body counts, and designed to achieve roughly the same thing: show statistical progress in a war effort where little existed. As a result of the April debacle, the Defense Department deleted the seventy-four thousand members of the Facilities Protection Force from its estimates altogether, conceding that the real number was likely tens of thousands of troops lower, their training was negligible to nonexistent, and, because they were hired and paid by Iraqi ministries, U.S. officials had little way of knowing whether they even showed up for work. The Iraq Defense Minister would later state that the roughly 15,600 troops of the Department of Border Enforcement were so corrupt and incompetent that they would have to be either dismissed or integrated back into police units.

An authoritative study by the Center for Strategic and International Studies (CSIS) would put the more likely number of warm bodies in actual service in Iraqi security forces at 62,822 in early fall of 2004, of whom just over half possessed authorized weapons and vehicles, and only 28 percent had adequate communications equipment. The core of adequately trained and equipped "combat ready" Iraqi security forces, the CSIS report would conclude, did not likely exceed 12,000 men.

After wasting most of a year in the critical task of standing up Iraqi security forces, the Pentagon would soon name one of the U.S. Army's most capable leaders, Maj. Gen. David Petraeus, to head the effort to train and equip Iraqi security forces. The Bush administration eventually asked Congress to reprogram $3.46 billion of the $18 billion appropriated for Iraq's reconstruction to help fund Petraeus's efforts and other near-term security programs, conceding that the Pentagon had badly mismanaged priorities by failing to first establish at least a modicum of security in Iraq.

In the spring of 2004, increasingly embattled Pentagon neoconservatives described all of those changes as a sign of tactical agility. Along with the Bush administration's plan to quickly transfer sovereignty to a still nascent and vaguely defined Iraqi interim government, the wholesale changes were still sold as steps toward the overarching strategic goal of establishing a viable democracy in Iraq as a beacon for reform in the Middle East.

"Everyone knows that prewar predictions never unfold perfectly, and in war you will face setbacks, so we've shown that we can be flexible," Douglas Feith told a gathering at the American Enterprise Institute that I attended in May 2004. "The essence of successful strategy is steadiness and not allowing yourself to be buffeted by the latest polls or news of the day," Feith continued, acknowledging that the level of violence in Iraq was likely to spike as the June 30 date for transferring power approached. "President Bush's steadiness has been described by some as unapologetic stubbornness, but I can only imagine what the same people would have said about Winston Churchill's 'stubbornness.' History teaches that steadiness is a gemlike trait in wartime leaders."

History was also replete with examples of major powers falling victim to the venerable bane of empire—hubris and imperial overreach. Many analysts saw that and worse in the determination of neoconservatives to bring democracy to Iraq at the point of a gun, with few allies and against a well-documented and surging tide of anti-American sentiment in the Arab and Islamic worlds. They detected arrogance in Rumsfeld's insistence on a historically small invasion force designed for speed and liberation rather than a lengthy occupation, nation building, and counter-insurgency war. They noted the Bush administration's prolonged reluctance to share decision making as well as burdens in Iraq with the international community. There was also President Bush's own conviction that the United States could accomplish such an ambitious undertaking on the cheap during a time of unprecedented tax cuts, saving him the bother of shifting the country to a wartime footing of shared sacrifices. All of those decisions were part of a strategic calculus by the Bush revolutionaries that had steered America into a very hard position.

A downside of all the belated and frantic course corrections in Iraq as the handoff of sovereignty approached, for instance, was that they could be interpreted by an already skittish Iraqi public as signs that the United States was looking for the exit doors. Steve Metz, a professor of strategy at the Army War College, believed such concerns accounted for the relative quiet of Iraqi moderates at a time when a show of hands was critical to their nation's future.

"In typical American fashion, we seem perplexed that we're not getting more support from the Iraqi street, because we obviously offer Iraqis a better future than the insurgents," Metz said. "If you look at the situation through Iraqi eyes, however, the most salient question they might be asking is, 'Who is more likely to be here in five or ten years' time, the armed insurgent groups or the Americans?' If you look at Iraq from that perspective, you might come up with a less ambitious and optimistic strategic assessment than the Bush administration has offered."

Like many other strategists, Metz had been struck by the great mismatch between the Bush administration's grand strategy and lofty rhetoric concerning Iraq and the follow-through on the ground. Even after the April insurrection and the spectacle of a prison abuse scandal perpetrated by an overworked chain-of-command and poorly trained and underqualified Reservists, for instance, the Bush administration steadfastly resisted calls in Congress and elsewhere to increase the size of the U.S. military and send more troops to Iraq.

"Bush has no shortage of vision, and I happen to agree that a democratic Iraq and reformed Middle East would represent a bold transformation benefiting not only the United States, but the whole world," said Metz. Unfortunately, the Bush administration never mobilized the country or allocated the resources necessary to achieve such a decisive victory. "That suggests that the actual strategy is one of managing problems as they occur. The choice now is to try and raise our commitments commensurate with our strategy, or to downgrade our strategy and expectations."

With anti-occupation sentiment running off the charts in Iraq, and the June 30 deadline fast approaching for transferring sovereignty, the Bush administration had decided in effect to hang on and hope that the course corrections already taken would see Iraq through what promised to be another long, hot summer of portent. By the spring of 2004, they determined that moves to delay the transfer date, rush thousands of more U.S. troops to Iraq, or take a more confrontational stance against Sunni insurgents and renegade Shiites could well ignite an already smoldering tinderbox. They may have been right.

"We've made so many mistakes and grotesque miscalculations that yesterday's good idea may not work any longer," Rick Barton, the head of the Post-Conflict Reconstruction Project at the Center for Strategic and International Studies in Washington, told me in May 2004. "There was a window of opportunity to capture the silent majority in Iraq. I don't know if it's closed yet, but it sure isn't letting in a lot of fresh air, and the temperature is getting hotter inside."

That point was underscored by an analysis that crossed my desk from Stratfor, a private intelligence and analysis firm whose assessments were typically provocative and often prescient. "Most wars reach a moment of crisis, when the outcome hangs in the balance and in which weakness and errors, military or political, can shape victory or put it permanently out of reach," read the Stratfor report. "The strategy of the United States in its war with radical Islam is in [such] a state of crisis. The situation is balanced on the razor's edge. The United States could recover from its tactical failures in Iraq, or suffer a massive defeat and strategic collapse. One thing is certain: The United States cannot remain balanced on the razor's edge indefinitely."

CHAPTER 25

Clouds in the West

ACROSS THE NARROW, blue depths of the Bosporus the remains of two ancient fortresses stand opposite one another on the fault line between East and West, the one in Europe and the other on the Asian continent. While in Istanbul to cover NATO's summit of June 28–29, 2004, I paid a few thousand Turkish dinars and took a ferry out to the well-preserved battlements. It is said that in AD 1453 the sultan Mohammed II would look across that narrow strait of water at the fortress walls of what was then Constantinople, eastern rampart of the Roman Empire, and curse the city he coveted.

Since moving his capital from Rome, Constantine the Great had used the walled city and namesake to control the strategic Bosporus, the only sea route between Asian Anatolia and the Balkan Peninsula of Eastern Europe, and from the fertile Black Sea region south to the Mediterranean. Constantine controlled sea traffic and the approaches to Constantinople with a giant chain that spanned the narrow strait and was raised or lowered at his whim. The Turkish fleet had tried and failed to break the chain across the narrow point in the Bosporus called the Golden Horn.

Mohammed II was not a man, however, easily dissuaded from his desires. His first act upon becoming sultan in AD 1451 at age twenty had been to send an assassin to drown his baby half brother and potential future rival for the throne. Mohammed's second act as sultan had been to execute the assassin. So Mohammed II devised a bold plan for seizing that which he coveted. Unable to break the chain of the Golden Horn, Mohammed went around it. On his orders, workers leveled land on the eastern bank of the Bosporus, laid and greased long wooden rails, and dragged seventy ships a mile over dry land. Now able to concentrate his fleet and two hundred thousand-man army wherever he wanted, Mohammed laid siege to Constantinople, overwhelming the outnumbered Christian garrison and eventually killing the city's namesake. Constantinople fell after six weeks of war.

As William Weir details in his fascinating book *50 Battles That Changed the World* the fall of Constantinople spelled the beginning of the end for a Roman Empire that in Constantine's day had ruled lands stretching between Britain in the north to Mesopotania, or modern-day Iraq, in the south. The war for Constantinople also heralded the rise of the Ottoman Empire, which established its capital in the city and began a centuries-long Islamic dominion that eventually encompassed much of Eastern Europe, the Balkans, and parts of the Middle East.

Wars change the course of history. They forge new international orders and chart the ascent and decline of empires. When I traveled to Istanbul in late June of 2004 in order to cover the critical gathering of Western heads of state there, I had no reason to doubt that the United States' war on international terrorism, with major fronts already opened in Afghanistan and Iraq, was destined to do the same. After all, it was a war led and waged by the only superpower on earth, and one designed from its inception to challenge and topple the orthodoxies of the old world order.

In retrospect the Bush doctrine, with its consequent revolutions in foreign and military affairs, represented a radical strategy wedded to a bold and ambitious premise: that American power, unconstrained by traditional bonds and honed to an insurmountable edge by military transformation, could not just check or contain, but decisively defeat the greatest threats confronting Western civilization at the turn of the twenty-first century—nihilistic Islamic terrorism, the spread of doomsday weapons and technology, growing global instability, and the proliferation of failed or rogue states that nourished those modern scourges.

Capping an extraordinary season of diplomacy, President Bush and his top foreign affairs and national security advisers were in Istanbul to make a final case for the campaigns that translated that doctrine into action—dealing decisive blows against the chief terrorist threat in Afghanistan and the most egregious rogue state threat in Iraq, and securing both victories with a long-overdue democratic reformation of the Middle East. Bush and his top advisers understood that Istanbul represented their last, best chance before the 2004 election to wrest back the initiative in the revolution that would define their legacy and the Bush presidency.

Certainly the White House chose the time and place for maximum effect. On June 29, Bush addressed the Western alliance just after the United States had transferred qualified sovereignty to Iraq's new interim government two days ahead of schedule, the better to avoid an anticipated wave of attacks by a still potent Iraqi insurgency. In Istanbul, NATO for the first time had issued a pledge to help in the critical task of training Iraqi security forces, and to increase its troop levels in Afghanistan in anticipation of fall elections.

Standing on the bank of the storied Bosporus, his back to the bridge linking the Asian and European continents, his feet firmly on the soil of a Muslim country where Islamic traditions and democracy coexist in relative harmony, Bush staunchly defended his vision of wars and regime change in Iraq and Afghanistan as victories in the larger war against terror, and harbingers of democratic reform throughout the Middle East.

"In this century NATO looks outward to new threats that gather in secret and bring sudden violence in peaceful cities. We face terrorist networks that rejoice when parents bury their murdered children, or bound men plead for their lives. We face outlaw regimes that give aid and shelter to these killers, and seek weapons of mass murder," Bush said, arguing that the growing dangers confronting the Western alliance should now be obvious to all. "The only question is whether we will confront them, or look away and pay a terrible cost."

Noting NATO's first "out of area" operation in Afghanistan, and pledge to help train Iraqi security forces, Bush rallied the alliance to do more by helping in the democratic transformation of the Middle East. "The historic achievement of democracy in the broader Middle East will be a victory shared by all. Millions who now live in oppression and want will finally have a chance to provide for their families and lead hopeful lives. Nations in the region will have greater stability because governments will have greater legitimacy. And nations like Turkey and America will be safer, because a hopeful Middle East will no longer produce the ideologies and movements that seek to kill our citizens. This transformation is one of the great and difficult tasks of history. And by our own patience and hard effort, and with confidence in the peoples of the Middle East, we will finish the work that history has given us."

In Istanbul, those most receptive to Bush's entreaties were the newly minted member states from the Baltics and Eastern Europe, nations who had only recently secured their own liberty against tyranny. Some took note of Libya's recent declaration and monitored destruction of its weapons of mass destruction programs. So through lofty rhetoric and dogged optimism, had Bush met the challenge he laid down for himself shortly after the 9/11 attacks, to "redefine the terms of the conflict and campaign in a way that leaders understand and in a way that the people of the world understand"?

In the face of increasing instability in Iraq and the region, many nations represented at the Istanbul summit rejected not only the Bush definition of the conflict, but his revolutionary doctrine for dealing with it. Instead, the general subtext of NATO's Istanbul summit was of a deeply unsettled and profoundly damaged Western alliance.

Far from a springboard to democracy, many European allies believed instead that the aftermath in Iraq—the utter failure to find weapons of mass destruction, the United States' continued inability to impose even a modicum of security, the Abu Ghraib prison scandal—had all confirmed their worst fears. Few shared Bush's fervent faith in Iraq as a catalyst for democratic reform. Most of America's closest allies worried that the Iraq intervention would prove to be a strategic debacle that destabilized and further radicalized the entire region.

That pessimism largely explained the reluctance of allies to come to the United States' aid even in an hour of great need. Before the ink was dry on NATO's pledge to help train Iraqi security forces, for instance, French president Jacques Chirac was denying that it even implied an actual NATO presence in Iraq. After precious months were lost in the ensuing debate, NATO would eventually find a few hundred trainers to send to Iraq as a fig-leaf gesture of support, hardly the decisive achievement touted at the summit. In response to Bush's call in his speech for the European Union to finally grant membership to Turkey as a strategic outreach to the Islamic world, Chirac publicly invited the U.S. president to mind his own business during a press conference I attended in Istanbul.

The most striking aspect of the Istanbul summit, however, was the fundamental loss of trust in the nature and character of American leadership. "We still need the United States, not only for its unique power, but also for its status as a special nation that can define Western values and lead us. Without U.S. leadership we cannot win the war on terror," one foreign minister of a major European nation said in an almost plaintive tone. "Having said that, I fear the positive options are increasingly fading away in Iraq. It is a tremendous risk for the United States to try and get NATO involved there now. I worry that the United States and NATO would become increasingly frustrated with one another in what may amount to mission impossible."

Even NATO Secretary General Jaap de Hoop Scheffer, a pleasant Dutchman and the anointed cheerleader for the alliance, could not resist a public dig at Bush administration neoconservatives who, after constantly downplaying the significance of the alliance in the war on terrorism, were now asking it to once again help clean up a mess in the aftermath of U.S. unilateralism, masked though it was with an ad hoc coalition of the easily led. "Extreme views that used to dominate so much of the Iraq debate have become increasingly discredited. Those U.S. unilateralists who thought the United States didn't really need allies have come to realize that the United States not only needs allies, but also the alliance," de Hoop Scheffer said at a conference in Istanbul sponsored by the German Marshall Fund.

In terms of Iraq, each handoff of power and responsibility by the Bush administration to the United Nations, to the Iraqi interim government, to the fledgling and unproven Iraqi security forces, and even to a wary and reluctant NATO alliance, also served to underscore just how hard a place the United States found itself in because of the myriad mis-

calculations surrounding the occupation. Increasingly, the Bush revolution and legacy, and the fundamental credibility of the United States on
the world stage, were staked on an endeavor that was slipping out of U.S.
control.

In Istanbul, the fear was also palpable that U.S. counterinsurgency operations in Iraq and the carnage of frequent terrorist and insurgent attacks
there, broadcast around the clock in grisly detail throughout the Islamic
world by Arab satellite television stations, were throwing fuel on the fire
of global jihad that Osama Bin Laden had spent his life trying to kindle.

Operation Enduring Freedom in Afghanistan had denied Al Qaeda
sanctuary, and roughly two-thirds of its top leadership had been captured
or killed. That represented major strategic gains, and for nearly three
years the terrorist organization had proven incapable of mounting the
type of terrorist spectacular that it had pulled off with years of careful
planning and uncontested preparation on September 11, 2001. After toppling the repugnant Taliban, the United States was also successful in enlisting the United Nations and NATO to help set that country on the path
to elections and democracy, though the new government's lack of control
outside of Kabul had resulted in an explosion of opium production that
accounted for more than 50 percent of Afghanistan's gross domestic
product. As nation building went, a number of experts I talked with worried that the operative model looked disturbingly like Colombia in the
1990s.

More importantly, Bin Laden and his second-in-command Ayman al-
Zawahiri had to date eluded capture. Even if the Al Qaeda terrorist leaders were "martyred" there were increasing signs that they had already
become less operational commanders than inspirational figures and models for a more loosely knit, autonomous, and widening network of Islamic
terrorist cells and groups. The fevered visions of world jihad that Bin
Laden nurtured had become a virus, and thanks in part to incubators of
violent conflict between the West and Islam in places such as Iraq, Afghanistan, and the occupied territories on the West Bank and Gaza, the
virus was spreading.

By the summer of 2004 outbreaks were occurring with alarming
regularity. They were felt among U.S. allies in the Middle East such as
Morocco, whose capital Casablanca was rocked by five simultaneous
bombing attacks on May 16, 2003. Four days earlier suicide bombers
struck brazenly in the Saudi Arabian capital of Riyadh in another coordinated attack bearing the hallmarks of Al Qaeda. On March 11, Islamic
terrorists had struck in the heart of Europe with four nearly simultaneous
rail bombings that killed 202 people in Madrid, Spain, leading to the fall

of the Spanish government and a pullout of Spanish troops from Iraq. That retreat was followed by the pullout of the troops of Honduras, Nicaragua, and the Dominican Republic from an already shaky U.S.-led coalition in Iraq, inspirational fodder for the terrorists. Before the year was out, a total of thirteen countries would announce plans to either pull their troops out entirely or reduce their presence in Iraq. Meanwhile, all of the Islamist terror cells responsible for those attacks reportedly pledged at least loose allegiance to Al Qaeda.

If he continued to elude capture or death in Iraq, Abu Musab al-Zarqawi was displaying the kind of tactical acumen and organizational talent, and his followers were gaining the type of operational experience and combat seasoning, that Bin Laden and his mujaheddin had gained from operations against the Soviet Union in Afghanistan in the 1980s. A new figurehead of Islamic terror and jihad, and a second wave of nihilistic holy warriors, might well be fomenting in the hothouse of violence and mayhem that was Iraq.

Certainly the scars of that ongoing war against Islamic terror were evident in Istanbul, where one day I visited the construction site that had been the British Consulate. In November of 2003 Islamist terrorists bombed the consulate, the headquarters of a London-based bank, and two synagogues, killing more than sixty people. Everywhere I went in Istanbul the Turks—taxi drivers, hotel porters, waiters—warned me to keep an eye out for terrorists, just as they were keeping eyes peeled. A large part of the central city had been essentially walled off and quarantined for the summit. My guide that day on the Bosporus ferry, a young Turkish college student named Cem Kantarci, had even suggested that I not wear a baseball cap given to me as part of the press kit because it had a tiny NATO emblem. An American traveling abroad in the summer of 2004 could have no doubt that the nation was at war, nor that the West and its allies were under a sort of siege.

Instead of having a decisive discussion in Istanbul about how the civilized world must respond anew to the growing threat of global terrorism and the proliferation of doomsday weapons, however, much of the official and unofficial discussion at the NATO summit was occupied with debates about the unchecked use of U.S. military power and where it had led the alliance. At a critical moment in its history, the West was badly divided.

"The struggle against Al Qaeda and the virulent strain of Islamic extremism that it represents cannot be won on the battlefield," Fawaz Gerges, the Middle East expert at Sarah Lawrence College, told me shortly before the summit. "This is a complex conflict that requires involving the world community, swaying world public opinion, and reaching out to the floating middle of Islamic and Arab public opinion. And initially the Bush administration achieved major progress in that campaign by focusing on multilateral political, security, and intelligence cooperation."

In Gerges's view that momentum had been squandered in the acrimonious controversy over Iraq. "Suddenly shifting gears in the midst of its war with Al Qaeda, and basically deciding to militarily preempt a country such as Iraq that had little, if anything, to do with terrorism produced the exact opposite of the intended effect. Far from hammering a nail into the coffin of Al Qaeda, the Iraq war has breathed new life into the organization by enabling Bin Laden and his ilk to recruit more alienated Arab and Muslim men and make inroads into the hearts and minds of Arabs who had previously rejected his message."

In the process, Gerges believed the Bush administration lost the moral high ground and credibility to pressure authoritarian regimes in the region to reform and liberalize, in effect undercutting its own strategic goals encompassed in the administration's stillborn Broader Middle East Initiative. "It's a great shame and pity, but the decision to extend the war on terror to Iraq set back the fight against Al Qaeda, and I fear it may actually hammer a nail into the coffin of Arab reformers."

In Istanbul, many European allies also echoed what friendly Arab governments had said all along, that in terms of reform in the Arab world the lynchpin remained finding a resolution to the Israeli-Palestinian conflict that continually inflamed Arab anger at the United States and, by proxy, the West. Yet by the summer of 2004 the Bush administration's policy of marginalizing Palestinian leader Yasser Arafat and hewing closely to Israeli hard-liner Ariel Sharon as a partner in the war on terror had devolved into stalemate and strategic incoherence.

Just before the Istanbul summit, for instance, President Bush publicly backed Sharon's plan to unilaterally pull back from the Gaza Strip and implicitly endorsed Israel's keeping some settlements on the West Bank and refusing Palestinians the right of return to Israel proper. Once again the Bush revolutionaries had reversed long-standing U.S. policy, which held that such matters should be left to final negotiations between the two parties themselves. By again positioning itself closer to Sharon, the Bush administration provoked another predictable outcry and backlash in the Arab world. In response, the Bush administration officials reversed course yet again, insisting that they had never meant to prejudge final status negotiations. Even the death later in the year of Yasser Arafat would fail to elicit a coherent plan from the Bush administration on how to get back on its own "road map" for peace, given that Sharon utterly rejected many of its contours.

Setbacks in the Middle East and the spread of terror attacks were not the only subjects that troubled alliance counsels in Istanbul. Concerns about

U.S. leadership also centered on the fact that after naming the "axis of evil" and putting North Korea and Iran alongside Iraq in the supposed U.S. crosshairs, the Bush administration seemed to have no immediate answer to the forces that it had helped unleash. Both Pyongyang and Tehran had responded to the implied threat of preemptive war, for instance, by apparently accelerating their programs to acquire nuclear weapons, both of which were far ahead of Saddam Hussein's moribund nuclear program.

In a deft bit of diplomacy the State Department had widened negotiations with North Korea into six-party talks that included China, Russia, Japan, and South Korea. However, the State Department's continued and familiar disagreements with hard-liners in the Pentagon and Vice President's office on what kind of deal to offer North Korea for abandoning its program, if any, had paralyzed talks for more than a year. The *Washington Post* would report that Vice President Cheney himself intervened decisively in those internal administration negotiations when he nixed a nascent deal. "We don't negotiate with evil; we defeat it," Cheney was quoted by two officials who attended the meeting. Yet the Bush revolutionaries had no plausible plan for regime change in Pyongyang that could be purchased at an acceptable price.

In the meantime, the world's most dangerous proliferator continued to reprocess eight thousand plutonium fuel rods into weapons-grade fuel, enough for perhaps eight nuclear weapons—weapons that North Korean officials publicly proclaimed were already in their arsenal. There was growing evidence that North Korea might test a nuclear weapon, possibly sparking a nuclear arms race in Asia. In the midst of the crisis, the Bush administration was announcing a withdrawal of U.S. troops from South Korea.

With U.S. forces clearly stretched thin in Iraq and Afghanistan, and the West badly split on the way ahead, signs were also increasing that the hard-line mullahs in Tehran smelled strategic weakness. Iran had initially showed pronounced signs of outreach out of fear following the United States' swift victory in Iraq. By the summer of 2004, however, Iran had cracked down heavily on internal dissidents and democratic reformers, and U.S. intelligence indicated that Tehran was funneling weapons and funds to Iraqi Shiites, working to influence planned Iraqi elections. Iran was even harboring known senior Al Qaeda operatives, the mullahs essentially thumbing their nose at U.S. threats to hold nations accountable for such support. Tehran's support for Hezbollah and terror groups who attacked Israel also continued unabated. Meanwhile, the Iranians were openly rebuffing Western demands that it abandon its nuclear program, publicly declaring its plans to process weapons-grade uranium, a threat verified by the International Atomic Energy Agency (IAEA), the United Nation's atomic watchdog.

Stepping into that vacuum, Britain, France, and Germany had begun negotiations to try and entice Iran into giving up its nuclear program in exchange for favorable trading agreements. After purposely undermining the architecture of nuclear nonproliferation treaties as unwanted constraints on U.S. power, denigrating the usefulness of U.N. inspections in Iraq that turned out to be prescient, and eventually bypassing the U.N. Security Council with a preemptive strike on Iraq based on badly flawed intelligence, the Bush administration was clearly in a weak position to rally the international community to confront Iran's nuclear program. The Europeans steadfastly rejected Bush administration attempts, for instance, to have the issue of Iran's nuclear weapons program elevated to the U.N. Security Council for possible sanctions. The Europeans I talked with were having none of it.

"Believe me, we have no illusions that Iran is in full compliance with the IAEA on its nuclear program, and when I look into the eyes of the Iranians I don't see the flowers of the orient reflected there," said one senior European member of the negotiating team. "Our negotiations with Iran are the toughest I've ever been involved with. If we complied with U.S. wishes and took the issue to the U.N. Security Council, however, we could be falling into the same trap that the Bush administration fell into with North Korea, namely addressing a crisis in a way that makes it even more dangerous."

From the counsels of Istanbul the situation regarding Russia and China seemed hardly more stable, though a senior White House official I spoke with characterized U.S. relations with these great powers as "the best any American administration has ever had."

In terms of China, common cause in the fight against Islamic terror and a mutual desire to see the Korean peninsula remain nuclear-free had quieted some of the bellicose rhetoric often heard on both sides of the Sino-American relationship. The Communists in Beijing, however, were world-class experts at sensing and exploiting weakness on the world stage. With the United States diverted by its struggles in Iraq and Afghanistan and the Western powers bitterly divided, Beijing had thus hastened its deployment of missiles opposite Taiwan, ratcheting up pressure on the island nation to find an accommodation or risk war. After being encouraged to take a more independent stance by neoconservatives early in Bush's term, Taipei was sufficiently alarmed by the new developments that later in the year a senior adviser to the president of Taiwan would take out a full-page advertisement in the *Washington Post* accusing the Bush administration's newfound love of the venerable "one China" policy as tantamount to appeasement on a par with Neville Chamberlain's accommodation with the Nazis in 1938.

In terms of Russia, after famously looking into the eyes of Vladimir Putin and recognizing the soul of a good man he could do business with, Bush had largely stood by silently while the Russian strongman used his increasingly bloody fight with Chechnyan terrorists as an excuse to reassert state control over Russian media, jail political opponents, and bring regional governors under his direct sway. Before the year was out Putin would openly meddle unsuccessfully in democratic elections in Ukraine, pushing a favored candidate who tried to steal the election through fraud and precipitating a major crisis. That suggested to many experts that Putin was interested in reasserting Russia's traditional dominion over its "near abroad." Thus the Western alliance's primary reclamation project of the post–Cold War era—bringing Moscow into the Western fold—was in danger of a decisive reversal.

"[Putin's government] has systematically undercut the freedom and independence of the press, destroyed the checks and balances in the Russian federal system, arbitrarily imprisoned both real and imagined political rivals, removed legitimate candidates from electoral ballots, harassed and arrested NGO [nongovernmental organization] leaders, and weakened Russia's political parties," read a letter that was released later in the year and signed by 115 European and American leaders, including former presidents and prime ministers and sitting Republican and Democratic senators. "The leaders of the West must recognize that our current strategy towards Russia is failing."

How did the United States find itself at such a perilous crossroads, challenged by existential dangers on numerous fronts, and with American leadership sounding an uncertain trumpet in the ears of so many allies? Such fateful moments in the life of a nation do not happen by accident or in a vacuum. In this case the predicament was the direct consequence of cataclysmic events and a revolutionary strategic vision, of high-risk policy choices and high-level personality clashes, and of a political movement that posited a new answer to the weightiest foreign policy question of the era: How would America wield its historically preponderant power? In Istanbul there could be no ignoring just how terribly wrong their calculations had proven. Instead of making America stronger and more secure, they had left the nation overstretched and increasingly isolated as real and potential enemies multiplied. The Bush revolution had failed. The West was weak.

In retrospect, no American President, early in his first term and still relatively inexperienced on the world stage, should have to confront a crisis of the magnitude of September 11, 2001. Presidents facing international crises early in their term are apt to stumble before gaining their balance. Think of the difference between John F. Kennedy's handling of the Bay of Pigs, and of the later Cuban missile crisis. Or of Bill Clinton's early missteps in Somalia, and his subsequent management of the Balkans crisis. Presidents don't get to choose, however, the timing and circumstances of the crises that will confront them and shape their legacies. As George W. Bush discovered, the American presidency is the world's most unforgiving on-the-job training program in foreign affairs.

It has become something of a cliché to say that the September 11 terrorist attacks on the United States changed everything. But certainly there can be no argument that they profoundly impacted the Bush administration's key players, and provided a historic opportunity for the revolution in U.S. foreign and military affairs that many of them had advocated from the beginning.

In those critical months, Bush's experienced foreign policy and national security teams for a time played to their strengths. The Bush doctrine for fighting the global war on terror was certainly strategically far-reaching and risky, but the need to change the paradigm in regards to catastrophic terrorism justified great risks. The Bush team also showed decisiveness and innovation in quickly taking the fight to Al Qaeda and the Taliban in Afghanistan, and they used the outpouring of support around the world to mend diplomatic fences splintered in their first, tumultuous months in office. They initially drew to the U.S. cause a very broad coalition that included Pakistan, India, Russia, China, and the major European powers, highlighting the fact that a global solution was required to combat a scourge that expertly traveled among the flyways and electronic byways of globalization. In rallying the world to the counterterrorism fight, the Bush administration found for a time the unifying theme and coordinated approach that had so eluded it early on.

In retrospect, the turning point in that remarkable stretch came in the 2002 State of the Union address, which served as the official unveiling of the Bush doctrine for fighting the war on global terrorism. The doctrine, fleshed out in the 2002 National Security Strategy document, could hardly have been more far-reaching in its scope. The United States was at war not only with Al Qaeda, but also with global terrorism writ large. Its enemies in that war were not only the terrorists themselves, but also any states that stood at a nexus of rogue behavior, weapons of mass destruction, and past or present ties to terrorists.

It was in how the United States apparently planned to deal with such a broad array of threats, however, that the Bush doctrine skewed badly off course. Allies who had scarcely been consulted once again detected a unilateralist impulse to unshackle the United States from the constraints of international law and norm that bound the world order, this time in existential matters of war. The United States would not merely sit back and wait for such threats to gather, Bush stressed in his speech, but was prepared to launch "preemptive" and, if need be, unilateral war against them.

Bush administration officials never seemed able to grasp the dramatic shift in momentum that occurred when they unveiled such a radical new doctrine and premise for waging war, with virtually no consultations with allies or interested parties, in a speech memorable primarily for its bellicose tone. It was not enough to put the world on notice that the Bush administration was anticipating a far broader war than most had anticipated; in his State of the Union speech, Bush explicitly put Iraq, Iran, and North Korea on notice as part of an "axis of evil." With that speech and follow-ups by senior administration officials, the Bush revolutionaries adopted a tone that alarmed friends and foes alike, emphasizing a values-based prism for looking at the world as a place of good and evil, where evil needed to be confronted and beat back with the sword of democracy.

"From the beginning, two aspects of the Bush doctrine really bothered me," Zbigniew Brzezinski, the author of *The Choice: Global Dominion or Global Leadership,* told me in an interview in June 2004. "First, it defined the war on terror in a rather theological way as a global confrontation between good and evil. That was troubling because as an approach, it was both very susceptible to exaggeration and even demagoguery, and it ignored completely the Middle Eastern context and specific nature of the terrorism that was directed at us. I also found troubling this repeated invocation of [Vladimir] Lenin's formula that 'He who is not with us, is against us.' That had a very divisive effect, because it transmuted alliance relationships into subordination."

Certainly with the "axis of evil" speech, the outpouring of goodwill and empathy around the world in response to the terrorist attacks began to quickly evaporate. It was replaced by growing concern over just how far the American superpower intended to take its doctrine of preemptive war, fears that senior Bush administration officials often seemed intent on gleefully stoking.

"I know some speechwriter looking for a pivotal phrase probably inserted 'axis of evil' into the State of the Union address, but it seemed to me to cloud the issue," Sen. Richard Lugar (R-IN), the Republican chairman of the Senate Foreign Relations Committee, told me in an interview. "It shifted the focus of the war on terror substantially. Suddenly, people were asking what these nations had to do with Al Qaeda and the terrorists who had attacked us. It seems to me that's where our diplomacy started to get difficult."

In retrospect, the "axis of evil" speech was also the first clear indication that the September 11 terrorist attacks had forged a powerful alliance between the neoconservatives and the hard-line nationalists—the "neo-Wilsonians with a sword" and "Don't tread on me" Jacksonians—in the Pentagon and in Vice President Cheney's office. Partly that was the result of power shifting naturally in times of war to the White House and Defense Department and away from the "Hamiltonian" diplomats in the State Department. Regardless, the strong emphasis on good versus evil, the focus on U.S. military power unconstrained by international law or norms, the implied unilateralism—all of it projected the warlike visage of a superpower run amok that was at odds with how members of the Western alliance had come to think about its standard bearer.

In the midst of this critical shift in the internal dynamics of the Bush administration, Vice President Dick Cheney emerged as the wild card in the debate on how to translate the Bush doctrine into action. The shock of the 9/11 attacks—of being physically lifted from his feet by Secret Service agents and hustled into the White House bunker, there to await possible destruction of the president's home by the American Airlines plane that eventually slammed into the Pentagon—the entire trauma clearly impacted Dick Cheney profoundly. With a policy portfolio unequaled in the history of the vice presidency, the inscrutable Cheney was suddenly free to indulge his own proclivities for perhaps the first time in a long career in public service, and what emerged was the *uber*-Jacksonian among the Bush revolutionaries. With little oversight and almost no transparency into his actions and critical role, Cheney operated in the shadows and transformed his large staff into a parallel National Security Council. Behind the scenes, Cheney became the administration's strongest proponent for war with Iraq and unilateral action in the war on terror, and an indispensable "trump card" for neoconservatives in the Pentagon who were in frequent and direct contact with his staff.

"Of all the key players in the Bush administration, Dick Cheney is the one who really surprised me," said a Republican with long ties to many senior Bush administration officials. "In the thirty years that I've known Cheney he always came at problems from a pragmatic, albeit very conservative perspective. In retrospect maybe because he was serving more moderate administrations. Or possibly the 9/11 attacks converted him to the cause of the ideological zealots in this administration. All I know for certain is that he had a profound influence on President Bush, and was a ringleader in pushing some of the more extremist policies."

In 2002, as those policies advanced and the war drums over Iraq grew louder, it became clear that after initially amplifying the strengths of the Bush administration's foreign policy and national security teams, the war on terrorism over time came to exaggerate the weaknesses and fissures evident in the administration's first months in office. The tendency to view things in terms of good versus evil became so pronounced as to blot out the nuance and subtle grays of diplomacy. Sometimes Bush's tone slipped into the almost messianic—at one point he even referred to the war as a "crusade"—raising concerns that the administration was playing into Osama Bin Laden's apocalyptic vision of a clash of civilizations.

The administration's early emphasis on the primacy of U.S. military power, and its downplaying of the importance of consensus building and alliances, also reappeared with a vengeance. When the Pentagon quickly dismissed NATO's landmark invocation of Article 5's clause on collective defense with the soon-to-be-familiar mantra that the "mission would define the coalition," the message was clear: The Western alliance that had triumphed in the Cold War had been downgraded to a debating society and military standards office.

The administration's confidence in the righteousness of its chosen path also increasingly crossed the line into arrogance. The humility that Bush had promised during the campaign was nowhere to be seen as the Bush revolutionaries wielded the hard spear of American military power. When Germany and France voiced opposition to a preemptive war against Iraq, Rumsfeld thus dismissed them as "old Europe," dividing the alliance at exactly the moment that a Bush administration acting in unison might yet have rallied it to the cause.

Perhaps most importantly, the philosophical divide between competing worldviews within the Bush administration also reappeared as the Iraqi crisis took center stage. By the fall of 2002, when the administration brought the Iraq matter to a head in the U.N. Security Council, the infighting had already drained the United States' substantial capital at the world body. Factions within the administration seemed to be working at cross-purposes, creating a foreign policy of dysfunction. Even as Secretary of State Powell was preparing Bush for his appearance before the U.N. General Assembly, Cheney was giving a speech denigrating a return to U.N. inspections in Iraq as worse than useless. Allies trying to decipher which of the conflicting messages revealed true U.S. intentions became increasingly confused as the crisis grew at the United Nations.

"Every time Powell would make significant progress at the United Nations or in building a coalition on Iraq, either Cheney, Rumsfeld, or Wolfowitz would do something to undercut him," Sen. Joseph Biden (D-DE), the ranking minority member on the Senate Foreign Relations Committee, told me in an interview in the summer of 2004. "Basically, this is the most fundamentally divided administration, in terms of opposing worldviews, of the seven that I've personally witnessed. There's a San Andreas Fault running down the middle of this group in terms of basic outlook."

The net result of those fissures and miscues was that the United States launched its controversial Iraqi front in the war on terror not from a position of maximum strength and leverage, but rather from a position of rare isolation resulting from a foreign policy debacle of monumental proportions. The Bush administration's miscues and maladroit diplomacy before the war denied the U.S. military a northern front launched from Turkey, the potential support of a broad coalition, and the political cover that would have come from participation by even a single major Arab allied army. As polling clearly indicated at the time, the failure to gain broad international backing also meant that domestic support in the United States for the war and its aftermath was far shallower than would have otherwise been the case.

"The standoff in the U.N. Security Council over Iraq, and the conflict and its aftermath, have created the lowest point in transatlantic relations since World War II," said Charles Kupchan, a professor at Georgetown University and a member of a task force on transatlantic relations sponsored by the Council on Foreign Relations. "The abrasive tone and substance of U.S. policy under the Bush administration set Europe on edge, and over time, the accumulated effect has been that Europeans find it increasingly difficult to accept what they see as a shift in quality and character in American leadership."

The net result, said Zbigniew Brzezinski in an interview, is a superpower firmly enmeshed in a region of 550 million people that is "ethnically combustive, religiously aroused, and seething with unrest and hostility toward the United States. If we stay on our present course, I'm worried we could become truly isolated and overwhelmed by problems that outstrip our ability to respond. Really, the dimensions of this problem are unprecedented, and not fully understood by the American people."

In the course of my reporting, and just before leaving for Istanbul, I visited National Security Adviser Condoleeza Rice in her West Wing office, in June 2004. She was charming and as intelligent as ever. Many national security experts put the failure to forge a strategically coherent policy out of the competing factions within the administration, however, directly at her doorstep. While much of the interview was off the record, Dr. Rice's reply to my question on that matter was not. At some point wasn't she, as National Security Adviser and the President's designated alter ego on matters of national security, directly responsible for instilling discipline and finding some consistent middle ground between the clearly divergent views at State and Defense?

You mean harmonizing the views of Colin Powell and Donald Rumsfeld?

Exactly, I told her.

At that point, Condi Rice just shook her head and had a good laugh at the question.

In researching my retrospective on the Bush doctrine and foreign policy, I also spent an hour with Colin Powell in March 2004 in his ornate office on the top floor of the State Department. Peppering him with questions and unable to get a single jab through his spirited defense of a foreign policy in clear disarray, I was reminded again why Powell was widely considered one of the most capable of Washington hands, and one of the most impressive Americans of his generation.

In Powell's telling, President Bush was a committed multilateralist and the "axis of evil" speech just Reaganesque plain speak. "I must say that I didn't expect quite as strong a reaction as we got, because I saw the 'axis of evil' line before it was delivered. It really put an exclamation behind the point, however, that President Bush was trying to make. He said there are policies and nations in this world that are evil, and he was absolutely right, and he fingered three of the worst," Powell told me. "The President understands the value of speaking clearly and directly when you want to send a message, and you don't want it to be confused. The 'axis of evil' phrase may not be headed for a diplomatic award, but it sure got everybody's attention."

Powell was equally adamant in defending the Bush doctrine of preemption. Despite exhaustive evidence from the 9/11 Commission of a mammoth intelligence breakdown prior to the September 11 attacks, a further intelligence debacle over Iraq's weapons of mass destruction, and Powell's own deeply flawed testimony before the United Nations based on bad intelligence, Powell's faith in the doctrine was apparently unshaken. He insisted that preemption remained very much in the U.S. toolbox even though the U.S. intelligence apparatus seemed manifestly incapable of supporting such an aggressive doctrine.

What nation, I wondered, was going to believe the United States the next time it cried wolf and threatened to preempt another country's WMD programs? Along with other Bush administration officials, Powell was also strangely silent on the issue of whether the United States believed other nation-states should also embrace a doctrine of preemption—India and Pakistan, for example, or North and South Korea, Russia and Georgia, China and Taiwan, or perhaps Israel and Syria—in order to settle their differences.

"Perhaps because of my military background, preemption is not something that seems all that extraordinary to me. In my view, preemption is just a tactic or strategy that states that you will preempt danger that is heading your way, whether it comes from a rogue, a terrorist organization, or another nation. If we had known the Japanese aircraft carriers were sailing toward Honolulu on that fateful morning in 1941, for instance, we would have preempted them," Powell told me. "In the case of my February 5, 2003, speech at the United Nations, it was the best assessment that was available to us, by people who worked very hard at it. And a lot of it, I think, has stood the test of time. Iraq was developing long-range missiles; they were developing unmanned aerial vehicles; they did have the intension and capability to have such weapons."

The only thing they apparently lacked were the actual weapons of mass destruction that the Bush administration had posited to the world as the primary reason for the war. When the United States' Iraqi Survey Group would release its final report later that year, it would confirm what virtually every expert had come to suspect, and what U.N. inspectors in Iraq were suggesting before the war: Saddam Hussein had no stockpiles of doomsday weapons, and there was no evidence that he had been able to meaningfully restart his nuclear program despite all the Bush administration references to "mushroom clouds."

"We haven't found the stockpiles," Powell admitted. "That's a surprise to me, to the intelligence community, to [chief U.S. inspector Dr. David] Kay, to all of us."

In talking to Powell, it was hard to square the Bush administration Secretary of State with the Bush '41 Chairman of the Joint Chiefs that I had interviewed a decade earlier. At that time, his doctrine cautioned that the United States should never go to war without committing overwhelming military force to secure decisive victory, and without the firm support of the American public. I admired the deep sense of loyalty that had characterized Powell's entire career, but as George W. Bush's first term drew to a close, I couldn't help but feel that loyalty had been poorly rewarded. Despite his iconic stature, there was something decidedly sad about the tarnished legacy Colin Powell would take with him when he resigned from the administration shortly after Bush's reelection in November 2004.

Even by the summer of 2004 the finger-pointing within the administration had already begun in earnest over who was most responsible for a foreign policy morass, and the neoconservatives and their allies were predictably pointing at Powell. His crime was apparently insufficient ardor in prosecuting the Bush doctrine, as if the tenets of that flawed doctrine were not at all to blame. Former House Speaker Newt Gingrich, a member of the Defense Science Board along with Richard Perle, and a close friend of the Pentagon neoconservatives, had written a much-publicized article accusing Powell of essentially betraying Bush's foreign policy agenda. Apparently that would not present a problem in Bush's second term, when Condaleeza Rice would ride herd over Foggy Bottom.

"I don't care what Newt Gingrich or any of them say! The only person whose view on my loyalty I care about is the President. But go ahead, have fun, write it! Because you all enjoy writing about this divide, and it's a constant in all the articles that come out. There's always the need to find some debate or disagreement," Powell said, obviously agitated for the first time in our interview. "And frankly, there *are* debates and disagreements. I've never been in an administration where there weren't. You know, I cut my milk teeth on similar debates between [Reagan administration Defense Secretary Caspar] Weinberger and [Reagan Secretary of State George] Shultz! I mean, this is not new to me! This is government. And it would be a very boring government if we all sat around agreeing with each other. We do have strong views and strong personalities in this administration, and we argue these things out."

During the interview I didn't have time to point out what many Reagan insiders believe: that legendary disagreements between Shultz and Weinberger led to flawed decisions such as putting U.S. Marines in Lebanon without a clear mission, a policy debacle that ended with the bombing of the Marine barracks by Hezbollah terrorists, the death of 241 Marines, and a demoralizing retreat of U.S. forces from Lebanon. Or that the policy paralysis at the top prompted by the Weinberger-Shultz feud opened the door for mischief making by an ambitious young Marine lieutenant colonel on the National Security Council staff named Ollie North. That mischief begot Iran-Contra, the worst scandal in Ronald Reagan's presidency.

After the interview, however, I did call two close associates who had known Powell for years and had worked under him in senior positions at the State Department before deciding to leave before the end of Bush's first term. Both confirmed that Powell's obvious frustration was not due to fights with Rumsfeld, against whom he felt fully capable of holding his own. Rather, Powell was frustrated by a Rumsfeld-Cheney axis that drew on the power of the Pentagon and the proximity of the Vice President to the Oval Office to thwart many Powell initiatives and dilute his influence. Both sources also talked about their own decisions to leave the State Department out of exhaustion over the constant infighting within the Bush administration.

I asked one of those sources when that clash in worldviews had become evident from within. "After I saw the lineup of who would get top jobs, it was obvious to me even before day one that there would be a fundamental split in approach within the Bush foreign policy and national security apparatus," said the source, who left the State Department after becoming tired of having to defend in public policies he and Secretary Powell opposed in private deliberations. "Everything that happened later reinforced my original prediction."

In Istanbul, senior Bush administration officials tried to convince skeptical allies that they were ready to turn a new page in relations, and indeed signs of a foreign policy in dramatic flux were evident in the obvious disgruntlement among the various Bush factions. Reporters traveling with Donald Rumsfeld said he was irritable even by his own irascible standards. Back in Washington, the usually composed Dick Cheney, president of the "greatest deliberative body in the world," was making headlines for telling a Democrat to fuck himself on the Senate floor. In a recent letter, an apparently weary Paul Wolfowitz had issued a public apology to journalists in Iraq whose courage he had directly impugned, despite the fact that so many had been wounded and killed covering an Iraqi campaign that Wolfowitz himself was instrumental in launching.

And in Istanbul, Bush officials conducted consultations and reached compromises that they conceded might better have come earlier. It was an admission that obviously came hard to a President and administration whose collective DNA seemed hardwired against acknowledging mistakes. That stubbornness may have played well into the spinmasters' image of George W. Bush as a man of firm convictions, but such a predilection made the Bush administration loath to reexamine a chosen course and slow to make corrections even when potential disaster loomed.

Time and again in Iraq, that unwillingness of the administration to confront in a timely manner the error of its initial judgments—on the size of the U.S. military force needed to subdue a fractious Iraq; on the dissolution of the Iraqi military and the radicalization of its jobless troops; on the de-Baathification program that alienated much of the Sunni community; on the resilience and ferocity of the insurgency—had narrowed the prospects of success and lasting democracy in Iraq. That, too, was part of the Bush foreign policy legacy.

Privately, senior administration officials seemed to understand that the failure to engage in frank consultations with U.S. allies in the critical period after the 9/11 terrorist attacks had been a costly mistake. "What I've said to my European friends about this period is that after the shock of September 11, we never really had a good chance to have a strategic dialogue because everything was happening so fast," a senior White House official told me. "I fully understand that the United States is a singular power, however, and when the allies were not quite sure how we viewed our strategic interests, it was unsettling for them. If I could do anything over again it would be to have those substantive discussions earlier."

In Istanbul, the fallout from a U.S. administration with no instinct for consultation even in the midst of war, and the anti-American backlash that resulted, was evident even in the roster of Western leaders who gathered there in the summer of 2004. You could see it in the person of a politically diminished Tony Blair, the British prime minister whose popularity had plummeted at home as a result of constant references to Blair as

George Bush's "poodle." It helped explain the presence of German Chancellor Gerhard Schroeder, who owed his office and place at the table to his calculated opposition to the United States and the Iraq war. The fallout was even revealed by the empty seats and the faces not present, such as former Spanish prime minister José María Aznar, who was ousted after the Madrid bombings by a majority of Spaniards who opposed his support for the United States in Iraq. It was evident in the squeals of delight by young Turks that followed French president Jacques Chirac wherever he went in Istanbul. In the summer of 2004, all it took to attain rock-star status in the eyes of many young Europeans was to stand up to the United States.

The subject of the long-term costs of such a loss of international prestige for the United States came up at a private dinner in Istanbul for senior American and European officials and a few journalists, which was hosted by the German Marshall Fund (GMF). A GMF survey of Americans and Europeans then under way would confirm what we all sensed: that the deterioration in U.S.-European relations first demonstrated in the aftermath of the Iraq war had hardened over the past year into a semipermanent distrust that was fundamentally redefining transatlantic relations. The survey showed that 76 percent of Europeans polled expressed disapproval of U.S. foreign policy, and a majority wanted to distance themselves from U.S. leadership in the world.

The dinner was held at the opulent, five-star Ciragan Palace Hotel, a marble palace on the European bank of the Bosporus that had served as the residence of the last of the Ottomon sultans. Over drinks on an outside patio, Simone Serfaty, the urbane head of the European Program at the Center for Strategic and International Studies in Washington, confessed his despair that attempts to explain America to European audiences increasingly fell on deaf ears. At that an elder European parliamentarian and foreign policy expert sitting with us recounted his early memories of America as a liberator of Europe, and his later extensive travels in the United States. His own daughter, by contrast, was coming of age in a time of anti-Americanism, and her formative memories would be of an America perceived as a threat to world order. "You shouldn't fight a war that you can't explain in a sentence or less," the elder statesman told our small group. "And when my daughter asked, I couldn't explain this war to her. America has lost my daughter's generation."

At that moment it was still too soon to judge whether the U.S. campaigns of nation building and counterinsurgency in Iraq and Afghanistan were the new beginning for the broader Middle East that the Bush administration envisioned, or the beginning of the end of an era of unchallenged American leadership and predominance. Yet the simple fact that the

United States stood at such a perilous tipping point, where either outcome was easily imaginable, spoke to fundamental flaws in the underpin-
nings of the Bush revolution.

The controversial reign of the Bush revolutionaries over U.S. foreign
policy was not a failure for trampling diplomatic sensitivities or the misty
memories of an elder statesman. Rather, the revolutionaries had fallen
woefully short of their own stated goals. Too many of the core precepts
of the neo-Wilsonians and Jacksonians simply proved false. The assumption that if America the superpower led assertively its allies would be
forced to follow was patently mistaken. The belief that the United States
could claim exception and unshackle itself from the constraints of arms
control treaties and multilateral agreements, yet still rally the world
against rogue state proliferators who violated those same norms, was
likewise misguided. The insistence that the "mission would define the coalition" in Afghanistan and Iraq had been followed by an admission in
Istanbul that the coalitions as assembled were woefully insufficient to the
tasks at hand, essentially leaving Bush administration officials in the un-
enviable position of beggars at the banquet of a parsimonious NATO.

At its core the Bush revolution was premised on a fundamental mis-
judgment about the nature of American power. In their ideological fervor,
the revolutionaries had convinced themselves and a goodly portion of
their countrymen that good intentions and U.S. military might make right
in world affairs. They failed to see how the perception of a superpower
run amok would diminish the greater source of American power: the
principles and ideals that others freely embraced and by which our good
intentions and leadership are judged. At a critical moment in the history
of the West, with storm clouds gathering all around, America's beacon
flickered.

Sitting on the patio of the Ciragan Palace Hotel at the literal edge of
Europe, I looked across the Bosporus and imagined the shock as the city
of Constantinople awoke on that long-ago May morning in AD 1453 to
find the entire Turkish fleet amassed outside its walls. As they sounded
the trumpets and engaged in desperate battle, could the soldiers have
guessed that the destinies of great empires and the scales of history hung
in the balance? I very much doubted it. Even if the notion had occurred,
what message could Constantine have possibly composed to awaken
Rome to its peril?

CHAPTER 26

Twilight Warriors

JUST OUTSIDE the small town of Josephina, the driver turned his battered car down a small farm road that ran parallel to the main thoroughfare. On the main street he could see a checkpoint and U.S. troops of the 4/27th Field Artillery Battalion clearing the road with a strange-looking contraption: an armored vehicle with a large mechanical claw that was snatching at clumps of trash and debris on the side of the road searching for hidden bombs. In Saddam's time, the largest employer in this dirt poor Sunni area just south of Baghdad had been a nearby factory that produced most of the commercial-grade explosives for the Iraqi military. The factory had been bombed by the United States and looted during the war, and the men who worked there no longer had jobs. What they had were grievances and time on their hands, and an intimate familiarity with explosives.

The soldiers of Second Brigade, First Armored Division, which was responsible for keeping the critical supply lines open that ran through the area, reaped the inevitable whirlwind. Their experiences in the hard-luck villages and towns south of Baghdad largely explained the nickname the Americans and many Iraqis had given the region: the "Triangle of Death." Second Brigade was averaging thirty attacks a week by IEDs in the triangle. In the previous week, Charlie Battery of the 4/27th alone had suffered ten casualties as a result of roadside bombs. One of its soldiers was now blind as a result. Another had lost his leg. Others were badly maimed. So when the unmarked car approached their clearing operations, a Charlie Battery platoon emerged from concealed positions in order to wave the driver off. They intended to brook no argument, and they got none.

As the soldiers approached the car the driver's bearded face was visible behind the windshield, but not his hands. No one saw him trip the igniter on hundreds of pounds of weapons-grade explosive, and when the smoke cleared from a blast that was heard for miles around, the Charlie Battery platoon was nowhere to be seen.

Forty-five minutes later Col. Rob Baker and one of his officers were walking through a field next to the bomb site, policing up body parts. As soon as Baker had seen the faces of the surviving Charlie Battery soldiers he had relieved them of the grisly job. After more than a year in combat Baker had acquired a sixth sense for when his soldiers had about all they could take of Iraq duty, and Charlie Battery exhibited all the telltale signs. In one corner of the field Baker and his companion approached a sodden lump in the weeds, their stomachs churning at what amounted to the worst part of the job. Instead of the remains of a C Battery soldier, however, they turned it over to reveal the severed head of the car bomber, his long dark beard matted and wet. And God forgive him, at that moment Rob Baker, the West Pointer and all-American optimist, felt the thrill of bloody vengeance and hatred stir in his heart. That, too, was part of Iraq duty.

Days later Baker was sitting in the front row at the memorial for the eight soldiers killed in the blast, one more among many he had attended over the past year. Only this time when he faced the row of eight helmets perched atop eight rifles, their bayonets embedded next to eight pairs of empty boots, Rob Baker suddenly had trouble breathing. For the last time on earth the names of each soldier were called out expectantly, and then swallowed in the echoes of the "missing man" tribute. Sergeant Patterson! Staff Sergeant Patterson!? Staff Sergeant Essau G. Patterson? Staff Sergeant Jeffrey F. Dayton? Sergeant Ryan M. Campbell? Specialist James L. Beckstrand? Private First Class Ryan E. Reed? Specialist Justin B. Schmidt? Private Jeremy R. Ewing? Private First Class Norman Darling? None present, all accounted for in the deafening silence of another bad day in Iraq.

As Col. Rob Baker rose to offer a solitary salute to the eight soldiers his breath was ragged in his chest, and then the sixth sense kicked in again and Baker retreated into that empty numbness where soldiers inured themselves against too much death. Some would carry that emptiness the rest of their lives. In the long, violent summer of 2004, that too was an inescapable part of U.S. military duty in Iraq.

When the April insurrection forced the Army to extend the First Armored Division's tour of duty in Iraq by three months, it committed the men and women of "Old Ironsides" to the longest sustained combat deployment by U.S. soldiers since Vietnam. At times it was also one of the most eventful. The division called back units that had already arrived at its home bases in Germany, and took control of a 12,400-square-mile area stretching from the outskirts of the Sunni stronghold and terrorist redoubt of Fallujah, all the way south to the Shiite holy city of Najaf. Over the ensu-

ing three months Colonel Baker and Second Brigade fought multiple battles to retake southern cities from the militias of Muqtada al-Sadr;
subdued insurgents in the Sunni Triangle east of Fallujah; and kept open
vital supply routes that were under constant attack by rebels in the "Triangle of Death." During that three-month extra extension, Second Brigade suffered more wounded and killed in action than during the entire
previous year.

In the process, Second Brigade, First Armored Division, offered a
brief glimpse into the future of a transformed U.S. military. After more
than a year in Iraq, technology and techniques that were novel as recently
as the Iraqi Freedom campaign were second nature to Colonel Baker and
his commanders. They planned and monitored operations using advanced computer and satellite communications systems that were evolving by the day. They took for granted the real-time integration of satellite
and airborne surveillance data into their daily operations. They honed
human intelligence-gathering skills such as running networks of informants, exploiting captured computer disks, and conducting interrogations. Joint operations integrating U.S. airpower and Special Forces
capabilities into brigade operations were routine.

That was the only way a U.S. Army brigade, operating largely autonomously, could cover so much ground and adapt so rapidly to the very
different demands of urban combat operations, targeted counterinsurgency strikes, and area security operations. Along the way, Second Brigade revealed the most transformative weapon in the entire U.S.
arsenal—officer and noncommissioned officer corps and soldiers that
were learning innovation and adaptability as survival skills in the hard
crucible of Iraq.

And all of that amounted to only the hard-power half of their campaign. Upon repositioning south, Col. Rob Baker was determined to
apply *everything* he had learned in over a year in Iraq. The Sunni tribes
south of Baghdad had received little of the largesse that Baker and other
commanders in the capital had doled out regularly through their emergency reconstruction funds. The First Armored Division was the fourth
military organization to take control of the fractious area since the end of
major hostilities, a direct outgrowth of the Pentagon's attempts to stretch
a too-small force over too much territory in Iraq. The triangle had just
fallen between the widening seams. As a result, no U.S. unit had been
around long enough to build the bonds of trust with the local population
that were essential to counterinsurgency warfare.

The tribal sheiks initially viewed the grassroots democracy of the district and neighborhood advisory councils as a direct threat to their hierarchal rule. Col. Rob Baker set out to change all of that. Modifying his
Religious Advisory Council concept into Tribal Advisory Councils called

"Nahias" and "Qadas," Baker reached out to the sheiks in the triangle. He shamelessly exploited relationships established with Sunni religious and political leaders in Baghdad to help him open doors and network down south. He personally chaperoned a group of sheiks to the trial in Baghdad of some of the U.S. soldiers accused in the Abu Ghraib prison abuse scandal, to show them firsthand that the U.S. military was dealing openly and quickly with the matter.

Baker also spent money as fast as humanly possible for a brigade commander in a war zone on whatever local projects the sheiks deemed a priority, doling out $3 million in a short three-month span. After retaking the town of Al Kut from Sadr's militia, Baker and his superiors had immediately given the local sheik several hundred thousand dollars to rebuild a local amusement park, and they instructed him to please hire as many of the young men as possible that Second Brigade had fought in retaking the town. To anyone who would listen, Baker explained that establishing security was his primary mission, but reconstruction was his main line of attack. Soon the Tribal Advisory Councils became must-attend affairs for tribal leaders, and Baker knew the sheiks had taken the bait. He then began asking for small favors in return. Before long, Second Brigade's intelligence on the insurgency in its new area of operations began to improve dramatically.

Almost from the outset Baker's outreach campaign provoked tensions with local representatives of the Coalition Provisional Authority in Baghdad. In Al Hillah the local CPA official wouldn't officially recognize his Tribal Advisory Council because some of its members had not completed recommended training, as if getting a tutorial in Western-style governance was the top priority in a country teetering on the brink of implosion. The CPA also overruled Baker's proposal to hold local elections as a jumpstart to grassroots democracy. The CPA official even wanted to fire one of the Tribal Advisory Council members for accepting a small kickback on a construction project, a standard of ethics alien in an Arab culture of barter where sheiks maintained their position by dispensing and calling in favors. Enforcing such strict ethical standards at the outset would require shutting down virtually the entire reconstruction effort. So let's not let our Western norms and emotions override our logic, Baker told the CPA official. I'm just happy the son of a bitch is working with the United States and not shooting at us.

The tensions pointed to a larger problem. With most CPA officials rotating through on ninety-day temporary tours, and mostly remaining holed up inside Baghdad's Green Zone, the U.S. occupation authority had lost touch with the reality in Iraq, at least in the minds of many military commanders who had to face that hard reality on the ground every day for over a year. Time and again the CPA would issue edicts from its secure compound that translated into trouble on the streets. A perfect example was the decision to close Muqtada al-Sadr's newspaper and arrest one of his top lieutenants the previous April, at a time when Grand Ayatollah Sistani was out of the country seeking medical treatment—and thus unable to provide his usual moderating influence on the younger renegade cleric—and U.S. military forces were in the midst of a difficult relief in place. That little snafu helped spark the Sadr militia's April insurrection around Najaf and Karbala, which helped send the country to the brink of anarchy, which in turn dictated that First Armored Division extend its tour in Iraq by three months and retake the southern cities in difficult fighting.

All of which helped explain why Col. Rob Baker and many other U.S. commanders in Iraq were privately relieved on June 28, 2004, when Ambassador Bremer handed over a blue folder representing Iraqi sovereignty to new Prime Minister Iyad Allawi, and then permanently closed the doors of the Coalition Provisional Authority. In one of his first acts as America's new ambassador to Baghdad, Ambassador John D. Negroponte would send a cable to Washington pleading for the flexibility to drop twenty federal acquisition regulations in order to speed Iraqi reconstruction projects. It was about time. As one four-star, active-duty general put it privately in summarizing the CPA's yearlong rule as designed and overseen by Pentagon civilians, "The CPA was largely a failed experiment, and by the time it closed most U.S. military leaders viewed it as only slightly less onerous than the insurgency itself."

For their part, a number of CPA officials privately blamed the U.S. military, with some justification, for its failure to grasp the true nature and scope of an insurgency they were slow to acknowledge in the first place. In the summer of 2004, U.S. military intelligence suddenly upped its rough estimate of the size of the insurgency from five thousand to twenty thousand rebels, and even that number was deemed conservative by many intelligence analysts.

With the handover of sovereignty to a new Iraqi government, and the shift of increasing security responsibilities to nascent Iraqi security forces, the insurgency predictably redoubled its campaign of terror and intimidation. In June and July of 2004, U.S. and Iraqi forces would be attacked with 759 roadside bombs, according to an analysis by *USA Today*. By the Pentagon's own figures, more U.S. soldiers would be killed and wounded in Iraq between May and September of 2004 than in the first thirteen months of the war. Given the bloody urban warfare to retake Fallujah, more U.S. soldiers and Marines would be killed in November 2004 than in any other month since the U.S. invasion save April, when the United States found itself on the bloody edge of a knife in Iraq due to the simultaneous Sunni and Shiite uprisings.

Meanwhile, kidnappings, hostage taking, and beheadings were becoming epidemic, with over seventy citizens from over two dozen countries seized in the first seven months of 2004. There were likewise more than one hundred documented assassinations and kidnappings of Iraqi doctors and academics, according to the Iraqi Health Ministry, causing an exodus of Iraqi professionals from the country so severe that it threatened to "abort scientific progress" in Iraq. Policemen throughout Iraq were slaughtered en masse or executed one by one with sickening regularity, having been targeted as the weak link in U.S. plans for a shift to Iraqi sovereignty.

Noting those trends, the National Intelligence Council, representing the consensus of the U.S. intelligence community, delivered the Bush administration a stark analysis on Iraq in the summer of 2004. Its gloomy tone mirrored that of a similar report given to the administration before the war. Even under a *best-case* scenario, the report concluded, Iraq and U.S. troops there could expect more of the same, achieving only a "tenuous stability" over the next eighteen months. The worst of three scenarios outlined in the report had Iraq sliding into a civil war that U.S. forces would find it difficult, if not impossible, to halt.

Meanwhile, in his first public comments after leaving Iraq, L. Paul Bremer belatedly noted what virtually everyone who had been on the ground in Iraq knew from firsthand experience: that from the start the Iraqi Freedom campaign and democratic transition had been hamstrung by a lack of sufficient U.S. troops, allowing an atmosphere of "lawlessness" to take hold. That gloom had only deepened as Iraq's reconstruction lurched ahead in fits and starts, and the insurgency steadily gained strength and experience.

As Ambassador Bremer was boarding an aircraft out of Baghdad, and President Bush was standing on the banks of the Bosporus in Istanbul outlining his vision of Iraq as the nascent flowering of democracy in the broader Middle East, Col. Rob Baker and Second Brigade were preparing to go home. On June 30, 2004, at a ceremony at the Baghdad airport, Second Brigade officially cased its colors and battle streamers. Even as he closed one of the most eventful chapters in the unit's history, Baker sensed that he and many of the soldiers gathered for the ceremony had not seen the last of Iraq. From their vantage point on the furthest redoubt of empire, America seemed truly in a state of perpetual war. Col. Rob Baker and his soldiers and the thousands just like them were its twilight warriors, sent forth time and again into the gathering gloom by a grateful but strangely detached nation.

"The global war on terrorism that we are waging is a seminal period in our nation's history," Baker told the assembled troops. "I believe we are closer to the beginning of this campaign than we are to its end. Many of us expect to return to Iraq in the future, and we are willing to fight in other parts of the world to defeat the evil elements that challenge our way of life and our national interests."

In closing Baker told his commanders and troops how proud he was of their accomplishments and sacrifices, never more so than when the soldiers took the news of their extension in Iraq with stoic determination, despite the fact that everyone knew the order surely condemned some among them to never return home at all. "There are many reasons for the grace and professionalism you displayed that day," Baker said. "I believe the sacrifices our wounded and fallen comrades made, and your intense desire to ensure that their efforts mattered, transcended the temporary sacrifice of staying here to fight for another ninety days. Regardless of your personal reasons, your sense of purpose and commitment to our mission during this period of extension is one of the most extraordinary acts of professionalism that I have ever witnessed. I have never been prouder to serve in the United States Army, and the reason I say that is the soldiers and leaders standing before me today."

Even as First Armored Division prepared to embark on the long trip home, however, Baker also knew that the U.S. Army was beginning to show cracks under the pressure of constant war. Just to keep its roster filled for the Iraq deployment, for instance, the division had to institute three stop loss decrees barring soldiers from rotating out of the division or leaving the Army even if their enlistments were up. In some instances that extended by more than a year the tours of soldiers scheduled and anxious to leave the Army. When Second Brigade's stay in Iraq was extended, it also prolonged the tour of a military police unit from the North Carolina National Guard that was attached to the brigade, and which had only expected to spend six months in Iraq. Instead, the Guardsmen spent nearly fifteen months in combat. So strapped was the Pentagon for fresh troops that fully 40 percent of the new rotation into Iraq were Reservists or National Guardsmen, America's traditional strategic reserve. An Army that was designed and built as a world-class sprinter was indeed mired in a bloody marathon. With Bush administration officials staunchly defending the doctrine of preemption and confrontation with rogue actors, and with crises brewing in Iran and North Korea, there was certainly no finish line in sight.

Signs that the Army might be beginning to buckle under those burdens had become too numerous to ignore. In the first thirty-day period of the new fiscal 2005 recruiting year, U.S. Army recruiters would fall 30 percent short of their goal for active duty enlistees, and 45 percent below target for the Reserves. Those monthly targets were used as guideposts by

the Army, and they spelled potentially serious trouble. Congressional offices on Capitol Hill were also receiving dozen of calls from active-duty
soldiers complaining that they had been threatened with a deployment to
Iraq unless they agreed to reenlist, essentially amounting to blackmail.
Rob Baker was anxious to find out what Second Brigade's own reenlistment rate would be once soldiers had a chance to reintegrate into families
that had worried about them and flinched at every newscast from Iraq for
fifteen months.

Tracking those trends, the Defense Science Board, a group of experts
that advised the Secretary of Defense, told Donald Rumsfeld in the summer of 2004 what anyone who spent time deployed with the Army should
already know: The U.S. military simply lacked the troops and force structure to adequately sustain current operations around the world without
undue stress on soldiers and families. Never mind provide prudent insurance against the unforeseen. It was one more among a host of warnings
that the all-volunteer force was in peril. Yet still Don Rumsfeld refused to
permanently increase the size of the U.S. Army lest it relieve the stress
and impetus for change within the military, and drain resources from his
cherished transformation project.

Instead, Secretary Rumsfeld was gambling the fortunes of the finest
military in the world on a bet that the situation in Iraq and Afghanistan
would markedly improve despite his own profound miscalculations, and
that no other crisis would boil over and further burden an already overstretched force. If another front in America's global war on terrorism and
rogue states did erupt, Rumsfeld's insistence on ad hoc coalitions and his
rough handling of the United States' traditional alliances would likely ensure that the U.S. military once again bore the overwhelming brunt of the
conflict alone. The lives of U.S. service members risked and lost, and the
fate of nations and nascent democracies such as Iraq and Afghanistan that
were imperiled by such a high-risk and parsimonious approach, would
ultimately prove as much a part of Secretary Rumsfeld's legacy as transformation itself.

As he decompressed on the long flight back to Germany, Col. Rob
Baker knew that the Pentagon had already informed First Armored Division leaders that it could expect to deploy back to Iraq in 2005. A former student of the Naval War College, he knew full well that a similar
cycle of back-to-back combat deployments during the Vietnam War had
broken the back of the professional Army. Leaders had crossed an ill-
defined line that they didn't even see until stepping into the abyss.
At some point, their senior noncommissioned officers, experienced
captains, and seasoned warrant officers—the backbone of a modern
Army—had given up and begun voting with their feet. The Army subse-
quently discovered to its dismay that it could draft warm bodies, but it

could not draft experience. The result was a spiraling descent of a once-proud Army into a self-perpetuating cycle of low morale, poor quality recruits, and gross incompetence. The United States was left at a critical period of the Cold War with a U.S. military that was hollow at its core, and the Soviet Union responded to that weakness with the 1979 invasion of Afghanistan.

Now it was the U.S. military overcommitted in Afghanistan and Iraq, and a familiar barbarian was once again rattling at the gates of empire. Indeed, it was part of Osama Bin Laden's genius that he always took the long view on such matters, saw the sweep of history as something that played out over decades and even centuries. Though the dream-quest of the arch terrorist still seemed delusional to Americans, by Bin Laden's reckoning much had already been accomplished in a short amount of time. The limits of the superpower's reach had been exposed, its position increasingly isolated and its strength sapped. The jihad was spreading. For the U.S. military, the ultimate destruction of Bin Laden and Al Qaeda remained another mission yet to be accomplished in a world of unfinished business.

Certainly Col. Rob Baker knew something about the strains back-to-back deployments could put on a marriage and family. Except for a few weeks captured between assignments, he had spent nearly two years away from Debbie and his two girls during successive combat tours in Iraq and the Middle East. There was every possibility that he would be going back again before too long. They were approaching the threshold, Baker could sense it. Another combat tour in a year or two, sure, but after that? At some point the great officers and soldiers he served with were going to say, "I just can't give any more." Baker needed to reacquaint himself with his own family before contemplating where his and Debbie's threshold lay.

The welcome home ceremony for Second Brigade, First Armored Division, was held at its home base in Baumholder, Germany, a remote village nestled below hills crowned with church steeples and the ruins of medieval castles. "Welcome Home" banners were strung over the village's main street, and on the hillsides above town the base's large white barracks buildings gleamed in the sun. Generations of U.S. soldiers had passed through those barracks and trained in the nearby fields to repel the Soviet hordes at Germany's Fulda Gap. The First Armored Division's next deployment out of Germany would likely be its last, however, as the Army pulled the bulk of its forces out of Europe in the process of transforming into a more expeditionary, less alliance-dependent force.

The troops of Second Brigade marched into the welcome home ceremony in formation, each soldier scanning the expectant crowd for the face of a loved one. Rob Baker immediately saw his wife, Debbie, and oldest daughter, Caitlin, but for some reason his youngest daughter was not there. When the signal was given, soldiers rushed into the crowd and at long last Baker clasped his wife and daughter to his side. Only then did he realize that the gangly girl standing next to them *was* his youngest daughter. In the almost two years Rob Baker had been away, his little girl had grown nearly a foot. Twelve-year-old Julianne Baker was practically a teenager now.

Debbie Baker would not let go of her husband. She and the other wives had prepared an earlier welcome home ceremony, had hung the streamers and signs, and then watched as it was all snatched away. Word of the brigade's extension in Iraq after a full year was greeted in Baumholder first by disbelief and then anger and then abject fear. In the ensuing months, every bit of bad news out of Iraq ignited a wildfire of rumor on the base, as cell phones trilled and Debbie Baker and the other wives of the Family Readiness Group struggled to determine which families would need their support and condolences this time.

In a grim ritual that was repeated over and over again, Baumholder's chaplain and a casualty notification officer would drive up to one of the large barracks buildings that housed as many as thirty Army families, and every spouse would pray, dear God, let it not be me and mine. Let it be someone else. A knock on the door would sound, sometimes followed by a wail, and then a collective sigh of relief and shame by all those who had been spared. Even after the unit had cased its colors and begun pulling out of Baghdad, the knock sounded twice more for Second Brigade soldiers killed on the dangerous march home, and the ritual was repeated all over again. That, too, was part of Iraq duty as served on the home front.

So Debbie Baker and the other spouses clung to the necks of their loved ones, finally surrendering their fear of the knock on the door that had stalked them for so many months, or the unexpected phone call in the dead of night. All of that was blessedly behind them now. At least until the next deployment.

Early in the twenty-first century, America is indeed fighting an extended global war, a war unlike any in its past. One day, historians will note that for the first time, most of the residual pain and suffering was quarantined on bases such as Baumholder, Fort Carson, Fort Bragg, or scores of other far-flung outposts just like them that serve as home to an army of volunteers. The President of the United States called it a generation-shaping struggle, but he had not called upon a generation of Americans to share its burdens. Those fell disproportionately on the nation's professional warriors, active and reserve. Someone who bore witness to even a fraction of the toll in deaths and maiming and psychological scarring at the front, or saw the constant fear and depression and broken marriages that defined life at home inside the quarantine, might be forgiven for questioning the nature of the bargain struck, and for worrying how it, too, was shaping America's destiny.

NOTES

Prologue

An analysis of the red and blue map of America can be found in a November 13, *Washington Post* article "Election Map Makers, Exercising Some Latitude." American attitudes on the Iraq war are cited from a December 3, 2004, article in the *Christian Science Monitor* entitled "Public Divisions Remain Deep and Fixed over War." An October 22 article in the *San Bernardino Sun* quoted 9/11 Commission member and former Navy Secretary John Lehman that terrorist mastermind Osama Bin Laden was hiding out in the South Waziristan region in Pakistan, and that the Pentagon knew this with certainty. The December 5 article quoting Pakistani president Pervez Musharraf to the effect that Bin Laden's trail had gone cold, and blaming the United States for the inability to capture the terrorist, was from the *Washington Post*. The November 21 article in the *Houston Chronicle* detailing the imminent deployment of the Bush administration's new national missile defense system is entitled "Putin's Nuclear Plans Signal New Arms Race; Bush's Critics Blame His Push to Build a Missile Defense System."

The accelerated efforts of Iran and North Korea to develop nuclear weapons are explored in October articles in the *Boston Globe* and *New York Times*, respectively. Reporting that President Bush wanted to expand the Pentagon's role in clandestine operations that often circumvent international law and are the traditional purview of the Central Intelligence Agency appeared in the November 13, 2004, *New York Times*. The confidential Red Cross report equating U.S. treatment of prisoners at Guantánamo Bay, Cuba, as "tantamount to torture" is discussed in a December 3, 2004, Associated Press dispatch entitled "Evidence Gained by Torture Can Be Used to Detain Enemy Combatants at Guantanamo." The article outlining the unprecedented proliferation dangers confronting the Bush administration appeared in the October 26, 2004, *Washington Post*.

As cited in the text, the *Washington Post* reported on successful elections in Afghanistan in October, while an October 22 article in *USA Today* noted Afghanistan's bumper crop of opium. A November *New York Times* report quoted Michael Scheuer, the former chief of the CIA's Osama Bin Laden unit, to the effect that Al Qaeda had morphed into a "global Islamic insurgency" after being largely driven out of Afghanistan. On November 12, the *Washington Post* reported that Abu Musab Al-Zarqawi, the most wanted terrorist in Iraq, had begun referring to his group as "Al Qaeda in Iraq." The page-one article in the December 6 *Washington Post* quoting U.S. generals in Iraq to the effect that great gains had been achieved against the Iraqi insurgency was entitled "Generals See Gains from Iraq Offensives." News that the U.S. embassy in Iraq had decided that the road to the Baghdad airport was too dangerous for its personnel to travel was reported in the December 3, 2004, *New York Times*.

The distillation of the Bush doctrine contained in the prologue was based on the administration's seminal blueprint for fighting the war on terror, "The National Security Strategy of the United States of America," released in September of 2002; and from interviews with various authors of the doctrine.

Chapter 1: Atlas Shakes

Details of the trial of Radislav Krstic for war crimes by the U.N.'s International Criminal Tribunal for the former Yugoslavia were taken from the author's May 13, 2000, article "Humanity's Court" in *National Journal* magazine. The author's analysis of the likely foreign policy differences between presidential candidates Al Gore and George Bush was originally published in the April 1, 2000, *National Journal* under the headline "Bush and Gore's Positions on Foreign Policy." The note from George H. W. Bush commending *National Journal*'s coverage of his son's campaign is described in the magazine's promotional materials.

Much of the historical detail on post–World War II U.S. strategy, and the Clinton-era doctrine for the post–Cold War 1990s, as well as quotes from experts such as Don Kagan, are taken from the author's April 17, 1999, article "Indispensable, Yet Uncertain" in the *National Journal*. The evolution of the Republican Party's foreign policy positions after the 1994 "Republican revolution" is detailed in the author's "A Return to Isolationism" in the October 9, 1999, *National Journal*. As noted in the text, the discussion of the historical roots of the Bush revolutionaries' views on U.S. power and foreign affairs draws from the analysis of historian and foreign policy expert Walter Russell Mead, and his book *Power, Terror, Peace and War*.

As noted in the text, the discussion of neoconservative philosophy is informed by interviews with Joseph Nye, a former dean of the John F. Kennedy School of Government and author of *The Paradox of American Power*, and a discussion with Jonathan Clarke, coauthor of *America Alone: The Neo-Conservatives and the Global Order*. Quotes from letters and mission statements of the Project for a New American Century come directly from the organization's website. References to the biographies and background of the Bush revolutionaries are from the author's biographical sketches in "The Decision Makers," in the June 23, 2001, *National Journal*.

Chapter 2: Three-Dimensional Chess

Discussion, analysis, and interviews involving U.S. Space Command operations, and their relevance to Defense Secretary Donald Rumsfeld's vision for transforming the U.S. military, are taken from the author's March 17 article "The Permanent Frontier," in *National Journal*, and from firsthand reporting. Likewise, the evolution of the proposed national missile defense system and quotes from experts such as Kurt Gottfried are included in "The Ultimate Bomb Shelter," from the July 8, 2000, *National Journal*. As noted in the text, biographical data on Donald Rumsfeld draws on many sources, including James Mann's book *Rise of the Vul-*

cans. Rumsfeld's embrace of the "Revolution in Military Affairs," the resistance from the services to such radical prescriptions, and the operations of the Pentagon's Office of Net Assessments are detailed in "A Small Study Carries a Heavy Burden" in the March 3, 2001, *National Journal.*

Chapter 3: A Darker Prism

The reaction of Russia to the Bush administration's new hard-line, and excerpts from the interview with Mikhail Gorbachev, come from the author's May 19, 2001, *National Journal* article "A Cooler Peace." The negative response of much of the international community to the Bush revolution in foreign affairs is likewise chronicled at length in the author's March 31, 2001, article, "In Foreign Policy, Bush II Is Like Reagan I," and in the May 19, 2001, article "The New World Disorder," both in *National Journal.* The warning to the Bush administration from British Parliament member Francis Maude is likewise taken from "The New World Disorder." Discussion of how the Bush approach to the Israeli-Palestinian peace process broke with numerous traditions is taken from "The Ties That Bind," in the April 20, 2002, *National Journal*, and the author's April 6, 2002, article "Oslo and Camp David Are Dead: Or Are They?" Details of the U.S. nuclear test site were originally reported by the author in February 21, 1998, in "At Ground Zero." The Bush administration's revolutionary approach to arms control, and John F. Kennedy's warning about the dangers of nuclear proliferation, are explored in the author's July 14, 2001, article "Is Arms Control Dead?" The response of Germany and France in particular to the Bush administration's revolutionary approach to foreign affairs, and potential pitfalls it could produce in transatlantic relations, are explored in the author's February 10, 2001, article "A Tale of Two Allies."

Chapter 4: Assassins at the Gate

Details on the run-up to the September 11, 2001, terrorist attacks are taken largely from the definitive *9/11 Commission Report: Final Report of the National Commission on Terrorist Attacks Upon the United States.* The Bush administration's early moves in responding to the attack are outlined in the author's September 15, 2001, article "The Coming Counterstrike," and his September 22, 2001, article "A New and Colder War." The lengthy section discussing the creation and evolution of Osama Bin Laden's Al Qaeda terrorist organization comes from the author's November 10, 2001, article "Osama's Learning Curve," which sites numerous sources, notably including Peter Bergen's *Holy War Incorporated* and Bruce Hoffman's *Inside Terrorism.* David Kay's quote was taken from an interview with the author. The significance of the anthrax attacks in the fall of 2001—the first attack on America with a sophisticated germ weapon—is outlined in the author's October 20, 2001, article "A New Threshold of Terror Crossed." The section outlining the dysfunctional divide between the FBI and CIA in terms of fighting terrorism originally appeared in the author's September 16, 2000, article "Covert Counterattack."

Chapter 5: A Fork in the Road

The divide within the Bush administration on whether to include Iraq and Saddam Hussein as targets in the immediate post-9/11 counterstrikes, including quotes by Colin Powell, were originally reported in the author's *National Journal* article of October 13, 2001, entitled "Next Stop—Baghdad?" The description of the seminal Camp David meeting following 9/11 is based on an off-the-record recounting by one of the participants. Counterterrorism czar Richard Clarke's part in these discussions is taken from the *9/11 Commission Report*. The reaction of the world community to the attacks, and potential for a favorable reordering of world affairs, is analyzed in the author's October 27, 2001, article "Ending State Terror." The potential for Russia to serve as a lynchpin in that reordering is explored in the October 6, 2001, article "Putin's Leap of Faith." The explanation of the Bush administration's early struggles to develop a coherent strategy and doctrine for winning a "global war on terror" first appeared in the author's October 27 article "Ending State Terror." All appeared in *National Journal*. Excerpts from President Bush's 2002 State of the Union address—the critical unveiling of the Bush doctrine for fighting the global war on terror—are taken directly from his speech, which is available on the White House website.

Chapter 6: A Familiar Nemesis

On-site reporting from Turkey on the U.S.-led Operation Northern Watch enforcing the Iraqi "no-fly zones"—and the steady unraveling of the international sanctions regime—originally appeared in the author's March 2, 2002, article "The Little War with Iraq." The lengthy analysis of Turkey as a potential model for a democratic transformation of the Islamic Middle East also first appeared in *National Journal* on March 2, 2002, in the article "The Turkish Model." The discussion of Ahmed Chalabi and the Iraqi National Congress as a potential democratic "government in waiting" for Iraq likewise is taken from "The Little War with Iraq," and informed by interviews the author conducted with Chalabi in 2002 and 2003. Chalabi's comments on the Afghanistan war serving as a useful model for Iraq were made at a conference hosted by the Council on Foreign Relations in early 2002. Paul Wolfowitz's advocacy for overthrowing Saddam Hussein is detailed in the *9/11 Commission Report*. The arguments that Saddam was behind the original 1993 World Trade Center attacks, and possibly 9/11, were advanced by Laurie Mylroie, the author of *Study of Revenge: Saddam Hussein's Unfinished War against America*, and explored in the author's article "Next Stop—Baghdad?" Ties between Pentagon neocons and Vice President Dick Cheney's office are detailed in numerous press accounts, as well as in James Mann's *Rise of the Vulcans*. Interviews and quotes from experts attesting to Saddam Hussein's clandestine programs for weapons of mass destruction originally appeared on October 13, 2001, in the author's article "Next Stop—Baghdad?"

Chapter 7: Pox Americana

European resistance and opposition to the Bush doctrine in general, and the looming war with Iraq in particular, is detailed in the author's reporting on the German elections from Germany in the September 28, 2002, article "A Suddenly Untethered Germany." Comments about the Bush doctrine and its adherence to neoconservative principles by Robert Kagan are from the author's November 2002 article "The New, New World Order." European alarm over the Bush doctrine and growing anti-American sentiment in Europe were originally reported in the author's April 6, 2002, article "Pox Americana?" The lengthy section reported from Poland on Defense Secretary Donald Rumsfeld's attempt to transform NATO are taken from the October 12, 2002, articles "U.S. to NATO: Change or Else," and from "Lessons from the New Poland," both in *National Journal*. The NATO section also draws from the author's reporting in the February 9, 2002, article "NATO Metamorphosis."

Chapter 8: A Perfect Storm

The initial section outlining the potential costs and pitfalls of an invasion and nation-building operation in Iraq, including the quote from Barry Rubin, is drawn from the author's November 2002 *National Journal* article "A New, New World Order." The unraveling of the diplomacy preceding the Iraq war, including on-and-off the record quotes from senior U.S. officials and their international counterparts in interviews with the author, was originally detailed in the author's March 8, 2002, article "Fractured Alliance" and his July 19, 2003, article "Damage Control." As noted in the text, Bob Woodward details at great length in his book *Plan of Attack* how Bush decided as early as late December 2002—and certainly by early January 2003—that war with Iraq was unavoidable. Dick Cheney's role in inserting "poison pill" language into the U.N. Resolution on Iraq is also recounted from *Plan of Attack*. The concluding section on the damage done to traditional alliances and the shakeup in the international order that resulted from the failed diplomacy preceding the Iraq war is taken from the author's article "Fractured Alliances."

Chapter 9: Fear City

Descriptions of Kuwait prior to the war are from the author's firsthand reporting, and draw on his March 15, 2002, article "An Important Moment for Kuwait." As noted in the text, this chapter also quotes excerpts from Michael Kelly's *Martyrs' Day* and Stephen Ambrose's *D-Day: The Climactic Battle of World War II*.

Chapter 10: Eve of Destruction

Descriptions of the journalistic embed process and Camp Virginia are from the author's firsthand reporting. Quotes from Lt. Gen. Scott Wallace, and Wallace's biographical information, are from interviews with the author. The lengthy section on Donald Rumsfeld's transformational battle plan for the Iraqi Freedom campaign, and the significant risks it assumed, is drawn from the author's March 22, 2003, question-and-answer interview with Brig. Gen. Daniel Hahn entitled "A Just-in-Time Force," and from the author's extensive reporting on the campaign's first stage contained in the March 29, 2003, article "The Army's Gamble" in *National Journal*. Descriptions of the "Black Hole" and depiction of U.S. intelligence operations in Iraq—as well as assumptions about likely Iraqi war plans and technological capabilities—are from the author's firsthand reporting and an extensive interview with Col. Steven Bolz, the chief of intelligence for V Corps.

Chapter 11: American Centurions

Michael Kelly's experiences as an embedded journalist with the Third Infantry Division are reconstructed through interviews the author and *Atlantic Monthly* correspondent P. J. O' Rourke conducted with Third Infantry Division officers in Baghdad, including Third I.D. commander Maj. Gen. Buford Blount; Deputy Commander Brig. Gen. Lloyd Austin; Operations Officer Lt. Col. Peter Bayer; Deputy Operations Officer Maj. Mike Todd; Chief of Plans Maj. Edward Bohemann; and Sgt. Frederico Alzerreca, Kelly's Humvee companion and driver through much of the war. The author also interviewed *ABC Nightline* correspondent Ted Koppel for this section.

The contrasts between the U.S. military force of 2003 and that which fought in Desert Storm in 1991, as well as advances in technology that were transforming the U.S. military that are explained by V Corps information officer Maj. Mark Shaaber, are taken from the author's March 15, 2003, article "The Same, But Different" in *National Journal*.

Chapter 12: March Madness

The depiction of the first days of the Iraqi Freedom campaign comes from the author's firsthand reporting as an embedded reporter with the V Corps Tactical Headquarters. The problems of maintaining communications on such a long road march, and the unfolding of the transformational war plan in its entirety, are detailed at great length in the definitive recount of Army operations in the war, *On Point: The U.S. Army in Operation Iraqi Freedom,* written by Col. Gregory Fontenot, Lt. Col. E. J. Degen, and Lt. Col. David Tohn and published by the Combat Studies Institute Press, Ft. Leavenworth, Kansas. The experience of the Eleventh Attack Helicopter Regiment in their first deep-strike mission of the war also draws from the detailed explanation in *On Point*, as well as from an interview the author conducted shortly after the attack with Lt. Col. Mike Barbee, commander of the Sixth Squadron of the Eleventh Attack Helicopter Regiment. Problems caused by the unexpected ferociousness of Saddam fedayheen paramilitaries and an unusually intense sandstorm are taken from the author's firsthand reporting, as well as his March 29, 2003, article "The Army's Gamble" in *National Journal*.

Chapter 13: Gates of Babylon

Details of the 3/7th Cavalry's fight in the sandstorm after crossing the Euphrates River are taken from *On Point* and interviews with several of the unit's members shortly after the fight. Details of how the Air Force was able to use a "Global Hawk" unmanned aerial vehicle to see through the sandstorm, and send data halfway around the world for development into actionable targeting information that was then relayed into the cockpit of a B-1 bomber on scene, were drawn from George Wilson's September 20, 2003, article in *National Journal* entitled "Will the Eyes over Iraq Soon Be over Us?"

The Battle for Jenkins Bridge and Al Kifl was reconstructed from interviews with a number of the participants—including First Brigade Commander Col. William Grimsley, 3-69 Armor Battalion Commander Lt. Col. Ernest "Rock" Marcone, and C Company, 2-69 Commander Capt. Carter Price—supplanted with details from *On Point*. The scene of senior commanders reviewing the Al Kifl battle after the fact was reconstructed from interviews with Lt. Gen. Scott Wallace of V Corps, Maj. Gen. Buford Blount of the Third Infantry Division, and ABC correspondent Ted Koppel. Michael Kelly's decision to change his embed unit and move to the tip of the invasion spearhead was recounted by his Humvee companions, Lt. Col. Peter Bayer and his driver Sgt. Frederico Alzerreca.

Chapter 14: The Enemy Votes

The experiences of the Thirty-first Air Defense Artillery Brigade are recounted from the author's interview with its commander, Col. Heidi Brown, and contained in his April 5, 2003, article "A Patriot Brigade Shares Success and Pain" in *National Journal*. The controversy over "the pause" and the section outlining changes in the battle plan to compensate for the fedayeen come from interviews with Gen. Scott Wallace and V Corps Operations Officer Col. Steve Hicks and their staffs, and from the author's firsthand reporting, much of it contained in his April 5, 2003, article "The Plan Unfolds." Intelligence that the Republican Guard Nebuchadnezzar Division moved south to reinforce the Medina Division and backstop Baghdad's southern defenses, and that two brigades of the Adnan Republican Guard Division had repositioned from the north during the sandstorm into the Karbala Gap and astride Highway 6 southeast of Baghdad, directly into the path of the intended U.S. advance, is taken from *On Point*. The activities of the Special Forces units are also recounted in *On Point*; quotes from Special Forces personnel are from the author's firsthand reporting.

Chapter 15: Fuel Masters, Water Dogs, and Gorilla Snot

The depiction of the logistics buildup at staging area Bushmaster is the result of the author's firsthand reporting, much of it published in his April 5 article "The Plan Unfolds" in *National Journal*. The March 31, 2003, launch of five simultaneous attacks south of Karbala in preparation for the final push to Baghdad is recounted in great detail in *On Point*. The seminal position that the Karbala Gap occupies in the U.S. war plan was explained in an interview with V Corps Operations Officer Col. Steve Hicks.

Chapter 16: Baghdad Calling

The passing of the Third Infantry Division's First Brigade Combat Team through the Karbala Gap in the early morning hours of April 2, 2003, is reconstructed through interviews with First Brigade Commander Col. Will Grimsley, and 3-69 Battalion Commander Lt. Col. Rock Marcone. The fratricide incident in the Karbala Gap that night was recounted in harrowing detail by Gen. John Keane, acting Chief of Staff of the Army, in an August 5, 2003, interview with the Defense Writers Group, which included the author.

The seminal Battle of the Euphrates Bridge at Objective Peach is reconstructed through interviews with Colonel Grimsley, Colonel Marcone, and embedded journalists Ted Koppel of ABC and Mario Decalvalho of CBS. Details of the fight were also taken from *On Point*. The discussion on whether to launch the attack early on Saddam International Airport was recounted by the participants in interviews the author conducted with Lt. Gen. Scott Wallace, Maj. Gen. Buford Blount, and Col. Will Grimsley and Col. Steve Hicks, and is also detailed in *On Point*. Much of this section is recounted from the author's April 12, 2003, article "Baghdad's Liberation" in *National Journal*.

Chapter 17: Brothers in Arms

The scene in V Corps TAC as UAVs are used to target Iraqi forces is taken from the author's "Baghdad's Liberation," and from firsthand reporting and discussions between the author and Lt. Col. Rob Baker and Lt. Col. Eric Wagenaar. In the twenty-four-hour period following the Third Infantry Division's breach of the Karbala Gap, the U.S. Air Force destroyed 25 percent of all the enemy targets it hit during the entire war up to that point, according to *The Iraq War: A Military History*, by Williamson Murray and Maj. Gen. Robert Scales Jr. The workings of "cluster bombs" are detailed in Michael Kelly's book *Martyrs' Day*. Descriptions of the destruction on the road to Baghdad in the Third Infantry Division's wake, and biographical information of some of the soldiers lost along the way, are from the author's firsthand reporting and recounted in "Baghdad's Liberation" in the *National Journal*.

Chapter 18: Iraq and a Hard Place

The description of V Corps TAC's road to Baghdad are from the author's firsthand reporting, and appeared in abbreviated form in his April 19, 2003, article "Life after Death" in *National Journal*. The decision to launch the thunder runs into Baghdad that ended the war is recounted from interviews with Lt. Gen. Scott Wallace and Brig. Gen. Buford Blount, and also depicted in great detail in *On Point*. The great difficulties the U.S. military had after the sudden collapse of Saddam's regime, as U.S. commanders found themselves still in a combat posture and struggling to make the transition to the "Phase 4" tasks of providing security, delivering humanitarian aid, and stabilizing a traumatized society, were reported by the author in "Life after Death" in *National Journal*. The controversy over the looting of the Baghdad Museum was recounted in an interview with General Blount. Gen. Scott Wallace's initial views on the success and limitations of the "transformational" war plan were recounted in a lengthy interview with the author that was published in *National Journal* on April 26, 2003, entitled "Attack Always." The section outlining the difficulties faced by retired Army Gen. Jay Garner as the commander of the Office of Reconstruction and Humanitarian Assistance is informed by an interview with Garner conducted at the offices of the *National Journal* by the magazine staff after the war. The death of Pfc. Joseph P. Mayek is recounted in "Life after Death" in *National Journal*.

Chapter 19: Homecoming

The description of the Eric Brindel Journalism Award ceremony in New York in June 2003, including the comments of Claudia Winkler, is the result of the author's firsthand reporting of the event. President George W. Bush's May 1 visit to the aircraft carrier USS *Abraham Lincoln* in a Viking warplane, where the president spoke before a banner proclaiming "Mission Accomplished," was documented in numerous press reports. Michael Kelly's column on the stakes of the Iraq war are taken from a *Washington Post* column published shortly before the campaign began. The post-Saddam death toll in Iraq, which included Kirk Straseskie and Rasheed Sahib, is detailed in a May 24, 2003, Associated Press story entitled "When the Dust of War Settles, the Dying Is Not Done."

Chapter 20: Transplanting Democracy

This chapter assessing the Iraqi reconstruction effort at roughly its six-month mark is taken largely from the author's November 1, 2003, *National Journal* cover story "The Ramadan Offensive." The opinions of Iraqi officials on the subject of Saddam's suspected weapons of mass destruction are detailed in the interim report by the Iraqi Survey Group headed by Charles Duelfur. The failure to find Saddam's WMD and discussion of how U.S. intelligence were so wrong on the issue are informed by the October 2004 congressional testimony of Charles Duelfur, the U.S. chief weapons inspector in Iraq (see NBC News, October 6, 2004, Federal News Service). Paul Wolfowitz's long advocacy for deposing Saddam Hussein is detailed in James Mann's book *Rise of the Vulcans*. Secretary of State Colin Powell warning to Bush that if the United States invaded Iraq it would become the owner of the "hopes, aspirations and problems" of twenty-five million people is recounted in Bob Woodward's book *Plan of Action*.

    The section outlining U.S. difficulties in managing a fractious Iraqi media and getting its message across to the Iraqi people is taken from the author's October 11, 2003, article "Muddling the Message" in *National Journal*. The difficult job of turning the electricity back on in Iraq despite a campaign of sabotage by insurgents was described by Brig. Gen. Steven Hawkins, commander of "Task Force Restore Electricity," in an interview with the author in Baghdad. Indications that Saddam may have planned all along to put up only nominal initial resistance to a U.S. invasion before going underground to orchestrate a guerrilla war are contained in the final report by the Iraq Survey Group, widely known as the Duelfur Report (see also, "Study Ties Hussein, Guerrilla Strategy," in the October 11, 2004, *Boston Globe*). Reports from Babylon, Kirkuk, Tikrit, and Baghdad are from the author's firsthand reporting in October 2003.

Chapter 21: The Ramadan Offensive

The events preceding the Ramadan Offensive are reported in the author's November 1, 2003, article by that name. Ties between Ahmed Chalabi, the Iraqi National Congress, Pentagon neoconservatives in the Office of Special Plans, and Vice President Dick Cheney's office have been explored in numerous news reports and investigations (see, for example, "Drinking the Kool Aid" by Patrick Lang in the *Middle East Policy Review* in June 22, 2004; "The Radical" by Spencer Ackerman and Franklin Foer in the December 1, 2003, New Republic; and coverage of the Senate Intelligence Committee's investigation into the Office of Special Plans by National Public Radio reporters Steve Inskeep and Mary Louise Kelly on February 24, 2004). The success of First Armored Division's Second Brigade in tracking down the perpetrators of the Al Rashid Hotel attack are recounted from later interviews with its commander, Col. Rob Baker. The comments of Abdel-Aziz al-Hakim were recounted by a source present at his dinner with Wolfowitz. The point that Defense Secretary Donald Rumsfeld's transformational war-fighting model had led the U.S. military into a manpower-intensive counterinsurgency campaign for which it was undermanned and poorly prepared was made by numerous military analysts, including prominently Andrew Krepinevich, director of the Center for Strategic and Budgetary Assessments.

Chapter 22: Transformation and Revolt

The history of the Army's National Training Center in the Mojave Desert is taken from the author's first book, *Prodigal Soldiers: How the Generation of Officers Born of Vietnam Revolutionized the American Style of War*. Interviews in this section were conducted in January and August of 2004. The analysis of the Office of the Secretary of Defense's attempts to use the impetus created by the Afghanistan and Iraq wars to hasten the process of transformation comes largely from the author's January 31, 2004, article "About Face" in *National Journal*. Details on the Rumsfeld vision for transforming the U.S. military were filled in during subsequent interviews by the author with Deputy Secretary of Defense Paul Wolfowitz; Undersecretary of Defense Douglas Feith; Army Chief of Staff Gen. Peter Schoomaker; Director of the Pentagon's office of Force Transformation, retired Navy Vice Adm. Arthur Cebrowski; and the Commander of Joint Forces Command, Adm. Edmund Giambastiani Jr.

The section on the discord between Secretary Rumsfeld and former Army Chief of Staff Gen. Eric Shinseki—what many experts consider the most serious civil-military breach since the post–World War II Revolt of the Admirals—draws from the author's September 6, 2003, article in *National Journal* entitled "Stress Fractures." Historical references to the Goldwater-Nichols Defense Reform Act of 1986, and the move to an all-volunteer military in 1973, draw on chapters in the author's book *Prodigal Soldiers*. Test failures and other problems with the Pentagon's national missile defense system are detailed in numerous news accounts (see the December 18, 2004, article in the *Los Angeles Times* entitled "Missile Defense System Won't Be Launched This Year," and the December 16, 2004, article in the *Miami Herald* "Crucial Test for Missile Defense System Fails").

Figures on the strains on Army manpower created by operations in Afghanistan and especially Iraq are also taken from the author's February 7, 2004, interview with Undersecretary of Defense for Personnel and Readiness David Chu, entitled "Military Manpower: Adjusting to New Stresses," and from his September 18, 2004, article in *National Journal* entitled "Army Anxiety." The refusal of an Army transport unit in Iraq to complete a delivery run is detailed in the December 6, 2004, *Army Times* under the headline "Convoy Controversy." The Pentagon's Global Posture Realignment reform is described in the author's articles "Promise, Not Presence" (April 3, 2004) and "Army Anxiety" (September 18, 2004), both in *National Journal*.

Chapter 23: Nation Building in a Time of Terror

This analysis of the Bush administration's epic campaign of nation building in a time of terror and insurgency—including the raids that netted Zulu Zero One—is drawn largely from the author's March 27, 2004, article "Building Up, Tearing Down," which was reported from Baghdad and filled in with additional firsthand reporting. Numerous news reports pointed to the fact that only a tiny fraction of the $18 billion Congress appropriated for emergency reconstruction funds in Iraq in 2003 was actually spent on actual projects (see "Iraq Cupboard Is Bare" in the July 9, 2004, *San Jose Mercury News*). The details of Operation Striker Elton and the terrorist pipeline were provided in interviews with Col. Rob Baker, and Second Brigade intelligence officer Maj. Larry Wilson. Problems and gross negligence in the stand-up of Iraqi security forces are detailed in the author's April 10, 2004, *National Journal* cover story, "Out of the Nest."

Chapter 24: Razor's Edge

This chapter on the badly deteriorating situation in Iraq in the spring of 2004 is drawn largely from the author's May 15, 2004, *National Journal* cover story, "The Moment of Truth." The description of testimony by Paul Wolfowitz and Richard Armitage before the Senate Foreign Relations Committee on May 18, 2004, is from firsthand reporting. The findings by the Schlesinger Commission that Defense Secretary Rumsfeld and senior OSD officials bore responsibility for the Abu Ghraib abuses were reported in numerous media (see the September 6, 2004, article in *Time* magazine entitled "The Verdict on Rumsfeld"). Steve Cambone's role in sending Maj. Gen. Geoffrey Miller, the commander of the detention facility in Guantánamo, Cuba, to Iraq to strengthen intelligence gathering at Abu Ghraib is likewise well documented (see "The Roots of Torture" in the May 24, 2004, *Newsweek*). The National Intelligence Council's reports before the launch of Iraqi Freedom warning of the likely postwar insurgency were recounted in numerous press reports, including an October 25, 2004, article in *USA Today* entitled "Prewar Intelligence Predicted Iraqi Insurgency," by Steve Komarow. Senator Richard Lugar's criticism of the Pentagon's management of Iraq are from an interview with the author.

Chapter 25: Clouds in the West

The analysis of the Bush revolution in foreign affairs and its doctrine for prosecuting the global war on terror are drawn from the author's July 10, 2004, retrospective in *National Journal* entitled "Daring and Costly." The failure of NATO to quickly live up to its commitment of trainers for Iraqi security forces is reported in the October 14, 2004, *New York Times* under the headline "NATO Vows to Speed Sending 300 Troops to Train Iraqi Forces." The evolution of Al Qaeda into a global jihadist movement is outlined in numerous analyses and articles (see the November 8, 2004, *New York Times* article entitled "Evolving Nature of Al Qaeda Is Misunderstood, Critic Says," and the September 9, 2004, *Philadelphia Inquirer* article "Al Qaeda Battered, But Others Rise"). The pullout of coalition troops from Iraq during 2004 was documented in numerous articles (see "The Creaky Coalition" in the November 1, 2004, edition of *Newsweek*). Dick Cheney's unusually powerful influence within the Bush administration is detailed in the *Washington Post* article of October 5, 2004, entitled "Impact from the Shadows: Cheney Wields Power with Few Fingerprints." Iran's increasing bellicosity and meddling in Iraqi affairs is revealed in numerous news reports (see "For Bush and Kerry, A Growing Arms Threat with No Clear Answers" in the October 27, 2004, the *Baltimore Sun*). The quotes from European officials are from off-the-record interviews with the author. The letter of alarm by Western leaders and analysts over Putin's drift toward authoritarianism is detailed in an October 3, 2004, editorial in the *Washington Post* entitled "The Truth on Russia."

Colin Powell's extensive comments on the Bush foreign policy are taken from an interview with the author, published in the March 13, 2004, *National Journal* under the headline "Tough Work Ahead." The article critical of Colin Powell written by Newt Gingrich appeared in the July 2003 issue of *Foreign Policy*.

Chapter 26: Twilight Warriors

Events surrounding the killing of eight soldiers from Second Brigade, First Armored Division, by a suicide bomber outside the small Iraqi town of Josephina are reconstructed through interviews with Col. Rob Baker and First Brigade documents. The operations of Second Brigade in Iraq following the extension of its tours in the spring of 2004 were reconstructed from interviews with senior officers following the brigade's return to Germany. Much of this chapter on the strains on the U.S. Army resulting from combat deployments was drawn from the author's September 18, 2004, article "Army Anxiety." The rising death toll in Iraq for coalition troops, and the deterioration in the security environment, are drawn from numerous news articles (see the December 1, 2004, *USA Today* article "Monthly Death Toll Reaches Record Set in April"; "Iraq Facing Health Crisis, Medical Group Reports" in the December 1, 2004, *Washington Post*; and the December 3, 2004, article in the *New York Times* that quotes U.S. officials to the effect that the size of the Iraqi insurgency has grown to twenty thousand).

The National Intelligence Council's classified report predicting that even under a best-case scenario the United States could expect more of the same insecurity and violence in Iraq is detailed in the October 2, 2004, article in the *New*

York Times headlined "CIA-White House Tensions Are Unusually Public." L. Paul Bremer clarified his statements that U.S. operations in Iraq were hindered at the beginning by too few troops in an opinion column in the October 8, 2004, *New York Times.*

Col. Rob Baker's comments on furling Second Brigade's colors in Baghdad are taken from a copy of his speech. The fact that the Army fell far short of its recruitment goals in the first month of the new recruiting cycle was revealed in an October 20, 2004, article in the *Wall Street Journal* entitled "Army Recruiters Miss Target for Enlistees in Latest Month." The historical passage of the Army's descent into a "hollow force" in the 1970s draws on the author's first book, *Prodigal Soldiers.*

INDEX

The Author

James Kitfield has reported on national security and foreign affairs issues from Washington, D.C., for nearly two decades. In 2004 the Military Reporters and Editors Association awarded him its first-place prize for excellence in overseas reporting for his coverage of the Iraq war. Mr. Kitfield is also the recipient of the 2002 Stewart Alsop Media Excellence Award for his reporting on intelligence-related issues following the 9/11 terrorist attacks, awarded by the Association of Former Intelligence Officers and the Spy Museum. He is likewise the recipient of the 2000 Edwin Hood Award for diplomatic correspondence given by the National Press Club for excellence in reporting on foreign policy issues, and the only two-time winner in the history of the Gerald R. Ford Award for Distinguished Reporting on National Defense. His work has appeared in the *National Interest*, *National Journal*, *Newsday*, *Omni*, *Army Times*, *Air Force Magazine*, *Stars and Stripes*, and other publications. His book *Prodigal Soldiers* was first published in 1995. Mr. Kitfield lives in Arlington, Virginia.